No solution

Manchester University Press

No solution

The Labour government and the Northern Ireland conflict, 1974–79

S.C. Aveyard

Manchester University Press

Published by Manchester University Press
Altrincham Street, Manchester M1 7JA, UK
www.manchesteruniversitypress.co.uk

British Library Cataloguing-in-Publication Data is available

ISBN 978 0 7190 9640 2 *hardback*
ISBN 978 1 5261 2170 7 *paperback*

First published by Manchester University Press in hardback 2016

This edition published 2020

Typeset by Toppan Best-set Premedia Limited

For Mum & Dad

Contents

Figures and tables

Figures

Tables

Acknowledgements

My first and largest debt is to Keith Jeffery, who supervised the doctoral thesis on which this monograph is based. Keith has been an inspiration throughout and continued to offer advice, encouragement and hospitality long after any obligations were fulfilled. It has been a delight conversing with such a fine scholar and I am eternally grateful to him. My parents, Susan and Andrew Aveyard, have been a constant source of support, accepting my prolonged absences without complaint and nudging me along during those moments when doubt set in. Ross Connor Aveyard offered amusing torment and perspective as any ideal sibling should.

I arrived in Belfast in September 2007 to study for a master's degree in the School of History & Anthropology at Queen's University Belfast. The quality of the company I found there accounts in large part for my remaining at that institution for eight years and I am particularly grateful to Evi Chatzipanagiotidou, Kieran Connell, Paul Corthorn, Elaine Farrell, Peter Gray, David Hayton, Seán Lucey, Fearghal McGarry, Sean O'Connell, Alexander Titov, Ioannis Tsioulakis and Immo Warntjes. I was very fortunate to have my doctoral thesis examined by Professor Lord Hennessy and Andrew Holmes. Their comments constituted the best preparation for writing this book.

I have been blessed with great friends and would especially like to thank Adam and Emma Child, Aidan Enright, Ania Beck, Conor Browne, Daniel Brown, Daniel Ritchie, Erica Doherty, Kacper Rekawek, Mark Benson, Mark Gray, Matthew Lewis and Stuart Irwin. One of the greatest delights of my time in Belfast has been meeting Pamela Linden and I thank her for her willingness to tolerate my company. Finally, James Greer and Shaun McDaid deserve a special mention, not least because they suffered through the entirety of the first draft and offered excellent advice and insights. All mistakes are my own.

Abbreviations

ASU	Active Service Unit
BBC	British Broadcasting Corporation
CBI	Confederation of British Industry
CDS	Chief of the Defence Staff
CDU	Campaign for Democracy in Ulster
CGS	Chief of the General Staff
CSJ	Campaign for Social Justice
CID	Criminal Investigation Department
CLF	Commander Land Forces
CPRS	Central Policy Review Staff
DAC	Divisional Action Committee
DCC(Ops)	Deputy Chief Constable (Operations)
DCI	Director and Co-ordinator of Intelligence
DUP	Democratic Unionist Party
EEC	European Economic Community
EPA	Emergency Provisions Act
ESC	Emergency Steering Committee
GOC	General Officer Commanding
HMG	Her Majesty's Government
HQNI	Army Headquarters Northern Ireland
HR	human resources
IMF	International Monetary Fund
INLA	Irish National Liberation Army
IRA	Irish Republican Army
IRC	Intelligence Review Committee
IRSP	Irish Republican Socialist Party
LSE	London School of Economics
MACM	Military Aid to Civil Ministries
MACP	Military Aid to the Civil Power
MOD	Ministry of Defence
MRF	Military Reaction Force

NATO	North Atlantic Treaty Organization
NEB	National Enterprise Board
NICRA	Northern Ireland Civil Rights Association
NICS	Northern Ireland Civil Service
NIDA	Northern Ireland Development Agency
NIEC	Northern Ireland Economic Council
NIES	Northern Ireland Electricity Service
NIFC	Northern Ireland Finance Corporation
NIO	Northern Ireland Office
NIOR	Northern Ireland Operations Room
NIPG	Northern Ireland Patrol Group
NUI	National University of Ireland
NUIG	National University of Ireland, Galway
NUM	National Union of Mineworkers
OIRA	Official Irish Republican Army
OPC	Operational Policy Committee
PA	Parliamentary Archives
PAC	Provisional Army Council
PIRA	Provisional Irish Republican Army
PRONI	Public Record Office of Northern Ireland
PSF	Provisional Sinn Féin
PS/SSNI	Private Secretary to the Secretary of State for Northern Ireland
PTA	Prevention of Terrorism Act
PUS	Permanent Under Secretary of State
RM	Republican Movement
RÓB	Ruairí Ó Brádaigh papers
RTÉ	Raidió Teilifís Éireann
RUC	Royal Ulster Constabulary
RUCR	Royal Ulster Constabulary Reserve
SAS	Special Air Service
SB	Special Branch
SDLP	Social Democratic and Labour Party
SF	Security Forces
SPG	Special Patrol Group
SRU	Special Reconnaissance Unit
TD	Teachta Dála
TNA	The National Archives (UK)
TUC	Trades Union Congress
UDA	Ulster Defence Association
UDR	Ulster Defence Regiment
UFF	Ulster Freedom Fighters

xii   ABBREVIATIONS

UFTM   Ulster Folk and Transport Museum
UPNI   Unionist Party of Northern Ireland
UUAC   United Unionist Action Council
UUC   Ulster Unionist Council
UUP   Ulster Unionist Party
UUUC   United Ulster Unionist Council
UUUM   United Ulster Unionist Movement
UVF   Ulster Volunteer Force
UWC   Ulster Workers' Council
VAT   Value Added Tax
VUPP   Vanguard Unionist Progressive Party

Introduction

It is no good ignoring facts however unpleasant they may be. The politician who thinks he can deal out abstract justice without reference to forces around him cannot govern. (David Lloyd George, 14 October 1921)[1]

In its broadest sense this is a book about the limitations of government power. As Lloyd George was aware, when abstract solutions encounter the context and conditions of whatever problem they are intended to resolve they rarely emerge unscathed. Just as the 1921 Anglo-Irish Treaty failed to fully realise the ideals of Irish nationalists or British/Irish unionists, so the more recent peace process in Northern Ireland failed to do the same for their modern-day counterparts. This book demonstrates the naivety of claims that a solution to the Northern Ireland conflict could have been imposed by the British state two decades before the 1998 Good Friday Agreement. It also argues that while there is a tremendous volume of material written on the Northern Ireland conflict, areas remain where there is a poverty of understanding. This is especially the case for the difficult years of the Labour administration of 1974 to 1979. The application of a distinctively historical methodology for this period offers insights into why the conflict lasted as long as it did. During these crucial years the power-sharing executive which emerged from the Sunningdale Agreement collapsed because of a general strike by loyalists. Afterwards the Labour government considered a variety of constitutional options before concluding that indefinite direct rule from Westminster would remain until a political settlement was agreed by the two communities in Northern Ireland. The British state was unable to impose a constitutional solution in the face of local opposition.

The Labour government engaged in dialogue with militant republicans during the Provisional Irish Republican Army's (PIRA) 1975 ceasefire. The content of the conversations that took place demonstrate that a serious negotiation between the two sides was not possible at that point in time and illustrate how far the Provisional movement was from accepting

constitutional politics. Labour used the ceasefire to bring an end to detention without trial. It then enacted policies of criminalisation and police
primacy. Some of the errors that characterised security policy in the first
half of the decade were corrected. Although violence levels reduced significantly, there were serious limitations to Labour's new approach. The
appeal of political violence remained strong for a large number of individuals in Northern Ireland and it was not possible for the British to remove
all of the various factors that contributed to this. Criminalisation led to
new confrontations in the prison system, there were accusations that the
police engaged in brutality to extract confessions during interrogation and
a number of killings by British security forces occurred in disputed circumstances that lent weight to claims of a 'shoot-to-kill' policy. The PIRA
showed that it was able to adapt to the new conditions of the conflict. By
the end of the decade key officials in the Northern Ireland Office were
emphasising in their advice to ministers that the conflict would be a lengthy
one. The events of 1974 to 1979 in many ways set the conditions for the
remainder of the conflict.

With the UK economy suffering acutely from a world recession there
was a shift in economic policy towards Northern Ireland which ran contrary to the experience in Great Britain. Dependence on the public sector
increased at a time of severe cuts in the British government's expenditure.
There was a desperate effort to encourage industrial investment in the
region. This had consequences for the regional economy that continue up
to the present day. Such efforts to conduct a more positive form of direct
rule did not create the conditions for a compromise between nationalism
and unionism. Indeed, the period was especially alienating for constitutional nationalists who, after the peak of the Sunningdale Agreement,
suffered great setbacks in their claims that non-violent politics could
deliver for the Catholic community. The belief that the Labour administration had become too sympathetic to unionism and struck a deal with the
Ulster Unionist Party at Westminster led life-long Labour supporter Gerry
Fitt to play a crucial role in its downfall.

This book places all of these key issues in context and undertakes a
focussed attempt to understand the problems faced by those involved in
formulating government policy and the options that were open to them.
This is all the more necessary because of the nature of existing accounts.
Brendan O'Leary, one of the foremost political scientists to write about the
conflict, conflates the nature of government policy with simplistic personality caricatures of the ministers involved. This is especially the case for
the two Labour Secretaries of State for Northern Ireland, Merlyn Rees and
Roy Mason. O'Leary's glib description of Rees as bearing the 'shambolic
gait of a badly dressed and over-promoted headmaster' stands next to his

similarly crass depiction of Mason, the blunt Yorkshireman and 'true political thug of the Callaghan administration'. O'Leary argues that the collapse
of power-sharing 'is the event by which Labour's ministers should be
judged' and emphasises 'the disrespect attached to the conduct of Northern Ireland policy' under Labour.[2] Here O'Leary straightforwardly endorses
the views of politicians present at Sunningdale who were naturally deeply
upset at the agreement's demise.[3] It is a common analysis, supported also
by the memoirs of two Northern Ireland civil servants. Kenneth Bloomfield, secretary to the power-sharing executive, writes that during the loyalist strike Rees 'was inhibited by humanitarian instincts and an inbuilt
irresolution'.[4] Robert Ramsay, one of Mason's private secretaries, describes
the Labour government, and Rees especially, as 'pathetically weak'.[5] The
prevalence of these views makes them important; the caricatures do
capture aspects of the two ministers' personalities. Personality plays an
important role, but there is also a need for academic authors to engage
more thoroughly with the parameters within which those at the Northern
Ireland Office operated. It is the absence of context in O'Leary's work
which needs to be redressed. In doing so this book shows his analysis to
be deeply flawed. Too often contemporary criticisms are repeated by academic authors without any consideration of the context of government
policy.

The emotional attachment to Sunningdale achieved new significance
following the success of the peace process. The Social Democratic and
Labour Party (SDLP) politician Seamus Mallon famously described the
1998 Good Friday Agreement as 'Sunningdale for slow learners', prompting
many to question whether the outcome of the conflict could have been
grasped more than twenty years earlier and with far less blood-shed in the
intervening period.[6] Michael Kerr's work is the academic embodiment of
this view; the subtitle of his book, *The destructors*, which considers both
Sunningdale and its downfall, portrays the subject as Northern Ireland's
'lost peace process'. Kerr further argues that the Labour government abandoned Sunningdale in 'a story of lost opportunities'. He claims that had the
Conservatives been in power the agreement would have been saved.[7] The
counterfactual seems to provide a particular draw to scholars of Northern
Ireland but here it is not especially useful. Shaun McDaid rightly argues
that Kerr's speculations lack 'a compelling evidential basis'.[8] While it was
of course intended to facilitate peace, Kerr's description of a 'lost peace
process' neglects the fundamental problem that it did not involve representatives of either the republican or loyalist traditions. Richard English
defends the 'slow learners' claim, pointing out that in the 1970s there were
those who 'preferred to kill in pursuit of unlikely victory'.[9] This is accurate
but an historical approach must grapple with the prevailing conditions that

made Sunningdale unsustainable; it would be unrealistic to conceive of the key paramilitary groups accepting defeat at that point of the conflict and acquiescing in institutions which they regarded as a sell-out. Similarly, that power-sharing has been deemed a desirable objective does not mean that the British government had the power to impose it on Northern Ireland. Mallon's remark stems from bitterness that his party would later be proved right in its claims that power-sharing offered the best constitutional form for a peaceful settlement. Being right or moral does not necessarily count for much in a political conflict.

Much of the academic literature has been limited because the application of historical method in its strictest sense has only become possible with the release of archival material. Michael Cunningham, writing in 2001, has effectively summarised official publications and drawn from official statements to depict policy as it was presented. As such, his account lacks analysis and fails to shed light on a much broader and more colourful picture.[10] Similarly, Paul Bew and Henry Patterson's *The British state and the Ulster crisis*, published in 1985, lacked access to archival material necessary to reconstruct government policy in detail and it is now necessary to revise a number of their claims.[11] There are many monographs on Northern Ireland which deal in part with the subject matter of this book. Some authors have been forced to rely on memoirs and other non-archival sources. In places they offer a very accurate picture, albeit with less detail because of the broader remit of their work. On other occasions the revelations of new material makes it possible to revise their judgements.[12] Other authors, such as Anthony Craig, Shaun McDaid and Cillian McGrattan have produced accounts drawing from similar sources, but which do not share the same focus of this book.[13]

In order to provide a full and proper appreciation of the context within which the British government operated between 1974 and 1979, this book investigates the complex relationships between ministers and civil servants across numerous government departments, senior army officers inside and outside of Northern Ireland, and senior police officers in the Royal Ulster Constabulary (RUC). It also grapples with the public and private discourse of politicians in Great Britain, Northern Ireland and the Republic of Ireland. The release of government archival material makes such an investigation possible and the backbone of this book is drawn from the correspondence of key protagonists and the minutes and memoranda of numerous committees in which policy was debated and shaped. In addition, there are a number of private papers which have proven useful. Merlyn Rees recorded his thoughts on audio tapes during his tenure in Northern Ireland. These were transcribed to assist the writing of his published memoirs and then made available through the London School of

Economics (LSE) after his death. They prove an excellent source, showing a very personal view of important aspects of government policy and of individuals involved in Northern Ireland politics.[14] Similarly, Ruairí Ó Brádaigh, President of Provisional Sinn Féin throughout the 1970s, has deposited papers at the National University of Ireland, Galway (NUIG). Alongside the papers of Brendan Duddy, the intermediary between the British government and the PIRA during its 1975 ceasefire, these compensate in part for the lack of British material on talks with republicans.

A structural analysis of Labour government policy in Northern Ireland is also necessary. Existing literature often fails to appreciate that the British state is not a monolithic institution. There is a need to unpick the various structures involved in formulating government policy and to delineate the views of those individuals contained within. It will be shown, for example, that the views held at the Ministry of Defence (MOD) and Army Headquarters in Northern Ireland (HQNI) often differed, with the MOD in many ways closer to the Northern Ireland Office (NIO). From the NIO's creation there was a degree of separation from the Northern Ireland Civil Service (NICS). The NIO, divided between offices in Belfast and London, held responsibility for political affairs and law and order. As such, NIO staff were principally drawn from the Home Office, the Ministry of Defence, and the Foreign and Commonwealth Office, in addition to unacknowledged input from MI5 and MI6.[15] The NICS, meanwhile, predominantly consisted of Northern Irish civil servants working in domestic departments such as Finance, Commerce and Agriculture. This is not simply a matter of administrative detail; it has a significant bearing on how the views of individuals should be treated. There was a substantial degree of mistrust of the NICS as the nature of its staff was perceived to render it susceptible to communal ties. Merlyn Rees at times felt unable to be completely free with his views for fear that NICS officials and policemen would pass information to loyalist politicians such as Ian Paisley. After one such occasion, when housing documents were published in Paisley's *Protestant Telegraph*, Rees privately remarked: 'This is why on very many basic issues in NI the stuff that comes to me is marked for UK eyes only and it does not go to the NI civil servants, not even the NI people in the security setup' (that 'UK eyes alpha' was used on documents to exclude Northern Irish officials rather than 'GB eyes alpha' is perhaps rather telling of the perceived constitutional relationship).[16]

The unwillingness to look beyond Northern Ireland has led authors to ignore occasions on which the British state faced similar problems. It is vital that the British context of the conflict is better recognised. Authors writing about Northern Ireland have made far too little effort to engage with contemporary British history and especially critical works on the process of British governance.[17] A cursory reading of monographs such as Peter Hennessy and Keith Jeffery's *States of emergency* reveals that some of the challenges faced in Northern Ireland were not unique.[18] A detailed study of government policy in Northern Ireland also has much to offer post-war British historiography. Richard Crossman claimed in 1963 that the post-war epoch saw 'the final transformation of Cabinet Government into Prime Ministerial Government' and likened this system to 'voluntary totalitarianism'.[19] This view has been too readily adopted. While Harold Wilson and James Callaghan did at times make important contributions, the argument presented here is that the views of both prime ministers had rather less of a role in shaping policy than has been assumed.

This book is focussed on the problems with which government ministers were most preoccupied: the need for a political settlement, the need to minimise violence and the need to prevent an economic crisis from making the conflict worse. The structure is a hybrid of the chronological and thematic. Until 1976 ministers were largely unable to disentangle the different elements of British policy in Northern Ireland and the constitutional and security spheres affected each other particularly deeply. There is thus a strong case for handling Home Secretary Roy Jenkins's support for withdrawal in the same chapter as his dealing with the aftermath of the Birmingham bombings. After the collapse of the PIRA ceasefire and the Constitutional Convention it was somewhat easier for the Labour government to deal with each sphere in turn. Thus, the second half of the book is more thematically organised to reflect this.

By necessity a number of elements have been neglected. The parliamentary context is a thread that runs throughout this book but it is not a study of the Labour party's response to Northern Ireland in the broadest sense. Party activists and dissenting backbenchers are worthy of further attention but after surveying relevant material it has become apparent that these groups had very little influence on the Labour government. The uneasy relationship between the British and Irish governments is addressed but a detailed historical account of British–Irish relations still needs to be written (Henry Patterson's excellent *Ireland's violent frontier* goes some way to address this with its focus on cross-border security).[20] A whole range of social matters in which Northern Ireland departments were involved, such as housing, require much further study. A final caveat is that the analysis presented here is inevitably provisional in nature because of the archival material that remains to be released. This is especially the case for intelligence matters and controversial questions such as collusion. The ability to reconstruct Northern Ireland's past is still heavily constrained by restricted access to government records, not all of which will have been preserved.

Notes

1 Michael Cox, Adrian Guelke and Fiona Stephen, *A farewell to arms? Beyond the Good Friday Agreement* (Manchester: Manchester University Press, 2006), p. 25.
2 Brendan O'Leary, 'The Labour government and Northern Ireland, 1974–79' in Brendan O'Leary and John McGarry (eds), *The Northern Ireland conflict: consociational engagements* (Oxford: Oxford University Press, 2003), pp. 199–216; Brendan O'Leary and John McGarry, *The politics of antagonism: understanding Northern Ireland* (London: Athlone Press, 1993), pp. 200–9.
3 Paddy Devlin, *The fall of the N.I. Executive* (Belfast: P. Devlin, 1975); John Hume, *Personal views: politics, peace and reconciliation in Ireland* (Dublin: Townhouse, 1996); Brian Faulkner, *Memoirs of a statesman* (London: Weidenfeld & Nicolson, 1978); Garret FitzGerald, *All in a life: an autobiography* (Dublin: Gill and Macmillan, 1991); William Whitelaw, *The Whitelaw memoirs* (London: Aurum, 1989).
4 Kenneth Bloomfield, *A tragedy of errors: the government and misgovernment of Northern Ireland* (Liverpool: Liverpool University Press, 2007), p. 48.
5 A number of Northern Irish civil servants have published memoirs but it should be noted that officials from Great Britain have been more circumspect. Ramsay in particular has been quite forthright in expressing his own political views, writing in his memoirs that he viewed the prorogation of Stormont in March 1972 as a 'betrayal': Robert Ramsay, *Ringside seats: an insider's view of the crisis in Northern Ireland* (Dublin: Irish Academic Press, 2009), pp. 106, 127. See also Kenneth Bloomfield, *Stormont in crisis: a memoir* (Belfast: Blackstaff, 1994); Maurice Hayes, *Minority verdict: experiences of a Catholic public servant* (Belfast: Blackstaff, 1995).
6 For Mallon's remark and a detailed comparison of the two agreements see: Jonathan Tonge, 'From Sunningdale to the Good Friday Agreement: creating devolved government in Northern Ireland', *Contemporary British History*, 14:3 (2000), pp. 39–60.
7 Michael Kerr, *The destructors: the story of Northern Ireland's lost peace process* (Dublin: Irish Academic Press, 2011); see also: Feargal Cochrane, *Northern Ireland: the reluctant peace* (New Haven: Yale University Press, 2013), pp. 95–6.
8 Shaun McDaid, *Template for peace: Northern Ireland 1972–75* (Manchester: Manchester University Press, 2013), p. 185.
9 Richard English, 'Review: Shaun McDaid, *Template for peace*', *Irish Historical Studies*, 39:154 (2014), p. 366.
10 Michael Cunningham, *British government policy in Northern Ireland 1969–2000* (Manchester: Manchester University Press, 2001).
11 Paul Bew and Henry Patterson, *The British state and the Ulster crisis: from Wilson to Thatcher* (London: Verso, 1985).
12 Paul Arthur, *Special relationships: Britain, Ireland and the Northern Ireland problem* (Belfast: Blackstaff, 2000); Peter Neumann, *Britain's long war: British strategy in the Northern Ireland conflict 1969–98* (Basingstoke: Palgrave

Macmillan, 2003); Henry Patterson, *Ireland since 1939: the persistence of conflict* (Dublin: Penguin Ireland, 2006).

13 Anthony Craig, *Crisis of confidence: Anglo-Irish relations in the early troubles 1966–74* (Dublin: Irish Academic Press, 2010); McDaid, *Template for peace*; Cillian McGrattan, *Northern Ireland 1968–2008: the politics of entrenchment* (Basingstoke: Palgrave Macmillan, 2010).

14 Merlyn Rees, *Northern Ireland: a personal perspective* (London: Methuen, 1985).

15 Peter Hennessy, *Whitehall* (London: Secker & Warburg, 1989), p. 470.

16 London School of Economics (LSE), MERLYN-REES/1/10, Transcript of tapes, undated, p. 2.

17 For example, Peter Hennessy's *Whitehall*; Rodney Lowe, *The official history of the British civil service: reforming the civil service*, volume 1: *The Fulton years 1966–81* (London: Routledge, 2011).

18 Keith Jeffery and Peter Hennessy, *States of emergency: British governments and strikebreaking since 1983* (London: Routledge & Kegan Paul, 1983).

19 Richard Crossman, 'Introduction' in Walter Bagehot, *The English constitution* (London: C.A. Watts, 1964), pp. 51, 56.

20 Henry Patterson, *Ireland's violent frontier: the border and Anglo-Irish relations during the troubles* (Basingstoke: Palgrave Macmillan, 2013).

1

Background: British Labour and Northern Ireland, 1964–74

The ten years prior to 1974 saw the outbreak of the conflict, a tremendous upsurge in violence, the removal of the Northern Ireland government and an attempt to bring about a political settlement between nationalists and unionists. For the purpose of this book, the period is also significant in that it illustrates how reluctant both the Labour and Conservative parties were to become involved in Northern Ireland. The Labour government of 1964 to 1970, and the Conservative administration that followed it, hoped that the Stormont regime could reform itself into being acceptable to the Catholic community. As the failure of the strategy became apparent, the Labour party found itself objecting to aspects of security policy under the Conservatives. The leader of the Labour party Harold Wilson also made a number of interjections which revealed a personal hostility towards unionism. As Labour's Northern Ireland spokesman, Merlyn Rees unsuccessfully pressed for a number of modifications to security policy. His criticisms were less strident than those of a number of Labour backbenchers and he feared the difficulties that the party would have outside of opposition. These various aspects are essential to understanding what followed after Labour returned to office in 1974.

Internal reform

Prior to the emergence of the civil rights movement in Northern Ireland the Labour party generally held to the convention that issues connected to the region could not be discussed at Westminster. This began to change with the formation of the Campaign for Social Justice (CSJ), who wrote to Labour leader Harold Wilson in an attempt to publicise discrimination against Catholics.[1] Prior to the 1964 general election which saw the formation of the first Labour government in thirteen years, Wilson promised CSJ that once in office he would introduce impartial procedures for housing allocation and bring in tribunals to deal with complaints about public appointments. After becoming prime minister, however, he left the governance of the region to the Unionist premier Terence O'Neill.[2]

A number of backbench Labour MPs objected to the Westminster convention and sought to debate the issues highlighted by the civil rights campaigners in Northern Ireland. In 1965 the Campaign for Democracy in Ulster (CDU) was founded and chaired by Paul Rose, also including fellow Labour MPs Stanley Orme and Kevin McNamara.[3] The CDU had very limited success as the convention was repeatedly asserted in the House of Commons. Wilson argued in private correspondence with the group that O'Neill was engaged in a programme of reform and had his support. Here Wilson exaggerated the scale of what the Unionist prime minister actually offered, which amounted only to symbolic gestures and minor reforms of local government.[4] He was rather more exercised by the tendency of Unionist MPs to vote with the Conservative party in the Commons. With such a small majority prior to the 1966 election, he asked that it be considered whether unionists could be excluded from votes that would not affect Northern Ireland. This was deemed unworkable but it marked the first major indication that the Labour leader was antipathetic towards unionists at Westminster.[5]

The desire to avoid intervention remained the dominant characteristic of British government policy towards Northern Ireland but this became increasingly untenable. In 1967 the Northern Ireland Civil Rights Association (NICRA) was formed and began more public forms of protest against the Stormont regime. In June 1968 Austin Currie staged a housing sit-in in the village of Caledon, County Tyrone. The first civil rights march took place in August, travelling from Coalisland to Dungannon.[6] Most significant, however, was the banned 5 October NICRA demonstration in Derry in which protestors were batoned by the RUC. Television cameras caught the clashes and the broadcasting of the images transformed the situation.[7] The Labour government was forced to take a greater interest in Northern Ireland but preferred to put pressure on Stormont ministers to carry out internal reform. In November Wilson pressured O'Neill to enact a number of reforms including adopting the same local government franchise that existed in Great Britain.[8]

Although internal reform followed, tensions in Northern Ireland increased. Young student radicals in the People's Democracy group staged a march from Belfast to Derry which was attacked by loyalists and off-duty B Specials. Riots followed in Derry. Protestant fundamentalist preacher Ian Paisley led counter-demonstrations and divisions emerged within the Unionist party over the extent and speed at which O'Neill planned to bring about change. The Northern Ireland Prime Minister was forced to resign in April 1969 and was replaced by James Chichester-Clark, who had resigned from O'Neill's cabinet five days earlier only to commit to the same reform programme upon succeeding him. Throughout all of these events the Labour administration sought to avoid becoming entangled in Northern Irish politics, hoping that the Unionist government at Stormont could do enough to satisfy all sides.[9]

The escalation of violence

On 12 August the Apprentice Boys march in Derry was stoned by Catholic youths. Violent clashes followed with the police in what became known as the Battle of the Bogside. Two days later the rioting spread to Belfast where it was more starkly communal. Seven people were killed in Belfast and around 1,800 families were forced out of their homes by the disturbances (roughly 1,500 Catholic and 300 Protestant).[10] The British army was deployed in both Derry and Belfast but direct rule was not imposed. After a meeting between Unionist and Labour ministers Downing Street issued a declaration that both governments were committed to reform.[11] When a report into the police recommended disarming the RUC and replacing the B Specials with a new locally-recruited regiment, loyalists rioted in October and killed the first RUC officer to die as a result of the conflict.[12] Divisions emerged within republicanism and a split took place in the winter of 1969–70. Although the IRA was active in parts of Belfast during the August riots it was not particularly prominent.[13] Traditional republicans who had objected to the Marxist turn of the IRA leadership and the lack of violent activity argued that it had failed to defend the Catholic community. In December an IRA General Army Convention voted in favour of a national liberation front with the radical left and also to drop parliamentary abstentionism. This led to the formation of the PIRA and a split then occurred at the Sinn Féin ard fheis in January 1970. While the Official IRA leadership did not believe that an armed offensive against the British state was realistic, the Provisional movement adopted a more straightforwardly militaristic stance.[14]

The Labour government, meanwhile, lost the June 1970 general election. While in opposition, the security situation deteriorated dramatically. The PIRA mounted an increasingly violent campaign and reactions from the British army brought an end to the initially warm relationship with the Catholic community. On 27 June 1970 rioting broke out on the Crumlin Road in North Belfast after an Orange Order march passed through in the afternoon. The PIRA opened fire, killing three Protestant civilians. In East Belfast rioting also occurred between Protestants from the Lower Newtownards Road and Catholics from the Short Strand. Provisional IRA men took up positions in the grounds of St Matthew's Catholic Church and exchanged fire with Protestant gunmen. Three civilians, two Protestant and one Catholic, were killed.[15] A week later on 3 July the British army searched houses in the nationalist Lower Falls area for weapons and ammunition. A riot developed and a military curfew was announced that lasted until 5 July. During the course of the searches the British army smashed up houses and were abusive to residents. Although a number of weapons were found, the alienation of the community was far more significant. Geoffrey Warner rightly argues that the incident 'marked only a stage in the evolution of Catholic opinion' towards the army but it is a useful example of how heavy-handed actions angered the nationalist population and helped armed republicans gain support.[16] By the end of the year twenty-nine people had been killed as a result of the conflict, sixteen by the PIRA and five by the British army.[17]

The year 1971 was yet more violent, seeing 180 deaths. Loyalist paramilitaries became more active, with the emergence of the Ulster Defence Association and a growth in attacks by the Ulster Volunteer Force (UVF). Together the groups were responsible for twenty-one deaths, fifteen of which were Catholic civilians murdered by the UVF's bombing of McGurk's bar in Belfast.[18] Republicans were responsible for a majority of the killings (106) with the PIRA emerging as the most significant group, responsible for eighty-four.[19] In February 1971 the PIRA killed its first British soldier.[20] The following month it executed three Scottish soldiers on a mountain road on the edges of Belfast.[21] This was a particularly shocking moment for unionists and the Northern Ireland Prime Minister Chichester-Clark told the Conservative government that he no longer felt credible enough to hold the post. He asked for a more overt army presence in nationalist areas but had already decided to resign.[22]

The new Northern Ireland Prime Minister, Brian Faulkner, was keen to see the introduction of internment without trial. The General Officer Commanding (GOC) Northern Ireland, Harry Tuzo, did not advocate it but the Conservative government approved it anyway.[23] On 9 August 1971 internment was introduced and violence escalated dramatically. Twenty three people were killed over the course of three days, nineteen of them civilians. Particularly shocking were the eleven killings of civilians by British soldiers in the Ballymurphy estate of West Belfast, two of whom died from their injuries later in the month.[24] Three-hundred and forty-two people were interned, all of them Catholic. The one-sided nature of the operation further fuelled support for republican paramilitaries. Before internment the PIRA had killed ten British soldiers. By the end of the year it had killed thirty more.[25]

These events prompted criticism of the Conservative government by Labour. On 1 September 1971 the Labour party issued a statement condemning internment, stressing that 'no realistic solution could even be envisaged' until it was ended.[26] In the Commons, however, Harold Wilson offended a number of his own backbenchers when he questioned the handling of internment rather than attacking it in principle. He complained that 'so far from being limited to a sober, cool, clinical counter-violence operation, it was carried out on a politically selective, factional basis'.[27] These comments formed the general line adopted by Labour's frontbench. The following day the Shadow Home Secretary James Callaghan adopted the same line of criticism, remarking 'I have always felt ... that people who unprovoked shoot at the British Army have no right to be at liberty ... But the evidence which we can glean is that the people who have been interned cover a far wider spectrum than that'.[28] A number of Labour backbenchers led by Kevin McNamara and Stanley Orme voiced disgust with this, condemning Labour's decision not to seek a parliamentary division on internment. McNamara declared: 'Internment is unacceptable. We want the release of the detainees and an end of the façade of a bipartisan policy'.[29] The dissenting MPs independently divided the Commons on the issue, losing the vote 74 to 203. Sixty-six of their number were from the Labour party.[30]

Two months later Wilson spoke in the House of Commons and announced a fifteen-point plan for a united Ireland with entry of the Republic of Ireland into the Commonwealth and the introduction of an oath of allegiance. The principle that Northern Ireland could not cease to be part of the United Kingdom without the consent of its population featured in his speech, but he argued that they should accept unification. This was inherently unlikely and Wilson was marked out by unionists as a threat to their constitutional position. The plan was also predicated on the idea that violence had to stop first and 'the men of violence must be either destroyed or compelled to retire', which was optimistic about the capacity of British security forces to deal with the violence.[31] Meanwhile, the shadow spokesman on Northern Ireland, Merlyn Rees, argued for 'a return to the rule of law and the abandonment of the present rules of internment'.[32] After it emerged that a small group of the internees had been subjected to the 'five techniques' (hooding, deprivation of sleep, deprivation of food and water, the playing of white noise and wall-standing), James Callaghan proposed a motion opposing the continuation of internment without trial and calling for the transfer of security powers to Westminster. The motion was defeated by the Conservative majority.[33]

On 30 January 1972 the British army fired shots during a demonstration against internment in Derry, killing fourteen innocent civilians.[34] Afterwards, the PIRA had more people willing to join the organisation than it was able to handle.[35] The organisation escalated its campaign in response and Northern Ireland descended into chaos. A total of 496 people were killed in 1972. Republicans were responsible for 277, with 229 killings carried out by the PIRA. Loyalist paramilitaries killed 121 while the British army was responsible for seventy-nine deaths.[36] Following Bloody Sunday Wilson argued there could be no military solutions and that all-party talks should take place alongside the transfer of security powers to Westminster.[37] On 3 March he made a speech in Lancashire which went further, stressing that no agreement would be possible until the progressive ending of internment was announced. If this happened, Wilson believed, all-party talks on an 'open agenda basis' could begin by the end of the month.[38] On 24 March, however, Conservative Prime Minister Ted Heath announced the suspension of Stormont after Brian Faulkner refused to accept the transfer of security powers to Westminster.[39]

Direct rule and security

Following the fall of Stormont the first Secretary of State for Northern Ireland, William Whitelaw, promised to investigate all internment cases and review the operation of the Special Powers Act, which provided for internment alongside many other security powers.[40] Six months later he appointed the Diplock commission to consider legal means other than internment for dealing with paramilitary organisations.[41] Before the commission produced its report, the Detention of Terrorists Order was brought in. It replaced internment with a quasi-judicial system of detention without trial, featuring legal commissioners. The Secretary of State for Northern Ireland could sign an interim custody order for the detention of a person for 28 days, after which legal commissioners would decide whether to release them or allow for indefinite detention.[42] As the Northern Irish political magazine *Fortnight* argued 'the mass of the Catholic population are unlikely to be impressed by the verbal distinction between old style internment and new style detention'.[43] Providing the Labour frontbench's response, the former Attorney General Elwyn Jones said the new provisions were an improvement but did not go far enough. He objected that the proceedings would be in private and only one commissioner would decide each case. He disliked that both the commissioners and the appeal tribunal had the power to hear witnesses give evidence in the detainee's absence, a measure adopted to avoid witness intimidation. Elwyn Jones recognised this was a problem but he deemed the power 'so contrary to the principles of natural justice' that he felt authorisation should be given in each instance by the president of the appeal tribunal.[44] Merlyn Rees reiterated the criticisms, lamenting that the system was 'still only quasi-judicial'.[45] Labour abstained but a small minority of the party's backbenchers opposed the Order.[46] Although this group could only muster thirty votes, Rees expressed concern in his diaries about 'the powerful forces' of Catholic Scotland and north-west England in the Labour party, recording: 'we would have great difficulty in running Ireland if there were a Labour Government, of that there is not the slightest doubt.'[47]

A similar process occurred with the Emergency Provisions Act (EPA) of 1973. Based on the recommendations of the Diplock commission, it established a system of trial without jury for terrorist offences, changed the onus of proof in relation to charges of possession and contained numerous other security provisions. Although the controversial Special Powers Act was repealed, many of its clauses reappeared in the EPA.[48] Rees expressed a greater reluctance to accept certain provisions than the Conservatives, while recognising that special powers were necessary and should be opposed in detail rather than principle. He felt the provisions should be renewed more frequently and criticised most of the clauses in the Bill for inadequate safeguards. For instance, he believed that only one judge for juryless trials was insufficient, the provisions for bail were too harsh, and the provisions for admissibility of written evidence too vague.[49] Most important were his remarks on detention without trial. Rees believed that 'the fundamental aim must be to end' detention but balanced this by recognising it could not happen immediately. He urged Labour backbenchers to 'work to improve the Bill in detail' rather than oppose it outright.[50] A number of amendments were attempted, but Rees was forced to admit that they had 'not achieved very much'.[51] Most significant was the cross-party support for a clause which ended capital punishment for the crime of murder in Northern Ireland, a change which took place for Great Britain in 1969 but which had been rejected by the Unionist government.[52] At the final reading of the Bill in the Commons the votes were low with the outcome not in doubt. Only six Labour MPs opposed the Bill.[53]

Sunningdale and Labour

Direct rule had never been desired by the Conservative government so Whitelaw set about formulating a constitutional policy which aimed to restore devolution with two new elements: power-sharing between both nationalists and unionists and an all-Ireland institution for co-operation with the Republic. It was hoped that the nationalist SDLP, formed in 1970 out of the civil rights activism of Gerry Fitt, John Hume, Paddy Devlin, Austin Currie and Ivan Cooper, could deliver the support of the Catholic community for a compromise with unionism.[54] A White Paper was produced in March 1973 and legislated for shortly afterwards.[55] Elections took place for the Northern Ireland Assembly with unionists split over

Whitelaw's proposals. Within the Ulster Unionist Party Brian Faulkner led those in favour and Harry West led 'un-pledged' unionists.[56] William Craig's Vanguard Unionist Progressive Party and Ian Paisley's Democratic Unionist Party (DUP) rejected Whitelaw's proposals. The pro-White Paper side (Faulkner's unionists, the SDLP and the Alliance party) won a majority but anti-White Paper unionists received more support than Faulknerites, outnumbering them 27 to 23.[57]

In December 1973 the Sunningdale Agreement was brokered by the pro-White Paper parties and the British and Irish governments. A power-sharing executive was to be established. On the unionist side benefits included a declaration from the Irish Taoiseach accepting the status of Northern Ireland and the promise of better security co-operation. For the SDLP the primary gain was the proposed cross-border Council of Ireland.[58] Merlyn Rees supported Whitelaw's constitutional proposals, stating in his diaries: 'the realities are that a million Protestants ... cannot be bulldozed into the South. The other reality is that the government of the South does not want them ... [we have] got to make it possible for the minority in the North to feel that they belong in Northern Ireland and that they can work for a united Ireland.'[59] Although Rees's memoirs state that he 'felt the chance of agreement was far greater than all the cliff-hanging reports suggested', his private diaries reveal a great deal of gloom throughout Whitelaw's attempts to restore devolution.[60] Such pessimism fluctuated according to immediate events. In September 1972 he rightly observed that direct rule had made unionists feel 'rather rudderless', noting growing disaffection amongst working-class Protestants.[61] Prior to the Assembly elections he observed that power-sharing as an abstract idea had merit but he could not see how the SDLP could be forced to work with unionists.[62] On 8 July, however, he remarked 'I have always felt that it is the Protestants who can prevent this working more than the SDLP.'[63]

The Northern Ireland Executive took office on 1 January 1974 but it received a number of blows in its first two months. The Fianna Fáil Teachta Dála (TD) Kevin Boland took the Irish government to court on the grounds that the Sunningdale communiqué was unconstitutional. Articles 2 and 3 of the Irish constitution claimed the right to legislate for the whole island and the government was only able to defeat Boland by arguing that the declaration merely stated present policy. Thus, its significance was watered down, making it difficult for Faulknerites to present this as a concrete acceptance of partition. There was also controversy over the Council of Ireland proposals. The title alone was enough to provoke opposition from unionists, who feared that it would be a stepping-stone to unification. In January Faulkner resigned from the Ulster Unionist Party (UUP) leadership after the Ulster Unionist Council voted against the concept. A heavier blow came when Edward Heath called the February 1974 general election in response to disruption caused by striking miners.[64] On the eve of the election Rees remarked, 'I should feel extremely angry if all this Irish business were to be thrown into the melting pot just because ... the suburbans in the British Cabinet over the coal dispute and so on were to throw it aside.'[65] In Northern Ireland the election was fought solely on the subject of Sunningdale. The DUP, Vanguard and Harry West's 'Official Unionists' formed the United Ulster Unionist Council (UUUC) and campaigned under the slogan 'Dublin is only a Sunningdale away.' The UUUC obtained eleven of twelve seats with 51% of the total vote.[66] Labour, meanwhile, returned as a minority government.

Notes

1 For a nuanced handling of discrimination see John Whyte, 'How much discrimination was there under the Unionist regime, 1921–68?' in T. Gallagher and J. O'Connell (eds), *Contemporary Irish studies* (Manchester: Manchester University Press, 1983), pp. 1–35.

2 Peter Rose, *How the Troubles came to Northern Ireland* (Basingstoke: Palgrave, 2000), pp. 11–17.

3 Paul Rose, *Backbencher's dilemma* (London: Muller, 1981), pp. 178–9.

4 Bew and Patterson, *The British state*, pp. 11–15.

5 Graham Walker and Gareth Mulvenna, 'Northern Ireland representation at Westminster', *Parliamentary History*, 34:2 (2015), pp. 238–9.

6 Simon Prince, *Northern Ireland's '68: civil rights, global revolt and the origins of the Troubles* (Dublin: Irish Academic Press, 2007), pp. 118–22.

7 Bob Purdie, *Politics in the streets: the origins of the civil rights movement in Northern Ireland* (Belfast: Blackstaff, 1990), p. 156.

8 Prince, *Northern Ireland's '68*, p. 182.

9 Paul Bew, *Ireland: the politics of enmity* (Oxford: Oxford University Press, 2007), pp. 492–5.

10 Bew, *Ireland: the politics of enmity*, pp. 492–5; Thomas Hennessey, *The origins of the Troubles* (Dublin: Gill and Macmillan, 2005), p. 264.

11 Bew, *Ireland: the politics of enmity*, p. 496.

12 Peter Taylor, *Loyalists* (London: Bloomsbury, 1999), pp. 71–2.

13 Brian Hanley and Scott Millar, *The lost revolution: the story of the Official IRA and the Workers' Party* (Dublin: Penguin Ireland, 2009), pp. 125–32.

14 Hanley and Millar, *The lost revolution*, p. 149; Richard English, *Armed struggle: the history of the IRA* (London: Pan, 2003), pp. 106–8.

15 David McKittrick, Seamus Kelters, Brian Feeney, Chris Thornton and David McVea, *Lost Lives: the stories of the men, women and children who died as a result of the Northern Ireland troubles* (Edinburgh: Mainstream Publishing, 2007), pp. 49–51.

16 Geoffrey Warner, 'The Falls Road curfew revisited', *Irish Studies Review*, 14:3 (2006), p. 337.
17 McKittrick *et al.*, *Lost lives*, p. 1553.
18 McKittrick *et al.*, *Lost lives*, pp. 122–5, 1553.
19 McKittrick *et al.*, *Lost lives*, p. 1553.
20 McKittrick *et al.*, *Lost lives*, p. 64.
21 McKittrick *et al.*, *Lost lives*, pp. 70–2.
22 Thomas Hennessey, *The evolution of the Troubles 1970–72* (Dublin: Irish Academic Press, 2007), pp. 80–1.
23 Bew, *Ireland: the politics of enmity*, p. 502.
24 McKittrick *et al.*, *Lost lives*, pp. 79–95.
25 English, *Armed struggle*, pp. 139–41.
26 Hansard (Commons), 823, col. 197.
27 Hansard (Commons), 823, cols 34, 36.
28 Hansard (Commons), 823, cols 188–9.
29 Hansard (Commons), 823, col. 247; Paul Dixon has defined bipartisanship as a general agreement between the two main parties at Westminster on constitutional policy, specifically on the principle that Northern Ireland's constitutional status could only change in line with the wishes of its population. There is merit in defining it more broadly to include security policy. Although it makes a clear definition much harder, this is revealing of the rhetorical nature of the term. Those advocating it used it to mean respectable political behaviour, while those chastising bipartisanship simply meant that the parties' leadership was too similar: Paul Dixon, '"A House divided cannot stand": Britain, bipartisanship and Northern Ireland', *Contemporary Record*, 9:1 (1995).
30 Hansard (Commons), 823, col. 328.
31 Hansard (Commons), 826, cols 1571–92.
32 Hansard (Commons), 826, col. 1667
33 Hansard (Commons), 827, col. 32; for detail on the interrogation procedures see Hennessey, *The evolution of the troubles*, pp. 152–67.
34 *Report of the Bloody Sunday Inquiry*, volume I, H.C. 2010–11 (29).
35 Richard English, *Armed struggle*, p. 151.
36 McKittrick *et al.*, *Lost lives*, p. 1553.
37 Hansard (Commons), 830, cols 38–9.
38 Bodleian Library, Oxford, MS Wilson c. 908, Statement by Harold Wilson in Prescot, Lancs., 3 Mar 1972.
39 Patterson, *Ireland since 1939*, p. 226
40 Laura Donohue, *Counter-terrorist law and emergency powers in the United Kingdom 1922–2000* (Dublin: Irish Academic Press, 2000), p. 122.
41 *Report of the commission to consider legal procedures to deal with terrorist activities in Northern Ireland*, Cmnd. 5185, H.C. 1972–3.
42 Donohue, *Counter-terrorist law*, pp. 132–4.
43 *Fortnight*, 5 January 1973
44 Hansard (Commons), 848, cols 54–62.
45 Hansard (Commons), 848, col. 92.
46 Hansard (Commons), 848, col. 103.

47 LSE, MERLYN-REES/1/2, Transcripts of tapes, undated, p. 31.
48 Donohue, *Counter-terrorist law*, p. 154.
49 Hansard (Commons), 855, cols 294–5.
50 Hansard (Commons), 855, cols 298–9.
51 Hansard (Commons), 859, col. 867.
52 Hansard (Commons), 856, col. 1142.
53 Hansard (Commons), 859, cols 877–80.
54 For histories of the SDLP see: Ian McAllister, *The Northern Ireland Social Democratic and Labour Party: political opposition in a divided society* (London: Macmillan, 1977); Gerard Murray, *John Hume and the SDLP* (Dublin: Irish Academic Press, 1998); Peter McLoughlin, *John Hume and the revision of Irish nationalism* (Manchester: Manchester University Press, 2010); Sarah Campbell, *Gerry Fitt and the SDLP: 'in a minority of one'* (Manchester: Manchester University Press, 2015).
55 *Northern Ireland constitutional proposals*, Cmnd. 5259, London, 1973; *Northern Ireland Constitution Act* (HMSO, London, 1973).
56 For the fracturing of unionism see: Graham Walker, *A history of the Ulster Unionist Party: protest, pragmatism and pessimism* (Manchester: Manchester University Press, 2004); Henry Patterson and Eric Kaufmann, *Unionism and Orangeism in Northern Ireland since 1945* (Manchester: Manchester University Press, 2007).
57 Brian Walker, *Parliamentary election results in Ireland: 1918–92* (Belfast: Institute of Irish Studies, 1992), pp. 82–87.
58 *The Sunningdale Agreement* (HMSO, London, 1973); for a detailed analysis of the negotiations see Shaun McDaid, *Template for peace.*
59 LSE, MERLYN-REES/1/1, Transcripts of tapes, undated, pp. 11–12.
60 Rees, *Northern Ireland*, p. 33.
61 LSE, MERLYN-REES/1/1, Transcripts of tapes, undated, pp. 12–13.
62 LSE, MERLYN-REES/1/2, Transcripts of tapes, 8 July 1973, side 4, p. 8.
63 LSE, MERLYN-REES/1/2, Transcripts of tapes, 8 July 1973, side 4, p. 11.
64 Gordon Gillespie, 'The Sunningdale Agreement': lost opportunity or an agreement too far?' in *Irish Political Studies*, 13 (1998), pp. 100–14.
65 LSE, MERLYN-REES/1/3, Transcripts of tapes, undated, p. 13.
66 Gillespie, 'The Sunningdale Agreement'.

2

The collapse of power-sharing

The electorate's endorsement of the anti-Sunningdale UUUC at the February general election and the high level of bombings and shootings by the PIRA undermined the moderate political parties in Northern Ireland. During the first three months of the Labour government Merlyn Rees tried to bolster the Northern Ireland Executive while conducting a reappraisal of security policy in line with Labour's criticisms in opposition. After the Ulster Workers' Council (UWC) strike in May 1974 led to the collapse of power-sharing, both Rees's conduct and that of Harold Wilson was called into question by the pro-Sunningdale parties, who claimed that Labour was not committed to the new institutions and had failed to face down loyalist opposition. This view has been accepted by a number of academic authors. The most aggressive criticisms have come from consociationalist political scientists Brendan O'Leary and Michael Kerr, who essentially hold Labour responsible for the collapse of power-sharing.[1] The analysis presented here is critical of the Labour government but less favourable to the pro-Sunningdale parties than other accounts on the basis that there has been insufficient engagement with the limitations experienced by the British state. Any consideration of the May 1974 loyalist strike must factor in practical logistics, the nature of security policy at the time and the broader British context of strikebreaking in the 1970s.

Reactions to the election

Rees presented his reading of the situation to the Labour government's ministerial committee on Northern Ireland three weeks after his appointment as Secretary of State for Northern Ireland. He identified three basic problems: the security situation, the need to restore confidence in the power-sharing executive, and the implementation of the Sunningdale Agreement. The PIRA increased violence to undermine the executive and Rees feared that if they were able to sustain their current efforts 'the risk of a more severe Protestant reaction must be high'. He noted that the general election had produced 'a sharp drop in the morale and credibility of the executive'. It also prompted division. The Faulknerites desired a more gradual approach to Sunningdale and hoped for greater security co-operation between North and South. The SDLP, on the other hand, sought releases from detention and the full implementation of the Council of Ireland. The Alliance party held a position approximate to Faulkner's, supporting the Council of Ireland provisions but believing they could not yet be sold in Northern Ireland. The Irish government, a coalition made up of Fine Gael and the Irish Labour Party, was keen for Sunningdale to be ratified.[2] Rees told cabinet colleagues that the political situation was worsening and the government needed to give assurance that the Assembly would last its full term and power-sharing would not be abandoned.[3]

After the election Rees told the Northern Ireland Executive that 'Sunningdale was still the basis for progress, and the House of Commons was firmly behind it', adding: 'If there was any disagreement, it was from a small group of MPs – few in proportion to the volume of public support behind them – expressing the view that the government should pull out of Northern Ireland altogether'. He remarked that there was 'no real leadership' behind the pro-withdrawal movement despite substantial public support for it in Great Britain. Of Northern Ireland itself he 'had been disturbed by the apparent apathy of a large number of the public', but said that the emergence of the UUUC in the Commons caused 'little difficulty as the three major parties [at Westminster] were united in their support for Sunningdale'. He offered the executive 'all possible help in re-establishing itself and re-asserting its authority'.[4] Rees did not need to mention that the Labour government's policy ran contrary to the wishes of the general public in Great Britain. Gallup polls did indeed show a majority favoured withdrawal, but those arguing for it at Westminster had very little influence and public feeling about Northern Ireland was never strong enough to threaten government policy.[5] Rees sought to reassure the Northern Ireland Executive but a simple rejection of the UUUC might have been more convincing to Faulkner's unionists and the SDLP. Rees's emphasis on the situation at Westminster did, however, serve its purpose by deliberately ignoring the very real opposition to Sunningdale in Northern Ireland. That the UUUC amounted to only 11 out of 635 MPs was less relevant than their claim to be the body most representative of opinion in Northern Ireland. What the executive needed was for the Labour government to declare its intention to ignore such claims and this assurance was delivered early after the election.

When Brian Faulkner saw Harold Wilson and Merlyn Rees in Downing Street at the start of April he expressed fear for his position. Faulkner said if he accepted a Council of Ireland there would be no public support for

ratifying Sunningdale. He hoped to convince the SDLP that it could be
worked towards more gradually. Similarly, Faulkner argued that there
would be a 'complete log jam' if the lack of progress on cross-border security was not fixed and asked Wilson to tell Irish Taoiseach Liam Cosgrave
that power-sharing might collapse because of the Irish government's
'pursuit of narrower objectives' and treatment of the executive as a tripar-
tite body rather than a thing of itself. Recent PIRA bombings weighed
heavily on discussion, with Faulkner arguing that the PIRA hoped to
change the will of the government and bring down power-sharing. Wilson
declared his 'full support'.[6]

The British Prime Minister raised Faulkner's points when he met Cosgrave four days later, pointing to the need for greater cross-border security
co-operation with a number of Faulkner's supporters having 'lost heart'.
Cosgrave played down the significance of the border, arguing that over the
last six months only 18 of 108 murders had taken place in the area and
that once Sunningdale was ratified 'the extremists would get the message'.[7]
In a larger meeting that included Merlyn Rees and Garret FitzGerald,
Minister for Foreign Affairs, the Irish government expressed frustration
with Faulkner: when Rees raised the difficulties with the Council of Ireland,
Cosgrave remarked that 'Faulkner was always raising a new issue'. FitzGerald, although acknowledging that practical measures could be taken to deal
with fugitives, described unionists' preoccupation with the border as a
facilitator of republican violence as 'the "Northern mythology"'.[8] Rees
pushed for monthly meetings between the two chief officers of police and
the two army Chiefs of Staff. Further down the line he hoped for regular
meetings between border units and technical experts from both sides. He
also sought for a network of secure communications to be established
between army units on both sides (the Irish army was not allowed to com-
municate directly with their British counterparts). The Northern Ireland
Secretary hoped this would eventually lead to automatic daily exchanges
of incident reports and regular weekly meetings. This was rejected in May,
however, when FitzGerald argued that the Irish constitution only permitted the army to operate in support of, and at the request of, the Garda.[9]
Faulkner was dealt a further blow that month when the Law Enforcement
Commission jointly established after Sunningdale reported against extra-
dition from the Republic to Northern Ireland. There were practical reasons
why this was deemed unworkable for the South but the political criticism
that Cosgrave's government would have faced from opposition party
Fianna Fáil was also a factor.[10] Despite these important limitations, when
Wilson and Rees stressed the need to bolster Faulkner's position, ministers
from the Republic showed little sympathy and pressed instead for a speedy
implementation of the Sunningdale Agreement.

Security policy

There was also a reappraisal of security policy in the first months of the Labour government. Some of the ideas reflected Labour's criticisms of the previous administration, though it should be borne in mind that a change in government and the need for officials to brief incoming ministers naturally gives encouragement for those involved to take stock of the situation. Rees proposed a number of changes in the field of security, including a review of the army's role, changes in the structure and organisation of the RUC, the tightening of firearms laws, the establishment of an inquiry into the Emergency Provisions Act, a phased programme of detainee releases and the legalisation of Provisional Sinn Féin and the UVF. Rees said the RUC's organisation was 'woefully out of date' and their morale patchy. He included a list of changes already in hand to increase the efficiency and the acceptability of the RUC. These included the reorganisation of the RUC operational command structure along the same lines as the three army battalions, with an Assistant Chief Constable for each area, the creation of administration, training and personnel departments and an increase in expenditure on community relations from £2,500 a year to £20,000.[11] Rees's proposals were approved.[12]

The Ministry of Defence was keen to reduce the number of troops committed in Northern Ireland because of financial constraints and commitments elsewhere. The Secretary of State for Defence, Roy Mason, recommended reducing the sixteen major infantry units in Northern Ireland to twelve or thirteen. The frequency with which army units were returning to the region had 'an adverse and cumulative effect, especially on the soldiers' families'. A high concentration of troops in the region also prevented normal training from taking place, making it difficult to maintain technical skills for the army's North Atlantic Treaty Organization (NATO) role. Mason argued that a reduction had 'been the aim for some time'. The Chief of the General Staff (CGS), Sir Peter Hunt, proposed that they remove one unit in late April, one in mid-June and a third in early July. Rees accepted the reduction but suggested that the second and third removals be postponed to the end of July and September.[13] Harold Wilson concluded that they should leave the first two withdrawal dates as they stood but have the third 'subject to further consideration'.[14] A month later Rees recorded that army headquarters in Northern Ireland held different views from the general staff and did not want the reductions. Noting that it was 'widely believed in the province that, in announcing troop withdrawals, I am rejecting army advice', he stressed to Mason that it 'must be made quite clear that force reductions were recommended by the army itself'.[15] Michael Kerr is mistaken in accepting as accurate the unionist fear that reductions occurred because of pressure from within the Labour party.[16]

In the long run, however, Rees hoped for a shift towards using the police. On 4 April he told the Commons that the Labour government's policies towards Northern Ireland would 'be firmly based on those followed by our predecessors in office', but argued that:

> the cornerstone of security policy should be a progressive increase in the role of the civilian law enforcement agencies in Northern Ireland. So long as so much of the burden is being borne by the Army, it is altogether too tempting to many members of the community to undertake less than their share of responsibility and to feel that law and order is a matter for the United Kingdom Government rather than for them. This is not a situation which can be allowed to continue indefinitely.[17]

This speech marked the beginnings of a move towards what became known as police primacy. Rees described his intention to legalise Provisional Sinn Féin and the UVF as a 'move in the same direction' as the Conservative government's legalisation of the political wing of the Official IRA. In the Commons he claimed there were 'signs that on both extreme wings there are people who, although at one time committed to violence, would now like to find a way back to political activity'.[18] Rees gave the Northern Ireland Executive a rather different line, claiming he 'was giving thought to the weakening of certain groups by involving them in politics'.[19] There was a difference between the Official IRA's (OIRA) Republican Clubs and the other organisations in that the OIRA was on ceasefire whereas the PIRA and the UVF were not.[20] The UVF further differed as it was an armed paramilitary group lacking a political wing to be legalised (one followed in June in the form of the short-lived Volunteer Political Party). There was therefore a variation between how membership of republican and loyalist paramilitary groups was treated, but for Rees the rationale was that membership was less legally significant than the acts of violence perpetrated by those in the organisation, which was already the focus of the legal system.[21] The Conservatives did not object to the change, nor did SDLP MP Gerry Fitt who spoke in favour, and so Provisional Sinn Féin and the UVF were removed from the list of proscribed organisations in May.[22]

Rees affirmed that detention without trial would be ended as soon as the security situation permitted, a commitment already contained in the Sunningdale Agreement.[23] In opposition the need to end detention was felt more urgently by Labour than the Conservatives. Once in government, however, they faced army pressure to maintain it. On 28 March the GOC, Sir Frank King, argued that 'no detainee should be released until violence ends'. King recognised that 'political needs may force you to other conclusions' and admitted the merit of a small number of releases, though only if it provided 'some positive advantage such as a ceasefire'. King also argued that the criteria for detention orders to be signed by ministers should be reduced and expressed disappointment with the commissioners operating the system, who released 40% of detainees at their first hearing.[24] Here we see a great difference in how detention without trial was perceived popularly and by the military; the army was not allowed to detain many of those that it sought to, a point which was understandably lost on those whose image of the policy was defined by the first swoops in August 1971.

Rees announced the appointment of Lord Gardiner as chairman of a commission to examine security legislation in the context of preserving civil liberties and human rights, a distinction reflecting Labour's line in opposition.[25] The choice of Gardiner is worth noting as he had a previous record of expressing sentiments similar to Rees. In November 1971 the Labour peer was appointed to the Parker committee, which investigated the procedures for interrogating the first internees in Northern Ireland. Gardiner submitted a minority report describing the techniques as 'illegal, not morally justifiable and alien to the traditions of what I believe still to be the greatest democracy in the world'.[26] By contrast, in 1973 he remarked that 'nearly all of the proposals of the Diplock Commission, however draconian, were justified by the exceptional conditions in Northern Ireland'. The criticisms he made of the Emergency Provisions Bill that year were the same as those made by Rees and Elwyn Jones, opposing specific clauses in detail rather than principle.[27]

The changes to security policy reflected the pragmatic line of the Labour frontbench in opposition. RUC reforms were primarily concerned with efficiency and establishing a more professional organisation. They carried no political content and did not represent any break from the previous Conservative administration. Similarly, attempts to establish greater security co-operation with the Republic merely continued previous policy. The reduction of army force levels had been a long-term aim and came from the most senior army officers in the MOD. Distinctions from the Conservatives did exist, however. Rees's request for an internal security review reflected his desire for a greater role to be played by the RUC. He placed greater emphasis on the phasing out of detention without trial and the establishment of the Gardiner commission maintained the distinction between the two Westminster parties on security legislation.

Contingency planning and withdrawal

On 10 April Rees told the cabinet he 'was bound to warn his colleagues that the political situation was extremely fragile and there was a danger of

political collapse'. In discussion it was agreed that contingency plans were
needed for if the executive fell. A return to direct rule 'would represent a
failure of policies and the prospects of reinstituting power sharing would
be remote'. The minutes record: 'In the worst circumstances there might
be strong pressures in this country for our withdrawal from Northern
Ireland and although the consequences of this would be very grave and
carry much danger… it would be advisable to examine those consequences
as part of the contingency'. Harold Wilson remarked, 'at this stage they
should not exclude plans on the ground that they were unlikely to be
adopted. This applied even to a policy of withdrawal, the objections to
which had been fully recognised in discussion.'[28] While this shows a preoccupation with the possibility of being forced to withdraw by British public
opinion, it is important to note that the discussion was couched firmly in
the language of contingency; the emphasis being on the possibility of the
government being pushed to do something undesirable.

The next day John Hunt, the cabinet secretary, wrote to Wilson suggesting the establishment of a small committee with similar composition to
the ministerial committee on Northern Ireland.[29] This would be supported
by an informal group of officials and would aim to submit a paper on contingency plans for the collapse of the executive. It is difficult to reconstruct
how far contingency planning went. Released cabinet papers do not contain
any meetings of such a committee. Some consideration of withdrawal was
definitely given, as evidenced by a letter from the Foreign and Commonwealth Office to the Cabinet Office on 26 April. The letter states that at a
'restricted meeting' to consider 'the various options open to HMG…you
asked if we could consider the international, legal and other repercussions
of a decision to disengage entirely, severing all constitutional links between
Northern Ireland and the rest of the United Kingdom'. The attached memo
was entirely dismissive, arguing that Britain would be viewed 'significantly
less attractive as an ally, as a political and economic partner…as a place
to invest in or a country to lend money to, or a country with a claim to
international influence.'[30] Radical constitutional change became a preoccupation of Harold Wilson in particular at periodic moments during his
administration when the situation in Northern Ireland deteriorated. The
temptation to resort to hypotheticals should be resisted, however. Investigations into constitutional options consistently came back dismissing
withdrawal.

Faulkner, meanwhile, expressed to Rees his inability to accept the ratification of Sunningdale and the Council of Ireland, arguing that he 'would
have no political following left'.[31] On 16 April Rees wrote to Mason, asking
that the scheduled removal of the army unit at the end of that month be
postponed until June.[32] Two days later Wilson and Rees met the Northern
Ireland Executive. Wilson said he 'had come to Northern Ireland to

demonstrate...the fullest support for the executive'. He claimed 'all hope of a solution' rested with them and 'no one could look forward with hope to any further period of direct rule'. Roy Bradford, Unionist representative for East Belfast and Minister for the Environment, noted that 'a large majority of people in Northern Ireland thought that the government wanted to disengage...[and] the Prime Minister should be aware of a serious malaise in the Protestant community'. In response, Wilson remarked that the British government had been consistent in its commitment to Northern Ireland 'in spite of public opinion'. He said it would 'be quite wrong to be committed to a date of withdrawal' and 'there was no chance that anyone would bomb the British Army out'. The record further states his fear that collapse of the executive might lead to civil war: 'Hence there was an absolute determination on the part of the British Government not to give in, or pull out. He recognised, however, that if our troops were caught in cross-fire between rival terrorist groups the pressure for withdrawal would be very strong.'[33] Wilson's caveat was foolish. The prime minister unnecessarily exaggerated the danger that popular opinion in Great Britain posed to Sunningdale while at the same time offering his commitment to it.

In late April fears about withdrawal were further raised after Roy Mason made a clumsy speech. Speaking to a meeting of the National Union of Mineworkers (NUM) in Newcastle-under-Lyme, the Defence Secretary said the Labour government was committed to power-sharing, but added that there was pressure in Great Britain to set a date for troop withdrawals in order to pressure unionists and nationalists into co-operating. The MOD quickly put out a statement saying there was no time limit to the deployment of troops. Gerry Fitt objected that Mason had given the impression to the PIRA that violence would bring them political benefits, while Ian Paisley claimed, inaccurately, that troops were being withdrawn at a rate of 1,000 a month. He contended that there were only 7,000 soldiers in Northern Ireland rather than the 15,500 claimed by the government.[34] Mason's speech contributed to the perception that Labour was not committed to the power-sharing executive at a time when rumours of withdrawal were disseminated by hostile figures such as Paisley. His remarks were not indicative of the Labour government's desires but rather its fears. Wilson, Rees and Mason failed to dispel suspicions about their government in Northern Ireland but all acknowledged that the collapse of Sunningdale would be a disaster.

The Ulster Workers' Council strike

On 14 May the UWC announced a general strike in opposition to Sunningdale. The organisation was far from an ordinary trade union. Its co-ordinating committee incorporated trade unionists from key industries such as electricity, gas and oil, but also included senior loyalist paramilitaries and UUUC leaders Bill Craig, Ian Paisley and Harry West.[35] They demanded fresh Assembly elections, knowing that this would damage Brain Faulkner's standing and weaken power-sharing. A fortnight later the Northern Ireland Executive collapsed because of the UWC action. There has been a general tendency to blame the Labour government's inaction for the success of the strike. William Whitelaw wrote in his memoirs that Wilson and Rees did not have the same attachment to Sunningdale as himself and Heath, and thus they were less willing to support the executive in its hour of need.[36] Paddy Devlin of the SDLP argued that the unwillingness to arrest those involved, 'caused thousands of law-abiding people who had earlier given support to the Executive to switch loyalties'.[37] Devlin's SDLP colleague Gerry Fitt described Rees's response as 'abject surrender'.[38] Garret FitzGerald later wrote of a 'failure of the British government to give adequate support to the Executive'.[39] Brian Faulkner, describing Rees as 'a sensitive and liberal man' and Minister of State Stanley Orme as a 'left-wing Tribunite', said the two ministers 'were more accustomed to viewing strikers sympathetically than taking action against them, and...this background seemed to leave them confused and ineffectual in their response until it was too late'.[40]

These arguments have been accepted by a number of scholars. Brendan O'Leary claims Rees 'was not only incapable of credible commitment; he simply lacked conviction'.[41] Michael Kerr concludes that 'it was not that the British were incapable of successfully taking on the strikers, or that they had lost control of the army: they simply chose not to act...if Heath had remained Prime Minister he would certainly have acted'.[42] Anthony Craig, meanwhile, confusedly states of the UWC that 'no one could have stood in their way' but the strike 'could and would have been controlled had British contingency plans not warned for years of the dangers of a Protestant backlash' (which was precisely what it amounted to).[43] Paul Bew and Henry Patterson offer a more nuanced analysis. Bew describes 'Wilson's decision not to support the executive with the army' but, importantly, adds that it 'became very difficult to think of any military strategy that would have broken it without serious loss of life, with incalculable consequences'.[44] Patterson argues that the government 'showed no desire to confront the strikers' while acknowledging army advice against taking action.[45]

These accounts lack a systematic appreciation of the context of the strike and the challenges involved in strike-breaking. O'Leary and Kerr in particular are wrong in emphasising that a simple application of will by the Labour government would have broken the strike. On the first day Stanley Orme met UWC representatives and insisted they 'would not get what

they wanted by attempting to intimidate the government.' He said that if
the strike continued the army would maintain essential services (hardly
the words of a sympathetic union man as depicted by Faulkner).[46] The following day Rees told Wilson that the strike might paradoxically put Sunningdale closer to ratification 'if the government stood up to this Protestant
action.'[47] There was not, at this point, a lack of will to succeed where Sunningdale was concerned.

The strike was conducted using two methods. Firstly, key employees in
essential services, particularly oil and electricity, restricted supplies to slow
industry to a crawl. Secondly, the UDA and UVF employed a campaign of
intimidation, threatening businesses if they stayed open and blocking
streets to prevent workers from reaching their jobs and supplies reaching
their destinations. These two methods presented different challenges and
army regulations reflected this, distinguishing between Military Aid to
Civil Ministries (MACM), i.e. provision of essential services, and Military
Aid to the Civil Power (MACP), i.e. maintenance of peace and public
order.[48] There is merit, therefore, in examining them separately.

Intimidation during the strike took a number of forms. Anonymous
threatening phone calls were made to businesses and youths stoned those
that remained open. Initially, an overwhelming majority of workers at
Harland and Wolff's shipyards turned out. At a lunchtime meeting the
predominantly Protestant workforce voted for a motion opposing the Sunningdale Agreement. An announcement followed that all cars still in the
car park at 2pm would be burned out.[49] Similar incidents occurred across
Northern Ireland and helped establish the strike. The chief form of intimidation, however, and the one which the British army was primarily criticised for failing to handle, was the barricading of streets. The UWC was
concerned at the start of the strike when the general population did not
heed its call to cease work and the reduction in electricity had not yet
affected businesses.[50] In response, Andy Tyrie, the Supreme Commander
of the UDA, ordered barricading to disrupt turnout.[51] On 16 May military
reports recorded fifteen barricades in Belfast.[52] These steadily increased
and on the sixth day of UWC disruption there were 170. Most of the blocks
consisted solely of people but vehicles were hijacked in some cases.[53] The
paramilitaries were careful to avoid direct confrontation with the security
forces. When the army approached the barricades, strikers often melted
away before returning shortly afterwards. As the strike progressed into its
second week women and children became heavily involved, linking their
arms to prevent access.[54] Three issues need to be addressed here: army
claims that barricades were not their responsibility, the importance of
political circumstances in responding to such subversion and the capacity
of the security forces to deal with it.

In a meeting with Rees on 17 May the GOC Frank King argued that the army was based largely in Catholic areas and was ill-disposed to strike-breaking.[55] Ten years later he told the BBC that soldiers armed with rifles and bayonets were not suited to handling such forms of disorder. King claimed the British army had acted similarly in every such circumstance since the Peterloo massacre of 1819. There is a vast difference between Peterloo and the UWC strike: the former was a peaceful meeting attacked without provocation, while the UWC strike was enforced by power cuts and intimidation.[56] The implication that the British army had avoided violent confrontation with protestors since 1819 is also demonstrably wrong. In August 1911 British troops fired on striking dockworkers and railwaymen in Liverpool and Llanelli, killing two in the latter case. Eight years later the British military commander of Amritsar, India, ordered troops to fire without warning on an unarmed and peaceful meeting of between ten and twenty thousand people, killing 379 and wounding over 1,200.[57] Furthermore, Bloody Sunday in January 1972 is a clear example of the army engaging protestors with lethal force without justification.[58] King is nonetheless right to argue that armed soldiers are not suited to such confrontations. As the historian Keith Jeffery rightly states: 'The rationale behind military organisation is the concerted use of lethal weapons. The army exists to fight other armies, not mobs.'[59]

King later told journalist David McKittrick that 'if Rees had ordered us to move against the barricades we would have said, "With great respect, this is a job for the police. We will assist them if you wish, but it's not ter-rorism".'[60] This meshes well with *The Queen's regulations for the army* which state that MACP requests should be referred to the chief officer of police unless a 'grave and sudden' emergency makes immediate interven-tion necessary to protect life and property. In such circumstances the soldier 'is to act on his own responsibility'.[61] Lieutenant-Colonel Robin Evelegh, who commanded an army battalion on two tours of Northern Ireland, observes that in internal peace-keeping operations soldiers are legally indistinguishable from common citizens. The soldier is 'seen in theory as being uncontrolled by the Government of the day and, in so far as he has a duty to respond to the civil authorities, as owing this response to the magistrates'.[62] In Northern Ireland the British army operated such that these legal positions were dramatically removed from events on the ground.

The GOC held overall responsibility for security operations, including co-ordinating the tasking of the RUC. Security operations were defined as 'operations to counter action... aimed at subverting the security of the state', 'action necessary for the protection of life and property in case of actual or apprehended civil commotion' and 'service assistance in the maintenance of essential services'. Crucially, 'offences by civilians arising from subversion or civil commotion remain offences against criminal law and are to be investigated and prosecuted by the police in the ordinary way'.[63] If the GOC deemed intimidation not to be threatening the security of the state or life and property, it was the responsibility of the RUC.

The British army was deployed, primarily in nationalist areas, because the RUC was unable to manage disorder. As the conflict developed they became focussed on combating the PIRA. An NIO official subsequently noted that 'for the first 4 years or so...the army command here operated largely independently of the civil power' and they consequently saw their function 'as organising a military campaign against a defined enemy'.[64] Meanwhile, the police continued their duties largely in Protestant areas. The reluctance of the army to involve itself during the strike should be seen as a consequence of this division of labour. The legal murkiness of military action against civil disorder and the open-ended nature of army regulations meant decisions were subject to personal assessments of military and political conditions. Jeffery aptly argues that the incidence of MACP 'to a very great extent depends, not on military action, but political circumstances'.[65]

Contrary to King's claims of army consistency since Peterloo, the British army had previously removed barricades during Operation Motorman, this time targeting republican no-go areas. The operation involved establishing a cordon around the Bogside and Creggan estates in Derry and the Andersonstown and Ballymurphy estates in Belfast on 31 July 1972. Reinforcements brought the army's strength to over 30,000.[66] Clearly this sets a precedent for the UWC strike, showing that the British army had previously been willing to remove barricades. There are important differences, however. Republican barricades in Derry and Belfast were allowed to remain for over a year. The operation was conducted only when the political circumstances were felt suitable. The fall of Stormont, the murder of a teenage soldier from Derry and the republican bombings of Bloody Friday all served to undermine the IRA, leading to approval of the operation by William Whitelaw.[67] Michael Kerr argues that if barricades had been removed in the first couple of days the strike would have failed.[68] This would have required an operation akin to Motorman within a dramatically reduced time span and across a wider geographical spread.

On 21 May the Trades Union Congress (TUC) General Secretary, Len Murray, led trade union back-to-work marches in opposition to the UWC. A total of 1,500 army troops and 500 RUC men were needed to keep the seven main routes into Belfast open.[69] At a security meeting, the Chief Constable of the RUC reported that 'they had not sufficient manpower or the capacity to deal with the blocks on the side roads'.[70] That same night, following the arrival of 2,000 troops from Great Britain, six battalions 'removed all road blocks in the Village, Sandy Row, Donegall Road, East Belfast, Shankill and most of North Belfast' between midnight and six in the morning.[71] Road blocks reappeared just two hours later, suggesting the success of the operation relied largely on the sleep-pattern of the strikers. During a later interview Ted Heath dismissed as nonsense the Chief of the General Staff's claim that keeping streets free of barricades would have required a force equivalent to the British Army of the Rhine, numbering around 55,000.[72] Any estimation of necessary numbers is of course specu- lative, but a presence on the side streets of Belfast would have required reinforcements the army believed to be impossible and may well have provoked an angry response from the Protestant community.

The police were even more ill-suited to deal with intimidation on this scale. Their force level was only 4,455.[73] In addition to not having sufficient numbers, further difficulties also existed because the RUC was overwhelm- ingly Protestant, placing its loyalty in doubt. Journalists claimed that some RUC officers fraternised with the UWC at barricades.[74] The political dimen- sion is vital in understanding the difficulties faced by security forces attempt- ing to maintain law and order. Rees later remarked, 'We couldn't do a Prague. You can't put down a popular rising by killing people. We're not Russia. The police were on the brink of not carrying out their duties and the middle classes were on the strikers' side. This wasn't just an industrial dispute.'[75] This exaggerates the scale of popular support during the first week of the strike, but the nature of loyalist barricades and the army's preoccupa- tion with nationalist areas made it logical that Rees chose not to antagonise his army advisors by insisting on an operation they deemed unfeasible.

Another method would have been to address loyalist fears of Sun- ningdale by abandoning the Council of Ireland or conceding the demand for assembly elections. The latter was not an option as the result would probably have been a loyalist majority. On 22 May it was announced that the Council of Ireland would have a phased implementation.[76] SDLP assembly members initially voted against this in a private meeting, and were only persuaded to accept it after Stanley Orme promised the ending of internment in the short-term future.[77] The concession was not strong enough and came at a time when the strikers already felt assured of success. It is doubtful whether a viable concession could have been made.

May 1974 proved to be an especially successful month for the loyalist paramilitaries. The UDA, who led the barricading, perceived a willingness of the general population to acquiescence in what they were doing. Intimi- dation did not produce a backlash from the Protestant community and the UDA's actions did not descend into major violence as during an earlier 1973 strike attempt. Such restraint did not extend to the Republic of

Ireland. On 17 May the UVF bombed Dublin and Monaghan, killing 33 innocent civilians. This was the worst daily death toll for the entire conflict. The UVF did not claim the attack but loyalists were triumphant, with a UDA spokesman commenting: 'I am very happy with the bombings in Dublin. There is a war with the Free State and now we are laughing at them.'[78] This was an extreme reaction but is arguably symbolic of a more general anger within the unionist community towards the Republic of Ireland. David Ervine described a perception in loyalist circles that the UVF was 'returning the serve', illustrating how they conflated the Republic with militant republicanism.[79]

The second element of the strike pursued by the UWC was a reduction in essential services such as electricity. Such disruptions were far from unique to Northern Ireland. While the precise political context of strikes in Great Britain were markedly different, usually taking the form of traditional disputes over wages and conditions, the logistical challenges in handling them were often very similar. The use of troops as substitute labour in Great Britain occurred on twenty-one occasions between 1945 and the UWC strike, fifteen of which took place under Labour (rendering the view that trade union sympathies made the party hesitant to tackle strikes rather simplistic). In all instances the work given to the military was manual and did not require specialist skills, but on six occasions the use of troops worsened the dispute. During the 1949 London power station strike troops were deployed to assist engineers, prompting a fourth, larger station to join the dispute. This led to widespread power cuts.[80] There is a need for sensitivity in using the army as substitute labour and the impact of the armed forces is seriously affected by the skills required for intervention. Analysing the experiences of strikebreaking throughout the UK, Jeffery and Hennessy make the distinction that troops 'can be used extensively where relatively unskilled work is involved'.[81]

As in Great Britain, the key problem in facing the UWC's restriction of electricity was the need for sensitivity and the right skills. Billy Kelly, a power station worker and union convenor at Belfast Station East, and Tom Beattie, an engineer at Ballylumford power station, produced plans designed to bring industry to a halt. On 15 May, as the strike began, labour was withdrawn from all but three generators at Ballylumford and there were similar walkouts at Coolkeeragh and the two Belfast stations. Pickets were mounted outside, stopping the supply of fuel and essential chemicals. The four electricity stations in Northern Ireland generated 725 megawatts of electricity and Kelly's plan was to reduce it to 400.[82]

The NIO considered various ways to increase the electricity supply. One possibility discussed was deploying a nuclear submarine in Belfast harbour. John Hume was adamant in a later British Broadcasting Corporation (BBC) interview that this would have worked and the navy were ready to carry the operation out.[83] Two days into the strike, however, the MOD noted difficulties in converting the supply to the electricity grid. Only a few hundred kilowatts would be provided in Belfast, where the two power stations were capable of producing 360 megawatts. They considered deploying a destroyer vessel but this would only have produced six megawatts at most, an insignificant amount.[84] Any attempts to increase the supply depended on the power stations in Northern Ireland.

The deployment of troops to run the power stations was given serious consideration. On 16 May Rees informed Wilson 'he had put on immediate notice troops capable of running power stations, and at short notice troops capable of running sewage plants'. He said there was enough power for twenty-four hours but 'it might be necessary to take a difficult decision the following day to bring in troops'.[85] The term 'immediate notice' was inaccurate. A Royal Engineers field squadron and an additional '500 or so personnel' were placed on seven days notice, except for '134 men, who might be required to maintain power stations' who were placed on forty-eight hours notice from 21 May. The following day discussions between the NIO and MOD led to the time frame being reduced to forty-eight hours from 20 May.[86] Intervention within the first week of the strike may not, therefore, have been possible.

On the afternoon of 17 May Rees informed Wilson that if troops were deployed middle management would probably walk out. He proposed that deployment should occur only on the basis of maintaining life.[87] At a meeting of officials including a representative of the Northern Ireland Electricity Service (NIES) it was observed that the army would require assistance from specialist technicians if it intervened.[88] An NIES representative was also present at a security meeting held between Rees, the GOC, and the Chief Constable. Rees asked how middle management would react to the use of service technicians in the event of a life and death situation. The NIES representative replied that 'bringing in the Services would alienate the whole of Protestant opinion, including his middle management' and he would prefer to try to keep electricity going without intervention.[89]

Dependence on middle management and the difficulty of using military forces to carry out skilled work is reinforced by the experience elsewhere. Gillian Morris points out that 'engineers have enormous industrial muscle as it has been clear for many years that they are indispensable to the supply system and cannot be replaced'. During an electricity manual workers' overtime ban in 1970 the secretary of state for trade and industry told the House of Commons that using troops in power stations was not practical. In 1977 the House of Lords heard that individual power stations were so specialised they could only be run by resident engineers with long-standing experience.[90] This situation existed in Northern Ireland as well: the Ballylumford station had twenty-four volumes of manuals of over 200 pages specific to the various boilers and turbines, while each engineer kept a personal notebook on modifications.[91]

In a meeting with the Irish ambassador, who conveyed the Taoiseach's desire for military intervention, Wilson remarked that if troops were moved in 'the amount of power produced might, in fact, be less than at present'.[92] On 24 May Wilson received a letter from the Electrical Power Engineers' Association. The union said that a majority of its Northern Ireland members would walk out if troops went in and that it had no choice but to back their decision.[93] That same day intervention was discussed by Wilson, Rees, Mason and the leaders of all parties on the executive. Wilson stated the dangers of intervention. Brian Faulkner and Gerry Fitt argued for it. Rees said he 'was placed in a difficult situation, when making his mind up about possible intervention...if presented with conflicting advice'. Rees was not firm enough in explaining the practical constraints to the executive. Despite his hand-wringing, the evidence was stacked against intervention and the decision against it did not stem from mere lack of political will. Wilson suggested that a threat to the pension rights of middle-ranking engineers 'might make them see reason'. This is a further indication that the claim Labour was unwilling to confront the strikers because of trade union sensibilities is unsubstantiated. Indeed, Wilson was prone to taking an aggressive line in Great Britain, as during the seamen's strike of 1966 when, much to the frustration of MI5, he publicly used intelligence material to accuse communists of orchestrating the strike.[94] His pension proposal fits into this pattern of behaviour but was judged counterproductive and rightly so.[95]

Another option was to ask Catholic workers at Coolkeeragh to increase the supply. The NIES opposed the plan on the grounds that it would provoke a walkout of the Protestant workforce at Ballylumford, with the chairman even threatening his resignation in response.[96] Counterfactual suggestions that the army could have maintained the electricity supply are borne of frustration rather than a realistic appreciation of what the government was capable of. Early in the strike the government sought advice on intervention in the power stations and placed army technicians on standby. The news was not encouraging and the UWC's tactic of keeping the electricity supply at a level that made military intervention risky discouraged Rees from deploying troops.

Meanwhile, the UWC controlled numerous other facets of daily life, including the distribution of petrol and bread. It issued passes to those who successfully argued that their work was essential.[97] A plan for the distribution of oil and petrol was approved by the executive on 22 May. Two days later the Labour government approved the use of troops to requisition the Belfast harbour estate and petrol stations spread across Northern Ireland.[98] Before the operation took place Wilson made a controversial television broadcast on 25 May which infuriated unionists. He spoke of the resources given to Northern Ireland, stating: 'people who benefit from all this now viciously defy Westminster, purporting to act as though they were an elected government; people who spend their lives sponging on Westminster and British democracy and then systematically assault democratic methods. Who do these people think they are?'[99] The speech had a devastating impact on support for the executive. While Wilson specifically attacked the strikers, his remarks were seen to be directed at the unionist community in general. By indulging in such an emotional response he failed to act in the balanced manner required in Northern Irish affairs.

Rees delayed implementing the oil plan.[100] He believed the unionist Minister for Environment Roy Bradford was leaking information in the executive and that 'anything we discussed in the Castle in [the] Emergency Committee' also leaked, displaying his distrust of the Northern Ireland Civil Service. Similarly, the RUC were not told about an army operation in Rathcoole for fear that they would leak to loyalist paramilitaries. Rees recorded in his diaries that 'one daren't talk in the Castle'. He felt that the executive 'just wasn't good enough to run a country in conditions like this'.[101] After the army carried out the oil plan on 26 May there was less petrol available than before. The UWC responded to the opening of twenty-one government-requisitioned petrol stations by closing over 140 that it previously kept open. Mistakes were made in distributing the exact grades of oil needed and at some stations paraffin was put in cars.[102] Pressure on the executive continued and on 28 May Faulkner asked Rees to negotiate with the strikers. He refused, leading Faulkner and his unionist colleagues to resign.[103] The executive collapsed and the following day the UWC ended its strike.

Conclusion

The failure of the first power-sharing executive has traditionally been seen as a black mark against the Wilson administration's record in Northern Ireland and against Rees in particular. Michael Kerr remarks that Rees 'had the power to tackle the strike and, *in what many observers regarded as a gross dereliction of duty,* totally failed the executive by not using it' [emphasis added].[104] These remarks are symptomatic of not just Kerr but other academic authors' tendency to confuse contemporary opinion with definitive argument. The challenges of handling a strike are substantial and present great difficulties for the security forces and government ministers. Simplistic accounts which attribute the collapse of the executive to Labour's lack of will or sympathy have failed to acknowledge the parameters within which the security forces could operate.

A greater emphasis is needed on the significance of unionist disaffection, which provided the UWC with an opportunity to bring down the executive. The general election result weakened Faulkner's position and while the Labour government sought to help him, there was little sympathy from the Irish government. Reducing the scope of Sunningdale to a more modest, acceptable form and delivering a level of cross-border security co-operation that would boost support for Faulkner was a project that presented real difficulties to nationalists and was an unlikely prospect. The SDLP faced a great challenge in taking their support with them in their support for power-sharing in the context of ongoing violence. The Irish government might fairly be accused of expecting too much of Faulkner's unionists, though it should also be remembered that the practicalities of some of the changes needed posed greater political problems in Dublin than they did in London. It is difficult to conceive of the Labour government overcoming these difficulties in a swift enough fashion to pre-empt loyalist opposition. With the strikers increasingly confident of success, however, Wilson's televised speech served only to exacerbate the problem. His preoccupation was with public opinion in Great Britain. Righteous indignation may have appealed outside of Northern Ireland but it was foolish to think it would elicit anything other than a hostile response from where it actually mattered.

Notes

1 O'Leary, 'The Labour government and Northern Ireland, 1974–79'; Kerr, *The destructors*.

2 UK National Archives (TNA), CAB 134/3778, IRN(74) memo 4, 28 March 1974.

3 TNA, CAB 134/3778, IRN(74) meeting 1, 1 April 1974.

4 Public Record Office of Northern Ireland (PRONI), OE 1/24, Executive Meeting with Secretary of State, 26 March 1974; Cf. Kerr, *The destructors*, p. 172.

5 An *Irish Times* article in 1972 recorded that 'half the population already favoured a withdrawal'. Later, in 1978, *The Times* stated that 'every opinion survey conducted in Britain' since June 1974 showed a majority in support of it: *Irish Times*, 15 April 1972; *The Times*, 20 Sept 1978.

6 TNA, PREM 16/145, Meeting between Wilson and Faulkner, 1 April 1974.

7 TNA, PREM 16/145, Meeting between Wilson and Cosgrave, 5 April 1974.

8 TNA, PREM 16/145, Meeting between Wilson and Cosgrave/others, 5 April 1974.

9 TNA, CAB 134/3778, IRN(74) memo 3, 28 March 1974; TNA, PREM 16/146, Meeting between Rees and FitzGerald, 13 May 1974.

10 McDaid, *Template for peace*, p. 64.

11 TNA, CAB 134/3778, IRN(74) memo 3, 28 March 1974.

12 TNA, CAB 134/3778, IRN(74) meeting 1, 1 April 1974.

13 TNA, CAB 134/3778, IRN(74) memo 5, 28 March 1974.

14 TNA, CAB 134/3778, IRN(74) meeting 1, 1 April 1974.

15 TNA, PREM 16/145, Rees to Mason, 16 April 1974.

16 Kerr, *The destructors*, p. 172.

17 Hansard (Commons), 871, cols 1463–8.

18 Hansard (Commons), 871, col. 1476.

19 PRONI, OE 1/24, Executive Meeting with Secretary of State, 26 March 1974.

20 The OIRA ceasefire declared in May 1972 was conditional and flexible, with the organisation mounting occasional retaliatory attacks: Hanley and Millar, *The lost revolution*, pp. 180–1.

21 Hansard (Commons), 871, col. 1476.

22 Hansard (Commons), 871, col. 1552; Hansard (Lords), 351, col. 1093.

23 Hansard (Commons), 871, col. 1471.

24 TNA, FCO 87/335, GOC to Rees, 28 March 1974.

25 Hansard (Commons), 871, col. 1471.

26 *Report of the Committee of Privy Counsellors appointed to consider authorised procedures for the interrogation of persons suspected of terrorism*, Cmd. 4901, H.C. 1971–2.

27 Hansard (Lords), 344, col. 697.

28 TNA, CAB 128/54, CC(74) meeting 11, 10 April 1974.

29 TNA, PREM 16/145, Hunt to Wilson, 11 April 1974.

30 TNA, PREM 16/145, Harding to Smith, 26 April 1974.

31 TNA, PREM 16/145, Note by Reid, 8 April 1974.

32 TNA, PREM 16/145, Rees to Mason, 16 April 1974.

33 TNA, PREM 16/145, Meeting between Wilson and Northern Ireland Executive, 18 April 1974.

34 *The Times*, 25 April 1974.

35 TNA, CJ4/504, 'The Strike in Northern Ireland', report by John Bourn, undated.

36 Whitelaw, *Whitelaw memoirs*, p. 122.

37 Devlin, *The fall of the N.I. Executive*, p. 15; Hansard (Commons), 874, col. 880.

38 TNA, PREM 16/150, Meeting between Rees and SDLP delegation, 29 Aug 1974.

39 FitzGerald, *All in a life*, pp. 243–4.

40 Faulkner, *Memoirs of a statesman*, p. 262.

41 O'Leary, 'The Labour government and Northern Ireland, 1974–79', pp. 215.

42 Michael Kerr, *Imposing power-sharing: conflict and coexistence in Northern Ireland and Lebanon* (Dublin: Irish Academic Press, 2005), p. 68.

43 Craig, *Crisis of confidence*, pp. 180, 194.

44 Bew, *Ireland: the politics of enmity*, p. 515

45 Henry Patterson, *Ireland since 1939*, p. 243.

46 TNA, CJ4/504, Meeting between Orme and deputation led by Paisley, 15 May 1974.

47 TNA, PREM 16/146, Butler to Bridges, 16 May 1974.

48 *The Queen's regulations for the army, 1975* (HMSO, London, 1976), pp. 11.1–11.3.

49 Robert Fisk, *The point of no return: the strike which broke the British in Ulster* (London: André Deutsch, 1975), pp. 59, 81.

50 Don Anderson, *Fourteen May days: the inside story of the loyalist strike of 1974* (Dublin: Gill and Macmillan, 1994), p. 148.

51 Taylor, *Loyalists*, pp. 130–1.

52 TNA, CJ4/501, STRIKEREP, 16 May 1974.

53 TNA, CJ4/501, Director of Operations Brief, 21 May 1974.

54 Anderson, *Fourteen May days*, p. 97.

55 TNA, CJ4/504, Meeting between Rees and GOC, 17 May 1974.

56 Ulster Folk and Transport Museum (UFTM), BBC Northern Ireland archive, #1663, 'A modern rebellion', 1984; the Peterloo massacre occurred at St Peter's field in Manchester during a mass meeting demanding the extension of the vote. A cavalry charge caused 11 deaths and over 600 injuries: Boyd Hilton, *A mad, bad and dangerous people? England 1783–1846* (Oxford: Oxford University Press, 2008), p. 252.

57 Keith Jeffery, 'Military aid to the civil power: an historical perspective' in Peter Rowe and Christopher Whelan (eds), *Military intervention in democratic societies* (Kent: Croom Helm, 1985), pp. 53–6.

58 *Report of the Bloody Sunday Inquiry* (London: HMSO, 2010).

59 Jeffery, 'Military aid to the civil power', p. 54.

60 David McKittrick, *Making sense of the troubles* (Belfast: Blackstaff, 2000), p. 103.

61 MOD, *The Queen's regulations for the army*, p. 11.1.

62 Robin Evelegh, *Peace keeping in a democratic society: the lessons of Northern Ireland* (London: C. Hurst, 1978), p. 3.

63 TNA, CJ4/1293, Directive for the General Officer Commanding Northern Ireland as Director of Operations, 14 March 1973.

64 TNA, CJ4/1208, Webster to Barker, 25 March 1976.

65 Jeffery, 'Military aid to the civil power', p. 64.

66 Peter Neumann and M.L.R. Smith, 'Motorman's long journey: changing the strategic setting in Northern Ireland', *Contemporary British History*, 19:4 (2005), p. 414.

67 Paul Bew and Gordon Gillespie, *Northern Ireland: a chronology of the troubles 1968–9* (Lanham: Scarecrow Press, 1999), pp. 53–5.

68 Kerr, *Imposing power-sharing*, p. 68.

69 LSE, MERLYN-REES/1/4, Transcripts of tapes, undated, p. 8.

70 TNA, CJ4/504, Note of a security meeting held at Stormont Castle, 21 May 1974.

71 TNA, CJ4/501, Director of Operations Brief, 22 May 1974.

72 UFTM, BBC NI archive #1663, 'A modern rebellion', 1984.
73 Hansard (Commons), 874, col. 268w.
74 Fisk, *The point of no return*, p. 71.
75 Under Communist leader Alexander Dubček there was a period of democra-
    tisation in Czechoslovakia during 1968. Moscow sent 500,000 Warsaw Pact
    troops to the country in response: Tony Judt, *Postwar: a history Europe since
    1945* (London: Heinemann, 2005), pp. 440–7; Taylor, *Loyalists*, p. 132.
76 Bew and Gillespie, *Northern Ireland: a chronology*, p. 86.
77 Paddy Devlin, *Straight Left: an autobiography* (Belfast: Blackstaff, 1993), p.
    239.
78 McKittrick *et al.*, *Lost Lives*, p. 447.
79 Taylor, *Loyalists*, p. 126.
80 Gillian Morris, *Strikes in essential services* (London: Mansell, 1986), pp. 51,
    100–2.
81 Jeffery and Hennessy, *States of emergency*, p. 241.
82 Fisk, *The point of no return*, pp. 19, 168-70.
83 UFTM, BBC NI archive, #1663, 'A modern rebellion', 1984.
84 TNA, PREM 16/146, Nicholls to Butler, 17 May 1974.
85 TNA, PREM 16/146, Butler to Bridges, 16 May 1974.
86 TNA, PREM 16/146, Nicholls to Butler, 17 May 1974.
87 TNA, PREM 16/146, Conversation between Wilson and Rees, 17 May 1974.
88 TNA, CJ4/504, Meeting of officials in Stormont Castle, 17 May 1974.
89 TNA, CJ4/504, Meeting between Rees, G.O.C. and Chief Constable, 17 May
    1974.
90 Morris, *Strikes in essential services*, p. 139.
91 Fisk, *The point of no return*, p. 172.
92 TNA, PREM 16/147, Meeting between Wilson and Irish Ambassador, 23 May
    1974.
93 TNA, PREM 16/147, Lyons to Wilson, 24 May 1974.
94 Jeffery and Hennessy, *States of emergency*, p. 232.
95 TNA, PREM 16/147, Meeting between Wilson and Chief Executive, 24 May
    1974.
96 TNA, CJ4/503, Meeting between Rees and senior commerce officials, 27 May
    1974; TNA, PREM 16/147, Meeting between Wilson and Chief Executive, 24
    May 1974.
97 Fisk, *The point of no return*, p. 74.
98 TNA, PREM 16/147, Meeting between Wilson and Chief Executive, 24 May
    1974; TNA, CJ4/504, Department of Commerce oil plan, undated.
99 'Text of broadcast made by Harold Wilson on 25 May 1974' (cain.ulst.ac.uk,
    accessed 8 April 2016).
100 TNA, PREM 16/148, Conversation between Rees and Wilson, 26 May 1974.
101 LSE, MERLYN-REES/1/4, Transcripts of tapes, 2 June 1974, pp. 9–11.
102 Anderson, *Fourteen May days*, pp. 138–9.
103 TNA, CJ4/501, N.I.E. news release, 28 May 1974.
104 Kerr, *Imposing power-sharing*, p. 69.

3

Drift?

With the collapse of the Northern Ireland Executive the Labour government needed to produce an entirely new constitutional approach. To many at the time, British policy for the remainder of 1974 was frustratingly static, both on the political front and in dealing with paramilitary violence.[1] Rees declared his plan for a consultative assembly in which politicians in Northern Ireland would be given the task of seeking an agreement without imposition from Dublin or London. This was hardly likely to succeed and there were fears that plans for withdrawal were being secretly developed. Rees's reputation suffered, with SDLP politicians calling for his resignation and anti-Sunningdale unionists showing no willingness to compromise. Bombings continued with the worst loss of life in Great Britain during the conflict occurring in Birmingham in November 1974. Though the period might be characterised as one of drift, significant developments occurred behind closed doors. Plans were developed for an expected PIRA ceasefire and the Gardiner commission produced its report, identifying many of the key changes that would follow and supporting Rees in his desire for a security policy which moved away from detention without trial and placed greater emphasis on the police.

Doomsday plans and the Convention

The question of what to do once the Northern Ireland Executive collapsed heavily exercised the minds of both officials and ministers during the UWC strike. On 22 May NIO permanent secretary Frank Cooper sent a top-secret memorandum to Downing Street after discussions with a 'very restricted circle of officials'. It dismissed integrating Northern Ireland with Great Britain. Legislating for Northern Ireland affairs at Westminster was considered unfeasible because of parliamentary timetable restrictions. Similarly, reducing Northern Ireland to county status and running it by local government would pose great difficulties. Although integration might have satisfied some unionists, Cooper argued that it would be opposed by nationalists, the Irish government and resented by the British public for binding Britain 'even more inextricably to the Irish problem'.[2]

Of particular interest is Cooper's consideration of withdrawal, forming the bulk of his paper. He remarked, 'the degree of planning necessary to accomplish withdrawal, and its complexity of execution, means that whatever its merits and demerits withdrawal would not be practicable as an immediate response to the crisis'. Withdrawal would either place 'Protestant Ultras in office' or, in the event of a handover to the Irish Republic, be resisted by Southern politicians. Economic withdrawal was considered impossible because of the damaging effects it would have on the country while military withdrawal would lead to greatly increased violence. Cooper also judged there would be international condemnation, with serious political and economic repercussions.[3] In essence, he argued that withdrawal from Northern Ireland would be disastrous. Both moral and practical difficulties rendered it unfeasible.

On 29 May John Hunt suggested to Harold Wilson that 'a small senior official group' be established to 'revise and refine' Cooper's paper.[4] Wilson responded that, while power-sharing remained 'an objective we must continue to proclaim', the government was in a position of power without responsibility and 'the press and an increasing number of MPs will soon be telling us that the Emperor has no clothes'. The government would have to face the possibility of another UWC-type strike if the Protestant majority rejected any future proposals. Wilson was convinced that the army was 'virtually powerless to maintain essential services'. He remarked, 'all this affects the drafting of any Doomsday scenario'. Wilson told Robert Armstrong (his Principal Private Secretary) that 'we should proceed to prepare a plan for Dominion status for Northern Ireland'. He wrote of the possibility of this having to be done over the following four months and involving negotiations between all political parties at Westminster and in Northern Ireland. Financially Wilson felt there should be a 'tapering off' period of three to five years and militarily a gradual removal of troops. If the new state backtracked on provisions for civil rights then financial support would be cut off completely. He also considered the possibility of economic sanctions, admitting that he was 'affected by Rhodesian negotiations' (sanctions had been introduced in Southern Rhodesia in response to white premier Ian Smith's unilateral declaration of independence in 1965).[5]

At a superficial level, there were some similarities between unionists and white settlers in Southern Rhodesia. As Donal Lowry notes, during the Irish Home Rule crisis Rhodesian settlers supported the unionist case, attacking the British government's proposed abandonment of the region to a hostile majority community. During the 1960s and 1970s the situation was reversed, with high-profile unionists such as Ian Paisley and Bill Craig expressing sympathy for Ian Smith.[6] Regardless of such affinities, there were tremendous differences between the two. In considering Southern Rhodesia a fitting analogy Wilson underestimated the willingness of Protestants in Northern Ireland to eventually acquiesce in direct rule. His dislike of unionists hampered his awareness of the precise context of Northern Ireland and contributed to his fears that the worst outcomes were probable.

Nevertheless, the 'doomsday' document requires careful treatment. Paul Bew argues that Wilson established a secret committee to consider withdrawal. He cites Bernard Donoughue, head of the Policy Unit in Downing Street, who claims in his 1987 memoirs that an official committee was established in the Cabinet Office to examine Wilson's doomsday proposals but that 'the whole enterprise was rendered academic' by the UWC strike.[7] Donoughue's recollections are incorrect; Wilson's memo was produced the day the strike ended. A different order of events is apparent in Donoughue's diaries, where he records that early in the strike Wilson expressed the need for a small contingencies committee to consider British withdrawal. During this discussion Wilson apparently told Donoughue that he favoured granting the region Dominion status.[8] There is no indication, however, that Wilson's committee was established.[9]

As for the document itself, although radical, it was predicated on a pessimistic analysis of what would occur over the following months. The letter envisioned a scenario where the British government was left with a painful choice. Anthony Craig describes the document as a 'subtly-veiled' indication of his desire for a united Ireland.[10] As the circulation of the document was restricted to Hunt, Armstrong, Donoughue and Joe Haines, a veiled approach was unnecessary.[11] Dominion status also did not logically imply progress towards a united Ireland; the creation of a semi-independent state with a Protestant majority would make an all-Ireland entity less likely to emerge. Wilson felt considerable antipathy towards unionism and may well have liked to be rid of Northern Ireland altogether, regardless of what was left behind. Such instincts should not, however, be misread as influential, even if they belonged to the prime minister.

A more accurate indication of constitutional policy after the fall of the executive is instead to be found in the discussions taking place amongst Northern Ireland Office ministers and officials, as these ultimately shaped the decisions taken. Merlyn Rees's thinking arose from his discussions with unionist party leaders on 30 May. Ian Paisley, Bill Craig and Harry West each separately said that they deeply resented the British government's attempt to impose a settlement on Northern Ireland. This led Rees to remark that there was 'a growing feeling that the British cannot solve the Irish problem and that it would be better to let them have a shot at it themselves'. He proposed a consultative assembly. The idea had merit simply because of the lack of other options; the formation of a new power-sharing executive would be impossible and the UUUC were demanding fresh elections in which they would likely do well. Any imposition by the Labour government would likely be rejected and they could not put elections off indefinitely.[12]

On 3 June Rees told the Commons that 'in recent years a new form of Protestant nationalism has been emerging in Northern Ireland which has culminated in the events of the past few weeks'.[13] He repeated this sentiment in his memoirs, claiming that 'the cry for independence was reverberating round the province at the end of the strike'. While his observation that the flag of Northern Ireland was increasingly preferred in East Belfast over that of the union, usage of terms like 'nationalism' misunderstood the frustration and anger being expressed by sections of the Protestant population. Even when calls for Ulster independence *were* explicitly made, these had more to do with anger at the actions of the British government than any conviction that severing the union offered a better prospect. He was, however, right to argue that Protestant feeling went 'deeper than a backlash'.[14] Rees appreciated that British involvement in Northern Ireland during the conflict had alienated large portions of the Protestant community. What he did not articulate was that they were alienated from British politicians rather than the union. Nonetheless, a reasonable and enduring element of his perception of the conflict was that London and Dublin were not in a position to impose a solution. This was not a view from which an effective set of policies could emerge in the short term. It was an acceptance of weakness, which in part accounts for the perception of him as weak. It was also, however, a realistic appreciation of the situation that the Labour government faced and a more persuasive analysis than that of the prime minister.

Hunt's officials produced a revised version of the Cooper paper for a ministerial committee meeting on 12 June.[15] Hunt informed Wilson that it was only to be used 'to clear out of the way any of the options which Ministers agree should not be entertained'; the main purpose of the meeting was to agree on Rees's short-term plan.[16] The revised paper dismissed Dominion status, judging that the 'act of abandonment' would not dissociate it from the policies pursued by an independent Dominion. It would be an illogical move as the government would retain a degree of moral responsibility with an even further diminished power to control the situation.[17] Integration was ruled out as unacceptable to public opinion. Similarly, immediate unilateral withdrawal was ruled out because it would lead to 'anarchy or a dictatorship'. A power-sharing executive remained the only attractive option. Any alternative would have to recognise 'that we could not divest ourselves of our obligations to leave behind as fair and stable a society as could be achieved'.[18] Rees agreed that integration and withdrawal should be rejected, reaffirmed that power-sharing should remain the aim of the British government and 'did not propose at this stage to examine other long-term options in any detail.' The ministerial committee agreed that Rees should proceed with his plans for a consultative assembly in Northern Ireland.[19]

In July 1974 a White Paper outlined the government's plans for what would be called the Northern Ireland Constitutional Convention, stating that 'the people of Northern Ireland must play a crucial part in determining their own future. No political structure can endure without their support.' The Convention members would be asked to consider what form of government would 'command the most widespread acceptance'.[20] Bew and Patterson argue that the Convention was not an indication of a new strategy but was 'specifically designed to keep local political and military forces harmlessly occupied whilst consideration was given to the possibilities of some new departure'.[21] Rees was instead firmly convinced that a solution had to come from Belfast rather than London.[22] In response to an article in *The Times* by Robert Fisk, which claimed that Wilson and his colleagues were considering withdrawal, Rees complained privately that Fisk had completely misunderstood; the Convention abandoned imposed solutions and there was no intention to withdraw if it failed.[23]

The adoption of this new approach did not mean that Rees held any illusions about the likelihood of success. It was expected that the UUUC would win a majority at the elections, the leaders of which Rees continued to hold in contempt.[24] In his private diaries he recorded his belief that Ian Paisley and Bill Craig were involved in 'a great deal that [is] evil in the Province.' Rees had a less venomous opinion of Harry West, describing him as 'a nice old man' but 'as thick as two short planks' (or, on another occasion, 'as dim as a Toc H lamp').[25] A crucial aspect of the UUUC leadership dynamic was that it restricted political manoeuvrability. The component parties of a coalition naturally resistant to accommodating other political traditions had even less impetus to do so. They feared being denounced as traitors and subsequently suffering electoral defeat, which placed limitations on Rees's Convention.

Relations with the SDLP were also difficult after Sunningdale's collapse. One meeting in August 1974 was recorded as 'tense, even hostile, in tone… and at times violent and abusive.' The SDLP complained that the White Paper proposing the Convention was vague on both power-sharing and all-Ireland institutions. They demanded explicit government support for both.[26] The SDLP wanted Rees to impose clear conditions for a settlement, which ran contrary to the ethos of the Convention. The party faced very

difficult circumstances in the absence of power-sharing. It had to convince
the nationalist community that it offered the best means to address their
grievances for fear that militant republicanism would replace it. This was
obviously a great challenge at a time when unionists had rejected nationalist participation in government. Rees was at times unsympathetic. In
October he described the party as lacking leadership, complaining that
they 'grew up under Whitelaw and find it difficult to face life without an
English nanny – the Torier the better'.[27] The general election of October
1974 returned Labour with a small majority but again confirmed support
for anti-Sunningdale unionism, with the UUUC taking ten of twelve Westminster seats and increasing its share of the vote from 51% to 58%.[28]

Even without much prospect of an agreement, Rees felt that both sets
of politicians needed to go through the process and that it might force
them to recognize common ground on socio-economic issues.[29] He noted
in his diaries, 'what I want is at least talk and if I can get them doing that
I shall be very pleased'.[30] As with Whitelaw's power-sharing initiative, the
participation of politicians from both communities was necessary and this
could only occur with compromise from both traditions. That it was
unlikely to succeed does not necessarily imply that Rees had an ulterior
motive. Indeed, he foresaw the need to play a balancing act in the build up
to the Convention just to get opposing political parties to participate.[31]
Legislation for the Convention was worded so that it was restricted without
imposing explicit conditions: any proposal had to be acceptable to Westminster and politicians in Northern Ireland were left to make their own
arguments about what acceptable might mean.[32]

Security policy after Sunningdale

The security review ordered by Rees before the UWC strike was dominated by army thinking and diverged sharply from his plans, amounting
to little more than a shopping list. It acknowledged the desire for a reduced
force level but recommended an increase of one battalion. The review
concluded that no detainees should be released for a lengthy period and
when this did occur the army should be reinforced by yet another battalion. The rest of the recommendations included tightening controls of
detonators and fertilisers, permission to use CR gas, the erosion of prisoners' privileges and the reduction of the criteria for detention without trial.
It also recommended a Director of Information Policy be appointed for
the 'immediate initiation of an aggressive information policy campaign to
publicise HMG's policies and denigrate terrorism', that a review be held on
the restrictions on questioning (it was argued that the present methods
produced 'remarkably little intelligence of value'), that 'a political lead' be

taken in establishing a better understanding of the term 'reasonableness' in connection with opening fire and that representations be made to the judiciary on the need for sterner sentences.[33] The majority of these recommendations were deemed within the remit of the Gardiner commission, left until its work was completed and ultimately ignored.

In July 1974 Rees sought the renewal of the Emergency Provisions Act. There was little doubt that the order would be passed with Conservative support, but it was the first major opportunity since entering government for Labour backbenchers to register their opposition. Despite Rees's previous fears, there was little resistance. The two most prominent critics of the party leadership's line on internment in 1971 had taken divergent paths. As Minister of State, Stanley Orme was prepared to sign detention orders in expectation that the system would later be phased out (causing a breakdown in his personal relations with backbenchers Tam Dalyell and Paul Rose).[34] Kevin McNamara, on the other hand, rejected such compromises and attacked the government for 'shuffling off responsibility [onto Gardiner], just as the Opposition shuffled off responsibility to Lord Diplock'. He claimed that the onus was on Rees to show detention had succeeded. Rees dismissed this, arguing that the introduction of internment had been a mistake but the system had been changed and many internees released. He asked McNamara if he 'should turn 600 internees out on to the streets at once'.[35] The renewal order was passed by 98 votes to 17. Including the two tellers, only 18 Labour MPs registered their dissent alongside Gerry Fitt. A similar situation arose five months later with a further renewal passed by 91 to 22 on 5 December 1974.[36] The low numbers needed to renew security legislation reflect how little concern there was at Westminster about juryless trials in Northern Ireland. When Ian Gilmour became Rees's Conservative shadow in June, he played very little role, not speaking in the July debate and merely stating support for the legislation in December.[37] At this stage the bipartisan relationship was sufficiently at ease such that Rees privately remarked in his diaries that Gilmour was 'not bothering much about Ireland'.[38]

Local politicians were more difficult. At the annual Twelfth parades the Ulster Unionist John Taylor called for a 20,000-strong home guard, while Paisley claimed it was Protestants' 'right to arm ourselves and to protect our homes and property'.[39] Five days later Rees warned that a loyalist militia would bring Northern Ireland closer to civil war.[40] The SDLP, however, were angry with the Labour government, claiming that it was not doing enough to end detention and that the army were deliberately harassing the Catholic population in order to build up support for the RUC. John Hume felt that no action was being taken against loyalist paramilitaries, while Austin Currie 'wondered' if the inclusion of a religious question in a current census 'was a plot to generate a ground-swell of protests calling for a with-drawal of the British army'.[41] SDLP trust in the Labour government plum-meted, while Rees recorded privately that though he respected the party 'their irresponsibility is unbelievable'.[42]

On 2 September Rees announced an expansion in the RUC regular force and the RUC reserve, raising the establishment target for the regulars from 5,500 to 6,500 (a long-term aspiration as the number of regular officers at this time stood at roughly 4,500) and the reserve force from 2,000 to 4,000, with up to 400 full-time female reserves (a new entity altogether) and an increase in male full-time reserves from 350 to 1,000. This fitted Rees's plans to expand the police role but was also seen as an attempt to coun-teract the unionist calls for an extra force. Unionists cautiously welcomed the proposals but SDLP member Seamus Mallon dismissed them as 'idiotic'.[43] In November Paddy Devlin wrote to Wilson demanding that Rees be sacked, largely on the basis of the collapse of Sunningdale, but Wilson brushed the criticisms aside.[44]

The interviews conducted by the Gardiner commission are revealing of the difference between the NIO and senior army officers on detention without trial. On 18 July Frank King told Gardiner that detention was vital to the British army because of the necessity of catching PIRA leaders, who planned operations but did not carry them out. He argued that the 'great phrase "detention without trial"' was really meaningless, as evidence of membership was not enough to convince ministers to sign detention orders and the commissioners released around 40% at the first hearing.[45] On 7 November, remarking on the increasing successes of the security forces, he stated, 'One reason for the progress is that the hard men are locked up…The improvement does not seem to us to constitute a good reason for letting the hard-line leaders out'.[46]

Frank Cooper, however, gave qualified support for ending detention. He showed distaste for purely moral arguments against its use, insisting that 'society has a right to protect itself' provided the procedures are kept 'as fair as possible in the circumstances'. Cooper remarked that 'to say "let us get rid of it" in the sense that it is abhorrent to a great number of people is almost a gambler's throw and does not assess the consequences'. Never-theless, he admitted, 'one must proceed on the basis of aiming to end detention'. As Rees argued, detention could not be ended with one single act and political circumstances would have to be taken into account. A slow, pragmatic change was Cooper's preference.[47]

Progress on the security front facilitated this gradual approach. In July Rees remarked that 'the security situation was quieter than it had been in 3 years'.[48] An October report gave statistics covering the July to September period of the last three years and showed a steady decline in explosions from 397 in 1972 to 122 in 1974.[49] As a result, Rees was able to make headway on detention. In June it was noted that the army continued to oppose large-scale releases but they would not object to the release of forty particular individuals.[50] In September Rees claimed half of the 600 detainees would be released by the end of the year.[51] 253 were released between 1 May and 22 December but the signing of 182 new detention orders meant a much smaller decline in the overall number.[52]

Cross-border security co-operation with the Republic of Ireland improved as well. On 19 September 1974 Rees held a meeting at Baldonnel military airport with the Irish Minister for Justice Paddy Cooney where it was agreed to set up technical panels on communications, exchange of information, advance planning and the detection of arms, ammunition and explosives. The British hopes for a communication link between the two armies was still not acceptable to the Irish, leaving the British army rather less pleased with progress than the NIO and RUC. British soldiers on the ground remained dismissive of their Irish counterparts and the border continued to be a major asset to the PIRA. The Irish government was highly sensitive to criticism. Fianna Fáil objections that Northern Catholics were being abandoned by the Fine Gael–Labour coalition caused serious problems. Nevertheless, the Baldonnel panels led to significant progress in 1975 and a better working relationship between the Garda and the RUC.[53]

Birmingham

There was a lull in the PIRA's campaign in Great Britain over the summer of 1974 but this was followed by an escalation in October and November. On 5 October two no-warning bomb attacks on pubs frequented by off-duty soldiers in Guildford killed five and injured seventy-five. On 7 November another pub bombing in Woolwich killed two and injured thirty-one. A week later a PIRA member was killed while attempting to blow up a telephone exchange in Coventry after his device exploded prematurely. On 17 November PIRA Army Council member Dáithí Ó Conaill was interviewed on television, warning the British public that they could not wash their hands of the 'terror they wage in Ireland' and that bombings would increase. Four days later twenty-one people were killed and 183 injured by two PIRA pub bombings in Birmingham. The Provisionals did not claim the attack.[54]

The response to the horrific violence in Birmingham included a dramatic rise in anti-Irish feeling in England. As McGladdery notes, petrol bombs were thrown into Irish clubs in London, thirty factories in Birmingham were forced to close and there were calls to bring back the death penalty.[55] Six days after the bombing, the Home Secretary Roy Jenkins presented the Prevention of Terrorism (Temporary Provisions) Bill in the Commons. It passed through parliament at a phenomenal speed after an all-night sitting and received royal assent within forty-two hours.[56] The Act proscribed the IRA in Great Britain, created exclusion orders from both Great Britain and the UK and allowed constables to arrest without warrant anyone 'concerned in terrorism' and hold them for seven days. Membership, financial support and assistance to proscribed organisations were made offences. The Act treated Northern Ireland differently, giving powers to exclude its residents from Great Britain.[57] This last provision was difficult for Merlyn Rees to accept and the Foreign Secretary James Callaghan supported him in his objections, but it was approved by the cabinet.[58]

Initially, Jenkins feared that a debate on the death penalty would lead to abolitionists being 'swept away as by an avalanche'. After a fortnight, however, the chief whip persuaded him that it would be safe to go ahead.[59] When the debate took place on 11 December it ended with a large majority for those against any reintroduction, though it still showed a hardening of attitudes. The debate began with two Birmingham MPs, one Labour and one Conservative. The Labour MP, Brian Walden, conceded that the majority of the British public favoured the imposition of the death penalty for terrorists, but warned that 'the whole of human history' stood in disproof of the contention that it would deter further acts. He pointed to the execution of the 1916 rebels and spoke of the danger of making yet more Irish martyrs. Conservative MP Jill Knight responded by pointing to the Irish Free State's execution of IRA members during the Irish Civil War, claiming that it had served to deter militant republicans where prison had not. This emphasis on deterrence rather than vengeance was reiterated by Keith Joseph, the most prominent Conservative calling for capital punishment. Joseph, previously an abolitionist, now drew a distinction between ordinary murders and political ones, arguing that 'in terrorism there is no question of impulse'. That he held the position of Shadow Home Secretary made his words more significant, but Joseph was forced to assert at the beginning of his speech that he was making it in a personal capacity. William Whitelaw, the Deputy Leader, instead spoke for the Conservative frontbench. Whitelaw had supported the death penalty until his time in Northern Ireland. In 1973 he had ended it for the region, believing it would only stimulate further violence. He reaffirmed this and declared the Conservative party's opposition to capital punishment.[60]

One of the key aspects of the debate was that those for the death penalty only proposed to apply it in Great Britain. This was argued on the grounds that non-jury trials in Northern Ireland made it unsafe there. The weakness of such a distinction is borne out by the miscarriages of justice which followed. The trials of the Guildford Four, Maguire Seven, Birmingham Six and Judith Ward (convicted of the February 1974 bombing of a coach on the M62) were conducted with juries but all of these convictions were in error. In each case, pressure on the police to secure convictions led to wrongful imprisonment. The parliamentary majority of 152 meant that these serious errors were not compounded by executing eighteen innocent civilians.[61]

It was in the heightened emotional aftermath of Birmingham that the ministerial committee on Northern Ireland returned to long-term constitutional options. In November a new committee of officials, set up to support the ministerial one, produced a paper covering repartition, cantonisation, majority rule, integration, dominion status and unilateral withdrawal. Each of these were dismissed and the paper instead supported 'playing it long', continuing direct rule 'to allow more time for Northern Ireland to come to its senses'.[62] This was Rees's perspective but other ministers called for more radical choices when they met on 4 December. Roy Jenkins was the most vocal supporter of British withdrawal, telling the committee that the region had nothing to do with the UK and the real danger 'was of the barbaric standards of Northern Ireland spreading to the rest of us'. As a Birmingham MP and the minister who had to handle the aftermath of the bombings in England, it is unsurprising that his was the voice most desperately keen to insulate Great Britain from Northern Ireland.[63] Edward Short, Lord President of the Council, called for integration instead. Bernard Donoughue's private diaries record that several of those present laughed at him for arguing that 'all the Irish needed was "good government"'. Donoughue himself thought Jenkins and Short had 'put the serious alternatives' and was critical of Rees and the NIO. He complained: 'All they have to offer is the Convention and they have little hope for that. Ahead stretches an endless period of direct rule – which is why HW wants to get some movement towards pulling out.'[64] Harold Wilson's position was far more opaque than Donoughue's diaries suggest, however. John Hunt later recalled that Wilson believed 'if only you could find the right constitutional gimmick or solution or whatever, this would solve it' and 'his inclinations were always towards disengagement of Britain and British troops'.[65] Within the ministerial committee, however, he did not push these ideas particularly far. The discussion remained within the parameters of a ruling out of long-term options to be pursued after the Convention failed.[66] It remained a contingency exercise and produced the outcome Rees and the NIO wanted; it confirmed that direct rule would remain.

Ceasefire preparations

Even prior to the Birmingham bombings, the weakness of the PIRA's position was regarded by some in the NIO as a potential basis for a ceasefire.
A meeting between Cooper and King led to the establishment of a working
group to examine how the British government should respond if one was
declared. The group chiefly involved NIO officials, but also included the
army's Chief of Staff, Brigadier Garrett, with whom there were sharp disagreements. NIO officials identified three key objectives of the PIRA: a
British declaration of intent to withdraw, that the future of Ireland be
discussed by all Irishmen, and the release of 'political prisoners', including
both those detained without trial and those convicted. Correspondingly,
officials proposed a markedly reduced level of military activity, an all-
Ireland conference, and the end of detention and 'some move' on releasing
special category prisoners (special category was given to those convicted
of crimes related to the conflict and carried greater privileges than for
ordinary prisoners such as free association and the right to wear their own
clothing).[67] Garrett insisted that 'we are now in a position of relative
strength and therefore have no need to concede any more than we want'.
He argued for a more gradual approach on each of the points, insisting
there should be no amnesty for special category prisoners. He also proposed the conditions that the PIRA cease all violence, accept policing
throughout Northern Ireland and respond well to an arms amnesty.[68] NIO
officials removed the reference to special category prisoners.[69]

Rees passed them on to the ministerial committee, claiming that the
PIRA was 'under heavy pressure from the security forces' and was in 'some
disarray'. He presented proposals to detain IRA military leaders before
January 1975 and to make a statement in parliament that month promising
a phased end to detention after a ceasefire, ending it within a year, a phased
reduction in the army profile, extended policing and the end of special
category status. He included a five phase plan produced by the working
group, laying out progressive reductions in army activity as the situation
improved.[70] In the ministerial committee on 17 December Rees said that
three out of thirty PIRA leaders had been arrested and 'a few more might
be detained before the end of the year but…it might not be desirable to
detain the whole group'. The committee stressed the ceasefire would have
to apply to all of the United Kingdom and distinctions drawn between
major ceasefire-breaking violence and sporadic outbursts. They also felt
detention policy should treat doves and hawks differently.[71] These points
raised very difficult challenges for the Labour government and the Northern Ireland Office that could only be handled on an ad hoc basis, but the
plan formed the core of security policy in 1975.

Another process that served to support the ethos of Rees's statements on security policy at the beginning of Labour's administration was the Gardiner commission, which completed its report at the end of the year.[72] The most important recommendation was that detention without trial should be brought to an end. It was recognised that in the short term it had been effective in containing violence but the long-term effects included a widespread sense of grievance and injustice which fuelled the conflict. This sense of balancing the level of violence made it 'impossible to put forward a precise recommendation of the timing' and so Gardiner recommended giving the Secretary of State complete responsibility, replacing the system of commissioners with an advisory board. Trial by jury was held to be the most desirable system but the Diplock courts received endorsement and many of the clauses opposed by Labour in the Emergency Provision Act 1973 were supported. The prison system was deemed to be failing. Gardiner recommended ending special category status at 'the earliest practicable opportunity', labelling the granting of it a mistake. It was also argued that all detainees should be held in temporary cellular accommodation at a separate prison from those convicted, ending the use of prisoner-of-war-style compounds. Extra measures were suggested, including a new offence of 'being concerned in terrorism', an offence of being disguised in a public place and a widening of the definition of terrorist to include those involved in recruitment. The Gardiner commission recommended powers 'to search for and seize communications equipment, unlawfully held or suspected of being used for an unlawful purpose'. An independent body was recommended to investigate complaints against the police, with consideration given to extending this to include the army.[73]

Conclusion

This large report took considerable time to be examined and implemented by the Labour government. New security legislation for Northern Ireland did not follow until the middle of 1975, detention without trial took until the end of that year to be brought to an end and special category status was phased out only from March 1976. Gardiner did, however, provide support for the kind of outlook on security policy adopted by Rees early on in the Labour government and offered a longer-term guide to comple ment the ceasefire plans. Both played a role in beginning a major shift in security policy that would not properly yield results until the late 1970s. Thus, while the aftermath of May 1974 was understandably seen at the time as a period of drift in which Labour seemingly had nothing to offer, important developments were taking place.

Constitutionally, the Labour government could not deliver anything substantial. The SDLP called for power-sharing to be imposed but the UWC strike and the electoral position of anti-power sharing unionists made this impossible. This prompted some within the Labour government to contemplate radical options. For the likes of Wilson, Donoughue and Jenkins there was a clear impulse to be rid of Northern Ireland, but Rees's Constitutional Convention idea should be regarded as the real basis for constitutional policy. Wilson's 'doomsday plan' might be eye-catching but it was not influential. It was predicated on loyalist disruption rendering direct rule impossible, a scenario that did not occur, and the idea of dominion status was demonstrated to be a deeply flawed concept in the investigations that followed. Discussions about withdrawal and dominion status would occur again but this period should be seen as one in which the British government was adjusting to the idea that direct rule was the least bad option. This adjustment would be a slow but ultimately successful one. The same can be said for security policy. The army was still the only force capable of acting in republican areas, new prisons had to be built and political conditions needed to allow for a steady release of detainees. A PIRA ceasefire would prove helpful on this last point.

Notes

1 For example: John Bew, Martyn Frampton and Iñigo Gurruchaga, *Talking to terrorists: making peace in Northern Ireland and the Basque country* (London: Hurst, 2009), p. 49.

2 TNA, PREM 16/147, Cooper to Armstrong, 22 May 1974.

3 TNA, PREM 16/147, Cooper to Armstrong, 22 May 1974.

4 TNA, PREM 16/148, Hunt to Wilson, 29 May 1974.

5 TNA, PREM 16/148, Wilson to Armstrong, 30 May 1974; for Wilson's handling of Southern Rhodesia see: Ronald Hyam, *Britain's declining empire: the road to decolonisation* (Cambridge: Cambridge University Press, 2007), ch. 5.

6 Donal Lowry, 'Ulster resistance and loyalist rebellion in the British Empire' in Keith Jeffery (ed.), *'An Irish empire'? Aspects of Ireland and the British Empire* (Manchester: Manchester University Press, 1996), pp. 191–215.

7 Bew, *Ireland: the politics of enmity*, p. 514; Bernard Donoughue, *Prime Minister: the conduct of policy under Harold Wilson and James Callaghan* (London: Jonathan Cape, 1987), p. 129.

8 Bernard Donoughue, *Downing Street diary: with Harold Wilson in no. 10* (London: Pimlico, 2005), p. 124.

9 None of the cabinet committees which discussed Northern Ireland fit the description given by Donoughue. In a Radio 4 interview he stated that Wilson had wanted a ministerial sub-committee, but he was not sure if it went ahead. The discussion of constitutional policy in the aforementioned committees suggests that it did not: *Wilson and Ulster*, BBC Radio 4, 11 September 2008.

10 Craig, *Crisis of confidence*, p. 182.

11 TNA, PREM 16/148, Wilson to Armstrong, 30 May 1974.

12 TNA, CJ4/491, Meeting between Rees and Paisley, 30 May 1974; TNA, CJ4/491, Meeting between Rees and West, 30 May 1974; TNA, CJ4/491, Meeting between Rees and Craig, 30 May 1974; TNA, PREM 16/148, Rees to Wilson, 31 May 1974; TNA, CAB 134/3778, IRN(74) memo 16, 10 June 1974.

13 Hansard (Commons), 874, col. 882.

14 Rees, *Northern Ireland*, pp. 91–2; cf. Bew and Patterson, *The British state*, pp. 75–7.

15 TNA, CAB 134/3778, IRN(74) memo 15, 7 June 1974.

16 TNA, PREM 16/149, Hunt to Wilson, 11 June 1974.

17 TNA, CAB 134/3778, IRN(74) memo 15, 7 June 1974; It is worth noting the Anglo-Irish settlement of 1921, which had Dominion status at its core. It was hoped that Dominion status would allow the British government to retain a degree of control over the Irish Free State. Such control or influence was immaterial and the status was dismantled over the following decades: Nicholas Mansergh, 'Ireland and the British Commonwealth: the Dominion settlement' in Desmond Williams (ed.), *The Irish struggle 1916–1926* (London: Routledge & K. Paul, 1966), pp. 93–101.

18 TNA, CAB 134/3778, IRN(74) memo 15, 7 June 1974.

19 TNA, CAB 134/3778, IRN(74) meeting 5, 12 June 1974.

20 *The Northern Ireland Constitution*, Cmnd. 5675, London, 1974.

21 Bew and Patterson, *The British state*, p. 76.

22 TNA, PREM 16/148, Rees to Wilson, 31 May 1974.

23 LSE, MERLYN-REES/1/4, Transcripts of tapes, undated, p. 33.

24 TNA, CAB 134/3778, IRN(74) meeting 9, 24 October 1974.

25 LSE, MERLYN-REES/1/4, Transcript of tapes, undated, pp. 5–11; LSE, MERLYN-REES/1/7, Transcript of tapes, undated, p. 22.

26 TNA, PREM 16/150, Meeting between Rees and SDLP delegation, 20 August 1974; TNA, PREM 16/150, Meeting between Rees and SDLP delegation, 29 August 1974.

27 TNA, PREM 16/151, Rees to Wilson, 28 October 1975.

28 Henry Patterson and Eric Kaufmann, *Unionism and Orangeism*, p. 175

29 TNA, CAB 134/3779, IRN(74) memo 22, 22 October 1974.

30 LSE, MERLYN-REES/1/6, Transcripts of tapes, undated, p. 39.

31 TNA, CAB 134/3779, IRN(74) memo 22, 22 October 1974.

32 *Northern Ireland Act* (HMSO, London, 1974).

33 TNA, CJ4/648, Joint Security Review, 17 May 1974.

34 *Independent*, 3 May 2005.

35 Hansard (Commons), 876, cols 1285–9.

36 Hansard (Commons), 882, cols 2102–3.

37 Hansard (Commons), 882, col. 2079; *The Times*, 20 June 1974.

38 LSE, MERLYN-REES/1/5, Transcript of tapes, 1 December 1974, p. 19.

39 *The Times*, 13 July 1974.

40 *The Times*, 18 July 1974.

41 TNA, PREM 16/150, Meeting between Rees and the SDLP, 29 August 1974.

42 LSE, MERLYN-REES/1/4, Transcript of tapes, undated, p. 39.

43 *Irish Times*, 3 September 1974.

44 TNA, PREM 16/171, Devlin to Wilson, 27 November 1974; TNA, PREM 16/171, Butler to Devlin, 2 December 1974.

45 TNA, CJ4/674, Meeting between Gardiner Committee and British Army, 18 July 1974.

46 TNA, CJ4/672, Meeting between Gardiner Committee and British Army, 7 November 1974.

47 TNA, CJ4/1033, Meeting between Gardiner Committee and Cooper, 2 October 1974.

48 TNA, CAB 134/3778, IRN(74) meeting 7, 17 July 1974.

49 TNA, CAB 134/3779, IRN(74) memo 24, 22 October 1974.

50 TNA, CAB 134/3778, IRN(74) meeting 5, 12 June 1974.

51 TNA, CAB 134/3778, IRN(74) meeting 8, 10 September 1974.

52 TNA, CJ4/1750, Abbott to Janes, 14 August 1975.

53 Patterson, *Ireland's violent frontier*, pp. 83–91.

54 Gary McGladdery, *The Provisional IRA in England: the bombing campaign* (Dublin: Irish Academic Press, 2006), pp. 86–91.

55 McGladdery, *The Provisional IRA in England*, p. 93

56 Hansard (Commons), 882, cols 451, 962.

57 *Prevention of Terrorism (Temporary Provisions) Act 1974* (London: HMSO, 1974).

58 TNA, CAB 128/55, CC(74) meeting 49, 25 November 1974; Roy Jenkins, *A life at the centre* (London: Macmillan, 1991), p. 396.

59 Jenkins, *A life at the centre*, p. 397

60 Hansard (Commons), 883, cols 518–640.

61 Hansard (Commons), 883, cols 518–640.

62 TNA, CAB 134/3779, IRN(74) memo 25, 21 November 1974.

63 TNA, PREM 16/152, Hunt to Wilson, 3 December 1974; TNA, CAB 134/3778, IRN(74) meeting 10, 4 December 1974; Donoughue, *Downing Street diary*, p. 253.

64 Donoughue, *Downing Street diary*, pp. 253–4.

65 Peter Hennessy, *Muddling through: power, politics and the quality of government in post-war Britain* (London: Weidenfeld & Nicolson, 1997), p. 261.

66 TNA, CAB 134/3778, IRN(74) meeting 10, 4 December 1974.

67 TNA, CJ4/1225, Webster to Garrett, 9 December 1974.

68 TNA, CJ4/1225, Garrett to Webster, 9 December 1974.

69 TNA, CJ4/1225, Bourn to PUS, 12 December 1974.

70 TNA, CAB 134/3779, IRN(74) memo 26, 13 December 1974.

71 TNA, CAB 134/3778, IRN(74) meeting 11, 17 December 1974.

72 TNA, CAB 134/3778, IRN(74) meeting 11, 17 December 1974.

73 *Report of a Committee to consider, in the context of civil liberties and human rights, measures to deal with terrorism in Northern Ireland*, Cmnd. 5847, H.C. 1974–5.

4

Negotiating the Provisional IRA ceasefire

The dominant issue for the Labour government for most of 1975 was the PIRA's ceasefire. The ceasefire had great implications for security policy and the political scene. It provided the backdrop to the Northern Ireland Constitutional Convention, which lasted from May 1975 through to March 1976, and deeply affected the Labour government's relationships with political parties in Great Britain and Northern Ireland, with the government of the Republic of Ireland and with senior British army officers. The public acknowledgement that the British government was in dialogue with militant republicans was highly controversial and heightened fears that Wilson's administration was considering withdrawal from Northern Ireland. Killings continued in spite of the ceasefire and this provided further evidence for the Labour government's critics that it was not aggressive enough in dealing with violence. This chapter looks at the changes made by the Labour government to security policy and the establishment of talks with senior PIRA representatives, both designed in order to secure the ceasefire. It also considers the expectations of Labour ministers and senior NIO officials going into the ceasefire and the ways in which it affected their relationships with other interested parties.

Responding to the Provisionals

Dialogue with the PIRA was not new in 1974–75. A variety of contacts had been made over the previous three years involving members of the British Labour party, sections of the British intelligence community and Conservative government ministers. In March 1972 Harold Wilson and Merlyn Rees met a PIRA delegation including Dáithí Ó Conaill, Joe Cahill and John Kelly. The meeting was facilitated by Irish Labour party TD Dr John O'Connell during a short-lived ceasefire.[1] John Hume and Paddy Devlin also facilitated contact between MI6 officer Frank Steele, Ó Conaill and Gerry Adams. In July 1972 this led to a group of the most senior PIRA men (Ó Conaill, Adams, Seán Mac Stíofáin, Martin McGuinness and

Seamus Twomey) meeting with Northern Ireland Secretary William Whitelaw. None of the meetings led to progress. At the Whitelaw gathering the republicans simply demanded British withdrawal. There were a number of additional contacts over the course of 1972 to 1974, but Whitelaw was extremely hesitant to allow them to develop very far.[2]

A greater willingness on the part of the British to talk became apparent in 1974. NIO assistant secretary for political affairs James Allan and Frank Steele's MI6 replacement Michael Oatley met with representatives of both loyalist and republican groups at Laneside. Conversations with the UDA and UVF during and after the UWC strike were used to gain information on the political perspectives within the organisations.[3] On the Provisional side, Allan and Oatley met with Seamus Loughran during the second half of 1974, meetings which would continue with Jimmy Drumm and Proinsias Mac Airt in 1975.[4] The most important contact for the ceasefire was Brendan Duddy, a Derry businessman and friend of Ruairí Ó Brádaigh, who had been in touch with Frank Steele from 1972 and had been passed on to Oatley.[5] This link served to confirm to the British that Ó Brádaigh and Ó Conaill were the two key doves in the Provisional movement. The Duddy link proved to be the most useful and so efforts were made to ensure that this was the focus for communications between the British government and the Provisional Army Council (PAC).

Prior to this, however, a third channel played a role in the actual initiation of the ceasefire. Protestant clergymen met with PIRA leaders in the village of Feakle, County Clare, on 10 December 1974. Eight days later they handed documents from the meeting to Rees. The clergymen produced proposals which stated that the government should reaffirm 'that it has no political or territorial interests in Ireland beyond its obligations to the citizens of Northern Ireland', that its prime concern was 'the achievement of peace and the promotion of understanding between the communities in Northern Ireland', that it would 'relieve the army as quickly as possible', but 'until agreements are achieved the army must remain in Northern Ireland', while the government recognised the 'right of all those who have political aims to pursue them through the democratic process'.[6] The PAC then responded with its own document. Seamus Loughran told the clergymen that it had been intensely discussed for eighteen hours and was designed to hold together the doves and hawks of the PAC, as well as ordinary volunteers.[7] It deemed any statement from the British government meaningless unless it was one which abandoned sovereignty in Ireland. The PAC proposed the establishment of an all-Ireland assembly to draft a new all-Ireland constitution, a public commitment by the British government to withdraw within twelve months of the implementation of this constitution and a declaration of amnesty for all political prisoners and wanted men (which accorded with the NIO's predictions in November). They requested a British response by 28 December and a cessation of operations by the army.[8]

Reverend William Arlow told Rees that the first point on sovereignty was a cosmetic one. He claimed that after the military representatives left the meeting Provisional Sinn Féin members admitted 'they could not hope to secure their aims by violent means'. The rest of the clergymen added that the political wing appreciated armed struggle could be continued indefinitely but 'they could never hope by those means to win struggle from men's minds'.[9] Arlow was naturally excited by such remarks but it would be an error to see much significance in them. Provisional Sinn Féin was very much the weaker partner in the republican movement and the balance of opinion on the Provisional Army Council counted in a way that the aspirations of the political wing did not. Indeed, only a few weeks later the Catholic Bishop of Derry, Edward Daly, told Rees and Cooper that his own meetings with the Provisional Army Council left him with the impression that they despised Provisional Sinn Féin.[10] Rees told the Protestant clergymen that a genuine cessation of violence would create a new situation but if the campaign continued in Great Britain 'each additional bombing incident would…constrain any positive response by the government'.[11] Two days later, the Provisional Army Council ordered a suspension of operations from midnight 22 December to 2 January 1975. It promised a permanent ceasefire if the British government responded to their satisfaction. In the meantime they demanded the British army cease raids, arrests and harassment, and the RUC be kept out of republican areas.[12]

Immediately after the PIRA announcement, the British Commander Land Forces (CLF) sent out new instructions to troops designed to reduce their overt presence. He ordered all brigades to reverse arms and reduce patrols. Arrests were only to occur for those who could be charged and brought before the courts or 'top leaders such as Toomey [sic]'. Armoured vehicles were to be used as little as possible and both house searches and identification checks were not to occur unless in hot pursuit after a clear breach of the ceasefire. Both vehicle check-points and searches on the perimeters of town centres were to continue to prevent PIRA attempts to move explosives and ammunition. The CLF emphasised that the army could not be seen to break the PIRA's ceasefire.[13] Rees sought to reassure senior army officers, telling Frank King: 'Clearly, there will always be a risk that a period of quiet will be used by the terrorists to re-group and re-supply their forces and I also appreciate that they will always be capable of breaking the ceasefire to suit their own short-term advantage'. He insisted there was 'no question of immunity for known criminals if found'.[14] Mindful of the potential damage that could be caused by media reports, Rees also circulated an instruction that it was 'absolutely critical that no minister or civil servant makes any comment in public' about the PIRA's ceasefire.[15]

The political demands of the Provisional Army Council were not addressed. On 23 December Frank Cooper met Stanley Worrall, spokesman for the Feakle clergymen. Worrall reported that Dáithí Ó Conaill was anxious about the 28 December deadline, but the all-Ireland Convention in the PAC document meant little and they would be satisfied if the government said it was out of their hands. Ó Conaill hoped for a statement on long-term British intentions to convince hardliners in the PAC, adding the importance of detainee releases and the army's low profile. The record states that he 'was sincerely trying for peace. He had problems of "face" and with his "hardliners". What he needed was some gestures.'[16] Rees's Christmas Eve statement announced six-day parole for 79 special category prisoners and three days' compassionate parole for 31 detainees.[17] He nonetheless was reluctant to get into political discussions with the IRA, remarking in his private diaries: 'There's no doubt that there is a great need for peace in Northern Ireland. What worries me is the political vehicle of doing it is not clear because if one looks at the list of the demands of the IRA they're not giveable [sic] by me. They're matters for the Irish when they meet together in the Convention.'[18] The church leaders wrote to Rees on 27 December asking for a bigger gesture.[19]

On the morning of 30 December Rees phoned Wilson. He proposed to release a small number of detainees and grant more paroles for the New Year. Wilson was supportive.[20] Meanwhile, Cooper again met Worrall and said the church leaders should make clear to Seamus Loughran that no negotiation would take place, but Rees would be making a statement and a gesture on parole and releases.[21] While the NIO opted for flexibility in military matters, Labour ministers and civil servants faced similar difficulties to the Provisionals in having to deal with varying internal enthusiasm for the ceasefire. While the army was not opposed to NIO plans to modify security policy, it oscillated between expressing support for the ceasefire and concern for what would happen as a consequence of it. Frank King wrote to Rees that he was 'wholeheartedly behind the line you are taking and agree entirely that we should show no sign of weakness'. The rest of his letter accentuated the second part rather than the first, asking that Rees make it 'crystal clear' they were only interested in a permanent ceasefire. The GOC was also anxious about the effect of detainee releases on the Protestant community, asking that the number be kept as low as possible.[22] King's letter to the Chief of the General Staff, Peter Hunt, was especially forthcoming. He told Hunt that he had expressed to Rees 'very strongly that any prolongation of a temporary truce is a retrograde step in the purely security sense since it predicates a regularly low profile by the Security Forces'. Admitting that the army had 'not changed our posture over much', he felt they had 'reached an interesting stage but it is messy from the soldiers' point of view'.[23]

Later that evening Rees met the GOC and Chief Constable James Flanagan to consider further responses to the PIRA demands. Both King and Flanagan confirmed the almost complete observation of the ceasefire. It was agreed that British security forces would continue their low profile, with an emphasis on intelligence-gathering and the closure of unapproved border crossings. If the ceasefire ended on 2 January they would immediately deploy the maximum number of men on the ground and resume normal operations. They agreed to three-day parole for roughly fifty detainees and sixteen detainee releases, two of whom would be Protestants. There was some haggling over the names and two further republicans were added.[24] Following this meeting the CLF issued new instructions to all brigades. The signal stressed they should 'begin operations with caution…in order to place the responsibility for starting violence clearly on the shoulders of the PIRA'.[25] On New Year's Eve Rees made another public statement. He re-emphasised the need for 'a genuine and sustained cessation of violence'. He stated that a permanent ceasefire would enable the army 'to make a planned, orderly and progressive reduction in its present commitment' and once violence ceased and was 'seen to have ceased' it would be possible to progressively release detainees. He reiterated that security force actions would be responsive to levels of violence.[26] At this point Rees was quite satisfied with civil–military relations, telling Wilson that the army 'let their hair down with me the other night, and their praise for your Government and support for them was really quite touching'. Rees said King was 'purring like a kitten'.[27]

On 2 January the PIRA extended their ceasefire for a fortnight, but adjustments to security policy were not enough for the PAC, which remarked: 'A satisfactory reply to the IRA peace proposals for a lasting peace was not received from the British government, and it is illusory and deceptive on the part of that government to pretend that the root causes of the conflict can be ignored.'[28] Four days later King told Rees that it was too early to assess whether the army's low profile was having an effect on intelligence operations. If the ceasefire ended on 16 January the army would resume normal operations, but arrests would be made more selectively according to local violence levels. They also discussed asking Flanagan to make plans for the progressive replacement of the army with military and civilian police. King argued that the RUC was too optimistic about the ceasefire, believing that the PIRA 'had been defeated everywhere except on the border'.[29]

A few days later the Chief of the General Staff wrote to the Chief of the Defence Staff, Michael Carver. Hunt informed Carver that force levels would remain the same, adding: 'if the "twilight peace" continues, and Rees can put his step-by-step plan for permanent peace into effect, there will come a time when the army will "withdraw to barracks"'. In a further remark illustrative of the priorities of the Chiefs of Staff, Hunt stated, 'a reduction in force levels may be imposed on us by the political require-ments of the time – a welcome reversal of form!' Relations with the RUC were described as 'now very satisfactory' but they were still 'woefully under-manned'. Recognising that the army had no other choice but to accept Gardiner's recommendation that detention be phased out, the CGS observed, 'The main point at issue at the moment is the time-scale of releases; we would like a much slower rate than [Rees] is contemplating, but a compromise can probably be worked out'.[30] Over the course of the ceasefire it became clearer that the general staff's willingness to compro-mise was not shared to the same extent by senior army officers based in Northern Ireland.

On 11 January the CLF yet again informed all brigades that it was 'imperative' that army operations could not be held to have prejudiced the continuation of the ceasefire. Previous instructions remained 'except that, unless caught in the act of committing a criminal act, no member of the PAC, or officer of the Provisional Sinn Féin, is to be arrested until the arrest has been cleared by this HQ'. This leaves open the possibility that key Provisionals had immunity during the ceasefire. Subsequent decisions suggest that this was not the case later on, though it may have been tem-porarily the case while the ceasefire was in its infancy. In a clear sign of the sensitivities involved, the signal further stated 'This policy has not yet been cleared with the RUC and the contents of this signal should not be discussed with them until other orders are issued'.[31] Similarly, on 31 December Rees told Wilson that they should be careful what was placed on paper about contact with the Provisionals as the RUC would find out and inform unionist politicians.[32] Relations might have improved between the army and the police but the latter remained politically suspect and decisions were not always shared with those from Northern Ireland.

Rees told colleagues in the ministerial committee that he wanted to delay publishing the Gardiner report. He planned to make a statement referring to detention and did not want this to be lost in discussion of other Gardiner recommendations.[33] Aspects of the report which might provoke the PIRA were slow to be dealt with. Six days later Rees told the Commons there had been no major incidents and he had not signed any orders for detention without trial since 22 December. Rees repeated his promise that the army's profile would be further reduced if the ceasefire continued, adding: 'Once I am satisfied that violence has come to a permanent end, I shall be prepared to speed up the rate of releases with a view to releasing all detainees.'[34] The following morning he told Wilson that the NIO planned to release twenty-five detainees and offer three days of home leave to fifty more.[35]

In spite of this the PIRA did not renew their ceasefire. Their statement claimed that nothing in Rees's speech related to their peace proposals, that the truce was not observed by the army, only three detainees were freed before Christmas, one of their volunteers died after repeatedly being refused medical treatment, there was a concerted campaign of brutality in the prisons, compassionate parole was refused by the authorities, the O/C of North Armagh was assassinated by a British 'execution squad' and senior Provisional Kevin Mallon was arrested in Dublin.[36] The NIO released a rebuttal. It pointed out that the particular areas where the PIRA claimed the truce was not observed had seen searches cut by 90%, the complaint that only 3 detainees were released completely ignored that 20 were released on 31 December and 25 on 15 January and compassionate parole was offered to 163 convicted prisoners and detainees.[37] On 17 January Rees argued the reasons for ending the ceasefire were 'totally unfounded' when meeting church leaders. Cardinal William Conway said that the vote on the Provisional Army Council had been very close and the government should 'try to restore the balance to the advantage of the "doves"'. He urged the Labour government to establish contact with Provisional Sinn Féin.[38]

A secret NIO memo recorded the basic strategy in handling the PIRA ceasefire up to this point: '(a) to string them along to the point where their military capacity went soggy and where Catholic community support disappeared; (b) to give the doves an excuse to call it all off without making substantial concessions. We recognised that a point was bound to come where our irreconcilable objectives came into conflict and where they read our intentions'. The author, whose name was omitted from the copy released to the National Archives, wrote: 'Detention is the hook they have got us on and they have recognised this. As long as this exists they can rally some catholic support. As long as the PAC do not stop violence we cannot end it.' The document did not offer recommendations, but stated two questions: whether to speak to Ruairí Ó Brádaigh and whether to continue releasing detainees.[39] Rees and the Labour government chose to do both.

Dialogue with the Provisionals

Reconstructing the dialogue between the British state and the Provisionals is made difficult by the lack of government source material. The chronological 'Situation in Northern Ireland' files of the Prime Minister's Office are currently withheld in entirety for the period between 21 January to 5 February and from early April to early August. For the files that are available, individual minutes between Merlyn Rees, Frank Cooper and MI6 officer Michael Oatley are retained. It is therefore hard to get a sense of what was privately said about the dialogue on the British side. The papers of Ruairí Ó Brádaigh and the intermediary Brendan Duddy do however offer insight into the republican perception of the discussions and substantial detail on the dialogue itself. On 17 January Duddy contacted Ó Brádaigh to say that the British had requested a meeting with him. Ó Brádaigh obtained approval from the Provisional Army Council and the following day he met with Michael Oatley and James Allan. It was agreed to proceed with two sets of meetings, the other being a continuation of the Laneside talks with Belfast representatives Seamus Loughran and Jimmy Drumm.[40]

On 19 January Oatley and Allan handed over a message from the Labour government which stated that they were prepared for the officials 'to discuss with members of Provisional Sinn Féin how a permanent cessation of violence might be agreed and what would be the practical problems to be solved'. They 'would not exclude the raising of any relevant question' but the dialogue would have to be within the terms of Rees's parliamentary statement about not negotiating with the IRA.[41] The distinction being made between the PIRA and Provisional Sinn Féin was cosmetic. The British knew that Ó Brádaigh and the two other republican representatives involved in the Duddy dialogue, Billy McKee and Joe McCallion, were representing the Provisional Army Council rather than the political wing; that was the essential purpose of the talks. McKee and McCallion were both on the Army Council themselves and while Ó Brádaigh served as President of Provisional Sinn Féin, his influence was hardly confined to the political wing. Understandably, however, the Labour government saw great risks in admitting to meetings with the military wing and was fearful in particular of any association with Seamus Twomey or Dáithí Ó Conaill (linked in the public mind with the Bloody Friday and Birmingham bombings respectively). It found it easier to publicly admit meeting with Provisional Sinn Féin. A belief in the distinction between talks and negotiation was perhaps more sincerely held on the British side but it was not straightforward either. The republicans had a clear hope that the dialogue would ultimately aid their objectives; the representatives warned that they would help if the Labour government if it 'wanted to disengage quietly from Ireland' but if it sought 'to restructure British rule in Ireland and make it more acceptable, then [the PIRA] would contest the ground'.[42]

The talks focussed on what was required for a renewed ceasefire. On 21 January the Provisionals handed Allan and Oatley a twelve-point document entitled 'Terms for bi-lateral truce'. The twelve points were: freedom of movement, cessation of civilian harassment, cessation of raids, cessation of arrests of members of the republican movement, an end to screening, photographing and identity checks, that members of the republican movement reserve the right to carry short-arms for self-defence, that neither side make provocative displays of force, that there be no reintroduction of the RUC or Ulster Defence Regiment (UDR) in designated (i.e. republican) areas, that an effective liaison system be established between both sides, that the army progressively withdrew troops to barracks, that discussion to secure a permanent ceasefire continue and that if any of these terms were violated, 'the Republican Movement reserve the right of freedom of action'.[43]

Continuing violence led the British to move slowly in responding to the republican document. On 19 January a 7-year-old boy was killed by a PIRA device while driving cattle. The next day a PIRA volunteer was shot dead by British soldiers while attempting to hijack a vehicle with other men. On 21 January two PIRA volunteers died while transporting a car bomb that exploded prematurely and a British soldier was killed by a PIRA bomb.[44] Early in the morning of 22 January Duddy was asked by the British to relay a message to Dáithí Ó Conaill that if the violence of 21 January had taken place earlier in the day the meeting probably would not have gone ahead and any further activity would lead the British to end the talks.[45] Rees put out a statement that as long as violence continued 'in the way that it has in the last few days' there was no point in detailed discussion of practical arrangements for a ceasefire.[46] Ó Brádaigh's instructions described Rees's statements as provocative and suggested that the British were evading agreement. They described the first point of their document as cardinal; a truce would rise or fall on whether there was an amnesty for all wanted men for the period of a new truce.[47]

Duddy continued to meet with Oatley and Allan in an attempt to get the British to support the twelve points, arguing that it was foolish to expect the Provisional Army Council to agree to a plan where PIRA volunteers could still be arrested. He recorded privately that the two agreed with him but said 'the British system did not leave room for an Irish type of agreement'.[48] This was the consistent line taken by the British representatives throughout much of the contact with the intermediary in 1975; sympathy was proffered while pointing to 'the machine' as an unfortunate obstacle. Duddy relayed to Ó Brádaigh that the British representatives could agree to many of the points, with the exception of freedom of movement and cessation of raids and arrests. These involved 'a massive law problem' for the British but a more elaborate liaison system should be used to deal with these points as well as the question of civilian harassment, searches and the right to carry short arms for self-defence.[49] Duddy, joined by Father Denis Bradley, also pressed the republicans to end violence, rowing with both Billy McKee and Seamus Twomey. On 30 January the British agreed to resume talks the next day, extending an invitation to Ó Conaill as well.[50] Ó Brádaigh was pleased that the British were willing to talk to Ó Conaill but the latter decided to stay out and the three republican representatives remained the same.[51]

When the talks resumed Allan and Oatley firmly insisted that the meetings should be the only channel of communication between the British and the PAC. This was supposed to prevent self-appointed intermediaries from causing confusion and misunderstanding between the two sides. The prime offender from the Labour government's perspective was John O'Connell, who sought to resume the role he had played in the earlier meetings between the Provisionals and Wilson. From the beginning of the ceasefire in December, O'Connell sought to involve himself. James Allan informed Frank Cooper that he had 'badgered' the private office for a meeting in the NIO.[52] He also passed messages to representatives of the Vatican and the USA, prompting Cooper to ask the British ambassador in Dublin to tell the Americans that O'Connell 'did not seem to be privy to the most recent events and it seemed likely that he was acting independently.'[53] The Vatican's representative in Dublin was told that 'Dr O'Connell is apt to try and get in on the act on occasions such as this.'[54] When he contacted the brother of Harold Wilson's political secretary, Allan told O'Connell that if he had anything to say it should be to him and not to people who had 'nothing to do with Northern Ireland.'[55]

During the break in the ceasefire Dáithí Ó Conaill sent John O'Connell to London with some proposals but, according to Duddy's diaries, the TD's claims to have met Wilson were false. Allan and Oatley very firmly sought to put the Provisionals off having anything to do with him.[56] The British were contemptuous: Wilson described him as having 'the enthusiasm of a self-opinionated salesman' and Rees told the Irish Ambassador that 'in all his dealings with Northern Ireland, nothing had made him more angry than Dr O'Connell's recent machinations.'[57] Andrew Mumford has criticised the British government's discouragement of unofficial efforts to instigate contacts and the desire to 'engage only in elite-level strategic dialogue' during the early 1970s, depicting an intransigence towards unsanctioned dialogue during the Whitelaw years.[58] The response to O'Connell shows continuity but also a basic logic to the approach; a single, controlled channel with direct contact between the two sides reduced the risk of miscommunication which could potentially end the ceasefire. The difficulties with O'Connell fed into a wider problem of public speculation about contact with republicans. Rees believed that the press seriously endangered the ceasefire, particularly Conor O'Clery (*Irish Times*) and Robert

Fisk (*The Times*), who the Provisional Army Council assumed had the ear of Stormont Castle.[59] In early January Fisk reported that a proposal for a permanent truce emanating from an Irish Labour TD [most likely O'Connell], a loyalist and the trade union leader Jack Jones was being considered by Wilson.[60] O'Clery reported that the army were advising against conceding anything to the Provisionals.[61]

In an attempt to make progress, Allan and Oatley suggested to the republicans that they should keep off principles and focus on practical arrangements. Frank Cooper asked officials to produce a scheme for monitoring the ceasefire. In a sign of friction to come, the army accepted the value of a 'hotline' between the PIRA and the NIO but said it did not want direct dealings over alleged violations of a ceasefire. A plan was produced for localised government centres manned by civil servants who would receive phone calls from republicans, which the Provisional Army Council then approved.[62] Seamus Twomey, however, continued to insist on total freedom of movement for PIRA volunteers.[63] This remained a sticking point in the discussions. On 3 February Allan and Oatley handed over a sixteen-point reply to the republicans' terms and suggested a solution lay between the two documents. The first point of the British version stated: 'In a situation of genuine and sustained cessation of violence, arrests under the Emergency Provisions Act would not be made and no organisation would be proscribed. There would be no restrictions on freedom of movement other than against those who are wanted for prosecution in the courts.'[64] Allan and Oatley said there was a possibility of meeting the republican demand for free movement 'provided the Vols do not flaunt themselves and there is no pursuit of them in designated areas.'[65]

The statement was not strong enough for hardliners like Twomey and it was not until a new form of words was found in the early hours of 7 February that the issue was dealt with. A revised British version stated: 'There would be no restrictions on freedom of movement and there is no question of those wishing to return home to live in peace being harassed by the security forces.' Another point in the document, however, stated that the 'only arrests will be arrests of people for breaking the law'.[66] At an impasse, Duddy records that he crossed out the 'difficult words' and an agreement was reached.[67] Precisely which words were crossed out is unclear but it would seem that even basic practical conditions for the ceasefire relied on constructive ambiguity, with the British wanting to satisfy the republicans without giving any real ground. Later disputes over arrests of PIRA volunteers are illustrative of how the basic principle of freedom of movement was not conceded. Other modifications to the original British document show similar signs of fudging; one point promised an end to screening, photographing and identity checks, with the deletion of the phrase 'as soon as practicable'. A message from Cooper was also added on the question of permits for firearms, in which he promised: 'if all that stands between us and the successful conclusion of our present arrangements is 24 permits – we shall find a way around that difficulty'.[68]

On 8 February the Provisional Army Council agreed to the modifications, with Ó Conaill telling Ó Brádaigh that they had got more than he expected.[69] Ó Brádaigh's instructions stated that the position was 'subject to review at regular intervals' and would depend on progress towards securing permanent peace through the talks. The following day the Provisional Army Council announced the suspension of offensive military action.[70] Seven government incident centres were set up and became operational from 15 February.[71]

This left Rees with the question of how transparent the government should be about the dialogue. In February his own view of the situation was firmly, but rather inarticulately, given in his private diaries. He recorded that he had instructed Frank Cooper 'to make sure that the 4 documents were brought back because it is the sort of stuff of history that people will believe that one had given in on something whereas my instruction was very firmly not to give in on any point and the point of this was discussion on politics but I am not prepared to talk on the political future of NI'.[72] He remained opposed to the idea that a settlement could be negotiated solely between the British government and republicans. John Bourn, under-secretary at NIO Belfast, tried to convince Cooper of the merits of going public on the documents, arguing that it would be better to do it of their own volition rather than have them announced by the republicans or dragged out under pressure. Bourn thought that there was nothing to hide; he believed that publication would 'nail any suggestion that the discussions were really "negotiations"'.[73]

When Rees spoke in parliament on 11 February he chose not to be explicit. He explained the plans for government incident centres to act as local points of contact, emphasising that peace and a political solution would not come quickly: 'There are many problems yet to overcome in a situation which is far from clear. There is no quick and easy solution and winding down from violence will not happen overnight'. He further insisted that talks with Provisional Sinn Féin were about practical arrangements for a ceasefire and there was 'no question of bartering away the future of the people of Northern Ireland'. When Conservative MP Julian Amery referred to reports that IRA volunteers would be allowed to carry side arms, Rees emphasised that the law would be kept. His response lacked an unequivocal denial: 'There is a law in Northern Ireland about carrying sidearms. Many people carry them. The right hon. Gentleman would be surprised at how many people who came to see me leave their guns at the door of Stormont Castle. Well-nigh everybody does. There are many people who are afraid.'[74] Rees's circling of the real issue would not have satisfied those suspicious of the Labour government's intentions. A blunt statement to the effect that guns required a legal permit would have been wiser.

His attempted assurances followed republican conversations with the press about the terms for the ceasefire. In mid-February Seamus Loughran told reporters it was agreed that there would be no searches in Catholic areas, that IRA men on the run would be allowed to return home and that all detainees would be released by 17 March.[75] Loughran also claimed that vigilante policing would begin in republican areas.[76] This was followed up at the end of the month with a claim in *An Phoblacht* that the Provisionals would arrange elections for a peace-keeping community force.[77] Allan and Oatley complained about Loughran to Ó Brádaigh and the others. They gave a formal statement that the press leaks were 'immediately and highly dangerous to the truce'. Billy McKee admitted that Loughran had gone beyond the terms of 'what it was agreed to tell the volunteers privately'.[78] Both sides were angered by his actions, but the Provisionals perhaps more so as there are hints that some within the movement had doubts about his intentions. Brendan Duddy's papers identified him as a 'suspected tout', while Rees recorded in his diaries a month earlier that Loughran had been sent on a fund-raising trip to the United States, adding 'I think he is lucky not to have been shot'.[79]

Ó Brádaigh's instructions showed that the Provisional Army Council was frustrated at the lack of gun permits and prisoner releases. They cited an article in the *Economist* which argued that the Provisionals had been 'conned and taken for a ride', further illustrating how press speculation could hamper the negotiations.[80] Allan and Oatley likewise said that there would be no movement on gun permits because of an article in *The Times* by Robert Fisk quoting a Provisional HQ source and a BBC radio broadcast about Sinn Féin claiming republicans were controlling their areas.[81] Despite this, permits were dealt with by the end of February. Frank Cooper asked officials for plans so that 'certain people' could 'move reasonably freely in green areas without too high a risk of arrest for carrying fire-arms' but without contradicting Rees's public statements. An identification scheme was drawn up for those engaged in maintaining the ceasefire. It did not grant immunity from arrest, with John Bourn remarking: 'It makes sense to put oil into the cogs of the ceasefire machinery; the documents are nothing more than oil of this kind'.[82] Rees and senior army officers met to discuss it on 25 February. Frank King opposed it on political grounds, arguing that the scheme would not give the bearer any greater freedom of movement and would only enhance the Provisionals' community status. According to the minutes, Rees sided with the GOC. Curiously, he added that Provisional Sinn Féin could produce their own document and make the government aware of its existence.[83]

This was another distinction that amounted to very little. On 28 February the British representatives agreed during the Duddy talks that a small number of documents would be issued to 'people connected with the truce', all of whom had to be members of Sinn Féin. In designated areas these would be recognised by the British army but not the RUC or UDR. Soldiers would be issued with orders that the holders should be 'allowed to go about their normal business as ordinary citizens' and would not be searched, though their vehicles might. The permits would not give legal immunity for firearm possession or where there was definite evidence against the person. Ó Brádaigh's record states, 'concealment is crucial to this arrangement.'[84] On 5 March the documents were made available. The meeting was Michael Oatley's last, having phased in replacement MI6 officer Robert Browning. Browning took Joe McCallion's photo for his permit with a Polaroid camera while Oatley handed out gold Cross pens for Duddy, Ó Brádaigh, McCallion, McKee and Mac Airt.[85] Army instructions suggest that the permits system did not offer immunity from arrest or contradict Rees's parliamentary statements: soldiers were told that the documents did not 'confer any rights on the bearer, whatever he may say' and they were only to treat the bearer as an ordinary citizen, unless the person could be charged with a criminal offence.[86] This worked in the context of the cessation of searches by the army. From the perspective of Rees and the NIO there were no substantive concessions made to the Provisional Army Council in securing a renewed ceasefire.

The reaction of the security forces

Sections of the media picked up on disagreements between the NIO and the army, though what passed between the two was often more complex and nuanced than what journalists were able to figure out. In April the *Observer* made much of an after-dinner speech by Frank King. King was asked whether the army would be in a better position against the PIRA if the ceasefire had not occurred and he replied that it would. The *Observer* described the gap between the NIO and the security forces as a gulf, claiming the release of detainees, the reduction of troop levels and the lowering of the army's profile were decisions made by Rees against army advice, representing a 'growing dichotomy between political and military thinking'.[87] Rees's diaries state this was not how he felt about the relationship: King apologised to him when the controversy broke and he believed that the GOC had been caught off guard, treating the question philosophically. He dismissed the reports depicting the two at odds as 'absolute rubbish'.[88] The three areas of disagreement described in the article are either inaccurate or too simplistically expressed: in the early stages of the ceasefire King was not opposed to releasing detainees in principle but was rather worried about the number of them; the reduction in troops was an MOD initiative pushed on both men, and King accepted the lowering of the army's profile.

A secret memo produced prior to the PIRA's declaration of an indefinite cessation on 8 February reveals the level of agreement at the top level of the NIO and HQNI in the early stages. It envisioned two scenarios. The first would see the PIRA return to violence on a significant scale. Here it was concluded that the British should seize back the military initiative while avoiding turning the Catholic population against them and protecting themselves from a loyalist backlash. As the experience of previous years showed, attempting to achieve all three of these objectives was easier said than done. To overcome this, a reversal of Theodore Roosevelt's dictum was suggested; they should 'speak loudly and carry a small stick', drawing up an arrest list that gave consideration to those within the PIRA who might exert a moderating influence while stopping detainee releases. The second scenario would be a 'no peace, no war situation' where a ceasefire progressively frayed at the edges. This would present much greater difficulties as they would still have the same objectives but find it harder to achieve them. The army would stick to their lower posture. Detention would not be used, except where major violence could be tied to PIRA volunteers believed to be hawks. Releases from detention would continue but be carefully judged 'so as not to conflict with the Secretary of State's stance that only a permanent end to violence will bring an end to detention'.[89] On 4 February King wrote to Frank Cooper that he agreed with the paper and that the British army was 'already operating largely on the lines that you suggest'.[90]

This is not to say that civil–military relations were comfortable during the ceasefire. Serious disagreements occurred but the timing was later than has been appreciated. At first disagreements were more narrowly focussed on the incident centres. On 19 February B.M. Webster, Assistant Secretary in NIO Belfast's security operations division, recorded that both the NIO and HQNI were initially surprised at the number of 'relatively trivial grumbles' claiming patrols and other minor operations were breaches of the ceasefire. The NIO stiffened its responses but the army believed that dealing with such trivialities gave ground to the Provisionals. It seems logical that this would be vexing for troops on the ground and Webster felt the NIO's strategy was unclear to army officers below the Chief of Staff.

Webster observed that the army 'were not used to being led by the NIO in an area which so closely affects their interests' and although personal relations were very good, he feared it might reach a point where they were unco-operative.[91]

The situation was not helped when Provisional Sinn Féin established their own centres (indeed, Paul Bew and Henry Patterson have confused them with the government centres, which they claim were manned by Sinn Féin).[92] D.J. Wyatt, Assistant Secretary in the NIO's liaison staff, concluded that the Provisionals could not be allowed to use the centres as a basis for vigilante policing. Otherwise, however, they were perfectly legal. The army had already visited the centre on Divis Street and questioned those inside, but the NIO asked them to refrain from searching and photographing the occupants.[93]

A month later Cooper wrote sympathetically to the GOC, noting that the ceasefire had been 'difficult for all of us'. He dealt chiefly with the incident centres, acknowledging that their inquiries were 'likely to raise eyebrows' with King. Cooper stated, 'The last thing in the world we want to happen is to give the impression that we are trying to do the army down or anything of that kind.' He added that the 'nub of the problem' was the need for their 'respective staffs to understand each other's problems rather more quickly than they do at the moment'.[94] Shortly after this P.T.E. England, NIO Belfast's Deputy Secretary, observed that the army 'do not seem to understand' that they needed to 'lay off generally and especially lay off the PSF incident centres even if wanted men are thought to be inside them'. There was still a need to persuade the army to only make arrests on hard and accurate information.[95] Cooper told England about a 'long private talk' with the GOC. King said he was 'much happier' with the incident centres and in general the ceasefire was going far better than he expected, although the army remained uncertain about long-term possibilities. He claimed to be 'very content' with NIO–HQNI relations, but was concerned that the army's low profile would provide a vacuum for criminals.[96] This reinforces Webster's argument that the problem with the army was lower down the ranks.

The chief impact of the ceasefire on the police was to bring out their enthusiasm for expanding their presence. In February King and Flanagan signed a joint paper titled 'Policing in a ceasefire situation'. It described Flanagan's intention to 'establish an increased, obvious, uniformed presence in green areas' using policemen released from static duties, some of which would be taken up by the army. It optimistically assessed that while a minority within the Catholic community 'will never consent to any form of policing...there is some evidence to suggest that faced with a fait accompli of an RUC presence in their area, a majority would indeed give tacit consent to RUC law enforcement.'[97] Rees's own position on this was contradictory. As we have seen, increasing the role of the police was a long-term objective of his but after the PIRA announced its temporary cessation in December 1974 he wrote to the Chief Constable that extending police operations during a truce would be wrong.[98] Any such move would be seen by republicans as provocation, a point reinforced by the talks with Ó Brádaigh.[99] In January, however, he asked Flanagan to produce a paper on expanding, which ultimately led to the joint paper with the army the following month. Such contradictions did not matter much at this point as there were serious questions as to whether the police were ready to play a larger role. Flanagan's ambitions were hindered by practicalities, which led John Bourn to conclude that the RUC 'may well not press forward too fast, whatever their plan might say.'[100]

Constitutional politics and the ceasefire

While it was clearly in the Labour government's interest to pursue the ceasefire, it had an overwhelmingly negative effect on relations with Irish politicians both North and South. The DUP were immediately suspicious of a sell out to the PIRA and refused to accept that Rees's efforts to sustain the ceasefire were not a threat to the union. On 7 January 1975 Ian Paisley told Rees that there was a simple choice to be made between demanding the unconditional surrender of the PIRA and defeating them militarily. He insisted on seeing proposals carried between the British government and the Provisionals. After Rees denied any such proposals existed, the NIO record states that the meeting 'departed from the norms of civilisation'. Paisley rose to his feet, verbally attacking Rees, who in turn said he refused to continue a meeting with anyone who called him a liar. The minutes note: 'In the ensuing mêlée, members of the delegation...were heard to question the Secretary of State's sanity, to wish that he and the entire British Government would leave the Province and to indulge in various forms of verbal abuse more worthy of a third-rate prep school.' Paisley refused to leave so Rees departed instead, taking his officials with him.[101]

Later in the year Rees recounted in his diaries how the DUP leader claimed bearded and hooded men had come to Stormont Castle and flown off in a helicopter. The men had actually come to sweep Rees's room for bugging devices. Rees believed that a policeman tipped off Paisley that the RUC had been given orders not to stop a van as it arrived. He compared Paisley's conspiracy theories to rumours in the 1920s that the IRA put poison in Protestant farmers' chicken runs and, referring to the logic 'you might expect from a graduate of Bob Jones' Academy in N Carolina [sic]', added: 'it is all so illiterate and low level.'[102]

The Ulster Unionists were similarly fearful of the ceasefire and appeared particularly suspicious of the incident centres, complaining to Rees that they were a cover for negotiating with the PIRA. Captain Austin Ardill argued that large numbers of UDA and UVF members should be recruited into the RUC Reserve and deployed in the largely republican Andersonstown (unsurprisingly, the minutes contain large exclamation marks next to this suggestion).[103] The SDLP, whose relations with the Labour government remained fraught, were also fearful. In September Gerry Fitt told Harold Wilson that several members of his party believed the government was planning with paramilitary groups for the failure of the Convention. Fitt said 'he thought that something should be said publicly to deny that the British government was about to abdicate its responsibility in Northern Ireland'. Rees replied that 'he would be saying that, for about the 58th time, in a speech tomorrow'.[104] So tired was Rees of denying that the government was seeking withdrawal that he compared the question in his private diaries to being asked 'have you stopped beating your wife?'; no answer would satisfy those asking.[105] Frustrating as it may have been, however, such distrust was only to be expected in the circumstances. The British government was engaging in dialogue with militant republicans and the distinction drawn between talks and negotiations was inevitably lost on those not privy to the conversations. To doubt the sincerity of government ministers was hardly beyond reason.

The Irish government was similarly scared that the British were contemplating withdrawal. After the UWC strike an interdepartmental unit was set up to consider the implications. The expectation was that loyalists would establish an independent state amidst great sectarian conflict and that an intervention from the Republic to protect Catholics would require a force of 60,000 (almost six times the size of the existing Irish military forces). Even then the unit concluded that armed intervention would only serve to provoke a violent loyalist response.[106] In October 1974 senior Irish politicians and officials expressed to the British ambassador to Dublin, Sir Arthur Galsworthy, their fear that the Convention would be dominated by the UUUC and the British would acquiesce in a 'new version of Protestant supremacy'.[107] The PIRA ceasefire inevitably raised the question for the Irish of whether the Labour government would negotiate with the republicans.

The British had to decide how honest they would be with the Irish government about the dialogue. Initial exchanges between the two governments were very positive, albeit with an emphasis from the Irish that there should be no negotiating. On 2 January Galsworthy met Garret FitzGerald. FitzGerald was satisfied with developments in the early stages of the ceasefire, saying they had judged releases and paroles well. He asked that they make clear no negotiation could happen with the PIRA and said the coalition government had decided the right posture for them was to say as little as possible publicly.[108] In a further meeting Sean Donlon, Secretary in the Irish Department of Foreign Affairs, said Irish ministers remained sceptical of the PIRA's motives. The Irish government would stay quiet but they were 'more than ever opposed to any suggestion of direct contact or negotiations between HMG and the Provisionals.'[109] On 19 January FitzGerald was interviewed on RTÉ. The British ambassador was happy with the performance: 'Despite several attempts to lead him to comments critical of HMG, Dr FitzGerald would not be drawn and the general impression left by the press reports of the interview is one of understanding and approval for our actions over the last three weeks.'[110]

Galsworthy told the Dublin government what they wanted to hear. Donlon and a civil servant from the Taoiseach's Department, Dermot Nally, were informed that the meeting with Provisional Sinn Féin was purely for the purpose of explaining Rees's public statements, that no negotiations would occur, and the government was 'very alive' to the fact the PIRA was seeking a means to claim they were negotiating with the British. He relayed to Cooper: 'They were entirely relaxed and raised no points of difficulty...I sensed that they had no criticism to make of the way in which we had handled the situation.' Later that day, Cosgrave again 'laid stress on the traumatic effect it would have throughout Ireland if the impression gained ground that [the British] were prepared to negotiate.'[111] Galsworthy continued to provide updates on the talks, reiterating that there were no negotiations. He said that 'our present assessment' was that the Provisionals were likely to revert to violence and their main objective was to appear to be in negotiations.[112] Here his assessment might more accurately be described as the Foreign Office's rather than the NIO's. As the head of the Foreign and Commonwealth Office's (FCO) Irish department stated months later: 'We have consistently taken a more sceptical view than the NIO of the chances that the ceasefire would hold more than a few weeks – wrongly, as it has turned out so far.'[113] Most importantly, these briefings spoke of Provisional Sinn Féin but not a dialogue with Ó Brádaigh.

In February the Irish government came to suspect they had not been told everything. Galsworthy told Cooper on 14 February that he had been summoned at short notice to brief FitzGerald. The ambassador noted that the Irish were suspicious. In particular they were concerned that there had been more than explanatory talks, that prominent Provisionals were directly involved in discussions and that they had been given assurances of personal immunity.[114] FitzGerald was also angry at the announcement of the incident centres being established.[115] Galsworthy wrote to Cooper:

> Up to now we have sought to keep the Irish government generally in the picture, and to allay any suspicions on their part by periodical briefings. But from now on it is going to be increasingly difficult to do this if we have to withold [sic] from them a part of the general picture which, were it ever to become public knowledge, would be especially sensitive from their point of view. If we continue on this tack of selective briefing we run the risk of being accused of having deliberately misled them.

Galsworthy argued this 'would have a worse effect on our general relations with the Irish than a charge of having kept them in the dark altogether'. He suggested telling the Irish government about the Ó Brádaigh talks as 'though they would no doubt bombard us with tiresome recriminations, that would in my view be preferable'.[116]

The ambassador was instructed to meet Cosgrave and inform him that discussions with Provisional Sinn Féin had 'broadened out to include one or two other people', but did not include 'leading terrorists such as [Dáithí Ó Conaill] and Seamus Twomey'. It was added: 'if the Taoiseach asks specifically whether [Ó Brádaigh] was involved, you should confirm this, for his personal information only'. Galsworthy was instructed to tell the Taoiseach that the government incident centres had no wider role and there was no question of permitting vigilante groups to police the community, nor any sign of their appearance on the streets.[117] He spoke to the Taoiseach as instructed; naming Ó Brádaigh when it became clear Cosgrave wanted to know if he was involved. Afterwards Dermot Nally said they had been 'virtually certain' of his involvement and the British could rest assured their suspicion was now dispelled. Galsworthy wrote that the Taoiseach 'expressed none of the criticisms of the incident centres that Dr FitzGerald had poured out last week'.[118]

Press reports added to difficulties in British–Irish relations and with FitzGerald in particular. The Irish Minister for Foreign Affairs was especially upset by Loughran's claims about vigilante policing and asked for a public promise that the PIRA would not be given immunity.[119] On 24 February Galsworthy met FitzGerald and pointed to the firm rebuttal of Loughran's statements in the press.[120] Robert Fisk, however, claimed in *The Times* that the Irish Cabinet had told the British Ambassador the incident centres were unacceptable.[121] FitzGerald told Galsworthy that Dick Walsh of the *Irish Times* had phoned him the previous day to comment on Fisk's allegations and he had denied the two governments were at odds. The next day Fisk reported that the British ambassador 'was told with some vehemence that political power should not be dispensed freely to the IRA'.[122]

Dick Walsh also claimed that Irish ministers suspected a secret deal between the British authorities and the PIRA.[123]

Galsworthy objected to the Secretary of the Department for Foreign Affairs, Patrick Keating, that any briefing on these lines was inconsistent with his discussions with Cosgrave and FitzGerald (a not entirely accurate claim for the latter case according to the ambassador's own reports). Keating said the Irish government 'had been (and remained) anxious about the position into which our contacts with Provisional Sinn Féin…might take us'. Galsworthy retorted that he had been at pains to explain the situation and reassure Irish ministers and such statements should not be made or even implied in press briefings. Keating accepted that the statement was untrue and promised to investigate the matter.[124] Galsworthy was taken to one side by Cosgrave at dinner the following day and assured that the briefing had not come from Foreign Affairs. Clearly not believing this, Galsworthy added to his report: 'I hope it may have the effect, at least for a while, of making the Irish more circumspect in their briefing.' He pressed for Rees to 'reinforce to [FitzGerald] personally our concern about some of his own personal utterances'.[125] There was something of a personality clash between the ambassador and the Minister for Foreign Affairs. Later in June Galsworthy reported on a meeting between Irish and British officials which was deemed to be far more productive and enjoyable because civil servants from the South 'recognised the futility of the kind of meetings which NIO Ministers habitually have to endure with Garret FitzGerald in which he occupies all of the available time gnawing away at old bones of contention'.[126] Nonetheless, while the ceasefire caused discomfort in Dublin and there were fears that the Labour government might seek withdrawal from Northern Ireland, the difficulties were not so great as to lead to public confrontations between the two governments and relations were generally affable.

Labour's expectations

The PIRA clearly wanted more than a temporary cessation and the overall thrust of the dialogue suggests a mutual desire for a permanent, peaceful settlement. This has led Niall Ó Dochartaigh to write of 'a missed opportunity for peace' in 1975. He emphasises that both republicans in the Provisional movement and elements within the Labour government showed a willingness to contemplate radical departures in the constitutional position of Northern Ireland. Ó Dochartaigh adds: 'Contrary to the received wisdom, the talks were neither a British ploy to weaken the IRA nor the product of a deluded IRA assessment that it had achieved victory.' He claims that the talks should be seen as negotiations which in the early stages 'promised so much.'[127] Nevertheless, internal correspondence suggests that Rees and the Northern Ireland Office were not optimistic. Rees's earlier rejection of negotiating with the Provisionals on constitutional matters is further supported by his outline of progress to the ministerial committee on Northern Ireland on 18 February. He described the government's immediate aims: to do whatever necessary to promote a ceasefire without conceding anything of substance to the Provisionals or provoking a loyalist backlash and 'to look for the outside chance of reaching some more substantial settlement with the Provisionals should they be sufficiently tired of violence to want to give up'. Rees stated, 'The Provisional leadership is still fighting the 800-year war against the English and are unlikely ever to abandon their objective of getting us out of Ireland. Capable of subtlety, they are a mixture of naivety and sophistication.' He noted that there were 'deep divisions' in the PAC about achieving their objective, but that, although these could be played on, they were not yet at the point of splitting. Rees told other Labour ministers that if the ceasefire lasted he would progressively end detention and 'lower the army profile while seeking to politicise the Provisional IRA through indirect talks'.[128] His plans for the ceasefire were rather more modest than the republicans' and aimed more at modifying security policy than the constitutional status of Northern Ireland.

A meeting of senior NIO staff chaired by Frank Cooper showed similar judgement. The record states, 'The longer it continued, the harder it would be for PIRA to resume violence.' Cooper stressed that the government had done nothing which could be regarded as a sell out, but recognised 'that the inevitable price paid in achieving the ceasefire was to have given inflated status to Provisional Sinn Féin'. The future of policing was one of the major topics of discussion. The record states, 'There must be no gap between the withdrawal of the army from hard republican areas and the introduction of normal policing. The army and the RUC were undertaking a joint study to consider how this could best be done.' Optimistic though this might seem it was agreed that 'the introduction of civil policing would take a number of years to implement'.[129] The British government's strategy remained much the same for the rest of the year: to end detention without trial, lower the army's profile and prevent a republican return to violence by engaging in talks. On 20 February the ministerial committee approved Rees's plan, with Harold Wilson congratulating him and Cooper for their success so far.[130]

Conclusion

The Labour government's response to the PIRA ceasefire initially followed the strategy developed in late 1974. The profile of the army was lowered, limited releases were made of those detained without trial and there was an emphasis on not provoking republicans into ending the cessation. The British had to go further in order to secure an indefinite break in the Provisionals' campaign and so dialogue was established, leading to the setting up of government incident centres as a grassroots point of contact. Immunity from arrest was not granted but rather an ambiguous set of plans was accepted by both sides which would later prove not to have truly resolved the issues at hand. In terms of the government's expectations, it was not thought that the talks would lead to a fundamental political transformation but rather they raised hope of reducing violence and bringing about changes to security policy that Rees already desired, such as the ending of detention without trial. Some of the changes posed problems for the British army, though the extent of its dissent from the government's strategy was overestimated by contemporary commentators. Far more worried were constitutional politicians in Northern Ireland and ministers in the Irish Republic, who feared that a negotiation would take place over their heads. Rees did not intend for this to occur and was personally dismissive of the idea but he was unable to convince them otherwise. Contained in all of these developments was a mix of tremendous difficulties that would grow the longer the ceasefire continued and frayed at the edges. The inability to be transparent about intentions meant it would prove very difficult for Labour ministers to convince the general public of its intentions. Suspicion and uncertainty dominated 1975.

Notes

1 Bodleian Library, Oxford, Harold Wilson papers c. 908, Note of a meeting with PIRA delegation, 13 March 1972; Peter Taylor, *Provos: the IRA and Sinn Féin* (London: Bloomsbury, 1997), pp. 132–3.

2 Freddie Cowper-Coles, '"Anxious for peace": the Provisional IRA in dialogue with the British government 1972–75', *Irish Studies Review*, 20:3 (2012), pp. 226–7; Tony Craig, 'From backdoors and back lanes to backchannels: reappraising British talks with the Provisional IRA, 1970–1974', *Contemporary British History*, 26:1 (2012), pp. 107–8.

3 Tony Craig, 'Laneside, then left a bit? Britain's secret political talks with loyalist paramilitaries in Northern Ireland, 1973–1976', *Irish Political Studies*, 29:2 (2014), pp. 298–317.

4 English, *Armed Struggle*, p. 178; Craig, 'From backdoors and back lanes', pp. 109–10.

5 Cowper-Coles, 'Anxious for peace', p. 228.

6 TNA, CJ4/860, Meeting between Rees and church leaders annex A, 18 December 1974.

7 TNA, CJ4/860, Meeting between Rees and church leaders, 18 December 1974.

8 TNA, CJ4/860, Meeting between Rees and church leaders annex B, 18 December 1974.

9 TNA, CJ4/860, Meeting between Rees and church leaders, 18 December 1974.

10 TNA, CJ4/860, Meeting between Bishop Daly and Rees, 7 January 1975.

11 TNA, CJ4/860, Meeting between Rees and church leaders, 18 December 1974.

12 TNA, CJ4/860, IRA ceasefire announcement, 20 December 1974.

13 TNA, CJ4/1225, CLF to brigades, 20 December 1974.

14 TNA, CJ4/864, Draft letter from Rees to GOC, undated; TNA, CJ4/864, England to the Private Secretary to the Secretary of State for Northern Ireland (PS/SSNI), 20 December 1974

15 TNA, CJ4/864, Rees to 'All Ministers', undated; TNA, CJ4/864, Jordan to 'All Information Staff', 23 December 1974.

16 TNA, CJ4/864, Meeting between Cooper and Worrall, 23 December 1974.

17 The Times, 27 December 1974.

18 LSE, MERLYN-REES/1/5, Transcript of tapes, 24 December 1974, p. 26.

19 TNA, PREM 16/515, Worrall et al. to Rees, 27 December 1974.

20 TNA, CJ4/864, Conversation between Wilson and Rees, 30 December 1974.

21 TNA, CJ4/864, Meeting between Cooper and Worrall, 30 December 1974.

22 TNA, DEFE 70/637, GOC to Rees, 30 December 1974.

23 TNA, DEFE 70/637, GOC to CGS, 30 December 1974.

24 TNA, CJ4/864, Meeting between Rees and GOC and Chief Constable, 30 December 1974.

25 TNA, CJ4/1225, CLF to brigades, 30 December 1974.

26 TNA, CAB 134/3921, IRN(75) memo 1, 3 January 1975.

27 TNA, PREM 16/515, Conversation between Wilson and Rees, 31 December 1974.

28 TNA, CAB 134/3921, IRN(75) memo 1, 3 January 1975.

29 TNA, CJ4/860, Meeting between Rees and GOC, 6 January 1975.

30 TNA, DEFE 70/637, CGS to CDS, 9 January 1975.

31 TNA, CJ4/1225, CLF to brigades, 11 January 1975.

32 TNA, PREM 16/515, Conversation between Wilson and Rees, 31 December 1974.

33 TNA, CAB 134/3921, IRN(75) meeting 1, 8 January 1975.

34 Hansard (Commons), 884, cols 201–3.

35 TNA, PREM 16/515, Wright to Wilson, 14 January 1975.

36 TNA, CJ4/860, IRA statement, 16 January 1975; John Francis Green was killed in controversial circumstances with claims that both the UVF and British intelligence were involved. At his funeral oration Ó Brádaigh described him as the O/C of North Armagh's 2nd battalion: McKitterick et al., Lost lives, p. 511.

37 TNA, CJ4/860, Ending of ceasefire, 17 January 1975.

38 TNA, CJ4/860, Meeting between Rees and church leaders, 17 January 1975.

39 TNA, CJ4/864, The end of the IRA ceasefire, undated.

40 National University of Ireland Galway (NUIG), Ruairí Ó Brádaigh papers (RÓB), POL28/67, Background to renewal of truce and subsequent negotiations, undated; NUIG, RÓB, POL28/67, Formal meeting, 18 January 1975; NUIG, Duddy papers, POL35/62, Diary entry, 17 January 1975.
41 NUIG, RÓB, POL28/67, HMG to RM, 19 January 1975.
42 NUIG, RÓB, POL28/67, Formal meeting, 19 January 1975.
43 NUIG, RÓB, POL28/67, Formal meeting, 21 January 1975; NUIG, RÓB, POL28/67, Instructions, 20 January 1975.
44 McKittrick et al., Lost lives, pp. 511–13.
45 NUIG, Duddy, POL35/62, Diary entry, 21 January 1975; NUIG, RÓB, POL28/67, HMG to RM, 22 January 1975.
46 NUIG, RÓB, POL28/67, Statement by the Secretary of State for Northern Ireland, 22 January 1975.
47 NUIG, RÓB, POL28/67, Instructions, 23 January 1975.
48 NUIG, Duddy, POL35/62, Diary entry, 23 & 24 January 1975.
49 NUIG, RÓB, POL28/67, S to M, 24 January 1975.
50 NUIG, Duddy, POL35/62, Diary entry, 29 & 30 January 1975.
51 NUIG, Duddy, POL35/62, Diary entry, 31 January & 1 February 1975.
52 TNA, CJ4/864, Allan to PUS, 24 December 1974.
53 TNA, CJ4/864, Note by Cooper, 30 December 1974.
54 TNA, CJ4/860, Callaghan to Holy See, 31 December 1974.
55 TNA, CJ4/864, Allan to Janes, 3 January 1975.
56 NUIG, Duddy, POL35/62, Diary entry, 31 January 1975.
57 TNA, CJ4/864, Wilson to Rees, 18 January 1975; TNA, CJ4/864, Meeting between Rees and Irish Ambassador, 28 January 1975.
58 Andrew Mumford, 'Covert peacemaking: clandestine negotiations and back-channels with the Provisional IRA during the early "Troubles", 1972–76', Journal of Imperial and Commonwealth History, 39:4 (2011), p. 639.
59 TNA, CJ4/860, Meeting between Rees and Protestant clergy, 18 January 1975.
60 The Times, 6 January 1975.
61 Irish Times, 4 January 1975.
62 TNA, CJ4/864, Bourn to England and PUS, 24 January 1975; NUIG, RÓB, POL28/67, Instructions, 1 February 1975.
63 NUIG, Duddy, POL35/62, Diary entry, 3 February 1975.
64 NUIG, RÓB, POL28/67, Untitled sixteen-point document, 3 February 1975.
65 NUIG, RÓB, POL28/67, Formal meeting, 3 February 1975.
66 NUIG, RÓB, POL28/67, Untitled sixteen-point document, 7 February 1975.
67 NUIG, Duddy, POL35/62, Diary entry, 7 February 1975.
68 NUIG, RÓB, POL28/67, Untitled sixteen-point document, 7 February 1975.
69 NUIG, Duddy, POL35/62, Diary entry, 8 February 1975.
70 NUIG, RÓB, POL28/67, Instructions, 8 February 1975.
71 TNA, CJ4/861, Allan to Dublin Ambassador, 24 February 1975.
72 LSE, MERLYN-REES/1/6, Transcript of tapes, undated, p. 17.
73 TNA, CJ4/864, Bourn to PUS, 10 February 1975.
74 Hansard (Commons), 886, cols 207–10.

75 TNA, CJ4/864, Note by Payne, 10 February 1975.
76 *Irish Times*, 14 February 1975.
77 TNA, PREM 16/517, Galsworthy to Cooper, 27 February 1975.
78 NUIG, RÓB, POL28/67, Formal meeting, undated.
79 NUIG, Duddy, POL35/63, Diary transcript notes, undated; LSE, MERLYN-REES/1/6, Transcript of tapes, 19 January 1975.
80 NUIG, RÓB, POL28/67, Instructions, c. 19–25 February.
81 NUIG, RÓB, POL28/67, Formal meeting, 25 February 1975.
82 TNA, CJ4/865, Bourn to PUS, 20 February 1975.
83 TNA, CJ4/865, Meeting at HQNI Lisburn, 25 February 1975.
84 NUIG, RÓB, POL28/67, Formal meeting, 28 February 1975.
85 NUIG, Duddy, POL35/62, Diary entry, 5 March 1975.
86 TNA, CJ4/865, Bourn to Wyatt, 19 March 1975.
87 *Observer*, 20 April 1974.
88 LSE, MERLYN-REES/1/7, Transcript of tapes, undated, pp. 11–12.
89 TNA, CJ4/864, Courses of action if the ceasefire ends, undated.
90 TNA, CJ4/860, GOC to Cooper, 4 February 1975.
91 TNA, CJ4/865, Webster to England, 19 February 1975.
92 Bew and Patterson, *The British state*, p. 82; Bew, *Ireland: the politics of enmity*, p. 519.
93 TNA, CJ4/867, Wyatt to England, 25 February 1975.
94 TNA, CJ4/1293, Cooper to GOC, 21 March 1975.
95 TNA, CJ4/865, England to PUS, 24 March 1975.
96 TNA, CJ4/865, Cooper to England, 25 March 1975.
97 TNA, CJ4/865, Policing in a ceasefire situation, 24 February 1975.
98 TNA, CJ4/864, Draft letter from Rees to Chief Constable, undated; TNA, CJ4/864, England to PS/SSNI, 20 December 1974.
99 NUIG, RÓB, POL28/67, Instructions, 20 January 1975.
100 TNA, CJ4/865, Bourn to England, 21 February 1975.
101 TNA, CJ4/1225, Meeting between Rees and DUP, 7 January 1975.
102 In 1966 Paisley was given an honorary doctorate from Bob Jones University in South Carolina, an institution known for a fundamentalist Christian ethos: Steve Bruce, *Paisley: religion and politics in Northern Ireland* (Oxford, Oxford University Press, 2007), p. 145; LSE, MERLYN-REES/1/9, Transcripts of tapes, undated, p. 12.
103 TNA, CJ4/858, Meeting between Rees and UUP, 17 February 1975.
104 TNA, PREM 16/520, Wright to Jordan, 19 Sept 1975.
105 LSE, MERLYN-REES/1/7, Transcript of tapes, undated, p. 34.
106 Patterson, *Ireland's violent frontier*, p. 82.
107 Quoted in McDaid, *Template for peace*, p. 162.
108 TNA, CJ4/864, Galsworthy to Cooper, 2 January 1975.
109 TNA, CJ4/864, Galsworthy to NIO Belfast, 7 January 1975.
110 TNA, CJ4/864, Galsworthy to NIO Belfast, 20 January 1975.
111 TNA, CJ4/864, Galsworthy to Cooper, 20 January 1975.
112 TNA, CJ4/864, Galsworthy to Cooper, 24 January 1975.

113 TNA, FCO 84/460, Harding to Sykes, 19 August 1975.
114 TNA, CJ4/865, Galsworthy to Cooper and Harding, 14 February 1975.
115 This is not referenced in the 14 February telegram but is referred to in a later meeting: TNA, CJ4/865, Galsworthy to Cooper and Harding, 21 February 1975.
116 TNA, CJ4/865, Galsworthy to Cooper, undated.
117 TNA, CJ4/865, Callaghan to Galsworthy, 20 February 1975.
118 TNA, CJ4/865, Galsworthy to Cooper and Harding, 21 February 1975.
119 TNA, CJ4/865, Galsworthy to Cooper and Harding, 14 February 1975.
120 TNA, CJ4/865, Galsworthy to NIO Belfast, 24 February 1975.
121 *The Times*, 24 February 1975.
122 *The Times*, 25 February 1975.
123 *Irish Times*, 28 February 1975.
124 TNA, CJ4/861, Galsworthy to NIO Belfast, 28 February 1975.
125 TNA, CJ4/861, Galsworthy to NIO Belfast, 1 March 1975.
126 TNA, FCO 84/460, Galworthy to Harding, 10 June 1975; Henry Patterson describes FitzGerald as 'famously prolix': Patterson, *Ireland's violent frontier*, p. 184.
127 Niall Ó Dochartaigh, '"Everyone trying", the IRA ceasefire, 1975: a missed opportunity for peace?' in *Field Day Review 7* (Dublin, 2011), pp. 50–77.
128 TNA, CAB 134/3921, IRN(75) memo 7, 18 February 1975.
129 TNA, CJ4/861, Meeting of NIO senior staff, 18 February 1975.
130 TNA, CAB 134/3921, IRN(75) meeting 3, 20 February 1975.

5

Fraying at the edges: the Provisional IRA ceasefire

Although the PIRA ceasefire lasted for most of 1975 the year was still a violent one. Sectarian killings were especially high with loyalist paramilitaries targeting innocent Catholic civilians and republicans carrying out their own horrific attacks against the Protestant community. Interfactional fighting was prominent with feuding between the UDA and UVF and a split within the Official IRA leading to the formation of the Irish Republican Socialist Party (IRSP) and what would become known as the Irish National Liberation Army (INLA). The Officials were targeted by PIRA volunteers as well as the new group in some of the worst feuding between republican groups during the conflict. Thus, although the ceasefire saw relatively few killings of police officers and British soldiers, 267 deaths resulted from the conflict in 1975.[1]

One indication of the frailty of the arrangement between the Provisionals and the Labour government was that the two sides were unable even to agree on the terminology for the stoppage. The Provisional Army Council and its representatives in the talks spoke of a bilateral truce. British security forces were chastised for not adhering to the principles of the proposals agreed in February 1975. Periodic retaliation followed with the republicans persistently frustrated by the lack of progress on their political objectives. For the British, the stoppage was a PIRA ceasefire and the strategy developed the previous year for how to respond to it remained in place. Detention without trial was phased out and the army's low profile kept in place.

In the dialogue facilitated by Brendan Duddy the British representatives made a number of statements to the effect that the government was willing to withdraw from Northern Ireland. The analysis presented here is that these remarks were made in order to drag the ceasefire out and that it did not amount to the bilateral arrangement they had hoped for. Bew, Frampton and Gurruchaga argue that there was 'little unity of purpose' within the Labour government, citing Wilson's doomsday proposals for withdrawal.[2] Ó Dochartaigh similarly points to Wilson as evidence that the republicans were not necessarily misled.[3] While one of the basic problems in analysing the ceasefire is the unavailability of material on the conversations between the British representatives conducting the dialogue and their superiors (Ó Brádaigh and Duddy's papers cannot shed light on this), there is reason to doubt that Wilson's predilections were relevant to the talks. He expressed them in 1974 and after the Convention failed to reach agreement, but they were not discussed for most of the ceasefire. Instead, Rees is shown here to be far more firm on what was expected of the ceasefire. Publicly, he was placed in the difficult position of being unable to make clear, definitive statements without endangering the ceasefire. Privately, he insisted there could be no negotiation with republicans and that the benefit of the ceasefire was that it enabled the Labour government to remove detention without trial and pursue a new policy of criminalisation. In the autumn it became apparent to the Provisionals that they were being strung along and the ceasefire collapsed.

The dialogue

With the practical arrangements for the ceasefire addressed, the talks with the PIRA began to include some political discussion. On 5 March the British representatives told Ó Brádaigh that the Convention was a sign the British government no longer wanted to dictate events in Ireland. They tried to encourage Provisional Sinn Féin's participation and offered to act as a sounding board for republican ideas. It was difficult for the republicans to see the value of participating in a six-county setup so they insisted on a thirty-two-county forum. When the British representatives argued they were unable to deliver this because it was beyond their jurisdiction, the Provisionals asked that the British publicly advocate it to force Dublin's acceptance. The British responded that Provisional Sinn Féin should put forward these views in the Convention.[4] Both sides held firmly to their established outlook on what constituted the legitimate democratic unit.

By the next meeting the talks meandered into disputes over the observation of the ceasefire, marking the beginning of perpetual disagreements about the truce proposals and whether they were being honoured. The arrest of republicans in Armagh led the Provisional representatives to warn that local units had considered reprisals after the incident centres gave no satisfactory reply to their protests.[5] A message was passed from the PAC stating that after four weeks of the suspension in hostilities the British government's response was 'unsatisfactory'. The arrests and other RUC operations were held to be in breach of the truce and negotiations on their basic political demands had 'not made any worthwhile progress'.[6] The British replied that they were 'unable to interfere in the processes of law' on arrests but accepted the complaints about political progress.[7] On 16 March the Provisionals were told that 'as a token of British sincerity' Marian and Dolours Price, convicted of bombing London in 1973, would be transferred from England to Armagh jail. Further detainee releases were promised before Easter.[8] The Price sisters were transferred after the meeting.[9]

In spite of this, the ceasefire almost collapsed again. Ó Conaill issued a public statement referring to a lack of a public apology for the shooting of two civilians in Belfast on 13 March, adding that because of RUC activities in Crossmaglen, instructions had been given to local units to 'repulse incursions by the RUC into designated areas'. The Provisional leadership would 'review the position with a view to resuming hostilities' if the British did not show a sincere desire to observe the truce.[10] Duddy felt that Ó Conaill was 'reading the position wrongly' as the British were temporarily exhausted in terms of what they could offer. He recorded that Ó Brádaigh attempted to get the statement stopped.[11] Duddy warned James Allan there was a danger that the ceasefire would break down in another month's time, privately recording that he was 'tired and dangerously close to giving in'. He told Allan that the British 'must show historic initiative to leave Ireland', noting in his diary that the NIO official agreed.[12]

The Provisional Army Council instructions for the meeting on 25 March focussed on the arrest of the Armagh volunteers, claiming that they had obeyed instructions and kept a low profile, thus leaving the British in breach of the agreement.[13] The British representatives again encouraged the Provisionals to participate in the Convention but Sinn Féin decided to boycott the elections. Allan and Browning promised that the British army had been told to 'cool it' and that only the Official–IRSP and UDA–UVF feuds had prevented reductions in activity. The rest of the meeting dealt with actions by both sides, including the additional arrest of Belfast PIRA volunteer James Kelly. The British argued that they lacked the centralised control of the Provisional movement because they had to operate in the context of a democratic society and could not dictate how the police acted. They promised that the Labour government's intentions had not weakened. They also referred to difficulties with the army, saying that they could only tell a small number of personnel the facts of the situation and a communications problem prevented messages travelling from the GOC to the rank and file.[14]

Duddy talked with the Provisionals after the meeting and recorded Billy McKee's remark that James Allan 'was only a message boy and he wasn't going to waste any more time on him'. Duddy himself argued that the British could not control the army and RUC but also 'wanted their cake and money back as well'. All agreed that the next meeting would decide whether the ceasefire continued.[15] Two days later Joe McCallion pressed Duddy to try to find a way through.[16] Duddy met Browning and told him that Ó Conaill was 'sad at going back to war' but felt he had no option. At Browning's suggestion Duddy composed a message for Harold Wilson that the MI6 officer could claim was sent by the Provisionals.[17]

The message said the British representatives on the talks were 'too close to the day-to-day problems of administrating Northern Ireland to fully appreciate the historic importance of the past one hundred days'. It was the leadership's 'compelling belief that our Irish problem will only be solved by Irish men, freed from British direction and political constraints', though they accepted it could not be solved at a stroke. Citing the lack of real movement, continuing arrests, the 'dribble' of releases and a 'discernible drift towards the restructuring of British Rule', the message concluded by asking for a positive initiative to prevent a return to hostilities.[18] Duddy was taking a risky action here in transmitting a message that claimed to be from the Provisional leadership but was not. Ó Brádaigh told Duddy afterwards that he approved but should see Ó Conaill.[19] Ó Conaill in turn said that he 'couldn't change a word'. He said that if the response from the British was not good enough there would be a slow return to conflict.[20] Duddy's act was to be considered by a later Provisional Army Council meeting.

Merlyn Rees took a very negative view of the message. Not knowing the real author, he privately recorded that Ó Conaill wanted 'a cosmetic way of saying he is in touch with the PM'. He decided to advise Wilson 'that in no way should he react to these letters', adding: 'There can be no question of negotiation.' Rees insisted he was 'not talking about ditching anybody...I allow officials to talk and our messages to fly about in this way because it is not negotiation but it is educational and when they talk about 800 years of history, it is not going to be undone overnight'.[21] Beyond sustaining the ceasefire, his expectations of what would come of the talks remained slim and he was opposed to a negotiation of the kind the PIRA desired. The British officials' response in the next meeting on 2 April was a defensive one, pointing out the risk of a collapse and holding out the prospect that the Provisional Army Council would get progress towards its objectives if it was patient. Browning told Duddy prior to the meeting that he was going to be tough on the Provisionals and tell them 'a few facts of life'.[22] He began by referring to a statement from the Provisional's Belfast Brigade claiming a bomb attack in the city centre the day before and warning that 'further violations of the truce by the British army will no longer be tolerated'.[23] Browning argued that the noises from the republicans appeared to be 'very warlike' while the meetings were being clouded by minor matters and had become like a 'glorified incident centre'. He warned that the cynics on the

British side were 'being proved correct' in their belief that the Provisionals were only using the ceasefire as a 'breather'. Browning reportedly said that the acceptability of the Provisionals 'as a respectable movement has greatly increased…It is now viewed as a serious political movement which should be listened to. This is an enormous gain. It will be lost if [the republican movement] goes back to war'.[24]

At the Provisionals' Belfast Easter parade Seamus Twomey repeated the traditional republican tenets of the movement: a permanent peace could not be achieved until the British declared their intention to withdraw, gave a general amnesty and withdrew troops to barracks.[25] Responding to this, Browning told Ó Brádaigh *et al.* that a public declaration was 'absolutely out of the question' as it would lead to a 'Congo-type situation'. If, however, the Provisionals helped the British 'to create circumstances out of which the structures of disengagement can actually grow, the pace quickens immensely once the ground work is laid'. Browning assured the republicans that the Labour government could not say they were leaving Ireland 'because the reaction will prevent that happening' but the 'tendency is towards eventual British disengagement'. He argued it was the interpretation of the ceasefire proposals which was in question and suggested both sides discuss how they perhaps misunderstood them. Crucially, Ó Brádaigh's record of the meeting notes that Allan remained silent 'as though he did not approve'.[26] Despite Browning's comments being favourable to the Provisionals' objectives, the reaction on the republican side was negative. Duddy's diary records McKee as saying afterwards that it was probably the last meeting.[27] Two days later, however, the Provisional Army Council agreed not to end the ceasefire. Duddy was censured for his writing to Wilson but there were no real consequences for stepping outside his authority.[28]

Sectarian violence and the Convention elections

In addition to the PIRA's problem of arrests, the ceasefire was also threatened by growing sectarian violence. The first half of 1975 saw few deaths of British army or RUC personnel, reflecting the PIRA's reduction in activity against those forces. Nevertheless, April saw thirty-eight deaths; almost as many as January, February and March combined and a monthly total that was only exceeded twice in 1974 and then only because of the Dublin/Monaghan and Birmingham bombings. The UVF were especially active, killing 105 people in 1975, its most violent year of the conflict.[29] Some of these were a result of a feud with the UDA but a majority were innocent Catholic civilians targeted solely for their religion. The PIRA's ceasefire was seen a threat to the union and one motivation of the UVF campaign was to force a breakdown in the talks between republicans and the British. Other attacks had a less strategic purpose, with Lenny Murphy's Shankill Butchers gang carrying out horrific killings that left the victims' bodies mutilated.[30] The high level of sectarian killing prompted retaliation from the PIRA, making inter-communal violence a prominent feature in 1975.

On 5 April nine people were killed in Belfast. Two Catholics died in a UVF bomb attack in North Belfast, another was shot by the same organisation, five Protestant civilians were killed by a PIRA bomb on the Shankill and an INLA member was shot by the OIRA.[31] The PIRA responded with a statement that new orders had been sent to its units; actions would 'be related to the level of violent and hostile activity by Crown and sectarian forces'. In the media this was interpreted as a compromise between hawks and doves which gave local leaders autonomy, with Belfast volunteers standing out as particularly sceptical of the ceasefire.[32] Duddy dismissed this supposed 'right to bomb as they please' as a misinterpretation, believing there would be 'no more violence'.[33] Provisional IRA units bombed Belfast city centre the following day but the deaths that occurred for the remainder of April were primarily carried out by other organisations.[34]

In a short meeting on 9 April Allan and Browning passed on a formal statement that the media briefing by the Provisionals encouraged sectarian violence and 'certainly gives the impression that all units can act independently'. They said they had no choice but to postpone meetings.[35] This only lasted a week, with meetings resumed because of the lack of PIRA activity. The British began to press the republicans on how to deal with Protestants, asking how they proposed to get across to them. A rather weak reply followed that there had been contact with loyalists in the past and lines were still open. Asked whether Provisional Sinn Féin would eventually stand for election, they said that this would be decided 'in the light of circumstances at the time'.[36]

The 1st of May was the date for the Convention elections. The UUUC campaigned for a complete rejection of power-sharing and all-Ireland institutions. It won a majority with forty-six of the seventy-eight seats. Rees privately commented, 'I am not worried about the election result. Anything that happens is not going to come from the moderates'.[37] His expectations were few and he followed the advice of his civil servants when they urged him 'not to lay stress on the "crisis" nature of the Convention', to respond only to queries by the chairman and not to make statements on the Convention until it produced its report.[38] Choosing to play such a passive role left him open to criticism. His insistence that a minister from Great Britain could not cajole the Northern Irish parties into a settlement had certain virtues, however. The conditions for compromise were not present and there was merit in pursuing a process where the parties themselves were more transparently to blame for failure. The Convention met from 8 May until 3 July, adjourning for informal inter-party talks. The discussion in this first phase offered little of significance. Rees noted that the atmosphere had been superficially harmonious, with the UUUC 'anxious not to appear intransigent' and the SDLP fearful of losing Catholic support to the Provisionals.[39]

The Convention influenced the dialogue with the Provisionals. Ó Brádaigh's instructions from the Provisional Army Council were to press the British to make a declaration of intent to withdraw and then ask the Convention to draft a constitution in this context. Rather impractically, considering the UUUC's majority, it was argued that this would 'rescue something from the shambles'. As before, it was asserted that permanent peace could only come with British withdrawal.[40] Duddy also made it apparent that he shared the traditional republican perspective on the conflict, telling the British representatives that 'the answer is to get out of Ireland and the Irish would soon have to settle quickly'.[41] The British representatives described the Convention as something that had to be gone through but about which the government was not too excited. They would not accept a return to majority rule but wanted 'to discover over a much longer period how Britain distances herself from here'. British policy, they said, would be stated *after* the Convention.[42] The Convention enabled the representatives to be guarded about long-term intentions, prevaricating when they were pressed by the Provisionals.

The dialogue was disrupted again in May after PIRA volunteer Shane O'Doherty was arrested in Derry, where he had served as the brigade's explosives officer.[43] Joe McCallion told Duddy that Martin McGuinness might use it as an excuse to break the truce.[44] Two days after the arrest the PIRA shot dead an RUC officer in Derry.[45] When Browning told Duddy that the British would be 'very reluctant to have any positive things to say' in the next meeting, Duddy thought they were 'playing the death' of the RUC man 'for political purposes' and complained that they had not 'honoured their part of the truce by refusing to curb the activities of the RUC'.[46] He was all the more angered on 14 May when only Browning showed up for a meeting because it was deemed 'not on' for Allan to be present.[47] Browning made a formal statement that the killing of the policeman was totally disproportionate to O'Doherty's arrest and the effect of the Derry Brigade Staff's actions was 'to put a stop to progress'. The MI6 officer again dangled the possibility of radical change in the future. Ó Brádaigh's record states: 'Personally B feels that [the republican movement's] major objective is in sight. He hopes [they] do not destroy their own case.'[48]

A meeting between the two sides did not occur for a fortnight afterwards but there were a number of contacts between Duddy and the British.

Duddy stressed that the Provisional leadership could not hold their position and the ceasefire would be lost. He added that they had moved far over the last three years; they were no longer looking for immediate troop withdrawals, agreed to steady progress through the talks and 'really wished for peace'. Duddy recorded a response from a British representative: 'The real problem is that Sir F Cooper is jealous of your power Brendan. He and not you wants to be seen running the show even if that means failure. So be it. Sir F Cooper privately admits that you are quite correct but that you are 10 years ahead of your time.'[49] These remarks are hard to assess as the name of the person concerned is blanked out in Duddy's diaries. It seems likely, however, that they were an attempt to appeal to his vanity, a tactic which the intermediary had attributed to Browning the previous day.[50]

Duddy made the case to Ó Brádaigh that renewed conflict would be tactically wrong: 'We must await the mistakes of the UUUC to become apparent to the Catholics in NI and then the Provos' cause would become accepted.' Ó Brádaigh agreed but told Duddy the British must act to keep the ceasefire intact.[51] Browning rang again to say that the government 'agrees with your thinking, though don't expect to see it in print. It is inevitable that the British are going – many things have happened in the last 48 hrs. All to your thinking.'[52] Duddy tried to get the British to meet the Provisionals. James Allan said they could not but he promised to end his disengagement from the contact between the intermediary and Browning. A further emotional message was sent by Duddy to Ó Conaill hoping for peace.[53]

There have been a number of statements thus far suggesting that the British were committed to disengagement or withdrawal. Ó Brádaigh's records and Duddy's diaries appear to accept these as sincere. Browning is recorded as being 'excited about the inevitability of the British leaving being accepted in the British establishment', with Ó Brádaigh's notes adding: 'he sees this as an on-going situation with victory for his diplomacy'. It was believed that this analysis was also accepted by James Allan: 'Both A and B concede that [the republican movement] has won; the job now is to get the British out gently. Their official straight [sic] jacket forbids them from saying this formally.'[54]

The withholding of government material related to the talks makes it harder to determine whether the British representatives were sincere or intended to deceive the Provisionals into continuing the ceasefire. It is also possible they went beyond their remit. There is some evidence to suggest that Browning's performance was not looked upon favourably. As we have seen, the other participants picked up on Allan being unhappy with some of Browning's remarks. Rees also recorded in his private diaries that Browning eventually departed the NIO 'because in some of the talks that had taken place it was put to me that people didn't think he was good enough'; he had spoken of 'independence and Britain at home getting fed up.'[55] Allowing for this still does not explain Ó Brádaigh and Duddy's perception that withdrawal was being seriously considered. While Browning was the most explicit and emotional voice, Allan also seems to have given this impression.

There was plenty of room for ambiguity in using the term 'withdrawal.' For the Provisionals the ideal scenario was a British declaration of intent to withdraw, a period of negotiations between Irishmen and the removal of British troops (leaving room for a certain flexibility on the constitution of a united Ireland and the timetable for soldiers leaving). Withdrawal could also mean the removal of troops following the end of conflict, leaving the union intact through some kind of internal settlement. The gap between the two was the difference between victory and defeat for republicanism.

Government records suggest a consistent British strategy that contradicts the republican perception of the talks. Rees argued in a 16 May cabinet memo that, having secured the ceasefire it was now time to use it to resist the PIRA's demands 'whilst seeking to persuade them that they must learn to work through political channels.' Far from desiring to empower them, Rees felt that if the ceasefire could be maintained for long enough, 'a number of factors may begin to weaken the Provisionals' power to dictate events.'[56] In a meeting of the ministerial committee on Northern Ireland Rees said that the Labour government 'faced the prospects of a prolonged period of direct rule.' Rather than withdrawal, he proposed a far more mild form of disengagement, appointing a Minister Resident or commissioner to give direct rule 'a greater Northern Ireland flavour' and increasing Westminster's distance from the governance of the region. Although fears were again raised in discussion that there might be growing pressure for withdrawal, Wilson approved Rees's approach.[57] The general thrust of these discussions suggests it is more likely that the Provisionals and Duddy were misled in the talks.

The army and the RUC

Violence during the ceasefire led to arguments between the NIO and senior army officers. Rees admitted that it remained high despite the Provisionals having almost ceased attacks on commercial and military targets. He identified four key categories into which most of the killings fell: sectarian violence emanating primarily from the UVF and UDA against Catholic civilians, gang warfare between the two main loyalist paramilitary groups over the spoils of criminal activities, factional violence between the Official IRA and the IRSP, and selective acts by the PIRA 'as an instrument of policy.' If, argued Rees, such violence reached a scale where the PIRA carried out major retaliation, he would have to face 'the dilemma of whether to re-start the cycle of detention orders, aggressive army patrolling and, in its wake, renewed "retaliatory" IRA violence.' He was weary of this and hoped instead to maintain the ceasefire and the release of detainees. Sectarian violence, he thought, had to be 'brought under control by careful, patient police work', while ways had to be found to assist in the 'long, slow job over a period of years to win the co-operation of the Catholic community for any form of policing.'[58]

Rees's desire to break away from past security policies was from this point more thoroughly criticised by the army. The longer the ceasefire remained intact, the more Frank King took a pessimistic view of its effect on the PIRA's military position. He argued that the PIRA were using the situation to 'refurbish their military strength' and 'the ceasefire itself was achieving nothing'. He said the pace of detainee releases was far too quick and suggested Rees return to using detention.[59] Frank Cooper responded by writing to King in a tone sympathetic towards the GOC but committed to Rees's approach. He said that 'none of us believe that it is all over bar the shouting', but the pattern of violence had changed for the foreseeable future and demanded a fresh look at security policy. In an important section which neatly tied the political and security context together, Cooper argued:

> the pattern of past security policy – in crude terms the army v the IRA and the RUC v the loyalists with totally different procedures – has imposed on us a situation which makes a political solution or even political progress difficult if not impossible.

He reminded King that he himself acknowledged the ceasefire had held well and argued that if the old pattern of operations was resumed they would run the risk of re-uniting the militant groups in both communities. If detention orders were signed again then violence might be temporarily contained but it would only mean a return to the treadmill.[60] It became increasingly clear that Rees and the NIO were keen on maintaining a softer approach and that the policy of responding proportionately to PIRA activity was more inelastic than the army desired. Rees's previous remarks that detention would only end with a permanent ceasefire were not held to.

A key reason for King and other army officers' frustrations with these developments was that they found it incredibly difficult to conceive of the RUC being in a fit state to take on army responsibilities. While Rees acknowledged the scale of the project and the time it would take, investigations tended to highlight the problems rather than identify solutions. In May a working party was established to review security policy.[61] It observed that the RUC lacked human resources (HR) and suffered from a 'two-generation problem'. Older commanders saw the RUC 'primarily as a security apparatus', while younger officers wanted to provide a more conventional police service like in Great Britain. B.M. Webster said the younger men might not appreciate the dangers of extending their kind of policing to republican areas.[62] The army felt the RUC were 'as yet making little or no progress in extending their activities'. The group recommended that the army's low profile be maintained, with no further troop withdrawals, but the RUC should take on more normal policing tasks with army assistance.[63] When John Bourn toured various RUC stations in August he recorded that nothing new arose from the discussions: all policemen 'insisted that they needed army support and none of them seemed to contemplate a life without the army'.[64] It was not until the following year that serious inroads were made into developing the RUC.

Stuttering contact

Public fears that the Labour government's dialogue with militant republicans might lead to withdrawal were given sustenance in mid-May after a series of statements from Reverend Arlow, one of the clergymen at Feakle. There were early indications that NIO officials disliked him. A January paper from the NIO contemptuously referred to him 'treating *Belfast Telegraph* readers to his spiritual and political odyssey'.[65] In April James Allan warned the British embassy in Washington that Arlow planned to visit the United States in the hope of establishing an international fund to turn paramilitary groups away from violence. He wrote: 'we have quite frankly not found him entirely reliable. Some discretion is therefore needed in dealing with him.'[66] He copied the letter to Cooper adding that the latter would want to watch this 'very carefully', warning of Arlow's 'potential for self-seeking and trouble-making'.[67]

During his trip Arlow gave a press conference alleging that the PIRA had been told by British representatives that if the Convention broke down there would be a British withdrawal.[68] The furore did not develop, however, until Arlow returned from the United States and repeated the accusation on BBC television.[69] The following day it was front-page news. Arlow's involvement at Feakle gave him public credibility and the clergyman did not dispel the assumption that he was still involved in talks, prompting Rees to complain that he was like John O'Connell. Rees further lamented the claim in some newspapers that a Labour minister was the source of Arlow's statement. He believed there was nothing in this and told Wilson: 'Unfortunately the Irish make bricks without straw.'[70] The Irish press were far from alone. A *Daily Telegraph* editorial speculated that

Arlow was tipped off by the Labour government to help them in their secret policy of 'consistently nudging Ulster towards a demand for political independence'.[71]

While Rees and the NIO had to suffer the fact that issuing official denials would do nothing to stifle Arlow's claims, the Provisional Army Council's instructions to Ó Brádaigh suggested that they could be put to good use: Arlow 'had conditioned the public mind towards withdrawal. Now is the time for public declaration by [the British government] to that effect'.[72] When this was pressed in the meeting, the British replied that 'informally the more one states the intention going the longer it is delayed'.[73] Duddy wrote to Ó Brádaigh offering two possible reasons for the British being unwilling to make progress: that they wished to return to conflict with the Provisionals to prevent a large scale loyalist takeover, fuelled by fear of a British–PIRA deal, or they were 'aware of the strength of the Republican Political position in that the average person just now believes that [the Provisional movement] have what they want... The Republican Leadership will not want to shatter that image by going back to war so the British need not give [the Provisionals] any visible sign to maintain the truce'.[74] Duddy's analysis was seriously flawed. There were certainly fears of another loyalist backlash, with Rees warning cabinet colleagues that the government must not 'provide a clear-cut issue around which Protestant passions can coalesce', but the threat was not great enough to prompt suggestions that the breakdown of the ceasefire would counteract this.[75] The second scenario Duddy envisioned overestimated the strength of the PIRA's position. Duddy does not at this point seem to have appreciated that the Labour government stood to gain from a more static situation, with reduced PIRA violence creating the context to bring detention to an end. That this context was seen by the British to be essential eluded the intermediary; Duddy did not appreciate the limit on the government's freedom to do what it wished.

The release of detainees was halted for most of May due to the killing of the RUC officer in Derry.[76] Duddy was especially concerned for Billy McKee's position and told the British representatives that the Belfast Brigade Commander needed help. 'Controlling Belfast', he wrote in his diary, 'is like working in a pit of poisonous snakes'.[77] James Allan told Duddy on 23 May that releases would begin again 'shortly'.[78] The following day another RUC officer was killed in Maghera. The PIRA denied involvement and the attack was claimed some months later by the INLA. More incidents followed, this time carried out by the PIRA but not admitted. On 1 June a Protestant woman was killed by a PIRA bomb at her home in Fermanagh which was probably intended for the previous occupant, a UDR member. Two days later three Protestant men (one a UDR soldier) were shot dead in County Armagh. Over the previous fortnight the UVF had killed five Catholic civilians.[79] From the government's perspective, this made releasing detainees very difficult but Duddy was unsympathetic, writing in his diary: 'I am not going to kill myself so that 600-day "wonders" can keep their jobs and go back to England saying, "Bloody Irish" they will never learn.'[80] On 2 June, after being told that detainee releases would start that week, he demanded numbers only to be told that if any more killings occurred everything would stop. Duddy recorded his reaction: 'I couldn't care if the British never met us again as we got nothing anyway.'[81]

A meeting between the British and Provisional representatives on 4 June produced little, with Allan and Browning saying that releases were due to take place but were postponed because of the Armagh killings the day before. Browning offered to get releases made immediately if the Provisionals could assure them that their organisation was not involved. The republicans replied that they did not know.[82] Duddy recorded his remark to Allan and Browning that 'the indecision of the last 3 weeks will cost you a kingdom'. His frustrations were borne of knowing the difficulties faced by the doves on the Provisional Army Council. Of the hawks, Seamus Twomey was particularly hostile, reportedly saying 'what have you got for 100 days of talking? Nothing, sweet fuck all.'[83] A written communication was sent from the Provisional Army Council to the British stating that the report of the last two meetings had been rejected because they made no progress.[84] On 11 June Allan and Browning replied that the government was 'sincerely anxious to make progress'. When the two asked for a Provisional statement that would help them release detainees, the republicans replied that this would only be given for a British declaration of intent to withdraw.[85]

Joe McCallion told Duddy that the Provisionals would give the British two weeks to produce a change. The intermediary thought this a mistake and 'all that would happen was a time-buying exercise'.[86] Ó Brádaigh and Duddy agreed that the British had decided to let the ceasefire 'slide away', making it easier to blame the Provisionals. Duddy suggested not meeting the British any more, 'thus causing Cabinet concern at the lack of "pulse-taking"'.[87] Six days later McCallion told Duddy that this suggestion had been accepted by the Provisional Army Council.[88] Relations were further damaged when Rees admitted in the Commons that the ceasefire 'is not complete, it is not genuine and sustained'. The admission was intended to qualify and thus strengthen his argument that PIRA violence was 'very much lower' and the bulk of killings taking place were 'sectarian, intra-sectarian, Chicagoesque', but the Provisionals saw the remarks as insincere and 'tantamount to a repudiation of the truce agreement'. They told the British there would be no further meetings 'at this time'.[89]

When Duddy passed the statement on to a British representative (whose name is blanked out in the diaries) he thought the official to be 'happy like a school-boy because he <u>now</u> had proof positive that he was correct, because he had been accused of being emotional and over-reacting by Sir F Cooper and the NI Office in general.'[90] Judging from previous remarks, this would suggest the words were Browning's. A day later, Duddy was told that Frank Cooper wanted James Allan present during the intermediary's conversations with the MI6 officer. Duddy took this to mean that 'MI5 [sic] was being squeezed out.'[91]

Duddy continued to meet the British, offering his analysis of the situation and reporting the conversations back to the Provisionals. He warned that the Provisionals would likely go back to war because morale was weakening on the ground, there was total disenchantment with the talks, detention remained in place and the Convention showed signs of restoring unionist rule with the SDLP on board. Duddy recommended that to prevent collapse a date should be given for the end of detention, prisoners in England should be steadily transferred and the British should issue 'a continuing flow of helpful statements, helping the Irish people to realise that the Provos had made an honourable effort for peace and deserved a place in the new Ireland'. Duddy complained that the British had a habit of developing the 'establishment': 'Praise for the judge, the RUC, the UDR and seldom a word of anything for the Rep Mov.'[92] It was naïve in the extreme to conceive of any British government issuing statements to bolster the PIRA. Duddy, however, was grappling with the basic problem that peace required the involvement and participation of militant republicans. His hopes were unrealistic because the importance of the Provisional movement to a resolution of the conflict was not matched by political influence. Duddy was contemptuous of the idea that the SDLP served as the voice for most nationalists but Provisional Sinn Féin could hardly make the claim convincingly either. This left little room for any serious negotiation between the Provisionals and either the British government or other parties in Northern Ireland. The context for a political settlement involving them did not exist. When a British representative suggested meetings should resume, Duddy rejected the idea, saying the last three meetings had been in vain.[93]

Security legislation and the return to talks

In an attempt to restart the dialogue, the British representatives made a series of suggestions which partially addressed Duddy's complaints. Donald Middleton was introduced to Duddy on 2 July by Allan and Browning (both of whom he went on to replace with Browning leaving Northern

Ireland and Middleton succeeding Allan as assistant secretary after the latter's promotion). The three men told Duddy of their wish to resume formal meetings 'but on a new level of co-operation' including publicity to show 'the major part' the Provisionals were playing in the situation. Crucially, this was conceived as something that would come after the Convention had ended and stretch to the British facilitating dialogue with loyalists. It was promised that detention without trial would be finished by 22 December and an offer was given to release a small number of detainees to be named by the Provisionals as an indication of British sincerity. Of the four remaining republican prisoners at Winchester, whom the Home Secretary Roy Jenkins had previously opposed transferring, two would be released within a fortnight with the remainder following a month or so later. It was put to Duddy that the package had been designed in Whitehall and approved by Harold Wilson.[94]

At the same time as these conciliatory messages were being passed on, however, the Labour government renewed security legislation and passed a new Act arising from the Gardiner report, both of which angered the Provisional Army Council. A continuance order of the Emergency Provisions Act 1973 was passed on 26 June as the new legislation would not get through parliament in time. Rees told the Commons that he did not want to return to signing detention orders but the power was still needed.[95] The new legislation, based on the Gardiner report recommendations, received its second reading the following day and was passed by the Commons on 14 July.[96] It contained new offences for paramilitary recruitment, training and obscuring one's face in public. It repealed the use of written statements from a witness absent at trial, as well as the change in the onus of proof for possession in summary trials. It also ended the commissioner system, making detention without trial solely the responsibility of the Northern Ireland Secretary.[97]

The consequences of this change were limited; the process was modified for a power which it was hoped would not be needed again. So far as Westminster is concerned, however, most significant was that the Bill's journey through parliament illustrates how uncontroversial Northern Ireland security legislation now was. The fact that it received all readings without a division in the Commons shows that Labour backbench opposition was insignificant. The outcome of the Gardiner review was to reconcile Labour to most of the 1973 measures about which they had doubts while in opposition. The Conservatives supported the changes. Their only dissent was on the decision not to create a new offence of being concerned in terrorism. Labour ministers argued that this was covered by incitement to violence and would need extra proof of political motivation on top of the act itself. Another important recommendation in the Gardiner report which was not implemented was the ending of special category status. Rees hoped to phase it out, but told the Commons he was limited by the prison facilities in Northern Ireland. Progress had been made in building cellular accommodation at the Maze and building was about to begin on a new prison at Maghaberry, but this was not far along enough to make special category possible.[98]

While the government had no difficulty passing security legislation, the combination of the ceasefire and Airey Neave's appointment as Conservative spokesman on Northern Ireland put bipartisanship under greater strain. Margaret Thatcher replaced Ian Gilmour with Neave as a reward for his managing her campaign to become Conservative leader in February. As elsewhere, this change heralded a far less consensual approach. Gilmour was a liberal Tory, critical of the ideological approach to politics.[99] Neave, however, adopted an aggressive tone. In May Neave attacked the Labour government's policy of releasing detainees.[100] The next month he demanded a statement that the army would remain in Northern Ireland until normal policing by the RUC was possible.[101] On 9 July the PIRA bombed office buildings in Derry and admitted responsibility. The next day Neave said that the PIRA was resuming violence and Rees should 'think again about continuing his policy of release of terrorists from detention'.[102] When Rees announced his intention to release all detainees by Christmas, Neave asked whether the risk was justified in sending 'experienced terrorists on to the streets'.[103]

The PIRA, meanwhile, said they were promised in February that the Emergency Provisions Act would not be renewed. They demanded visible signs of progress including the full implementation of the truce agreement (meaning by this no more arrests of republicans), withdrawal of troops in Belfast to the peace-lines, complete withdrawal from designated areas of Derry, no more identity checks, an end to helicopter surveillance and the evacuation and dismantling of two army forts in the Andersonstown and Turf Lodge areas of Belfast. It was argued again that there was no prospect of peace without a public declaration of withdrawal, Irish self-determination and a general amnesty.[104] To add to their problems, Dáithí Ó Conaill was arrested in the Republic on 9 July and sentenced to a year in prison for IRA membership.[105]

Duddy discussed with the British representatives how best to reply. When Middleton handed him the approved version on 16 July he refused to pass it on, describing it as the 'usual British humbug'. Middleton said that Cooper and Rees had insisted on changes but he eventually agreed to retype the answer.[106] The version delivered to the PIRA acknowledged that the drift away from the ceasefire had to be corrected. Regret was expressed at the death of a Catholic civilian shot by the British army in West Belfast after the car he was in backfired. On security legislation, it was put that the government 'have said publicly we do not wish to use these laws and hope there will soon be no need for them'. Each of the Provisional demands was addressed in a conciliatory manner but without promising change. While not referring to the most important demand of a declaration of intent to withdraw, the reply pushed against the idea by stating: 'There is no quick solution to the problems of Northern Ireland, and we are concerned, as we believe are the representatives of the Provisional Sinn Féin, to avoid the emergence of a Congo-type situation.'[107]

The following day Ó Brádaigh informed Duddy that the Provisional Army Council had agreed to resume meetings, though the former was worried that these might be rejected after the killing that morning of four British soldiers in South Armagh by a PIRA bomb.[108] Duddy reassured him but was then angered when Middleton said that 22 July might be too soon after the deaths.[109] Dealing with the incident in the House of Commons, Rees noted that the Crossmaglen PIRA had claimed the killings and that two of the big questions for him were 'whether the leaders of the PIRA are able to control their followers, for example, in South Armagh; whether such actions do not make the ceasefire meaningless'.[110] That he posed the questions but did not answer them was not a particularly effective response, reinforcing the public perception that he did not really have a clear mind as to what to do.

The meeting with the Provisionals did take place, with McKee telling Duddy that if it had not then bombings would have occurred in Belfast. Middleton took Browning's place in the talks. Duddy's account was very positive: 'It has saved the peace, DM agreed to almost everything. Talked about a private declaration of intent, reduction of British army to 300 in Belfast on the ground, 300 in rest of NI. Exciting stuff.'[111] The record in Ó Brádaigh's papers was less effusive, however, merely stating that a declaration had been discussed and the 'importance of retaining confidentiality was stressed'.[112] Duddy increasingly saw his role as being defined by personal conflict with the Northern Ireland Office and Frank Cooper in particular. When Middleton did not ring him for two days he began to 'wonder if the long distance duel between myself and Sir F Cooper is about to go another 15 rounds'. He was unsure whether Middleton simply had a different style from Allan or if Cooper had 'decided that I have been permitted to get too close to the British machine and in the process have got too clever'. He thought the NIO knew it had been his plan rather than the Provisionals' to break off talks and that Cooper would have been infuriated by it.[113] Middleton tried to reassure Duddy that he was simply overworked but the intermediary was not persuaded.[114] In a particularly emotional diary entry he wrote:

> What will I do, I still don't know, but to the students of history I say this: If Ireland is to gain, I must win this and many more similar tactical battles with the British Soviet of the NI office. I am sure by now that Sir F Cooper has a personal desire to prove me less tactician than he is. He may be correct! If he wins, Ireland loses and the Rep Mov is crushed. I will either be dead or written off as an emotional crank! What if I packed it up before Sir FC has a chance to put his little personal plan to work? Well student, what would you do. Let it happen and see the truce go out the window? Do nothing. Threaten to resign and <u>do it</u>. Or try and win? If I get the help of the PAC, I can win. I must.[115]

On 31 July the British representatives once more gave reasons why a declaration of intent could not be made: the Convention had to be given a chance, a Congo-type situation might occur and the government was 'waiting for a convergence of opinion in Britain'. When the Provisionals asked why continue to fight when withdrawal was on, they received the response that 'there is no British De Gaulle on the horizon'.[116]

The comparison with the French premier's rather swift conversion and declaration of support for Algerian independence conveyed the usual point that the British representatives had to suffer Labour ministers who lacked the conviction to make a drastic change.[117] A clearer strategy was nevertheless presented by Rees to other ministers. He acknowledged the real difficulties that the Provisionals faced in maintaining their ceasefire but was unsympathetic. In early July Rees said the Provisional Army Council's problems included 'how to maintain the cohesion of their movement with few if any gains from the ceasefire to show to their violent followers'. He added that the PIRA faced fundamental questions of how the ceasefire would lead to a new, united Ireland, what part they would play if the British left, what their future would be in the South and whether the Protestant community was in fact the real enemy. Rees argued there were 'signs that they despair of answering such questions and are prepared to return to a campaign of violence because they cannot cope with the real world in any other terms'. He described his strategy as being to 'increase their dilemma by taking every opportunity to drive deeper the wedge between the Provisionals' yearning for violence and the now manifest desire of the Catholic (and indeed the whole) community for peace'.[118]

Reflecting on the course of the ceasefire at the end of the month, Rees wrote that the 'strategy from the start of the ceasefire has been to play it long, on the basis that the longer it lasts the less support there will be for the PIRA in the Catholic community'. It would be hard for the Provisionals to return to the violence of 1972 to 1974 and the organisation would 'suffer from internal disruptive pressure and a developing sogginess'. This, in Rees's view, had 'provided the best possible background for the Convention and forced Northern Ireland politicians to think more for themselves'. Rees exaggerated the impact on the Convention though he rightly admitted that violence had a 'deep hold' and policing had made little progress in nationalist areas. He proposed to keep up releases and focus on depriving the Provisionals of any 'plausible excuse' to return to violence.[119]

The drift back to violence

There were two meetings with the Provisionals in August, a month which saw the deaths of over thirty people. July ended with the Miami Showband killings, in which UVF volunteers (some of whom were also members of the UDR) staged a road block and attempted to surreptitiously load a bomb into the back of the musicians' van. When it prematurely exploded killing two UVF volunteers the band were fired upon to eliminate witnesses, murdering three of them.[120] On 2 August the PIRA shot dead a UDR man in Tyrone. The weekend of 8–10 August proved particularly violent, falling on the fourth anniversary of internment. A 17-year-old PIRA volunteer was accidentally shot dead by another of the same age, a 15-year-old OIRA volunteer was killed, most likely by the Provisionals, and a 4-year-old girl was shot dead during a gun battle between republicans and British soldiers. All three occurred in West Belfast.[121] Co-ordinated attacks were made on security force bases in Belfast, Armagh, Lurgan and Newry. The British army described them as 'largely co-ordinated and pre-planned by the PIRA', but said that in Belfast the areas affected were those where the PIRA 'are believed to be restless under the ceasefire'. As other parts of the city were restrained it was not seen as part of 'an overall intention to break the ceasefire'.[122]

The Labour government was also accused of promising PIRA leaders immunity from arrest in early August. Bill Craig claimed that Seamus Twomey had been sighted in West Belfast on 28 July but the security forces did not arrest him. Craig claimed that Twomey had been removed from the list of wanted men and his photograph and dossier taken from RUC stations.[123] Rees's response matched the army's incident report: an army foot patrol spotted a man that looked like Twomey entering a shop. Reinforcements were sent but by the time an armoured vehicle arrived, the man escaped in a taxi. An attempt to catch it with road blocks failed.[124] Naturally those suspicious of the government's intentions were more inclined to believe the press. Brendan Duddy's information was that Twomey was not in Belfast on the day.[125]

The violence formed the starting point in the dialogue with the Provisionals. They objected that an anti-internment demonstration in Derry had been attacked by the army and RUC. No bail was given for fourteen people charged in Belfast. Blast bombs in Lower Falls and Clonard were blamed on the Official IRA. James Allan and Donald Middleton responded that government policy would not be affected by what happened. The Provisionals again pressed for a declaration of intent, deeming the cause of the weekend's violence to be British rule. Middleton is recorded as replying that 'no-one' he was 'in touch with sees the British presence in Ireland continuing.'[126] Duddy felt that Allan and Middleton 'had come with nothing' to deal with the Provisionals' demands.[127] Later that day the Provisionals launched a bomb and gun attack on the Bayardo Bar on the Shankill Road, killing five civilians. The sectarian character of the attack was reinforced by the firing upon women and children standing at a taxi rank along the escape route. Four more Protestant civilians were killed by the PIRA two days later.[128] The PIRA seemed to be deliberately targeting civilians on a sectarian basis in response to loyalist paramilitaries doing the same.

Prior to a 25 August meeting Duddy had a number of conversations with Middleton. The intermediary put forward his own proposals including giving a private declaration of intent 'immediately', with a public one to follow within a year, Rees to set up a civilian police force after 'secret agreement with Provos' and the early release of PIRA volunteers in the Republic. In return the Provisionals would destroy or hand in their explosives and withdraw other weapons from Northern Ireland.[129] Although they were unrealistic, Duddy reported in his diaries that Middleton showed him a secret document a few days later containing fifteen points on future British policy, 'all centred around withdrawal'.[130] When the two sides met, Middleton read extracts from the document, reportedly titled 'Strong Trends'. It was agreed that Duddy would make notes on its contents and transmit them to the Provisionals (though in the end this did not occur).[131] The intermediary felt all on the Provisional side were impressed, with McCallion reportedly saying it 'ties up in "red ribbon" all we want'.[132] The Provisional Army Council met the following day and was pleased. Duddy opted for another personal intervention and 'decided not to tell the British until next Tues or Wed as I think the PAC is a little too eager'.[133]

The proceedings were again thrown into chaos after a pub bombing in Caterham, Surrey (400 yards from a Welsh Guards barracks) on 27 August.[134] Another bomb followed in London the next day. Middleton rang Duddy to ask for a PIRA statement denying responsibility. Duddy thought the act 'totally out of character' and said that he was 'certain that the PAC were as baffled as I was'.[135] Duddy produced a statement with the aid of

Father Denis Bradley and attempted to get Billy McKee to release it but the Belfast Brigade Commander responded that 'Twomey was the boss and he couldn't put anything out'.[136] On 1 September Duddy promised Middleton that a statement would come. When Middleton said that Rees was holding despite the pressure, Duddy impatiently replied that the Northern Ireland Secretary 'must not only hold but move!' He insisted that if the SDLP and UUUC reached an agreement in the Convention there would be 'instant war'. Duddy recorded his advice in his diary: 'settle the national question with the PIRA and the rest will fall into line'.[137] That evening five Protestant civilians were killed at Tullyvalen Orange Hall. The South Armagh Republican Action Force, a cover name used by the South Armagh PIRA brigade, claimed the attack.[138] The *Irish Times* reported that the killings did not have the consent of the leadership but were carried out by dissident members of the organisation.[139] Duddy told Middleton that he thought the Provisionals were responsible, as McCallion had said that retaliation was on the agenda for the recent Provisional Army Council meeting.[140]

The Convention and the ceasefire

Rees objected that the media and local politicians were building up the security situation as a crisis when it was not. He told Harold Wilson there was no indication the PIRA wanted to terminate their ceasefire immediately and although the Provisional Army Council's control had become less effective they were seeking to re-establish their authority. The UUUC and SDLP, meanwhile, were falling back 'on the well-established practice of "bashing the Brits"' to obscure their failure to reach an agreement in the Convention.[141] On 29 August Ian Paisley produced a leaked army document claiming that Seamus Twomey was 'no longer a wanted man'. Paisley said this proved Rees had done a deal with the Provisionals and that he had lied in the Commons when denying immunity had been granted.[142] Rees responded to the allegations with a series of radio broadcasts. Speaking on Irish radio, he dismissed withdrawal as a possibility: 'Any ideas that there are of us pulling out and leaving a Congo-type situation, of us abdicating our responsibilities, are not true. They cannot be. There is no other form of government here other than the very proper one with the United Kingdom.'[143] Withdrawal was denied in increasingly forceful terms, which inevitably angered the Provisionals.

Paisley continued to demand that Rees be sacked and on 11 September the Convention passed a motion deploring the failure of the British government 'in dealing with the intolerable security situation'.[144] The next day Downing Street issued a denial that Rees was about to be moved to another post. He followed this by defiantly announcing the release of three more suspected PIRA members from detention.[145] According to Bernard Donoughue, Wilson had considered moving Rees to Education while planning a reshuffle earlier in June but Rees refused when the idea was put to him by James Callaghan.[146]

Rees certainly seems to have been keen to stay in the job. In late August he wrote to Wilson, arguing that when he left Northern Ireland it would 'inevitably be seen as heralding a change in policy'. After defending his approach of ending detention and establishing the Convention he concluded: 'Given the situation and with no political will to stay in the political graveyard of NI – I simply wish to indicate that I would be content to stay in NI until next year.' Rees also stated: 'The Airey Neave business is an added complication – he apparently believes that you are only waiting the moment to declare a pull out of Northern Ireland!' Noting that Orme desired a move, and had earned it, he suggested Parliamentary Under-Secretary Jack Donaldson as a replacement, followed by another peer 'unencumbered by three line whips'.[147]

The references to Neave and three-line whips are indicative of the souring of bipartisan relations at Westminster.[148] With the erosion of Labour's majority in the Commons, Margaret Thatcher also decided there would be no compromise on pairing arrangements at Westminster for Northern Ireland ministers, forcing them to return to London for key votes. This infuriated Rees and on one occasion Minister of State Don Concannon, flown in by helicopter, threw his bag on to the table between the Commons benches upon entering and swore at Conservative MPs. Rees remarked in his memoirs that the changes meant that 'bipartisanship was a thing of the past'.[149] This was an overstatement. The tone of debate became markedly more hostile but the basic principles underlying policy were still shared, even if Neave displayed a basic distrust that they were being adhered to. Labour's approach was not under threat but rather the daily task of NIO ministers was made more difficult. Rees received some small succour from Neave's more liberal Conservative colleagues. His diaries state that the former Solicitor General, Sir Michael Havers, branded Neave 'a disaster', while Ted Heath's former Parliamentary Private Secretary, Sir Timothy Kitson, went much further, calling the former Colditz escapee an 'effing fascist'.[150] Similarly, later in March 1976 when Rees complained to Whitelaw 'if only we could stop AN beefing on', the former Northern Ireland Secretary 'explained to me he is rather stupid and there is not much you can do about it'.[151]

The British met the Provisionals on 5 September despite the Tullyvalen killings, though there were further doubts about whether this would go ahead after the Hilton hotel was bombed in London earlier in the day, killing two civilians.[152] James Allan stressed British sincerity but admitted that 'the delivery or outcome of meetings is not enough for the people on the ground'. The Provisionals asked if they would be sold out should the SDLP and UUUC agree on devolution. The British replied that 'any solution must stick', prompting the republicans to say that British rule in any shape or form had to end.[153] Ó Brádaigh's notes state that Middleton's secret document, quotes of which had been received so enthusiastically in the last meeting, was still being considered and had to be cleared before it could be passed to the republicans.[154] In the end, this did not take place.

During the private inter-party meetings of the Convention Bill Craig surprised many by proposing a temporary voluntary coalition with the SDLP.[155] The clerk to the Convention chairman observed, 'this was a tactical move rather than a change in strategic objective. Craig still wanted [majority rule], but was prepared to accept a voluntary coalition with the SDLP for a few years in order to get it.'[156] It is unlikely that this would have been sustainable for long. If the SDLP and UUUC agreed on it, however, the British government would have found it difficult to reject any scenario advocated by both nationalists and unionists. The UUUC negotiating document left room for a temporary agreement for parties to join together in 'the national interest for the duration of the crisis'. Vanguard split, however, with Ernest Baird rejecting Craig and later forming the United Ulster Unionist Movement (UUUM). The DUP were hostile. The Ulster Unionist Party was divided, with Harry West cautiously supporting a continuation of negotiations but Enoch Powell and James Molyneaux providing strong opposition to Craig's proposal. Powell and Molyneaux argued that the Labour government might enlarge on a deal with the SDLP, co-operation between unionists would unravel and the UUP would be most vulnerable in the election that would have to follow. On 8 September the UUUC rejected Craig's initiative by 37 to 1.[157]

Duddy was delighted when he found out, believing that failure in the Convention would lead to British withdrawal. The day after the UUUC vote John Hume told Duddy that the SDLP were finished with it. Duddy's diary states, 'No power-sharing. No deals with Catholics. Now the road is clear for the solution of the Irish problem. British OUT, Irish IN!' After informing Ó Brádaigh of the conversation with Hume, the former agreed to meet Glen Barr of the UDA to tell him the Provisionals did not want war with loyalists, which Duddy regarded as 'a most important step forward towards a real peace in Ireland'.[158] He believed there would either be an agreement or repartition with an independent Protestant state.[159] On 12 September Duddy told Middleton: 'For 700 years the British have, time and time again failed to grasp the opportunity to readjust the relationship between our two countries. This time, the British must not do anything which would result in another phase of strife and turmoil.' He argued that the essence of the problem was Irish nationalism versus British colonialism. Again he insisted there should be a private declaration of withdrawal, which would be followed by direct rule while the Provisionals negotiated independence in a private deal with West, Paisley and Craig.[160]

The likelihood of this was slim in the extreme. Even if the UUUC were somehow able to negotiate successfully with the Provisionals (despite failing to do so with the SDLP), the belief that the Protestant community would accept the outcome because the British government had declared its desire to leave denied autonomy to a body of opinion which had successfully overthrown power-sharing the previous year. It is in this context that one should doubt the sincerity of Middleton's response. According to Duddy's diaries, he agreed but said Rees was too weak to produce movement in any direction and Wilson would only step in 'to accept the applause'. Duddy recorded: 'The British Cabinet system does not make de Gaulle-type decisions and is simply incapable of solving the Irish problem.'[161] He similarly blamed John Hume and the SDLP, believing that at the Convention they should have offered '6 seats, as a gesture of peace, to the Provos, thus bringing them into the democratic field' (another unworkable scenario).[162]

When the British representatives met the Provisionals on 16 September the republicans yet again said they needed a declaration of intent and that not giving it was 'prolonging the agony'. The British said that if the Convention produced a report which did not have wide acceptance or provide safeguards for the minority, the government would have to 'devise some method of governing the Province in the short term' as any dramatic move would result in violence. Added to this, the bombings in England, for which the Provisionals denied responsibility, were given as justification for not transferring any more republican prisoners to Northern Ireland.[163] McKee was furious with the meeting, believing the Provisionals were 'being conned'.[164]

The breakdown of the ceasefire

After the meeting Duddy offered his analysis to the PIRA: the British had no policy other than buying time and peace in the British mainland, Rees lacked the personality to effect change, Wilson wanted withdrawal but according to British timing and the will was not present in England to solve the Irish problem. A transcript of Duddy's diaries states that he suggested 'that the war be resumed on a limited basis', bombing three centres in England and three in Northern Ireland; the targets should be economic and no lives should be lost, while Mac Airt and Drumm 'should be "too busy" to see the British'. There should be no declaration of an end to the truce. According to the same transcript, he wrote: 'This is the first time I have ever given in to violence. I hope to God no one gets injured.' On 19 September McCallion saw Duddy after a Provisional Army Council meeting. Duddy recorded in his diaries: 'Bombing will start on Mon 22nd Sept. It will be as I suggested.'[165] When Duddy and Middleton met in Belfast the intermediary criticised the British, saying they had no policy and had squandered the opportunity for change. Middleton reportedly said: '"You are so right". Nothing but nothing matters except "Westminster". Rees is "Wet" and we are "powerless".'[166]

Rees, meanwhile, made public remarks that further suggested the Provisional Army Council was being strung along. During a speech in Cardiff on 20 September he stated that the ceasefire was the PIRA's, not the government's, and so demands for him to call it off were 'unreal'. He dismissed 'those who glibly talk about independence', arguing that it would result in a bankrupt society as well as a divided one. His final remarks offered little hope for the Provisionals engaged in the talks: 'I give this assurance again the government will not abdicate its responsibilities. But it is only in Northern Ireland that the ultimate decisions can be taken. We have given the politicians there a chance to look to the future.'[167]

On 21 and 22 September the PIRA carried out twenty bomb attacks across Northern Ireland. The PIRA's Belfast Brigade admitted attacks in the city, claiming they were in retaliation for 'the killing of a young man and a 10 year old child, the numerous attempted murders on innocent civilians, the organised torture of innocent people and a step-up of house searches and intensive screening operations' (the killings referred to were Leo Norney, an innocent civilian shot by an army patrol which claimed to have come under fire, and Stephen Geddis, a 10-year-old schoolboy fatally injured by a rubber bullet fired by soldiers trying to disperse a crowd of children throwing stones).[168] On the second day a hotel in London was bombed and a further pub bombing occurred on 25 September.[169] The Provisionals issued further statements that the bombings should not be taken as the end of a truce but as a response to the British government's failure to observe it.[170] Rees put out a statement that 'opportunities are still there to be grasped but the events of the last few days are a mockery and a travesty of any ceasefire.'[171] The next day a message was sent to the Provisionals which stated: 'The PIRA planned and deliberate display of violence, coupled with a public slanging match is leading inevitably to renewed conflict. The Secretary of State's policy as set out in the House of Commons and to which he is committed publicly has not changed.'[172]

On 30 September Duddy again gave his analysis to the Provisionals, arguing that British policy was 'in ruins'. He claimed they had hoped the

Convention would buy them time so they could 'complete their policy of "silent withdrawal"', but the failure of the inter-party talks left them with nothing other than a 'strong desire to get out'. He further argued that Labour's position was delicate: 'Nothing that happens in Northern Ireland…can equal the desire of the Labour party to stay in power in England [sic].' The memo dramatically concluded: 'To deliberately break the Truce when we have won a magnificent victory by the total break-down of the Convention and when the Loyalists are demanding the closing of the incident centres and an end to talks with the Republican Movement would be very unwise.' On the other hand following Westminster's pace was too slow and so he recommended that they cease both strands of meetings with the British without giving any reason.[173] In reality, the September bombings marked the beginning of the end of the ceasefire.

On 2 October the Provisionals wrote to the British defending the bombings and claiming the 'slanging match' had been started by Rees's speech in Cardiff. They saw his public statements as 'blatant denials of the factual position' and his insistence that there was 'merely a unilateral ceasefire' had 'not helped matters, to say the least'. Their conditions for resuming meetings were full implementation of their original twelve-point document and that the purpose of the dialogue 'be the devising of structures of British disengagement from Ireland'.[174] A series of bombings followed in West London during October and November. On 9 October a civilian was killed and twenty-one others injured by a bomb near Green Park tube station. Another civilian died in a car bomb on 23 October, eighteen were injured in another explosion on 29 October and on 12 November the bombing of a restaurant saw one death and fifteen injuries. Six days later another restaurant bombing killed two and injured twenty.[175]

The PIRA's return to armed struggle contributed to disagreements over security policy between Rees and senior army figures. Frank King was replaced in August with a new GOC, David House, and relations began cordially, with Rees informing Harold Wilson that the general 'assured me personally that he agrees with our policies'.[176] When Rees was attacked by the UUUC on security policy in September, House lamented the 'local political machinations to manufacture a political crisis out of the security situation'. This, he felt, encouraged people to believe that military action could 'compensate for a continuing lack of local political agreement'. The new GOC acknowledged that they could not 'make significant security progress in conditions of continuing local political infirmity'.[177] He did not, however, agree with Rees on what the British army's response should be if the ceasefire ended. Early in October House said that once the government's incident centres were closed he wanted to carry out a number of operations, such as raiding Provisional Sinn Féin's offices and arresting a large number of suspected PIRA members.[178]

Douglas Janes, Deputy Secretary at NIO London, said the army thought the centres would 'be full of incriminating documents, arms and explosives', but sensibly argued that the locations were 'too obvious and vulnerable'.[179] Meeting Rees on 14 October, the GOC went further. House agreed that the government centres should not be closed until the Provisionals carried out another day of violence comparable to the September bombings but suggested using detention without trial. He claimed it had worked before, leaving the PIRA 'on their knees just before they had offered the ceasefire'. With the MOD unwilling to send more than thirteen battalions to Northern Ireland, he argued it was the only hope of containing the threat. House also suggested the Labour government 'should pay more heed to the views of the majority'. Chief Constable James Flanagan warned of the risk of adverse publicity, proposing that this could be lessened if it was brought in after the PIRA claimed a 'particularly horrendous incident'. Rees was completely opposed, insisting that a full-scale war against the PIRA would not end violence.[180]

Meanwhile, Middleton pressed Duddy to arrange a meeting but the intermediary said the Provisional Army Council needed movement first.[181] Duddy's discussions with Joe McCallion and Father Bradley showed how desperate he was to secure a settlement. Duddy pressed for the idea that 'British out is our main aim, everything else is secondary'. Convinced that McKee and Ó Brádaigh could support a deal with Paisley, he phoned Middleton to say that the Provisional Army Council 'will come to an agreement with the UUUC...if you get out!'. He wrote in his diaries: 'No power sharing – majority rule, British out!'[182] On 21 October he went to Belfast and thought Middleton and MI5 officer John Walker were 'visibly excited' at his suggestion that the Provisionals would accept a loyalist-run six county state.[183] Duddy reported in his diary that the next day Ó Brádaigh agreed to the idea and so Middleton was told that the Provisional Army Council 'agreed completely with my stated position last night'.[184] Ó Brádaigh's support illustrates considerable flexibility but the idea was again an unlikely one, requiring not just the Provisional Army Council but ordinary PIRA volunteers to accept a loyalist dominated independent state. The outcome for the Catholic community was unlikely to be a positive one. If British money were stopped the state would fail and if it were to continue then British influence could hardly be said to have ended satisfactorily for republicans. The moral responsibility that follows financial support would have meant repeated intervention from London and a resumption of conflict.

When Duddy spoke to Proinsias Mac Airt he found him sceptical, talking 'continually of being "conned" by the British'. Duddy believed he was 'mentally justifying his position' because the Belfast Brigade had already decided to renew the conflict.[185] On 27 October Duddy met Middleton and Walker again, having been told by McCallion that he 'must get something from the British'. In his diaries he wrote of the frustration of going over the same points again, insisting that the Provisional Army Council wanted the conflict to end and was willing to work with loyalists in a six county state. The Provisionals were described as having only one aim: eventual British withdrawal. When he demanded an answer, Duddy was dismayed at Middleton's response, recorded in his diaries: 'I have been instructed to tell you... from the very top – dramatic pause – that the most careful consideration has been given to your "proposal" and that we are most interested.' Duddy and McCallion decided they had to devise 'a method of putting this as soft as possible to the PAC', that 'the position was simply one of discussion of "possibilities"'.[186]

At the PAC meeting on 28 October a motion to resume conflict was averted and Ó Brádaigh's instructions were that there should be no meeting unless the British would discuss the truce agreement and how to devise structures of withdrawal.[187] McKee is reported as wanting 'our own house put in order first'.[188] Between 29 October and 12 November a feud saw the deaths of six Official IRA volunteers and one Provisional. The Officials killed two civilians in connection with the feud, while the Provisionals killed a 6-year-old girl while attacking her father. They disappeared another civilian, Columba McVeigh, from County Tyrone.[189] By 8 November the British had still not offered a reply, prompting Duddy to tell Middleton that 'the only rational conclusion I could come to was that the British wanted to push the [Provisionals] over the brink or at the very least that the British were indifferent to the lives and values which would be lost as only a few would really know how the Provos had held out for peace and how the British had squandered every opportunity time and time again'. Middleton said a reply was ready but had to be finalised by London.[190] According to a transcript of his diary, Duddy wrote: 'I have firmly decided to put war as the only course open to the PAC.' He bitterly asked Middleton to 'tell Sir F Cooper that this decision will cause the break up of his United Kingdom and please remind him that I told him that some 7 months ago when the co-operation and progress between the [republican movement] and the British Government was turned into his personal chess game'.[191]

On 10 November the PIRA's Derry Brigade blew up the building containing the government's incident centre and two days later the NIO closed the rest.[192] Duddy was furious that 'silly bastard Rees' made the decision 'without asking about the possible consequences in the IRA'. He was handed a reply to the Provisionals on the day of the closure but believed it 'had been deliberately worded to cause confusion'. When Duddy asked whether the Labour government was 'prepared to back up its desires with positive moves', Middleton replied that he could not answer that. Duddy blamed the British for having 'neither the will, nor the desire to settle the Irish question', further shocking Middleton and Walker when adding: 'Some day the last British soldier will be driven out of Ireland and History will judge the Provisionals' sacrifice.'[193] The representatives continued to press for contact but Duddy recorded privately that he would 'only move if the British show a willingness to treat the Irish as equals'.[194] On 18 November the Provisional Army Council agreed on a return to conflict but without a public declaration of the ceasefire's end.[195]

Conclusion

The nature of the dialogue between the PIRA and the British government during the ceasefire supports the argument that 1975 was hardly a missed opportunity for peace, despite Ó Dochartiagh's claims.[196] It was incredibly difficult to sustain and the talks between the two sides regularly stumbled and came close to collapse. While British representatives may have spoken about a desire to disengage from Northern Ireland, this was not the strategy of Rees and the NIO and the raising of republican hopes is more likely to have been a ploy to prevent a resumption of the PIRA's campaign. Modest expectations of the ceasefire remained. Rees's emphasis that the British could not impose a solution remained the core aspect of the Labour government's constitutional policy. Both the Convention and the ceasefire trundled along with little prospect of agreement between unionists and nationalists, and with militant republicans still fixated on the idea that a declaration of British withdrawal would end conflict. More substantial change was made to security policy and this brought Rees and Cooper into conflict with senior army officers as it became apparent that limitations on the army's means of operating in Northern Ireland were to be more lasting than the cessation that brought them about. These arguments would continue as the new approach of criminalisation was refined and developed over the following year.

Notes

1 McKittrick *et al.*, *Lost lives*, p. 1552.
2 Bew *et al.*, *Talking to terrorists*, p. 57.
3 Ó Dochartaigh, '"Everyone trying"', p. 57.
4 NUIG, RÓB, POL28/67, Formal meeting, 5 March 1975.
5 NUIG, RÓB, POL28/67, Formal meeting, 11 March 1975.
6 NUIG, RÓB, POL28/67, Per Sinn Féin, 10 March 1975.

7 NUIG, RÓB, POL28/67, Formal meeting, 13 March 1975.
8 NUIG, RÓB, POL28/67, Formal meeting, 16 March 1975.
9 *The Times*, 19 March 1975.
10 NUIG, RÓB, POL28/67, Public statement, 19 March 1975.
11 NUIG, Duddy, POL35/62, Diary entry, 19 March 1975.
12 NUIG, Duddy, POL35/62, Diary entry, 21 March 1975.
13 NUIG, RÓB, POL28/67, Instructions, 22 March 1975.
14 NUIG, RÓB, POL28/67, Formal meeting, 25 March 1975.
15 NUIG, Duddy, POL35/62, Diary entry, 25 March 1975.
16 NUIG, Duddy, POL35/62, Diary entry, 27 March 1975.
17 NUIG, Duddy, POL35/62, Diary entry, 27 March 1975.
18 NUIG, RÓB, POL28/67, Message to Wilson, 29 March 1975.
19 NUIG, Duddy, POL35/62, Diary entry, 29 March 1975.
20 NUIG, Duddy, POL35/62, Diary entry, 30 March 1975.
21 LSE, MERLYN-REES/1/7, Transcript of tapes, 30 March 1975, pp. 7–8.
22 NUIG, Duddy, POL35/62, Diary entry, 2 April 1975.
23 *The Times*, 3 April 1975.
24 NUIG, RÓB, POL28/67, Formal meeting, 2 April 1975.
25 *The Times*, 31 March 1975.
26 NUIG, RÓB, POL28/67, Formal meeting, 2 April 1975.
27 NUIG, Duddy, POL35/62, Diary entry, 2 April 1975.
28 NUIG, Duddy, POL35/62, Diary entry, 4 April 1975.
29 McKittrick *et al.*, *Lost lives*, p. 1553.
30 Steve Bruce, *The red hand: Protestant paramilitaries in Northern Ireland* (Oxford: Oxford University Press, 1992), pp. 172–89.
31 McKittrick *et al.*, *Lost lives*, pp. 529–31.
32 *The Times*, 8 April 1975.
33 NUIG, Duddy, POL35/62, Diary entry, 7 April 1975.
34 *The Times*, 9 April 1975; McKittrick *et al.*, *Lost lives*, pp. 533–9.
35 NUIG, RÓB, POL28/67, Formal meeting, 9 April 1975.
36 NUIG, RÓB, POL28/67, Formal meeting, 17 April 1975.
37 LSE, MERLYN-REES/1/7, Transcripts of tapes, undated, p. 22.
38 PRONI, CONV/7/16, Meeting in NIO London, 5 March 1975; TNA, CAB 134/3921, IRN(75) memo 14, 15 May 1975.
39 TNA, CAB 134/3921, IRN(75) memo 17, 3 July 1975.
40 NUIG, RÓB, POL28/67, Instructions, 6 May 1975.
41 NUIG, Duddy, POL35/62, Diary entry, 5 May 1975.
42 NUIG, RÓB, POL28/67, Formal meeting, 7 May 1975.
43 A.R. Oppenheimer, *IRA: the bombs and the bullets* (Dublin: Irish Academic Press, 2010), pp. 267–73.
44 NUIG, Duddy, POL35/62, Diary entry, 9 May 1975.
45 McKittrick *et al.*, *Lost lives*, p. 540
46 NUIG, Duddy, POL35/62, Diary entry, 13 May 1975.
47 NUIG, Duddy, POL35/62, Diary entry, 14 May 1975.
48 NUIG, RÓB, POL28/67, Formal meeting, 14 May 1975.

49 NUIG, Duddy, POL35/62, Diary entry, 16 May 1975.

50 NUIG, Duddy, POL35/62, Diary entry, 15 May 1975.

51 NUIG, Duddy, POL35/62, Diary entry, 19 May 1975.

52 NUIG, Duddy, POL35/62, Diary entry, 20 May 1975.

53 NUIG, Duddy, POL35/62, Diary entry, 22 May 1975.

54 NUIG, RÓB, POL28/67, Report and assessment, 24 May 1975.

55 LSE, MERLYN-REES/1/8, Transcript of tapes, undated, p. 14.

56 TNA, CAB 134/3921, IRN(75) memo 15, 16 May 1975.

57 TNA, CAB 134/3921, IRN(75) meeting 5, 19 May 1975.

58 TNA, CAB 134/3921, IRN(75) memo 15, 16 May 1975.

59 TNA, CJ4/1293, Cooper to Rees, 9 May 1975.

60 TNA, CJ4/1293, Cooper to GOC, 7 May 1975.

61 TNA, CJ4/966, Young to brigade commanders, 27 May 1975.

62 TNA, CJ4/966, Webster to Bourn, 6 June 1975.

63 TNA, CJ4/966, Interim report, 14 June 1975.

64 TNA, CJ4/966, Visit to RUC stations, 12 August 1975.

65 TNA, CJ4/860, Abbott to Burns, 31 January 1975.

66 TNA, CJ4/861, Allan to Walker, 18 April 1975.

67 TNA, CJ4/861, Allan to PUS, 18 April 1975.

68 TNA, CJ4/861, Walker to Allan, 12 May 1975.

69 TNA, CJ4/861, Verbatim transcript of BBC TV news, 25 May 1975.

70 TNA, CJ4/861, Rees to Prime Minister, 4 June 1975.

71 *Daily Telegraph*, 6 June 1975.

72 NUIG, RÓB, POL28/67, Instructions, 26 May 1975.

73 NUIG, RÓB, POL28/67, Formal meeting, 28 May 1975.

74 NUIG, RÓB, POL28/67, S to M, 31 May 1975.

75 TNA, CAB 134/3921, IRN memo 15, 16 May 1975.

76 *The Times*, 2 June 1975.

77 NUIG, Duddy, POL35/62, Diary entry, 31 May & 1 June 1975.

78 NUIG, Duddy, POL35/62, Diary entry, 1 June 1975.

79 McKittrick *et al.*, *Lost lives*, pp. 542–5.

80 NUIG, Duddy, POL35/62, Diary entry, 1 June 1975.

81 NUIG, Duddy, POL35/62, Diary entry, 2 June 1975.

82 NUIG, RÓB, POL28/67, Formal meeting, 4 June 1975.

83 NUIG, Duddy, POL35/62, Diary entry, 4 June 1975.

84 NUIG, RÓB, POL28/67, Instructions, 5 June 1975 .

85 NUIG, RÓB, POL28/67, Formal meeting, 11 June 1975.

86 NUIG, Duddy, POL35/62, Diary entry, 11 June 1975.

87 NUIG, Duddy, POL35/62, Diary entry, 12 June 1975.

88 NUIG, Duddy, POL35/62, Diary entry, 18 June 1975.

89 Hansard (Commons), 893, cols 956–7; NUIG, RÓB, POL28/67, Note, 19 June 1975.

90 NUIG, Duddy, POL35/62, Diary entry, 19 June 1975.

91 NUIG, Duddy, POL35/62, Diary entry, 20 June 1975.

92 NUIG, Duddy, POL35/62, Diary entry, 22 June 1975.

93 NUIG, Duddy, POL35/62, Diary entry, 24 June 1975; NUIG, RÓB, POL28/67, Report, 1 July 1975.
94 NUIG, RÓB, POL28/67, Report, 3 July 1975.
95 Hansard (Commons), 894, col. 819
96 Hansard (Commons), 895, col. 1202
97 *Northern Ireland (Emergency Provisions) (Amendment) Act* (London: HMSO, 1975).
98 Hansard (Commons), 894, cols 819–912.
99 Ian Gilmour (www.oxforddnb.com, accessed 8 April 2016).
100 Hansard (Commons), 892, col. 644.
101 TNA, CJ4/861, Neave to Rees, 5 June 1975; Hansard (Commons), 893, cols 955–8.
102 Hansard (Commons), 895, cols 743–4.
103 Hansard (Commons), 896, col. 760–1.
104 NUIG, RÓB, POL28/67, Note, 7 July 1975.
105 *Irish Times*, 10 & 26 July 1975.
106 NUIG, Duddy, POL35/62, Diary entry, 16 July 1975.
107 NUIG, RÓB, POL28/67, Untitled, 16 July 1975; see the death of Charles Irvine in McKittrick *et al.*, *Lost lives*, pp. 552–3.
108 NUIG, Duddy, POL35/62, Diary entry, 17 July 1975; McKittrick *et al.*, *Lost lives*, p. 553.
109 NUIG, Duddy, POL35/62, Diary entry, 19 July 1975.
110 Hansard (Commons), 896, col. 39
111 NUIG, Duddy, POL35/62, Diary entry, 22 July 1975.
112 NUIG, RÓB, POL28/67, Formal meeting, 22 July 1975.
113 NUIG, Duddy, POL35/62, Diary entry, 24 July 1975.
114 NUIG, Duddy, POL35/62, Diary entry, 25 July 1975.
115 NUIG, Duddy, POL35/62, Diary entry, 27 July 1975.
116 NUIG, RÓB, POL28/67, Formal meeting, 31 July 1975.
117 Robert Gildea, *France since 1945* (Oxford: Oxford University Press, 2002), pp. 29–30.
118 TNA, CAB 134/3921, IRN memo 16, 3 July 1975.
119 TNA, CAB 134/3921, IRN memo 19, 31 July 1975.
120 McKittrick *et al.*, *Lost lives*, pp. 555–8.
121 McKittrick *et al.*, *Lost lives*, pp. 559–60.
122 TNA, PREM 16/520, Assessment by HQNI of violence 8–10 August 1975, undated.
123 *The Times*, 6 August 1975.
124 Hansard (Commons), 897, cols 413–4w; TNA, CJ4/1750, Middleton to Dublin FCO, 6 August 1975.
125 NUIG, Duddy, POL35/62, Diary entry, 13 August 1975.
126 NUIG, RÓB, POL28/67, Formal meeting, 13 August 1975.
127 NUIG, Duddy, POL35/62, Diary entry, 13 August 1975.
128 McKittrick *et al.*, *Lost lives*, pp. 560–3.
129 NUIG, Duddy, POL35/62, Diary entry, 18 August 1975.

130 NUIG, Duddy, POL35/62, Diary entry, 22 August 1975.
131 NUIG, RÓB, POL28/67, Formal meeting, 25 August 1975.
132 NUIG, Duddy, POL35/62, Diary entry, 25 August 1975.
133 NUIG, Duddy, POL35/62, Diary entry, 26 August 1975.
134 *The Times*, 28 August 1975.
135 NUIG, Duddy, POL35/62, Diary entry, 28 August 1975.
136 NUIG, Duddy, POL35/62, Diary entry, 29 August 1975.
137 NUIG, Duddy, POL35/62, Diary entry, 1 September 1975.
138 McKittrick *et al.*, *Lost lives*, pp. 571–2.
139 McKittrick *et al.*, *Lost lives*, pp. 571–3.
140 NUIG, Duddy, POL35/62, Diary entry, 2 September 1975.
141 TNA, PREM 16/520, Rees to Wilson, 26 August 1975.
142 *The Times*, 30 August 1975; according to *The Times* an internal inquiry ordered by the GOC found the document to be genuine: *The Times*, 10 September 1975.
143 *The Times*, 1 September 1975.
144 *The Times*, 13 September 1975; *Report, together with the proceedings of the Convention and other appendices: Northern Ireland Constitutional Convention*, H.C. 1975–6, p. 113.
145 *The Times*, 13 September 1975
146 Donoughue, *Downing Street diary*, p. 404.
147 TNA, FCO 87/460, Rees to Wilson, 27 August 1975.
148 *The Times*, 18 August 1975.
149 Rees, *Northern Ireland*, p. 301.
150 LSE, MERLYN-REES/1/8, Transcript of tapes, undated, p. 20.
151 LSE, MERLYN-REES/1/11, Transcript of tapes, undated, p. 5.
152 McKittrick *et al.*, *Lost lives*, pp. 574–5.
153 NUIG, RÓB, POL28/67, Formal meeting, 5 September 1975.
154 NUIG, RÓB, POL28/56, Formal meeting, 5 September 1975.
155 TNA, CAB 134/3921, IRN(75) memo 20, 19 September 1975.
156 Hayes to Burns, 5 December 1975 (PRONI, CONV/1/9).
157 Patterson and Kaufmann, *Unionism and Orangeism*, pp. 177–81.
158 NUIG, Duddy, POL35/62, Diary entry, 9 September 1975.
159 NUIG, Duddy, POL35/62, Diary entry, 11 September 1975.
160 NUIG, Duddy, POL35/62, Diary entry, 12 September 1975.
161 NUIG, Duddy, POL35/62, Diary entry, 12 September 1975.
162 NUIG, Duddy, POL35/62, Diary entry, 15 September 1975.
163 NUIG, RÓB, POL28/67, Formal meeting, 16 September 1975.
164 NUIG, Duddy, POL35/62, Diary entry, 16 September 1975.
165 NUIG, Duddy, POL 35/63, Diary entry, 18 & 19 September 1975.
166 NUIG, Duddy, POL35/62, Diary entry, 21 September 1975.
167 TNA, PREM 16/520, Speech to the Association of Ulster Societies in Cardiff by Merlyn Rees, 20 September 1975.
168 TNA, CJ4/867, Webster to PS/SSNI and PS/PUS, 23 September 1975; McKittrick *et al.*, *Lost lives*, pp. 567, 577–8.

169 *The Times*, 23 & 26 September 1975.
170 *The Times*, 24 & 26 September 1975.
171 TNA, CJ4/1750, Press Notice, 24 September 1975.
172 NUIG, RÓB, POL28/67, Message, 25 September 1975.
173 NUIG, RÓB, POL28/67, S to L, 30 September 1975.
174 NUIG, RÓB, POL28/67, Untitled message, 3 October 1975.
175 McGladdery, *The Provisional IRA in England*, p. 102.
176 TNA, PREM 16/520, Rees to Wilson, 27 August 1975.
177 TNA, CJ4/1293, GOC to Rees, 22 September 1975.
178 TNA, CJ4/867, Cook to England, 9 October 1975.
179 TNA, CJ4/867, Janes to England, 10 October 1975.
180 TNA, CJ4/867, Meeting between Rees and GOC, 14 October 1975.
181 NUIG, Duddy, POL35/62, Diary entry, 18 October 1975.
182 NUIG, Duddy, POL35/62, Diary entry, 20 October 1975.
183 NUIG, Duddy, POL35/62, Diary entry, 21 October 1975.
184 NUIG, Duddy, POL35/62, Diary entry, 22 October 1975.
185 NUIG, Duddy, POL35/62, Diary entry, 23 October 1975.
186 NUIG, Duddy, POL35/62, Diary entry, 27 October 1975.
187 NUIG, Duddy, POL35/62, Diary entry, 28 October 1975; NUIG, RÓB, POL28/67, Instructions, 28 October 1975.
188 NUIG, Duddy, POL35/62, Diary entry, 28 October 1975.
189 McKittrick *et al.*, *Lost lives*, pp. 590–5
190 NUIG, Duddy, POL35/62, Diary entry, 8 November 1975.
191 NUIG, Duddy, POL35/63, Diary entry, 9 November 1975.
192 Taylor, *Provos*, p. 196; TNA, CJ4/867, Webster to PS/Secretary of State, 12 November 1975.
193 NUIG, Duddy, POL35/62, Diary entry, 12 November 1975.
194 NUIG, Duddy, POL35/62, Diary entry, 16 November 1975.
195 NUIG, Duddy, POL35/62, Diary entry, 18 November 1975.
196 Ó Dochartaigh, '"Everyone trying"', pp. 50–77.

6

After the ceasefire

With the PIRA ceasefire over and the inter-party talks of the Convention having ended without agreement, the Labour government's focus turned to long-term plans for constitutional and security policy. The period up to March 1976 marked a phase in which the great uncertainties that had dominated since the collapse of Sunningdale were replaced with clearer plans for the future. Some Labour ministers sought to discuss radical changes to Northern Ireland's relationship with Great Britain. Rees was dismissive and, after the Convention concluded, these debates ended with the affirmation of indefinite direct rule. Brendan Duddy continued in his attempts to direct the British government towards making a deal with the PIRA but it resumed its armed campaign. Sectarian violence led Wilson to announce the deployment of the Special Air Service (SAS) to County Armagh but longer-term plans were also made more publicly clear. Rees's commitment to what became known as criminalisation was announced with the ending of detention without trial, a declaration that special category status for prisoners would be phased out and an emphasis on operating through the court system. Continuing earlier patterns, this led to internal disagreement with senior army officers but officials in the Northern Ireland Office were supportive and the basic principles developed during the ceasefire were to inform security decisions for the remainder of the Labour government.

The Convention

The report of the Convention was based on the UUUC manifesto. It stated that the system of government should be the same as in Westminster. As before, it was argued that under majority rule a government would be expected to carry out commitments made to the electorate and would then be judged accordingly, whereas under power-sharing this principle would be diluted by the presence of parties in government with contradictory commitments. The UUUC argued that Sunningdale was a rejection of the principles of democracy. This deliberately ignored the inevitable outcome of majority rule in Northern Ireland where political parties would be judged only by their commitments on constitutional issues and unionists would be perpetually in power. The offer of representation on a committee system 'to give real and substantial influence to an opposition' was supposed to address the objection that the Catholic community would have little say under majority rule. Nevertheless, the exclusion of nationalists from having any serious influence was explicit in the argument 'that no country ought to be forced to have in its Cabinet any person whose political philosophy and attitudes have revealed his opposition to the very existence of the State.'[1] The SDLP was rejected not because of democratic principles but, rather, because of its nationalism.

It was obvious what the report would advocate before it was even completed and so Labour ministers returned to considering constitutional options in September. The official committee on Northern Ireland produced a paper that once more ruled out withdrawal, repartition and integration as unrealistic. It suggested a policy of 'distancing', a modified form of direct rule which would gradually transfer responsibilities in a 'progressive process of local participation.'[2] Bernard Donoughue angrily intervened in a letter to Harold Wilson before the ministers met to consider it. He stated, 'there is not an ounce of vision or political judgement in this paper... Something more radical is required. We have to move to a different constitutional arrangement which unwinds the British imperial legacy in that island.' He pushed Wilson to return to Dominion status, asserting that it 'at least begins to combine political reality and our human democratic principles.'[3] Again Donoughue showed scant appreciation of the problems involved. Northern Ireland appears to fit into the pattern identified by historian Rodney Lowe that the Policy Unit 'was arguably most effective when Donoughue was the conduit for the ideas of experts... and rather less so when Donoghue's own instincts were to the fore.'[4]

The ministerial committee discussed all of the options again on 24 September and Donoughue was happy with the outcome, recording in his diaries that Wilson pushed Dominion status, Roy Mason argued for integration, Denis Healey for repartition and Roy Jenkins for eventual withdrawal.[5] The committee decided not to exclude withdrawal or integration from further consideration. Officials were instructed to examine majority rule and 'distancing', but with the addition of Dominion status. The Central Policy Review Staff (CPRS), the Cabinet Office think tank, was also instructed to produce a report on the options.[6] Donoughue wrote, 'Nice to go to a good lively meeting, where the ministers have independent views, where the grey official line is overturned, and where the PM is committed and impressive.'[7]

It was not, however, a victory for Donoughue's analysis. The official committee report, produced on 7 November, again dismissed radical options as impracticable and continued to support 'distancing'. Some executive powers could be devolved to local authorities and a regional council could be created as a forum for local politicians. The entire policy was devised to relegate the importance of Northern Irish problems in 'the British political scene'.[8] The CPRS report concluded that 'it would be in Great Britain's political and economic interest if Northern Ireland were to cease to be part of the United Kingdom', but it would be too harmful to Northern Ireland. CPRS argued that unless both communities were in agreement, 'separation would be neither an honourable nor a profitable objective'. They ruled out reunification, negotiated independence, unilateral withdrawal, handing over to the United Nations, repartition and condominium. Consent from both communities was required for 'proof against overthrow'. Three options were suggested: direct rule, distancing and a last chance for the Convention to agree, combined with an announcement that failure would mean direct rule. CPRS favoured the third option.[9]

Wilson was disappointed with CPRS, commenting in the margins that 'although this report purports to be radical, its conclusions are not'. He argued there was not enough serious consideration given to Dominion status and 'the report underestimates the GB desire to see the back of them'.[10] Cabinet Secretary John Hunt replied that if they were to disengage, the right way would be through 'a process of gradual devolution or distancing through a new form of direct rule for a stated period' leading to 'majority rule in the form of something akin to Dominion status with entrenched safeguards for the minority'. To this he added, 'I understand however that Mr Rees will not want to reach any hard and fast conclusions today, and this is probably right'.[11]

Hunt was correct. Rees told the ministerial committee that many of the long-term options were irrelevant for the period ahead of them.[12] Rees resented the involvement of CPRS even though they supported his analysis. He remarked in his memoirs that it was useful for economic valuations but not political judgements, noting: 'once more we had covered old ground and drawn the same conclusions'.[13] In his own memo he restated the same views as in June 1974, adding: 'The "English disease" is to look for a "solution of the Irish problem"; our aim must be to find a Northern Irish solution. It will take time'.[14] Ultimately, Rees, backed by officials, won the argument because the other options were inherently unrealistic. Wilson offered little resistance, summing up the discussion by saying that there was no need to make decisions on any of the policy options and the continuation of direct rule remained the only practical option.[15] That Rees thought the prime minister's preferred option irrelevant is illustrative of the nature of the discussion. Even though ministers had varying views on the ideal relationship between Great Britain and Northern Ireland, these did not really matter; long-term preferences had no bearing on constitutional policy. The immediate context counted far more.

On 17 November Rees began talks with the Convention parties. He reported that the UUUC claimed to accept Westminster sovereignty but wanted it limited so that devolution could not be abolished, as in 1972.[16] A devolved government in which unionists would be effectively guaranteed control, supported financially and morally by the British government and with little capacity for the latter to influence how it governed would have been a tall order under any circumstances, but against the backdrop of the conflict it was extremely unrealistic. Rees concluded it was important to avoid a flat rejection of the Convention report, which might produce another strike.[17] Instead he advocated recalling the Convention with an offer of restoring devolution if there was genuine agreement between both sides.[18] On 17 December the ministerial committee agreed to Rees's proposals.[19] He then wrote a letter to the chairman of the Convention, later published as a White Paper. It stated that devolution remained the optimum system of government and institutional arrangements like the Council of Ireland should not be imposed but develop naturally. It also stressed that Westminster would retain complete sovereignty. Most importantly, the letter stated that majority rule would not receive the broad support it required. The Convention was to be reconvened for one month to seek broader agreement.[20]

Security policy

Late 1975 also saw the ending of detention without trial and Rees offering a much clearer sense of where security policy was headed. On 4 November he praised the RUC in the Commons, asserting 'that the full processes of the law are a much more effective deterrent and are more acceptable to the community as a whole than any emergency procedures'. He described perpetrators of violence as 'criminals'. Rees's support for increasing the role of the police ran in parallel with the idea that political violence should be treated no differently from criminal violence. With the prison building programme having progressed, he outlined a plan to phase out special category status. To end it completely was not an option as more cells were still needed but he proposed to stop granting the status from 1 March 1976. It would continue to be phased out 'both because of the present successes in bringing people before the courts…and because there is a price to be paid for detention. It undermines the law. It alienates part of the community. It is a fertile ground for recruitment to the paramilitaries'.[21]

Criminalisation would be the focus of security policy both in terms of how the army and RUC were to operate and how convicted paramilitaries were to be treated in the prison system.

Airey Neave called for more aggressive measures, arguing that Rees should make Provisional Sinn Féin illegal. He advocated implementing the Republic of Ireland's system of dealing with membership charges, which allowed conviction solely on the testament of a senior police officer. Rees rejected this as 'moving away from the processes of law'. He argued it would be wrong to proceed 'on the basis of "think" or "maybe" in Northern Ireland'.[22]

There was an inconsistency here in that modifications to the law under the Emergency Provisions Act, such as the use of non-jury trials, were deemed to be acceptable and yet they had been brought in on the basis that the normal criminal justice system did not work for political violence. Those imprisoned were well placed to argue that as they were treated differently in the court system, they were entitled to be treated differently in the prison system. Nevertheless, there was logic in the argument that testimony on the word of a policeman carried the same dangers as detention without trial.

A much angrier exchange occurred in the Commons on 24 November after the killing of three British soldiers in South Armagh. An NIO report described the scene as 'an angry, confused, hostile and packed House'. Neave asked why the army had not been 'given clear orders to counterattack and clean [South Armagh] up?' He said the Conservatives were astonished at Rees's claim that releasing 'committed and dangerous terrorists' had nothing to do with South Armagh when a 'great many' came from there. Stanley Orme retorted that Neave was 'playing politics with the British Army' and the security forces were 'completely free and always have been to take what military action they deem necessary to overcome this problem... there is not one shred of evidence to refute that'. An NIO official recorded that Winston Churchill, grandson of the former prime minister, 'unwittingly came to the Government's assistance' by describing Labour ministers as 'spineless and gutless' politicians betraying the sacrifice of British soldiers. Orme dismissed the comments as 'too despicable to answer'.[23] The releases continued in spite of the hostility and on 5 December the final forty-six detainees were let out. Neave said he had 'very deep misgivings' about detention without trial coming to an end.[24]

Rees recorded in his diaries that GOC David House was 'absolutely furious and angry and bitter about the way he has been attacked by the politicians'. The Northern Ireland Secretary felt that the decision to end detention was understood by the army, 'maybe not amongst the soldiery but almost completely amongst the officers and certainly amongst the generals.'[25] This did not amount to senior army officers' approval of the new approach. The army was uneasy with the new emphasis on RUC successes in the courts. In October House discussed the RUC with Frank Cooper, stating that he found the police difficult 'to talk [to] freely and substantively'. He found Chief Constable James Flanagan 'an engaging character' but not a decision maker. House showed some sensitivity in responding to complaints that the army had recently been acting too aggressively, admitting that 'the army was a "blunt instrument"' and 'if there was a particularly nasty incident the soldiers were human beings and there was a tendency to "draw the sword"'. He promised to speak to his brigade commanders.[26]

Shortly after the last detainees were released, however, there was a row about the new approach during a security meeting including the army, the police and the NIO. Frank Cooper wrote to him afterwards, noting that House argued 'we must beware of euphoria about our success rate in the courts'. He had 'emphasised the real enemy was PIRA'. Much of the disagreement centred on the NIO's emphasis that violence had become more sectarian. Cooper responded: 'The PIRA are certainly the main threat and no-one would dispute this in anyway.' He stressed, however, that they needed to make the Catholic community hostile to the PIRA. Cooper pointed out that more people died in Northern Ireland because of road accidents and the murder rate was much worse in a number of American cities. He concluded, 'this is not in any sense to condone the amount of violence here...nevertheless, it is helpful sometimes to have a wider perspective.'[27] It seems unlikely that House would have thought the comparisons pertinent.

On 10 December House wrote to Rees recommending a 'cold, hard look' at security. He acknowledged the RUC had improved a great deal but said they were still unable to operate in strong republican areas. The GOC acknowledged his support for Rees's policies, admitting the '"ceasefire" had to be given a whirl' and claiming he understood the political motivation for ending detention. House remarked: 'in no sense do I feel that I am being forced by political restraints to operate "with my hands tied behind my back"'. He nonetheless felt that ascribing recent successes to the police served to 'induce a state of euphoria that was positively dangerous'. The Provisionals remained the main enemy and the RUC were not in an adequate position to deal with them. As a result, they should face up to the probable need to return to detention or 'some other process' which made it easier to obtain convictions for membership.[28]

Cooper replied that everyone accepted they 'must avoid unrealistic beliefs and statements about the work of the RUC' but argued that the statistics showed a more favourable picture than House allowed for, even though the RUC had a long way to go. Cooper emphasised that Protestant violence was considerable and Rees's strategy was to 'bring back the rule of law throughout Northern Ireland and to treat all who break it as criminals not potential political martyrs'. He stated, 'The involvement of the paramilitaries in *both* communities in crime of all kinds makes it impossible to draw a real distinction between the political fanatic and the common criminal. If we approach the war on terrorism as simply one aspect of the war against crime we shall avoid two pitfalls; that of concentrating our efforts too exclusively against one community; and that of ignoring forms of lawlessness which are not bombings or shootings'. Cooper promised that if violence reached such a stage that this strategy became insufficient then Rees had the power to reintroduce detention, remarking 'if it *has* to be, this will be our loss and PIRA's gain'.[29]

Cooper's letter effectively sums up the new security approach that was to follow. On 17 December Rees told the ministerial committee that, with detention ended and increasing success in the courts, he proposed an investigation to 'consider specifically how best to achieve the primacy of the police and the reduction of the army to garrison strength as soon as practicable'. Rees's plans emphasised the need to limit public knowledge of what was decided. A public announcement would follow but the likelihood that this would stimulate pressure to publish the conclusions led him to suggest the review be conducted by a committee of ministers serviced by a secret working party of officials ('an internal matter not requiring public mention').[30] Rather than an inquiry like Gardiner's the year before, the principles had been explicitly outlined and it would be the task of officials to work out the details.

The resumption of conflict

Brendan Duddy maintained contact with the British but without any significant developments. His diaries suggest a particular antipathy for John Walker and a belief that the MI5 officer had little interest in maintaining the liaison.[31] Duddy expected the Provisionals 'to unleash many bombs in London and other centres in England'.[32] On 7 December the PIRA unit responsible for much of the violence in London was spotted while carrying out a gun attack on the same restaurant they had bombed on 12 November. A six-day siege followed before they surrendered. This marked the end of intense PIRA activity in England for over a decade.[33] Duddy noted in his diaries that the 'ability to strike at will in England has been shattered and my bluff has been called. I really didn't think we were so so weak as to be depending on 4 men in London'.[34]

The year 1976 began with plans for a meeting between Ó Brádaigh *et al.* and the British representatives but the NIO withdrew after some of the worst sectarian violence of the conflict.[35] On 4 January the UVF killed six Catholic civilians in County Armagh.[36] The following day the PIRA reacted by killing ten Protestant civilians near Kingsmill, South Armagh, claiming the murders under the same cover name as the Tullyvalen Orange Hall killings.[37] In response, Harold Wilson held a meeting in London. Bernard Donoughue records that after a breathless account by Rees, Wilson 'said that he wanted a military initiative, even an over-response, to stress that we are doing something'. Rees balked at this, arguing that there were only thirty individuals on each side responsible for the violence. The Defence Secretary Roy Mason, on the other hand, 'suggested sending in the SAS; using computerised intelligence information, closing the border; and designating a Special Security Area under martial law'. Wilson ordered the dispatch of extra troops, the deployment of the SAS to Armagh and the closure of the border 'to a few checkpoints'. Later that day he expressed great satisfaction at a press headline about Rees's recall from Belfast, remarking: 'It's always good when people are coming and going to No. 10. Gives the impression of things happening'.[38]

The SAS already had a controversial reputation in Northern Ireland. Republicans alleged that the regiment had been used to carry out assassinations before its deployment in January 1976.[39] A cabinet memo on plain clothes patrols produced in March 1974 described their actual involvement. At the end of 1969 and the beginning of 1970 soldiers from the regiment made two covert visits to conduct surveillance on 'suspected gun-running activities and thefts of explosives from quarries, for which Protestants were thought to be mainly responsible'. When the PIRA bombing campaign gained momentum in 1971 the RUC and army formed small joint covert teams. Later that year they were reformed and expanded without RUC participation and named Military Reaction Forces (MRFs). This system was unsatisfactory as the men assigned left with their parent units, forcing continuous change. At the end of 1972 the Special Reconnaissance Unit (SRU) was established. As a result of 'persistent allegations from Irish propaganda sources', the MOD opted to exclude SAS members from the SRU 'the more easily to rebut these claims'. They were instead tasked with selecting and training the unit. The SRU comprised 130 troops carrying out covert surveillance on 'terrorists, their haunts and contacts and their couriers within Northern Ireland'. In 1973, when recruitment fell short, the embargo was waived and thirty SAS members were asked to first return to their original regiment and then join the SRU individually. They were deployed in January 1974 on a four-month tour.[40]

By contrast, in January 1976 Wilson chose to make the deployment of the SAS public, a first for the regiment and telling of the prime minister's preoccupation with appealing to the British media. Dublin was informed beforehand, with Liam Cosgrave providing an 'unexpectedly and encouragingly low-key' reply.[41] Galsworthy recorded the Dublin newspapers' use of emotive language when the decision went public, but felt the treatment of Wilson's decision was 'more sympathetic than might have been expected given the local myths about the SAS'. The most objectionable response, so far as Galsworthy was concerned, was a Raidió Teilifís Éireann (RTÉ) radio broadcast with Robert Fisk, who was described as 'generally hostile to the SAS' in an interview that the ambassador thought 'vicious even by his standards'.[42] On 12 January Wilson told the Commons of further measures in County Armagh, declaring it a 'special emergency area'. This amounted to an increase in check-points, more extensive personal identity checks, an increase in surveillance operations, greater use of powers to question people within a mile of the border, an increase in house searches, full use of arrest powers in the area and the promise of new measures for the border including a new information system to handle records more quickly.[43]

The Kingsmill massacre focussed the British media's attention on the border, with some commentators arguing that the Republic was a 'safe haven' for the PIRA. Garret FitzGerald and the Irish Department of Foreign Affairs denied that there was proof that republicans had crossed the border after the attack.[44] When he met with Galsworthy, FitzGerald complained about Wilson's remark in the Commons that those who committed the atrocity at Kingsmill were in Northern Ireland for less than an hour. Galsworthy responded that the van used in the attack had been hijacked in the Republic the afternoon before, seen by a witness crossing back into the country just after the attack and then found abandoned there, which seemed 'pretty conclusive'. He described the meeting as a 'remarkable nitpicking session' because of the 'trivial nature' of FitzGerald's complaints, but also the tone: 'without any of his petulance and indeed with some good humour'.[45]

Moments like Kingsmill raised tensions between the two governments but this was more to do with mutual fears of how the press and public were reacting. The development of cross-border co-operation between the Labour government and the Irish coalition was rather a story of quiet but steady progress. From May 1975 there was a direct radio link between all Garda and RUC patrols on the border and the British army was able to tune in. Rees met Justice Minister Paddy Cooney in London three days after the Kingsmill attack to discuss the progress of the Baldonnel panels established in September 1974. He was happy with the discussions between the two police forces but still wanted direct contact between the British and Irish armies. Cooney remained firm in rejecting this but he suggested new ideas for covert co-operation the following month, such as parallel patrols of the border and using the Gardaí for observation in areas where the British position would be particularly exposed.[46]

Meanwhile, Brendan Duddy continued to press upon Donald Middleton that the key to solving the conflict was to 'deflower' republican violence by reaching an agreement with the Provisionals.[47] Duddy lamented the rising influence of individuals like Martin McGuinness: 'he objects to what he cannot understand and would like a clear cut military battle between the Republican movement and anyone who disagreed.'[48] At the start of February the British requested another meeting with the Provisional representatives.[49] Duddy's diaries record that a Provisional Army Council meeting confirmed that there would be no declaration of a formal return to conflict and the meeting with the British would go ahead regardless of conditions. Provisional IRA volunteer Frank Stagg, imprisoned in England for bombing Coventry, began a hunger strike in December 1975 demanding his transfer to Ireland. It was decided that 'if and when' Frank Stagg died the Provisionals would resume bombing in England and increase attacks on British soldiers.[50] The Provisional Army Council's policy at this point left the initiative to local units, such that the PIRA was still responsible for the deaths of six regular army soldiers and three UDR members in November and December 1975.[51] Further sectarian attacks also followed after the Kingsmill massacre with the UDA/UFF carrying out a series of killings of Catholic civilians and the PIRA killing a Protestant civilian on 30 January with a no-warning pub bombing in Sandy Row.[52] On 6 February a PIRA attack led to the deaths of two RUC officers.[53]

In the context of this violence the British hesitated on whether to go ahead with the meeting. According to Duddy, who met with Middleton and Walker in Belfast the day before it was due, Frank Cooper wanted to go ahead but Rees 'had taken cold feet'. When the approval was finally given, Duddy told McKee and Ó Brádaigh: 'the message must go out from this room tomorrow, the PIRA want peace. The PIRA will work for peace, there will be more violence, but it can end and PIRA will play its part.'[54] Duddy and Ó Brádaigh's records of the meeting on 10 February are divergent; whereas the intermediary believed it to be 'highly successful' with 'everyone happy', Ó Brádaigh merely noted that the talks consisted of updates by both sides and there was no 'concrete result'.[55] Two days later Frank Stagg died, triggering several days of rioting. Republican anger extended also to the SDLP, with Gerry Fitt's house repeatedly attacked and the party's headquarters in Derry destroyed by a bomb.[56] Meetings between the British and the Provisionals came to an end with no sudden break in the contact; the Provisional Army Council decided to await developments, Duddy continued to press for the British to adopt a more radical policy but the NIO offered no indication that it was coming.[57] In March Duddy wrote that his advice to the Provisional Army Council was to 'renew the campaign totally' and 'forget the NI office.'[58] Contact between Duddy and Middleton continued for a number of months but the conversations consisted mostly of the intermediary attacking the Labour government for their 'non-policy.'[59] In July 1976 Rees proposed that the NIO distance themselves from the intermediary and on 30 January 1977 Duddy was told that his role would be brought to an end.[60]

Indefinite direct rule

After the Kingsmill attack Harold Wilson made another intervention on constitutional policy. He wrote to Rees and Denis Healey that there had been 'ominous warnings of a resort to extra-constitutional action' and that the loyalist paramilitaries were considering a 'revival of the strike weapon.' He feared a repetition of the UWC's success and therefore asked Rees and Healey to provide financial figures, stating: 'Somewhere here there should be items, the withdrawal or threatened withdrawal of which might possibly make the Ulster Workers' Council and others pause and think.'[61]

The following day Wilson wrote an 'Apocalyptic note' on the 'ultimate situation...if all present policies fail.' Wilson envisioned a situation of either civil war or widespread industrial action 'on a scale where the civil power becomes impotent.' He wrote that the government would be forced into total separation from Northern Ireland. Wilson further considered the possibility that loyalists would make a unilateral declaration of independence. Referring to William of Orange, he argued: 'they would prove as their actions have long suggested, that they are loyal to no monarch except a long-dead Dutchman, who on practical grounds would find it difficult to assume the operative position of Head of State.' The consequences of this were judged to be a total withdrawal of British armed forces and an end to 'the inordinate financial position which we have maintained at the expense of the tax payers.' Wilson wrote that the various sanctions he envisaged arising from such a situation might well be unacceptable to the British public, particularly in Glasgow and Liverpool. He anticipated the possibility of 'Ulster-inspired terrorism' emanating from such cities. Wilson acknowledged that his note raised 'frightening prospects', adding that he sought 'to sound a warning and to ensure that we are prepared for, but not to attempt to prescribe, a solution which would profit no one either in Northern Ireland or in Britain – or for that matter in the international community.'[62] As with all of his previous interventions, it was a dramatic response that lacked a serious appreciation of the situation. It was also predicated on a declaration of independence that was unlikely to come.

Both Rees and Cooper told Wilson that a strike was unlikely. Cooper rightly dismissed the use of financial sanctions, which risked driving the paramilitaries into an alliance with loyalist politicians.[63] Rees and Healey's joint reply to Wilson provided the financial figures he requested but began by stressing that the chances of a strike were small.[64] Donoughue recorded in his diaries that the Northern Ireland Secretary and the Chancellor conceded 'the enormous flow of money to Ulster' but that Rees 'made a passionate and convincing plea for not taking a tough financial line'.[65] Wilson's desire for punitive economic measures was foolish and failed utterly to contemplate the possibility that their burden would fall on the general population, a body hardly synonymous with the loyalism which so roused his antipathy. After requesting Wilson's permission, John Hunt discussed the 'apocalyptic' paper with Cooper and passed their conclusions to the prime minister. The cabinet secretary wrote that there were still a number of people who believed in negotiated independence but: 'Their only fundamental argument is that if they were independent the two sides would have to live together. The contrary argument is that there would be a lot of dead people before this happened.' Hunt added that if it was possible to persuade unionists to accept a voluntary coalition, this would be preferable. Otherwise, he felt, consideration might have to be given to some form of 'semi-independence' with safeguards for the minority, if direct rule failed.[66]

No breakthrough was expected of the reconvened Convention. The UUUC was firm in its unwillingness to compromise on power-sharing and the SDLP were despondent, only taking part in order to appear constructive.[67] Rees emphasised that the Labour government should be ready to intervene but that 'it would be wrong during the course of the Convention to have too much drama'. He was opposed to the idea of a Lancaster House conference, a device often used while negotiating the independence of Britain's overseas colonies and which would have involved Margaret Thatcher, Airey Neave and Liberal leader Jeremy Thorpe as well as Labour ministers; Rees was 'still deeply concerned about their lack of knowledge of the problem and of the people with whom they would be dealing'.[68] Instead, he advocated that the Labour government intervene alone at the point when the UUUC and SDLP reached an impasse. Each Northern Ireland party would then meet Rees and be informed that the British government could not agree to devolution without widespread agreement. Wilson might reinforce this with further meetings but there would not be 'an occasion for negotiation' or involvement from the Conservatives or Liberals. This was agreed by the ministerial committee on Northern Ireland.[69]

At the UUUC–SDLP meeting on 12 February Harry West gave three 'overriding conditions' for the talks. These were no negotiation on all-Irish institutions, no negotiation on power-sharing and a refusal to serve in government with the SDLP. The SDLP cited Rees's statement that devolution would require support from both parts of the community. The two groups continued to clash and the SDLP walked out, telling the UUUC it would be willing to talk again when the unionists accepted Rees's instructions.[70] Rees met with Wilson and informed him that the Convention was effectively over and there was little merit in talking to its members. When Wilson raised the possibility of a Lancaster House conference, Rees said there would be risks if the government was not able to offer something constructive. As before, his emphasis was on the Northern Irish parties failing and Westminster having minimal involvement. Wilson asked him 'to think very carefully' as the Commons 'would be increasingly bored and intolerant of the Northern Ireland question' and there was a 'real risk' of losing parliamentary support for direct rule without a 'glamorous' initiative coming first. He thought such a conference might serve the real purpose of making the 'insufferability' of Northern Irish politicians clear to the Conservatives and Liberals.[71] Characteristically, he overestimated the threat of Westminster MPs to direct rule.

The conference idea was raised at the ministerial committee meeting on Northern Ireland the following day with Rees arguing that the Commons did not sufficiently understand that local politicians 'were totally incapable of running the country' and adding that there was 'no analogy with the situation in a colony moving towards independence'.[72] On 19 February Rees wrote to Wilson that he thought a conference 'would be a great mistake' immediately after the Convention as the UUUC would use it to appeal to some Conservative MPs. He was not alone in the view that bipartisanship at Westminster would be endangered, citing William Whitelaw's 'particularly vigorous' advice against Margaret Thatcher attending a meeting involving politicians from Northern Ireland.[73] The following week Rees proposed to dissolve the Convention and make a statement to parliament. Again, he insisted that the government should not do anything to 'stir up false hopes'.[74] When the Convention returned to plenary debate the UUUC passed a set of motions restating its position. Rees announced the end of the Convention on 4 March.[75] He told the Commons that there was 'no instant solution to the problems of Northern Ireland'. Devolution was still the Labour government's aim but it did 'not contemplate any major new initiative for some time to come'.[76]

Conclusion

On 16 March Harold Wilson announced that he was resigning and would remain as prime minister only until his successor had been decided. He had made a number of passionate interventions on Northern Ireland during his final administration. Few of them were to the benefit of either the British government or those affected by the conflict. His 'spongers' speech during the UWC strike served only to bolster the loyalists he opposed. His consideration of dominion status, though grounded in contingency scenarios that did not arise, was impractical and displayed little sympathy for those that would be affected by it. His sending of the SAS to Northern Ireland, though arguably a useful contribution due to the damage that would later be inflicted by the regiment on the PIRA, was framed with both eyes firmly on the British press's likely reaction rather than on what would be most effective.[77]

The important point to be made about the Labour prime minister's role, however, is his general irrelevance for much of his tenure. Wilson's instincts and ideas rarely influenced government policy, which was instead shaped primarily by Merlyn Rees and the Northern Ireland Office. When differences emerged, the arguments presented by Rees and his department formed the basis for decisions. The basic context of the conflict was key in shaping them. Radical constitutional options were always unlikely to be implemented because their flaws were so great. Between the end of the PIRA ceasefire and March 1976 the various threads of Labour government policy in Northern Ireland were woven into a much clearer approach that would last for the remainder of the 1970s and beyond. On constitutional policy, the Convention came to its natural end and a commitment was made to continue direct rule indefinitely until politicians from both communities could reach agreement. Criminalisation was outlined with a new emphasis on the police and the court system in place of executive actions like detention without trial. The collapse of the power-sharing executive and the PIRA's ceasefire made political and security decisions between 1974 and 1976 messy, difficult to disentangle from each other and hard to address openly in public. When James Callaghan replaced Wilson as prime minister, the Labour government was in a position to approach each aspect of policy in Northern Ireland separately and with a particular set of principles. Criminalisation and police primacy would form the backbone of security policy. Indefinite direct rule would continue until Northern Ireland's politicians could reach an agreement.

Notes

1 Report, together with the proceedings of the Convention and other appendices: Northern Ireland Constitutional Convention (HMSO, 1976).

2 TNA, CAB 134/3921, IRN(75) memo 21, 19 September 1975.

3 TNA, PREM 16/520, Donoughue to Wilson, 23 September 1975.

4 Lowe, *The official history of the British civil service*, pp. 218–19.

5 Donoughue, *Downing Street diary*, p. 506.

6 TNA, CAB 134/3921, IRN(75) meeting 7, 24 September 1975.

7 Donoughue, *Downing Street diary*, p. 506.

8 TNA, CAB 134/3921, IRN(75) memo 25, 7 November 1975.

9 TNA, CAB 134/3921, IRN(75) memo 26, 7 November 1975.

10 TNA, PREM 16/521, Hunt to Saville, 7 November 1975.

11 TNA, PREM 16/958, Hunt to Wilson, 11 November 1975.

12 TNA, CAB 134/3921, IRN(75) meeting 8, 11 November 1975.

13 Rees, *Northern Ireland*, pp. 209–10.

14 TNA, CAB 134/3921, IRN(75) memo 24, 7 November 1975.

15 TNA, CAB 134/3921, IRN(75) meeting 8, 11 November 1975.

16 TNA, CAB 134/3921, IRN(75) memo 28, 12 December 1975.

17 TNA, CAB 134/3921, IRN(75) memo 28, 12 December 1975.

18 TNA, CAB 134/3921, IRN(75) memo 28, 12 December 1975.

19 TNA, CAB 134/3921, IRN(75) meeting 9, 17 December 1975.

20 *The Northern Ireland Constitutional Convention*, Cmnd. 6387, London, 1976.

21 Hansard (Commons), 899, cols 233–41.

22 Hansard (Commons), 899, cols 245–8.

23 Hansard (Commons), 901, cols 486–9; TNA, CJ4/1750, Abbott to Wyatt, 24 November 1975.

24 Hansard (Commons), 902, col. 31.

25 LSE, MERLYN-REES/1/9, Transcript of tapes, undated, pp. 26–7.

26 TNA, CJ4/1293, Note for the record by Frank Cooper, 22 October 1975.

27 TNA, CJ4/1293, Cooper to GOC, 8 December 1975.

28 TNA, CJ4/1293, GOC to Rees, 10 December 1975.

29 TNA, CJ4/1293, Cooper to GOC, 12 December 1975.

30 TNA, CAB 134/3921, IRN(75) meeting 9, 17 December 1975.

31 NUIG, Duddy, POL 35/62, Diary entry, 5 December 1975.

32 NUIG, Duddy, POL 35/62, Diary entry, 25 November 1975.

33 McGladdery, *The Provisional IRA in England*, pp. 103–4.

34 NUIG, Duddy, POL 35/62, Diary entry, 9 & 12 December 1975.

35 NUIG, Duddy, POL 35/62, Diary entry, 1 & 8 January 1976.

36 McKittrick *et al.*, *Lost lives*, pp. 609–11.

37 McKittrick *et al.*, *Lost lives*, pp. 611–14.

38 Donoughue, *Downing Street diary*, pp. 621–2; TNA, CAB 130/908, MISC 115(76) meeting 1, 6 January 1976.

39 English, *Armed struggle*, p. 172.

40 TNA, CAB 134/3778, IRN(74) memo 2, 28 March 1974.

41 TNA, PREM 16/959, Galsworthy telegram, 7 January 1976; TNA, PREM 16/959, Wright to PM, 7 January 1976.

42 TNA, PREM 16/959, Galsworthy telegram (10), 8 January 1976; TNA, PREM 16/959, Galsworthy telegram (11), 8 January 1976.

43 Hansard (Commons), 903, cols 28–9.

44 Patterson, *Ireland's violent frontier*, p. 97.

45 TNA, FCO 87/582, Galsworthy telegram, 15 January 1976.

46 Patterson, *Ireland's violent frontier*, pp. 96–7.

47 NUIG, Duddy, POL 35/132, Diary entry, 22 January 1976.
48 NUIG, Duddy, POL 35/132, Diary entry, 31 January 1976.
49 NUIG, Duddy, POL 35/132, Diary entry, 1 February 1976.
50 NUIG, Duddy, POL 35/132, Diary entry, 4 February 1976.
51 McKittrick *et al.*, *Lost lives*, pp. 592–603.
52 McKittrick *et al.*, *Lost lives*, pp. 618–22.
53 McKittrick *et al.*, *Lost lives*, p. 624.
54 NUIG, Duddy, POL 35/132, Diary entry, 9 February 1976.
55 NUIG, Duddy, POL 35/132, Diary entry, 10 February 1976; NUIG, RÓB, POL28/67, Formal meeting, 10 February 1976.
56 *Irish Times*, 13 & 18 February 1976.
57 NUIG, Duddy, POL 35/132, Diary entry, 5, 7 & 9 March 1976.
58 NUIG, Duddy, POL 35/132, Diary entry, 17 March 1976.
59 NUIG, Duddy, POL 35/132, Diary entry, 22 May 1976.
60 TNA, PREM 16/1343, Mason to Callaghan, 9 February 1977.
61 TNA, PREM 16/959, Wilson to Rees and Healey, 9 January 1976.
62 TNA, PREM 16/959, Apocalyptic note for the record, 10 January 1976.
63 TNA, PREM 16/959, Meeting between Wilson and GOC, 11 January 1976.
64 TNA, PREM 16/960, Rees and Healey to Wilson, 15 January 1976.
65 Donoughue, *Downing Street diary*, p. 678.
66 TNA, PREM 16/960, Hunt to Wilson, 16 January 1976.
67 PRONI, CONV/1/3, Meeting with UUUC, 19 January 1976; PRONI, CONV/1/3, Meeting with SDLP, 19 January 1976.
68 TNA, PREM 16/960, Rees to Wilson, 30 January 1976.
69 TNA, CAB 134/3921, IRN(76) memo 6, 30 January 1976; TNA, CAB 134/3921, IRN(76) meeting 1, 4 February 1976.
70 PRONI, CONV/1/3, UUUC-SDLP meeting, 12 February 1976.
71 TNA, PREM 16/961, Wright to Stewart, 17 February 1976.
72 TNA, CAB 134/3921, IRN(76) meeting 2, 18 February 1976.
73 TNA, PREM 16/961, Rees to Wilson, 19 February 1976.
74 TNA, PREM 16/961, Rees to Wilson, 25 February 1976.
75 PRONI, CONV/1/3, Chairman's phone conversation with Cooper, 4 March 1976.
76 Hansard (Commons), 906, cols 1715–16.
77 For the long-term impact of SAS operations in Northern Ireland see Mark Urban, *Big boys' rules: the SAS and the secret struggle against the IRA* (London: Faber and Faber, 1993).

7

Police primacy and the myth
of Ulsterisation

Over the course of 1976 plans were prepared to adjust security policy in line with Rees's desire for police primacy, leading to the professionalisation of the RUC and a marked change in the responsibilities and actions of the security forces. By placing greater emphasis on police work and proceeding through the courts, as well as limiting the way in which the army operated, it was hoped that support for paramilitary groups would be undermined. The military historian Hew Strachan aptly describes the fundamental difference in approach of police and soldiers: 'Minimum force is a key feature of British policing: it reinforces the liberal application of the law, and removes any justification for a terrorist backlash. Maximum force is the natural response of the soldier: its rationale in this case is that a show of strength implies resolution and thus constitutes its own deterrent.'[1] That the arms-bearing RUC did not fit into the model of a typical British police force was one major difficulty with the proposals. Senior army officers also continued to doubt the practicability of handing the RUC a greater role.

Many of the changes that followed were misunderstood by the media and general public, in large part because of the quite natural suspicion of government intentions. It has been commonplace to describe the shift as 'Ulsterisation', a term which draws parallels with the US withdrawal from Vietnam by handing responsibility to local security forces. This has usually been regarded as a move to reduce the deaths of British soldiers by placing Northern Irish recruits at the front line, thereby limiting pressure from the public in Great Britain to withdraw. The approach was rather less cynical and the episode is revealing of the failure of the Northern Ireland Office to convince outsiders of its motivations and long-term objectives.

The new prime minister James Callaghan was very close to Rees, describing in his memoirs how he chose to speak only to his 'closest friend' about standing for the leadership. Rees ran his campaign, while another NIO minister, Stanley Orme, did so for Michael Foot (prompting much amusement between the two when they were able to compare their lists of MPs pledging support and found a number appearing on both).[2] After

Callaghan's victory he maintained his distance from Northern Ireland. Although he had been deeply involved in the early years of the conflict as Home Secretary, he left Rees to the job. In July 1976 a newly appointed Director and Co-ordinator of Intelligence (MI5's top officer in NI) was left with the impression that Callaghan 'found the problem of Northern Ireland dispiriting and frustrating and that it was not one that was likely to engage a great deal of his personal attention'.[3] Economic problems offered plenty to be concerned with and he was not prone to Wilson's emotional interjections on the subject.

In September 1976 Rees moved to the Home Office and Roy Mason took his place. Some authors have depicted this changing of the guard as heralding a more confident and aggressive security policy. In 2004 the *Daily Telegraph* paid tribute to Mason as 'a living reproach, a demonstration that capitulation to the Irish brand of fascism called "republicanism" was not inevitable'. Martin McGuinness memorably remarked of successive Northern Ireland Secretaries: 'The only one who impressed was Roy Mason. He impressed some of the unionists, because he beat the shit out of us'.[4] Henry Patterson writes that 'the tough ex-miner…pursued the policies of criminalization and Ulsterisation with a crude vigour'.[5] While his rhetorical efforts were effective in securing confidence from unionists, his contribution to security policy was minimal.[6] Rees's approach formed the basis for security policy and when the army exerted pressure for a tougher stance, Mason followed the advice of his officials and resisted it.

The Bourn proposals

On 28 January 1976 the ministerial committee set up to develop the police primacy strategy met for the first time, chaired by Merlyn Rees and including Defence Secretary Roy Mason, the Attorney General Samuel Silkin and Ministers of State from the Foreign and Commonwealth Office and Home Office.[7] It established a working party of officials drawn from these departments and chaired by the NIO's John Bourn.[8] The officials' interim report claimed there was 'no likelihood of violence being eliminated over the next few years'. To achieve police primacy, they recommended specialist RUC teams for murders, fraud, surveillance and bomb disposal; the creation of Special Patrol Groups (SPGs); an expansion in community relations work; improved arrangements for handling intelligence; the transfer of RUC and army responsibilities for police station, protection and escort duties to the RUC Reserve and an expansion in local police centres providing resources to local communities. The officials proposed an increase in the maximum number of regular RUC officers by 1,000, raising it to 7,500 by 1980/81, and the same increase for full-time reservists. It was hoped that the army's force level of thirteen major units would be reduced to seven and a third by March 1979, with an expansion of full-time UDR soldiers by 800 to 2,400.[9]

When ministers met to discuss the interim report Rees emphasised that police primacy 'was not an aim that could be achieved overnight'. Especially significant was that he did not want the changes to be misinterpreted as a return to the set-up before troops were deployed in 1969, with an equivalent to the B Specials playing a major role. He asked that the UDR proposals be re-phrased to simply describe 'minor increases for several years'. In discussion the ministers emphasised Catholic recruitment and the need to avoid turning the RUC into a semi-military force.[10] Senior army officers based in Northern Ireland were pessimistic. In late March the Chief of Staff remarked that the 'army were not engaged in Northern Ireland to do the work of the police but to fight terrorism'. It was still incredibly difficult to get the army to adjust to the ethos of military aid to the civil power. NIO official B.M. Webster warned that army officers were struggling to maintain morale while the government attempted 'to "civil-ianise" the emergency here'.[11]

David House continued to hanker after a more aggressive approach. Ending detention left attrition in the hands of the courts and the RUC, rendering the army's day-to-day task as 'essentially defensive'. This was 'neither an enviable nor a particularly rewarding position', which required more troops than available to suppress disorder with 'real effectiveness'. Citing the high number of deaths in the first three months of 1976, House argued it would have been better if detention without trial had been retained. Despite this, he then went on to offer his support to the reliance on the courts, claiming that the general security situation was slowly improving. Professing support for police primacy, he suggested a cessation of routine army activities in loyalist areas. Similarly, he felt the RUC should take on 'fringe green areas', with the army gradually withdrawing to a supporting role.[12] The remarks are intriguing in that they reflect House's preference for detention, tempered by recognition that it would not return, and his support for the extension of police primacy to areas less dominated by republicans. His analysis could be a confused one, subject to immediate problems.

The police, on the other hand, were quite comfortable with the prospect of their elevation. James Flanagan's designated replacement as Chief Constable, Kenneth Newman, said his first priority 'must be to create a strong and efficient crime fighting machine designed to erode and ultimately overthrow the power of the PIRA'. Senior policemen hoped that the PIRA could be defeated with the RUC at the centre of the effort. He proposed 'a systematised joint [Special Branch] and [Criminal Investigation Department] criminal intelligence system', area crime squads, the reorganisation and expansion of forensic teams, and the establishment of crime centres 'for applying scientific method to the processing of large volumes of information and evidence relevant to multiple major crimes'. Newman believed that the intensification of Special Branch and Criminal Investigation Department (CID) activity would gradually make uniformed patrols of republican areas possible.[13]

The new approach was viewed sympathetically by the Director General of MI5, Sir Michael Hanley. Following a three-day tour of Northern Ireland in May, he remarked: 'Since the NIO was formed in 1972 I have followed a policy of helping the army first. Of course we must still help the army, but henceforth our first priority must be to the RUC, and we ought to pursue an active and positive policy towards them and be on the alert for any ways in which we can be of assistance.' Like others, Hanley recognised the process of securing police primacy 'would inevitably be a gradual one', but added: 'at least it held out the prospect of success in the long term, lowering the security temperature as it progressed'.[14]

The language of criminalisation was dominant in the ministerial committee on Northern Ireland. In May Rees spoke of the need to 'eradicate terrorism' by using the criminal law to 'demythologise the cult of the terrorist'. Although sounding bullish, he stressed the need to avoid IRA traps set to provoke Catholic alienation.[15] Four days later he described the best strategy as seeking 'to drive a wedge between the terrorists and the great majority of people on both sides of the community who are heartily sick of violence'. He believed the concentration on convictions was paying dividends and terrorists were 'increasingly perceived as criminals and not as wayward political heroes'. Rees and the Attorney General looked for ways in which to modify the law to further enhance this, but the efforts produced little. It was decided that the focus of reform should be on the police.[16]

By May 1976 Airey Neave wrote to Rees expressing deep dissatisfaction that 'no new security initiative had yet been announced'. He pushed for the creation of an anti-terrorist unit incorporating regular troops with the UDR and RUC.[17] Neave claimed they could not 'afford the present world-weary and negative attitude in official circles'. He wanted an aggressive response, including the introduction of identity cards in Northern Ireland: 'The Government's policy towards guerrilla warfare...seems to involve a half-hearted containing operation. We think that the Government should go over to the offensive and declare war against terrorism.'[18] Rees was dismissive of Neave's short-termism: 'There is no ingenious mechanism or sudden new initiative that will make the problem disappear overnight.' He brushed aside Neave's proposed combining of different security forces into one unit:

> The value of the Government's approach lies in the combination and inter-dependence of the various elements of the security forces...interdependence does not mean integration. It would be wrong...to establish the police as a paramilitary force, for the police to conduct military style operations or for the police and the Army to merge in whole or in part.[19]

Rees privately described the idea as 'illiterate rubbish'.[20] Any fears he might have held that the army would look more favourably upon Neave were put to one side when the Conservative shadow suggested extending soldiers' tours in South Armagh and officers responded with 'four letter words to describe him'.[21]

The following month the final report of the officials' working party on police primacy was discussed by Labour ministers. It later became known publicly as the Bourn report or 'The Way Ahead' but bore the more anodyne title 'Report of the Official Working Party on Law and Order in Northern Ireland'. The conclusion repeated verbatim Rees's desire 'to drive an increasing wedge between the terrorists and the great majority of people'. There was 'a traditional sensitivity and aversion towards the police' in Ireland and the RUC would have to overcome not only the effects of the last seven years of violence but 'the legacy of the distant past'. It needed to 'extend the range and scope of civilian policing services and activities to establish themselves within both communities'. Resident units of the army should return to barracks to act as a reserve, roulement units (major combat units on six month tours) should be redeployed to areas requiring a stronger military presence and the UDR increasingly used to relieve regular units of mundane tasks such as operating vehicle check-points. The recommendations for professionalising the RUC remained the same as in the interim report, though the targets for recruitment were put back a year to 1981/82. A number of possible changes in the law were rejected, including measures favoured by Airey Neave, such as the Republic's system for membership convictions and the creation of an offence of terrorism. Both were ruled out for the same reasons that Rees had given earlier. The Bourn report did not successfully grapple with the problem of how to improve Catholic recruitment. The hope of a virtuous circle of increasing success leading to Catholic recruitment was expressed, but with the additional remark that 'it is certain that there will always be a majority of Protestants in the RUC' because they were a majority in Northern Ireland. Higher priority was given to the professionalisation of the force.[22]

The report had large financial implications. The Public Expenditure Survey conducted in 1975 planned for the RUC to receive £59.9 million annually until 1979/80 after which its budget would decline to £58.6 million. Under the Bourn proposals, however, police spending would rise incrementally from £60.8 million in 1976/77 to £75.8 million in 1980/81. These costs arose from the increase in the size of the force and the purchase of 300 extra vehicles (to maintain a fleet of 1,400), 8 helicopters and a £2 million computer command and control system. Recruitment costs were also outlined for the UDR, showing a progressive rise in expenditure from £500,000 to £2.74 million. The implications for regular army expenditure were more complicated. Pay and allowances of military personnel and ordinary maintenance costs were not included in Northern Ireland costs, only those extra costs that were required because of the conflict. Until 1974 these had 'reserved item status', meaning that the Treasury accepted them on top of the defence budget in order to limit the damage to the army's 'primary commitments'. After the most recent defence review, however, this status was removed, leading to an addition £7–9 million annual cost. The Ministry of Defence had already set the target of reducing the army such that the reductions in the Bourn report would not offset the new costs for the RUC and UDR. The MOD therefore claimed it was impossible for them to pay to expand the UDR.[23] Negotiations to agree the financing of the changes took considerable time.

Rees decided there would be no White Paper for the final report, continuing with his preference to keep details on the new approach internal to the government. Instead he would give Conservative leader Margaret Thatcher an expurgated version omitting figures and the annexes and explain the general gist of the report to the House of Commons.[24] On 2 July Rees told the Commons that 'by their nature it would not be in the public interest to disclose the details' of the report.[25] Samuel Silkin outlined minor changes in the law including an increase in the maximum penalty for membership and a new offence of assisting a member of a proscribed organisation. He added that 'scrutiny has shown again and again that the weakness is lack of evidence.'[26] Margaret Thatcher returned her version of the Bourn report without comment.[27]

A week later Rees informed James Callaghan that action to implement the Bourn proposals was underway.[28] Bourn did not want to set targets, or for meetings to be too formal, arguing that 'the essence of the plan is its flexibility' and that it was important 'to avoid leaning too heavily on the Chief Constable, and checking his every move.'[29] He formally asked Newman to proceed with implementing the report on 26 July. In dealing with the army, he proposed to leave changes to the Ministry of Defence in order to avoid the question of whether the NIO should pay for the expansion of the UDR.[30] The MOD had already written to Bourn claiming that they could not pay for the expansion out of their existing budget.[31] Bourn objected that his group had 'watered down' references to army savings on the assumption that the MOD had adjusted their figures to take this into account 'since, to put it shortly, you will not get the army savings unless you expand the UDR and we expand the police'.[32] In August the MOD turned to the Treasury. They warned that 'unless some easement is negotiated' the expansion would be indefinitely postponed.[33] The Treasury sent a blunt rejection, placing their opposition in the broader context of the government's economic difficulties and the 'trivial size of the sums in question which are within any possible margin of error on a defence budget of the order of £6000 million'.[34] UDR expenditure was not fully resolved until a year later. The process of obtaining funds for the RUC, however, went smoothly and by November the Treasury approved the NIO's bid.[35]

Army frustration

Despite agreement on the strategic approach to security policy, the high number of killings in 1976 prompted David House to call for harsher measures. A total of 308 people were killed in 1976, making it the second-worst year of the conflict. In contrast to 1972, which saw the deaths of 496 people, the proportion of civilians killed was much greater (71% to 52%). Republicans were far less successful in attacking British soldiers, with only 14 dying in contrast to 108 four years earlier. Loyalists matched their murder rate of the previous year (126), which was their highest of the conflict, while the PIRA was responsible for 139 deaths.[36]

In June 32 civilians were killed. That same month the GOC told Frank Cooper's replacement Brian Cubbon of his 'respect for your judgement that, despite the generally worsening figures for killings and woundings since the "ceasefire"...there is not yet a political case for changing course'. Nevertheless, a change of course was precisely what he wanted, claiming that the level of violence 'must be gathering almighty close to overwhelming the RUC's...capability'. House wanted intelligence material to be used for convictions and advocated something 'in the sphere of administrative or executive action' since the courts would not do so.[37] Ken Newman was opposed, arguing that a return to executive action would only 'make police work harder'. House said time was running out and there should be a system like the special tribunals in the Irish Republic. He accepted that this 'would be seen as detention by another name' but did not want the army to 'remain indefinitely in their present reactive and defensive posture'. Cubbon wrote that this would be 'a complete reversal...of existing policy, so soon after ending detention and publicly nailing their colours to the mast of the rule of law'.[38]

In one of his last acts at the NIO, Rees sent House a passionate defence, describing detention without trial as 'the hated symbol of a negative repressive policy'. He said 'it was always realised that a ceasefire would be temporary and that there would be a return to violence' but it had allowed him to show 'the PIRA are criminals to be dealt with through the courts'. He claimed to have 'removed the emotional shadows of detention'. Rees argued that to diverge from their current path would 'destroy the gains we have made over the last year and a half. It would take us back into the rut out of which we have broken'.[39]

House agreed 'without qualification, that there is no respectable long term aim other than reliance on the courts'. He instead disputed the method by which this stage could be reached, claiming that violence had to be reduced first.[40] A week later he wrote: 'right now, the soldier has to tread a particularly delicate, difficult and vulnerable path – and soldiers are not ballet dancers'. House insisted that he 'always accepted the strength of the case' for ending detention and was convinced of the need to isolate PIRA from the Catholic community. Nevertheless, he felt it was wrong to dismiss modifications of the law as a return to detention under another name and asked for a study for 'some such solution, for application on a contingency basis, should the level of violence not subside'. House said he had never argued 'that the army should somehow or other be enabled to 'go hard; counter-attack; root out the gunmen; take off the political kid gloves' etc. . . . I do not consider that I have been shackled, in the direction of Army operations and policy, against my wishes or inclinations, by political constraints'.[41] Nevertheless, he still felt an instinctive dislike of the army operating on a defensive basis. While showing some willingness to accept the pattern of army activity since the ceasefire, House continued to hold out for a legal method which would take known paramilitaries out of the conflict. His was the frustration of those who felt certain of particular individuals' involvement in violence but saw them left relatively unhindered in their activities by the legal system.

House's request for another study into legal changes was not pressed for particularly firmly. This was because the exchange with Rees reached its conclusion at a point where the general himself admitted it was perhaps an inopportune time to suggest change. August 1976 was a month of greater optimism: the foundation of the Women's Peace movement, a stronger anti-IRA stance in the South, and the 'very recent spate of significant arrests by the RUC' led to the 'first real stirrings of hope' felt by him and he accepted they should wait to see how the situation developed.[42] The first of these grew out of the tragic deaths of three young children in West Belfast. Provisional IRA volunteer Danny Lennon was involved in a car chase with British soldiers when he was shot dead and his car mounted the pavement, crushing an 8-year-old schoolgirl and her two brothers, aged two years and six weeks old. The mother survived but committed suicide three and a half years later. Two Belfast women, Betty Williams and Mairead Corrigan, founded the Peace People movement, with rallies attracting tens of thousands and international publicity. They were given the Nobel Peace Prize for 1976 and there were high hopes that the group would have a major impact that summer. These were not realised, with criticism coming from politicians as the movement tried to grapple with wider political issues beyond a simple desire for peace.[43] The PIRA was particularly hostile, issuing a threat to 'any member of the peace movement' who co-operated with the British army.[44]

The second point, that the Republic of Ireland's government was taking a tougher stance on the IRA in the South, was borne of more violent deaths. On 21 July the newly appointed British ambassador to Ireland Christopher Ewart-Biggs and NIO official Judith Cook were killed by a PIRA bomb attack on the car in which they were travelling in Sandyford, County Dublin. Brian Cubbon was also in the car, narrowly surviving the attack along with the driver. Merlyn Rees would also have been inside had there not been a last minute cancellation of his visit.[45] The attack was humiliating for the Irish government. The *Irish Independent* alleged that a major lapse in the efforts of Irish security forces had allowed the killings to occur. British ministers and officials cautioned against criticising the Irish state. It was hoped that greater security co-operation would naturally ensue and that the Irish government would adopt an aggressive approach in the months that followed. To be seen to try to extract concessions from the Irish government was deemed very risky and liable to provoke a backlash from the public in the South.[46]

The Irish government's response was to increase the maximum penalty for membership of an illegal organisation to five years from two, to allow for suspects to be held for seven days, to increase the penalties for possession of firearms and explosives and extend Garda search and arrest powers to the Irish army. The legislation was not brought forward until a special session of the Dáil on 31 August. Irish public opinion had shifted such that Fianna Fáil and sections of the media felt able to condemn the Fine Gael–Labour coalition for infringing civil liberties. A constitutional crisis followed with the President Cearbhall Ó Dálaigh refusing to sign one of the Bills and referring it to the Supreme Court. He was forced to sign the legislation but on the same day the PIRA killed a Garda officer with a booby trap bomb to mark the occasion. Coalition ministers, who had a difficult relationship with Ó Dálaigh, saw the president as bearing some responsibility for the death of the policeman and Minister for Defence Patrick Donegan's description of him as a 'thundering disgrace' during a visit to

Mullingar barracks triggered a series of events that ended in Ó Dálaigh's resignation.[47] From the British perspective, the changes after the ambassador's death were minimal. The legislation treated the problem as an internal one and few gains were made on the key British priority of cross-border security co-operation. The persistent attacks on the coalition from Fianna Fáil show how difficult the Irish government's position was.

Meanwhile, Merlyn Rees was attacked for placing constraints on the British security forces. In August Vanguard member David Burnside demanded the reintroduction of internment without trial while UUUC MP Robert Bradford called for Rees to be sacked and the death penalty brought back.[48] Airey Neave described security policy as 'weak', complaining to the press that the Labour minister was not willing 'to listen to new ideas from us or from anyone else'. He had been 'utterly deluded' by the ceasefire, had adopted a 'failed policy of conciliation' and now, without detention without trial, lacked the legal powers to round up the ringleaders of terrorism.[49] Upon his appointment as Home Secretary in September, however, Rees bequeathed to his successor a security strategy that would lead to greater attrition against paramilitaries from both communities.

Roy Mason and 'semi-detention'

After Roy Mason replaced Rees on 10 September personality differences were very quickly observed by NIO staff. Douglas Janes, Deputy Secretary at NIO London, noted that whereas Rees had 'the habit... [of] ringing up Duty Officers at all hours and of listening to every radio news bulletin on every channel as sources of information', Mason was 'clearly accustomed to a much more orderly existence' and expected information 'to be served to him on a plate'.[50] Rees's enthusiasm for informal discussion with Frank Cooper and others was replaced with a formal, correspondence-driven approach. Mason's arrival did not, however, result in any dramatic adjustment to security policy. In his first press conference he surprised many journalists by saying the economy was Northern Ireland's biggest problem. *The Times* noted his 'Yorkshire bluntness' in dismissing the idea of involving local politicians in direct rule or ordering a sudden increase in the army's profile.[51]

With a particular eye on Airey Neave's complaints, Brian Cubbon suggested to Mason in December that the time had come to 'go a little more on to the offensive in dealing with the critics'. They 'should meet head-on the basic proposition that "men who are known to be the godfathers of terrorism are walking the streets free and should be behind bars"'.[52] This had been the focus of Neave's attacks on the Labour government for much of the year.[53] Cubbon pointed out that everything turned on the phrase 'are known to be'; if evidence was available the law was sufficient to deal with them, but as knowledge was usually based on intelligence, hearsay and suspicion, it was only natural that men thought to be murderers would not be convicted. The permanent secretary also sought to address some of the GOC's complaints. He suggested a study of 'some determinate system of detention', provided this was only a contingency study and the report was produced quickly. Cubbon doubted 'whether there is any half-way house...to detention' but wanted this demonstrated to the GOC.[54] The process that followed was shaped by Cubbon to reinforce the commitment to existing security policy.

Mason did not initially share Cubbon's certainty about the merits of the status quo and expressed concern at the Conservatives having 'something to snipe at'. He wanted to 'say something positive about the "godfather" law' in the upcoming debate on the Emergency Provisions Act. Cubbon responded that it was better 'to face up to the reality that the only solution lay in continuing and increasing police success'. When Mason suggested the possibility of obtaining outside advice from a criminal lawyer, Cubbon said he 'felt that we ought to be able to tackle this problem from within our own resources'. Mason agreed to Cubbon's proposed semi-detention investigation 'on the clear understanding that it was only a contingency study'.[55] Cubbon asked Anthony Stephens, Under-Secretary at NIO Belfast, to chair it. He modified the terms of reference from assuming a condition of higher violence than at present to the 'less specific formula' of 'a contingency basis', in order to 'avoid an unnecessary conflict with the GOC'.[56] Ambiguous language served only to delay disagreement.

On 17 December Mason used Cubbon's advice to address Neave's criticism of the inability to convict the 'godfathers' of terrorism. Pointing out that known criminals in Great Britain were also able to walk the streets free, he argued that '"Known" in this sense...does not constitute guilt in a court of law...In no circumstances must we allow myths and misconceptions to lead us into false moves which would lower the standard of justice'.[57] Neave objected to the 'constant repetition of the legal difficulties'. He complained that someone charged under the Explosive Substances Act could only be given fourteen years imprisonment, arguing that they should be convicted of terrorism and given life.[58]

Meanwhile, Cubbon prepared for disagreements with David House. P.W.J. Buxton, Webster's replacement as Assistant Secretary for security operations, informed Cubbon that House had recently discussed the Southern system with him. Buxton told House that even if the police agreed to it the Director of Public Prosecutions and the courts would not. House also said he missed the informal conversations he had with Rees and felt 'a little "unloved" at present'.[59] Cubbon advised Mason that to modify policy would 'be seen as vacillation and give an enormous boost to the Provisional morale'[60] Mason was not entirely convinced, saying that they 'might need to ask ourselves if we were content that we were getting on top of [the security situation] fast enough'[61]

Stephens's report concluded that 'barring a wholly new situation, the balance of advantage would lie in trying to ride out the storm'. The law had already been 'modified as far as it can be towards facilitating convictions' and they should 'avoid putting at risk the independence and reputation of the ordinary criminal courts'. The 'least unsatisfactory' alternative was detention without trial, but Stephens warned that, if introduced, 'waning sympathy for the Provisional IRA would be revived'[62] On 28 February Cubbon met House and Newman together. The Chief Constable supported Stephens's conclusions but the GOC said he '"hated" the report'. He accepted its conclusions but objected to 'the "cosy and cosmetic" argumentation' by which they were reached. House rejected the assumption 'that detention was counter-productive when it was tried last time'. He complained that the report and the advice given to Mason by his officials 'did not show sufficient concern with the gravity of the present situation'. Cubbon said he would personally have gone further than the report, arguing that detention represented a reversal of the professional orientation of the RUC and would have 'drastic consequences' for the removal of special category status.[63]

In March Cubbon held another meeting of officials to discuss how to brief Mason. It was argued that the minister 'should be advised to try to deal relatively quickly' with the Stephens report and 'postpone the GOC's set piece speech on the security situation until the next item on the agenda'[64] Mason took the advice of his officials and, when House complained of 'the doctrine that detention had been counter-productive', replied that 'if it were indicated that detention was even being considered, it would turn the clock back'. He insisted that the situation was much calmer, both in Northern Ireland and in parliament.[65] The pattern of violence over the winter of 1976/77 leant particular weight to this conclusion (see figure 1). The Stephens report served to affirm the commitment to the security strategy inherited by Mason. Although the army's most senior officer in Northern Ireland continued to call for a more aggressive approach and Mason was fearful of parliamentary criticism, officials in the Northern Ireland Office proved persuasive in advising the minister to stick to the policies of his predecessor.

Implementing the Bourn proposals

New directives were written to reflect changes in the relationship between the GOC and Chief Constable. Sociologists Graham Ellison and Jim Smyth

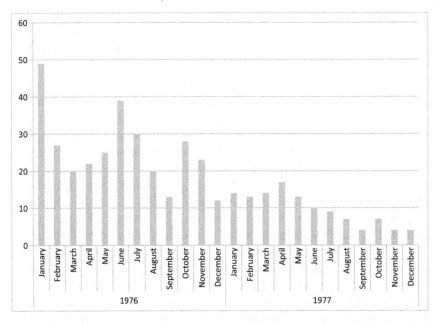

Figure 1 Total deaths resulting from the conflict, 1976–77

claim that 'police primacy came into operation officially on 1 January 1977', when Newman and the GOC 'signed a joint directive to relegate the army to a "military aid to the civil power" role and to position the RUC in the front line in the maintenance of internal security'.[66] This is simplistic; the army had always been deployed under the rules of MACP. Prior to the new directive, the GOC's responsibilities included co-ordinating the tasking of the RUC for security operations. This relationship was only confined to that one area and did not subordinate the police to the army as they continued to operate independently on other activities.[67] The new document (signed on 12 January) defined the army's role straightforwardly as being in support of the police. The RUC was 'to be fully concerned' with army operations, agreeing to the frequency and tasking of army patrols and vehicle check-points, and the army seeking authorisation from the police for house searches, identity checks and arrests. The Director and Co-ordinator of Intelligence was to continue directing intelligence efforts and hold responsibility for developing a close association between CID/ Special Branch and military intelligence.[68]

Ellison and Smyth also exaggerate the significance of the directive. Commenting on an earlier draft, Brian Cubbon noted that the two signatories regarded it in a very different light: 'The GOC is apparently intending it to be viewed as an important change of direction; the Chief Constable sees it as of no great significance.' Cubbon himself thought the document lay somewhere between the two. The relative responsibilities of House and Newman were 'at the heart of the government's approach' but there were still areas in which the police were unable to operate.[69] The implementation of the Bourn proposals was a long process and the directive was more aspirational than real.

More significant were draft documents produced by the CLF and Deputy Chief Constable for Operations (DCC(Ops)). As the second most senior officers, their roles were more closely tied to directing how soldiers and police officers operated on the ground, while their superiors dealt more with wider, strategic issues. The CLF felt the RUC had grown in strength and expertise throughout the year; the new regional crime squads had 'become increasingly successful' and some areas had been transferred to the RUC, with military support from the UDR. The draft directive, therefore, outlined further measures to achieve police primacy. An Operational Policy Committee (OPC) was proposed, chaired jointly by the CLF and DCC(Ops) with the aim 'to review, assess and formulate joint operational policy'. Where the RUC were unable to operate without the army's assistance there would be overall co-ordination between the relevant Assistant Chief Constable and Brigade Commander and between equivalent ranks at lower levels. Where the RUC were able to assume full responsibility they would 'determine the pace and pattern of operations'. In all areas the local policy for routine operations (the frequency and tasking of army patrols and vehicle check-points, and the authorisation of house searches, identity checks and arrests) would be agreed in the RUC's Divisional Action Committees (DAC). The intelligence effort would be co-ordinated by the RUC with close association between CID/SB and army units. In order to improve co-ordination, studies were carried out by the Intelligence Review Committee (IRC) (relevant files on this committee are withheld from the National Archives).[70] The various committees for co-ordinating a new relationship between the army and RUC only went so far, however. The expansion of the RUC and its professionalisation was to be a lengthy process.

Ulsterisation

Following the Labour government's public commitment to police primacy and criminalisation, 'Ulsterisation' became a common term in the media to describe the new strategy.[71] Some expressed support for the idea: in February 1977 Enoch Powell brought a motion to the Commons in favour of expanding the 'strength and effectiveness of the Ulster security forces' and fellow unionist MP James Kilfedder expressed a 'demand' for

Ulsterisation.[72] Others, such as Paddy Devlin of the SDLP, warned that it was an 'incontrovertible fact' that military withdrawal was at an advanced stage and in the future all operations would be carried out by the UDR and RUC.[73] Devlin's perception of Ulsterisation is more obviously aligned with the implicit comparison with the USA government's policy of Vietnamisation, which suggested that the British government was concerned to avoid the costly impact of soldiers' deaths on public opinion in Great Britain.

The term is generally accepted in scholarly accounts. Sociologist Robert White argues that it 'shielded the British public from the war'.[74] Henry Patterson notes that it 'avoided the possibility of a Vietnam syndrome in British politics' but the effect was to deepen sectarian divisions because of the PIRA's increased focus on killing policemen and UDR soldiers.[75] Former PIRA volunteer Tommy McKearney has argued the same; it was 'difficult to accept that Britain [sic] was unaware of the consequences arising from placing locally recruited militias (Protestant and Unionist for the most part) in direct conflict with the IRA'.[76]

By contrast, Peter Neumann has described Ulsterisation as a myth. Unfortunately, his argument is to a large extent predicated on statistical errors. Neumann's figures on the composition of the RUC are inaccurate as he mistakenly thought that figures for the RUC regular force included full-time and part-time reservists. He bizarrely records that in 1975 there were 83 regular RUC officers when there were 4,902.[77] On the Ulster Defence Regiment he argues that the overall strength 'had been decreasing in almost every year since 1972', but this gives insufficient weight to the expansion of *full-time* recruits, which more than quadrupled between 1972 and 1979.[78] The expansion of local security forces was substantial. Less satisfactory from the British government's perspective was that this was not matched with the reduction hoped for in regular army troops. The number of regular British soldiers deployed in the province remained between 14,000 and 15,500 until July 1978 when it was cut to 13,480, while the figure remained over 10,000 for every year of the conflict running up to the Good Friday Agreement bar the one exception of 1985 when it dipped to 9,700.[79]

Thus there is a limit to the validity of Patterson and McKearney's claims that the strategy exacerbated the sectarian dimension; the prominence of the army did not change dramatically, especially on the 'front line' of strongly republican areas where it remained dominant. It is more accurate to view the increase in attacks on the softer targets of the RUC and UDR as stemming from the PIRA's wider frustration at failing to kill ordinary soldiers, which had more to do with its own difficulties after the ceasefire. Indeed, the trend towards these attacks occurred before the shift in British strategy was implemented, with a sharp rise in killings of policemen and

UDR soldiers in 1976 (the worst year of the conflict for the RUC with 24 deaths).[80]

Within the NIO the term Ulsterisation was not looked upon favourably and its ubiquity says something of the inability of the Labour government to successfully convince the media and general public of its intentions. In March 1977 NIO Belfast Deputy Secretary Anthony Pritchard prepared a paper for Brian Cubbon in which he objected that the various strands of the Bourn proposals had 'been woven together into an accusation of "Ulsterisation"', which was 'inextricably involved with allegations of withdrawal'. He said it was not enough to protest that this was wrong and suggested that a more positive argument 'is that the policy is one of a return to normality'. The hope was that this would separate the changing balance in the security forces from the idea of withdrawal or disengagement by the British. The restoration of normality, he argued, 'is based on the principle that this can only be achieved by pursuing terrorists through the normal processes of the law' and the 'only effective instrument for achieving this is the RUC'.[81] Throughout his analysis there was an overwhelming emphasis on the professionalisation of the RUC and the basic principle of police primacy which had informed the Bourn proposals.

The plan to expand the UDR gave credence to the Ulsterisation concept. What NIO ministers did not convey was that the plans for the regiment were much less ambitious than assumed. Pritchard envisioned the UDR as a 'cost-effective' military back-up to the RUC only in areas where they were thought acceptable.[82] In his response, Cubbon wrote that the locally recruited regiment was 'the feature of our present policy which most needs study', with the Bourn papers 'not very illuminating on the basic future of the UDR'. He admitted that the thinking in the NIO had not 'advanced very much from the original idea of the UDR as a creation that enabled us to disband the "B" Specials'.[83] Though it was not said publicly, the UDR was seen in the NIO as having very little role in security strategy and remained a force to be kept away from republican areas. The rhetoric of police primacy was a sincere reflection of the Labour government's intentions, even though the term failed to achieve the prevalence of Ulsterisation in public discourse.

Westminster

Airey Neave began the New Year by declaring that 'The government should make 1977 the year of victory over terrorism in Ulster.' He continued to insist on a tougher security policy, calling for a larger deployment of SAS troops.[84] In March Mason promised to consider increasing the maximum penalty for offences under the Explosive Substances Act.[85] Two days later

Neave called for 'emergency tribunals, meeting in camera, to provide better protection for witnesses' (something already catered for with the Diplock courts), the creation of a 'Young Ulster Community Service' to keep young people away from violence and the declaration of, 'if not a State of Emergency, a "State of Urgency"', a rather nebulous and bizarre concept.[86] On 2 April he demanded Provisional Sinn Féin be made illegal, asking: 'Why should they be allowed to abuse our democratic freedoms to endanger lives?' For Neave 'human rights should be the foremost concern of all democratic politicians' but the terrorist constituted the major threat to these 'not the security forces sweepingly maligned in the correspond- ence columns of London newspapers far from the front line'.[87] Two days later both House and Newman expressed irritation at his 'habit of going public with his latest anti-terrorist rostrum... without the real experience or knowledge to develop his ideas'.[88]

In May he claimed that 'the whole concept of a long, defensive, "war of attrition"' was 'completely wrong', attacking the government for failing to go on the offensive. Neave asked for 'a major "search and destroy opera- tion" over the next 12 months followed by a mopping up'. As part of this, the government should arrest 'at least 100 of the most dangerous mer- chants of terror, the "<u>Bonzen</u>" of the assassination squads'. He recom- mended an 'anti-terrorist brigade of specially trained regular troops' with 'training and experience in clandestine operations', remarking: 'It was Napoleon who said that the only way to beat guerrillas is by operating as guerrillas'.[89] The suggestions were extreme and incompatible with the Labour government's desire to avoid actions which would alienate the general population in Northern Ireland.

In early March James Molyneaux, UUUC leader at Westminster, requested a meeting with the prime minister because of 'the appalling casualties continuing unabated in Northern Ireland'.[90] Although the overall number of deaths in the first three months of 1977 was relatively low, some of the victims were more prominent than usual. On 2 February the manag- ing director of the local Du Pont plant, one of Northern Ireland's largest industrial establishments, was killed by the PIRA. Four further business- men were killed over the next six weeks. February also saw the killings of four members of the local security forces: two RUC reservists, one RUC officer and one UDR soldier.[91] On the same day that the UUUC meeting was scheduled the press reported that a unionist delegation would demand a fundamental review of security strategy. According to the News Letter, Ian Paisley warned that 'if the government continues to "opt out" of its security responsibilities, businessmen could opt out of their responsibili- ties by refusing to pay taxes and rates in a "passive protest"'.[92] In the meeting Paisley complained that 'during the period in which 26 people had been assassinated, and 245 injured, only one IRA terrorist had been shot in action'. James Callaghan replied that although the ratio was disappointing 'we should not overlook the fact that the government had to operate on a legal basis'.[93] The next month a section of the UUUC, in tandem with loyalist paramilitaries, sought to bring Northern Ireland to a halt in an attempted repetition of the UWC strike.

The UUAC strike

The political context of the 1977 strike was very different from three years earlier. In April 1977, the United Unionist Action Council (UUAC), formed by Ernest Baird of the United Ulster Unionist Movement (UUUM) and including the DUP, the UWC and all major loyalist paramilitary groups, organised a demonstration in support of five members of the Ulster Service Corps, a small paramilitary organisation, charged with mounting an illegal road block. Ian Paisley 'called for the expenditure of "blood, sweat and tears" in a campaign which would restore Stormont, return control of security policy to local hands, and lead to the extermination of the IRA'.[94] A special security meeting in the NIO surmised, however, that Paisley had been overtaken by the paramilitaries with whom he was dabbling and the emotional impetus would be dissatisfaction with the security situation.[95] Paisley and Baird were also left politically isolated by vocal opposition from the Ulster Unionists and Bill Craig. Craig and Harry West issued a joint statement expressing dissatisfaction with the government's security policy but condemning 'any loyalist action which might embarrass the security forces'.[96] Another key issue limiting support for the strike was the ongoing economic crisis in the UK and the fear of job losses in this climate. Negotiations in November and December 1976 between the Labour government and the International Monetary Fund brought home just how precarious its economic position was and few regions of the UK suffered from as precarious a position as Northern Ireland.[97] Just before the strike began it was announced that Shell had placed a £70 million order for two liquefied petroleum gas tankers from Harland & Wolff, which Mason believed was 'a critical factor' in preventing shipyard workers from supporting the strike.[98]

Three years of planning were conducted in anticipation of a second strike. After the collapse of the power-sharing executive all departments in the Northern Ireland Civil Service were asked to prepare reports on their experiences.[99] Frank Cooper established the Emergency Steering Committee (ESC) in June 1974. Senior army officers told ESC that since committing troops to one service had 'almost inevitably led to their involvement in others... the initial commitment of troops might only have real advantage as a delaying tactic'. Similarly, contingency plans for police involvement were hampered because of the dependence on public co-operation.[100]

A civil service report in November 1974 concluded that it was 'not possible to seek to maintain the general continuance of most commercial, industrial and essential life' if a major strike occurred again. It might be possible to maintain a lower level of services while letting industry come to a halt, but this required negotiation with the strikers and was sustainable for only a fortnight.[101] Frank Cooper told the ministerial committee on Northern Ireland that there were 'no conventional means of dealing with a full scale strike'.[102] By September 1975 each of the relevant Northern Ireland departments had produced contingency plans for industrial action.[103] The RUC made preparations for road blocks but only for 'priority routes', as in the Belfast operation in May 1974.[104] In October the NIO conducted 'Exercise Fastball', a simulated strike to test the operations room designed to co-ordinate responses by civil service departments and the security forces.[105]

A revised assessment of the government's strikebreaking capability concluded that if there was 'determined industrial action by the majority community, the armed forces would not be able to sustain essential services'. The government was unable to prevent a breakdown in electricity and gas; substitute labour from Great Britain would be unavailable, or unwilling, in sufficient numbers to strikebreak. They would also be unable to protect Catholics, as any attempt to guarantee supplies in, for example, West Belfast, would 'precipitate violence and sabotage which would effectively cut off the supplies'. The only real option was to 'nip such a strike in the bud' by arresting the ringleaders. In applying legal powers, it was recognised that action would need to be 'speedy and selective, employ minimum force, and concentrate on the arrests of local ring-leaders'. Intimidation, however, was difficult to combat because it required 'an inefficiently large manpower commitment' and as soon as the security forces' presence diminished the intimidators could move back in. The best response was deemed to be intensive publicity to encourage people to give information. The possibility of some sections of the RUC, UDR and Northern Ireland Civil Service choosing not to co-operate was raised. The government was advised to describe in public statements 'what was possible; to express a determination to do what could be done to deal with acute distress; but to make clear that what the government could do generally to alleviate suffering and hardship would be very limited indeed'.[106] There was little to suggest, despite the prevailing popular understanding of the handling of the UWC strike, that decisive ministers would easily overcome logistical difficulties.

On 25 April the contingency preparations were outlined to Mason, alongside recommendations to activate machinery such as the ESC and the operations room.[107] Mason emphasised that if a strike did take place the burden would remain with the police.[108] There was less doubt about the RUC's loyalty this time because of its centrality to the government's security strategy. The UUAC issued an ultimatum which appeared in the press on 26 April; if Mason did not begin 'a powerful and effective offensive against the IRA and announce steps to implement the Convention report' within seven days 'Ulster loyalists' would act.[109] Deputy Chief Constable Jack Hermon agreed with the NIO assessment that roads were the top priority. He said, however, that there were limits to police resources and a lot would depend on the nature of barriers – if they were heavy and physical, army equipment would be needed. Furthermore, 'many awkward decisions would be faced' as the removal of barriers could either provoke violence or weaken the strike. Newman believed it would be harder to 'talk down' the barricades this time round as 'the strikers appeared more fanatical' and knew their strength.[110]

Unlike in 1974, the GOC prepared in advance for a re-deployment of troops. He planned to request three regular battalions and call out the UDR to relieve three further battalions from routine duties. Minister of State Don Concannon expressed doubts about the reliability of the UDR but both Mason and House said their contribution was essential. It was agreed 'there was no chance of keeping Ballylumford out of the hands of the paramilitaries' and the West Belfast and Coolkeeragh stations, although operated by a 50% Catholic workforce, would be subject to intimidation. The Northern Ireland Electricity Service was confident that middle management would remain in place but, as in 1974, were unsure if they would stay there if the army was deployed to work in the stations. The idea of importing middle management from Great Britain was 'not "on"'.[111] On 28 April it was revealed that House's request for three battalions would be granted, with arrival set for noon on 2 May. Specialist troops, however, had to be assembled from different units all over Great Britain and would take longer to arrive. Once present their ability to maintain essential services would be 'strictly limited' without co-operation from middle management.[112]

On 30 April Paisley announced that if the strike failed he would leave politics.[113] When Mason met both the DUP leader and Baird on 2 May, the minister expressed surprise that they did not find it embarrassing to be linked with the UVF.[114] Mason and Paisley conducted a public exchange of letters at the beginning of the strike. Mason warned: 'You are playing the IRA game and you should realise it.'[115] He received an abusive reply in which Paisley claimed he would 'fight to the death' for 'the devastated

Province which I love'. Paisley attacked 'the drunkenness, lewdness, immorality and filthy language' of British politicians, declaring that 'Ulster Protestants are not interested in gaining the goodwill of such reprobates'. Mason wanted 'to crush the Protestant majority, destroy Protestant liberty, foist republicans into the government of Northern Ireland, and eventually bring Ulster into a united Ireland'.[116]

The importance of the machinery developed for handling the strike is reflected in the sheer wealth of records produced throughout its duration. The operations room kept a continuous log of events and issued thrice-daily situation reports.[117] The ESC met at 0730 each morning, with Mason briefing the media at 0900 and three press statements timed to catch the lunchtime, evening and following morning's news. Cubbon held a stock-taking meeting at noon each day to prepare the agenda for the special security meeting at 1800, immediately preceded by a meeting between House, Newman and himself.[118] Despite all these preparations, the first day of the strike was a difficult one for the government. On the night of 2 May the operations room recorded numerous instances of intimidation, including threats to the night shift at Harland & Wolff shipyards and the cutting of railway lines between Bangor and Belfast.[119] The following day electricity supplies remained normal with an extremely high turnout but major industrial concerns were heavily disrupted.[120] Although there was little open violence, threatening phone calls were made, bus services were seriously affected and flying pickets intimidated small businesses. Larne harbour closed after dockers walked out and fuel tanker drivers agreed to confine deliveries to hospitals, health centres and homes for the elderly.[121]

Speaking to Newman, Mason commended the RUC for their presence on the streets that morning and asked 'whether [it] might now be the time for action against the intimidators'. Newman replied that the RUC 'had a three-line whip out all day on intimidation' and most of the intimidation was by telephone, with 'nothing physical to meet on the streets'.[122] After a nervous first day the situation improved. On 4 May all main roads were open and industry reported an increased turnout. Bus services continued to be disrupted and minor roads were still blocked but a major effort to obstruct the Newtownards Road leading from East Belfast into the city centre was cleared by the police.[123] The GOC watched the Newtownards Road confrontation from a helicopter and 'thought that the RUC performance had been first class', though it was agreed there was 'still every chance of the paramilitaries precipitating a proper punch-up'.[124]

The power stations were again a focal point in the tug-of-war between the government and the strikers. Workers were unhappy with the idea of troops being used so assurances were given that this would not happen.[125] On the first day the General Secretary of the Electrical Power Engineers

Association, John Lyons, 'reiterated his belief that the troops would <u>never</u> have a role in the power stations' and complained about media attention.[126] The following day both Lyons and the head of the NIES, Jim Smyth, complained that attendances were being announced on the radio. The NIES's transport provision for workers was defeated in one instance when a crowd of roughly 100 stopped a bus on the Newtownards Road.[127]

On 5 May Mason met a deputation of Ballylumford staff. The workers felt they had 'become a political football between the government and the strikers'. The deputation said that the vast majority supported the aims of the UUAC but had doubts about their methods and did not want to be manipulated by either side. Security was the most important issue and they wanted evidence that the government had a will to defeat terrorism.[128] NIO officials considered how to present security policy in order to garner support, suggesting a concentration on surveillance and covert activity.[129] Mason issued a number of statements, sections of which were misleading. The week prior to the strike Mason publicly claimed that the number of SAS troops in Northern Ireland had been doubled. The MOD complained that this was untrue and Mason's private secretary promised it was based on a misunderstanding. On 2 May he claimed that 'the number of special security forces such as the SAS had been substantially increased and this trend would continue'. Joleon Dromgoole, Assistant Under-Secretary in the MOD, objected that this implied SAS numbers had increased, which was untrue, and that they would increase in the future, which was 'not feasible'.[130] When Mason met the Ballylumford workers he said that 'SAS type operations' had been doubled and 'this trend will continue'.[131] Both Dromgoole and the Deputy Under-Secretary for the army, P.T.E. England, advised the Defence Secretary Fred Mulley to send a letter to Mason 'pointing out, yet again, that what he said about the SAS is not true'. England, formerly Deputy Secretary of NIO Belfast, also could not help 'observing wryly' that much of the remaining content in Mason's statements was based on decisions made before his appointment.[132] Not knowing this, Ballylumford voted to continue working by 286 votes to 171.[133] Mason seized the opportunity to capitalise on doubts at Ballylumford but especially important was the difference in attitudes there from three years earlier.

The failure to secure support for the strike at Northern Ireland's biggest power station was crucial. The UUAC recognised this and intimidation increased on 7 May. Some of this took the form of picketing but most of the pressure came via telephone calls. As the situation became increasingly tense the RUC promised the workers protection. The workers decided that, because of the threat to them and their families, the day shift would walk out unless assurances came from the UUAC that they would not be subject to force. The Ballylumford workers received public statements of support from leading trade unionists, the Mayor of Larne, Bill Craig and James Molyneaux. The following morning attendance was sufficient for the power station to operate as normal.[134] Cubbon and Newman agreed that, in addition to keeping the roads open, their chief priority was to maintain protection for Ballylumford.[135]

The failure to gain sufficient support in the power stations meant the paramilitaries increasingly dominated the strike. The UFF declared: 'It is with great reluctance that we find ourselves in the position of having to coerce the loyalist people to support themselves.' Two buses were attacked in Protestant areas of Belfast on 8 May, with one driver wounded by a gunman.[136] On 10 May Paisley took part in a tractor blockade in Ballymena. Paisley, Baird and ten others were arrested around noon when they refused to cease obstructing roads and the blockade dispersed that afternoon.[137] Moments later the UDA shot dead a Protestant bus driver on Belfast's Crumlin Road.[138] Reports on attitudes in North and East Belfast recorded that Paisley's arrest had failed to arouse any sympathy, with some noting 'that he took care to be out of Belfast when the bus driver was murdered'.[139] Bus drivers ceased work in response to the murder but voted to return to work after the funeral of their colleague on 14 May.[140]

There was a more pronounced effort by Labour ministers to strengthen the resolve of various industries to keep operating. Don Concannon kept in close contact with trade union officials, making numerous phone calls.[141] This gave the NIO a greater knowledge of the situation, as well as allowing them to reassure workers that the government was responsive to their plight. On 4 May Concannon met a deputation of workers from Shorts and Harland & Wolff. As with the Ballylumford workers, the deputation 'did not object to the UUAC's end, only their means'. Although unable to satisfy their frustrations about the security situation entirely, Concannon and Jack Hermon were able to put the government's position with the meeting ending 'on a cordial note'.[142] This approach was not so successful with the Larne harbour dockers. By 9 May John Freeman of the Transport and General Workers' Union felt there was a chance the dockers would end their strike if Concannon met them to repeat Mason's assurances at Ballylumford. After Concannon arrived with a letter from Mason they still voted against re-opening.[143]

Another key area was the supply of petrol. The Department of Commerce held meetings with the oil companies. On 4 May the BP refinery manager said that only 30% of his staff had reported for work. Esso and Shell drivers were delivering supplies to UUAC-approved users but BP and smaller companies were not supplying at all – only 2–5% of Northern Ireland's consumption was delivered. The managers believed that the attitude of the drivers was motivated primarily by fear of intimidation and established a liaison with the UUAC.[144] NICS officials argued that the oil plan might have to be put into action but they were hesitant because soldiers would not be able to supply ordinary motorists.[145] The following day the UUAC relaxed its list of essential users and news came through that all drivers would revert to normal delivers on 6 May.[146] On 12 May, however, a petrol tanker driver was attacked. Concannon was given the unusual task of keeping union leaders inside Stormont Castle for as long as possible to prevent them declaring a cessation of work.[147] They arrived at 0915 on 13 May and had a series of meetings with officials, senior army officers and policemen, tempered by recesses for discussion amongst themselves and with senior oil managers. The timing of involving managers was deliberately set to coincide with the beginning of BP's afternoon shift. At 2130, twelve hours and fifteen minutes after arriving, the deputation left Stormont.[148] At midnight Paisley announced the end of the strike and said he would not leave politics because the strike had been a partial success.[149]

Callaghan congratulated Mason in a personal minute, declaring that he had 'displayed courage and firmness against these dangerous men'.[150] Mason proudly quoted the document in his memoirs, though he claimed the victory was not his but that of the ordinary men and women who 'kept alive a hope for Ulster that might otherwise have been crushed beneath the hobnailed boots of Ian Paisley and the forces behind him'.[151] Even after three years of preparation the strike was a close-run affair. Many of the difficulties experienced in May 1974 were repeated. Mason's post-strike request for improvements in army training so they could operate power stations was rebuffed by his security advisors.[152] The NIO concluded they had been successful for a number of reasons: the mass of unionist opinion was not convinced that the strike would solve their problems; unionist leaders were unwilling to cede ground to Paisley and fought back 'with some skill and tenacity'; trade unions proved far more effective; there was mutual suspicion between the groups comprising the UUAC; and the government's response was unified in the absence of a power-sharing executive.[153] The great improvement in machinery for handling the strike should be added to this list, but what stands out most is the political context. Direct rule seemed far less threatening to the union than Sunningdale.

Intensification

Mason continued his publicity efforts to obtain support for the Labour government's security policy, declaring after the UUAC strike that there would be an 'intensification' of the existing strategy.[154] He told Fred Mulley that although the Ulster Unionist Party had rejected the UUAC they made it 'very clear that they are no less concerned about the security situation'. He judged that, while the essential features of security policy should remain the same, they needed to be seen to have reinforced its effectiveness. As part of this he raised the issue of the UDR expansion. After the Treasury refused to help the MOD it agreed in December 1976 to an increase of only 200 recruits, rather than the 900 proposed. Mason told Mulley that the GOC believed there were 'good military reasons' for 'finding a way through the financial difficulty'.[155] On 10 May Cubbon gave Mason a list of possible measures for a security package. Cubbon thought an extra SAS squadron might be possible, or a 'stepping up [of] covert, SAS-type activities' by regular army units. In terms of presentation, Mason was advised to point to a more independent and stronger police force, showing increasing professionalism, improved arrangements for feeding army information into CID (emphasising that this included information gathered from covert observation posts) and the declining importance of troop numbers because of reductions in street disorder. Cubbon also suggested meeting political parties to 'patiently and confidentially' run through security policy.[156]

As the strike approached its end Mason met House and Newman. Newman described progress in establishing a special RUC squad dedicated to 'home in on the ringleaders of violence'. He was convinced that this would yield good results but progress was slow and he had difficulty 'getting across the concept of a gradual build up of dossiers on selected targets' and the careful sifting of material for acceptable evidence'. The GOC expressed 'some disappointment' that Mason did not propose 'a "root and branch" review', suggesting they should concentrate 'on "cutting corners", particularly in regard to the rules of evidence'. He was hopeful, however, that the suggested improvements were possible.[157]

As part of this 'intensification', Mason wrote to Merlyn Rees seeking the support of police forces in Great Britain. He compared the difficulty of bringing 'so-called Godfathers' to trial with the experience of gang bosses such as the Krays in London, noting that the use of experienced detectives had yielded success in England. Newman's detectives were overstretched and could not concentrate exclusively on two or three cases so he asked that a Detective Chief Superintendant sent by New Scotland Yard to assist during the UUAC strike be retained for another six months.[158]

Four days later he wrote to Rees again, arguing that the rapid expansion of the Special Branch and CID had caused the proportion of uniformed officers to decline to 37%. This practice of 'creaming off experienced men for specialist tasks' left the uniformed branch young and inexperienced with 50% of the force having served for less than five years. Following discussion with Newman, he told Rees that the RUC needed 100 CID members and 24 further staff for support services such as fingerprinting.

There had previously been ad hoc recruitment from Great Britain but in small numbers (forty-nine since 1973). Mason therefore asked Rees to encourage Chief Constables in Great Britain to respond favourably to approaches from the RUC and to encourage promising policemen to volunteer for placements.[159] Rees said the Home Office was keen to help and left the matter to his officials.[160] Bruce Millan, Secretary of State for Scotland, described how both Scottish and English police chiefs felt the proposed package was not attractive enough. The Scottish chiefs also had 'grave doubts' about the desirability of encouraging experienced CID officers to leave 'undermanned' forces when crime was rising in their own areas.[161]

Mason had similar difficulties with the MOD. Noting the belief 'almost universally held in Protestant circles' that progress against the PIRA would be greater if there were more troops, Mason agreed with Mulley that public opinion had to be educated to accept 'that numbers alone are relatively unimportant now'. The problem was obtaining evidence against 'small groups of terrorists' rather than handling riots. He argued that the best way to do this was to convince the public that counter-terrorist skills were improving by publicising an intensification of covert operations. Mason spoke of the 'tremendous and lasting boost for public morale' caused by the SAS's involvement in Northern Ireland, 'borne out by the satisfaction which has greeted every hint...of a build-up in "SAS-type" operations'.[162] On 24 May the NIO produced a text on covert operations. It stressed that more was being done in the field of covert activity than the public realised but specialist detachments from the Royal Marine Commandos and the Parachute Regiment would be deployed in a covert role, training in covert operations would be increased with regular troops being used in this area more often, and a 'special command and control group' formed to co-ordinate special operations (known as 615 Intelligence Group).[163]

When Mason met Mulley the latter complained that the NIO 'had been forcing the pace on a number of issues and made a plea that he be bounced "only once per week"'. The two ministers decided it was unnecessary to call a meeting of the ministerial committee on Northern Ireland (which met only three times in 1977) and instead opted to write to James Callaghan.[164] The letter set out an agreement on the extra 700 UDR troops. The Treasury insisted there could be no overall increase in public expenditure until 1979/80. As the MOD continued to refuse to budge and the only expected financial difficulty was now restricted to the 1978/79 period, Mason agreed that if the MOD went over budget because of UDR costs the NIO would contribute 50% of the amount. As for the increase in covert operations which had been so prominent in Mason's public statements, the latter informed Callaghan there would be a genuine increase in activity but the details would not be made public. Mason was persuaded that no more SAS troops were available. He instead outlined the attachment of platoons from the Royal Marines and the Parachute Regiment described above, effectively doubling the size of the Northern Ireland Patrol Group (NIPG). The NIPG's task, Mason wrote, was to mount covert patrols, though these did 'not go as far as SAS type operations'.[165]

On 1 June Mason gave Callaghan a breakdown of the 'intensification' package. He proposed to give 'pride of place' to the steps to strengthen the RUC. These included a lengthy list of measures such as the reorganisation of the RUC's HQ crime squad and the introduction of three new regional crime squads, a new criminal intelligence section at headquarters with criminal intelligence units in each region and division, the strengthening of the fingerprints branch and an increase of 'about 150' detectives and other experts working on terrorism.[166] Although the description given to Callaghan did say that these were measures already taken, it was not acknowledged that they had actually been implemented the previous year as a result of the Bourn proposals.[167] The new steps to improve the RUC were in reality rather small, including 'efforts to attract further specialists from police forces in Great Britain', the successful secondment of a senior officer from New Scotland Yard (as in Mason's correspondence with Rees), a statement that the present RUC establishment of 6,500 was not 'an all-time ceiling' (merely an explicit statement of policy since the Bourn proposals), and an examination of further civilianisation of backroom posts. Lastly, Mason proposed small changes in legal provisions. These were to increase the maximum penalties for conspiracy to murder and possession of explosives with intent to life imprisonment and to increase the maximum penalty for membership of a proscribed organisation from 5 years to 10.[168] As such the 'intensification' package amounted to an explicit description of decisions already taken, with further, relatively small improvements.

It was more significant for its political impact. When he made his speech on 8 June, Airey Neave claimed that almost every measure proposed by Mason had been suggested by the Conservatives over the past three years. Other responses were far more positive. The Times reported 'a much greater emphasis on the intelligence gathering activities of the army' and that Mason had 'again demonstrated an outward determination to stamp out terrorism'.[169] The Ulster Unionist Party was pleased, privately telling the NIO that they 'were delighted, both with the Secretary of State and with his current security policy'.[170] Austin Currie of the SDLP said he was worried about the emphasis on 'SAS-type activity' because 'many of these people are a law unto themselves', while the party issued a statement that Mason had sought to 'appease the growing clamour from loyalist leaders and from the Conservative spokesman on Northern Ireland'.[171] It was in the aftermath of May 1977 that Mason earned his reputation as a tough minister. This was based not on changing security policy but on the success against loyalist strikers and his willingness to capitalise on this by appealing specifically to unionists. This emphasis on courting the unionist community made his tenure particularly alienating to moderate nationalists in the SDLP.

The Pritchard review

Just prior to the UUAC strike, Brian Cubbon expressed his desire for a review of the implementation of the Bourn proposals, particularly concerning the capability and human resources of the various security forces. The GOC and Chief Constable agreed, though Cubbon tellingly reminded House that it would be purely concerned with implementation rather than the basic concepts of Bourn's report.[172] Anthony Pritchard was asked to undertake the study.[173] The committee conducting the review included Jack Hermon, the army's Chief of Staff Brigadier Body as well as a senior official from the MOD.

On 19 May the secretary circulated a progress report. It recorded that RUC strength was, as of 30 April, at 5,408 against the Bourn recommendation of 7,500. Full-time RUC reservists stood at 925 against the Bourn figure of 2,200. At the end of 1976 a new Special Patrol Group had been established in Omagh bringing the total to nine with a strength of 305 officers. Two mobile support units were operating in rural areas and others were in training. Criminal Intelligence Units were formed with a network of local offices overseen by a Chief Inspector. A fraud squad had been established and some surveillance teams formed with others on the way. Only 7.6% of the intake in 1976 had been Catholic. There had been a reduction of one major army unit since June 1976 bringing the figure to twelve. UDR strength was 1,693, against the Bourn figure of 2,400 (representing almost full recruitment when taking into account that the financial disagreements had stopped the upping of the limit to Bourn's recommendation). The regiment operated one permanent vehicle check-point on a full-time basis and two on a part-time basis. Finally, a public relations group was established leading to 'extensive advertising on the TV and in the press on the theme "7 years is enough"', a campaign which the NIO felt had been well received.[174]

When the group held its first meeting they discussed RUC recruitment. It was reckoned that an establishment of 6,500 regular officers could be achieved by 1981/82, despite the Bourn committee's hopes that by this time it would be 7,500. The group believed a significant increase in recruiting could not happen without a better response from Catholics.

Furthermore, although the regional crime squads were deemed to have been successful, they were also 'over-worked'. Four key requirements were identified: to improve the effectiveness of the RUC reserve, to increase police acceptability in Catholic areas, to establish the role of the RUC in riot situations, and to expand the role of the UDR.[175]

The discussions led D.R. Ford, under-secretary for information, to tell Cubbon they were 'over-optimistically pinning our hopes' on the 'intensification' package and that their 'prospects of getting more policemen from the UK [*sic*] are fading'. He asked whether they could not look into raising RUC pay and incentives to bring policemen across from Great Britain.[176] Pritchard told Cubbon that an increase in pay seemed extremely unlikely as they were already well paid by British standards and he was 'not convinced that higher pay would induce the type of man we want to join'. Electing not to include Ford in the correspondence but instead to speak to him separately, Pritchard remarked 'time can be wasted and false expectations raised by wild ideas which could more sensibly be dismissed as a result of a few minutes discussion between room neighbours'.[177] Such tension reveals how the specialisation of under-secretaries prompted disagreements when they raised other issues with superiors.

Recruitment remained at the heart of discussion. A meeting chaired by Brian Cubbon concluded that the recruitment rate 'would prove insufficient to fulfil the Government's objectives'. It was agreed that HR requirements should be separated into two elements: those needed to undertake policing in nationalist areas (primarily uniformed) and those needed to deal with paramilitary activity (primarily CID, Special Branch and Special Patrol Groups). In early July Cubbon held another internal meeting to discuss differences between army headquarters and the NIO over the UDR. The army believed the regiment should have a role in urban crowd control and riot situations, whereas the NIO felt they were unfit for this role 'for political and operational reasons'. Whereas the army hoped to extend UDR operations as a means to relieve the regular army, the NIO's position 'implied that in the medium term the UDR would continue to be restricted to relatively humdrum and unattractive duties; and that in the longer term as violence diminished, the police would take on an increasing proportion of the duties carried out by the UDR...with the regular army in support'. The NIO also wanted 'to avoid premature momentum building up behind the idea of further reductions' in troops.[178] It was becoming apparent that Bourn's projections for recruitment were unlikely to be achieved.

Pritchard's interim report updated the threat assessment from 1976. It recorded that while violence and its 'underlying historical causes' remained, demonstrations and marches leading to riots had declined, as had shooting incidents, the number of explosions and the weight of explosives used. Pritchard's group identified four areas for further study: the future HR requirements and capability of the RUC, the future size and employment of the RUC reserve, the future role of the UDR, and the future size of the army. It proposed to conduct the first three of these.[179] The group wanted to include the army study but the Chief of Staff insisted that it was the GOC's responsibility and should be left to him.[180] Cubbon, House and Newman agreed.[181]

By mid-October the Pritchard group completed its studies. The UDR paper concluded that the ban on involving them in civil disorder should not be relaxed and the regiment should not be used to aid the RUC in 'the hard urban areas of West Belfast and West Londonderry'. The primary role of the UDR would continue to be military patrolling, searching and guard duties, with a relaxation in these activities as security improved. The responsibilities given to UDR battalions in some areas, primarily in the North and East, meant that regular army units operated under their command, except in public disorder situations. Pritchard informed Cubbon that such direct support 'by a predominantly Protestant force will arouse misgivings amongst the minority as this extension spreads across mixed or predominantly Catholic areas'. As a consequence, any proposals to extend UDR responsibility would have to be judged against opinion in that area, making the judgement as much a political as a security matter.[182] As in 1976, the Ulsterisation concept was misleading and the position within the NIO was one of opposition to putting the UDR in the front line of the conflict. This was not publicly appreciated because the Labour government could not be so transparent as to assert that the regiment was unacceptable in mixed or nationalist areas. This would have undermined UDR morale and brought great criticism from unionists and possibly Airey Neave.

The RUC study recommended no change in the roles of regular officers or reservists. In HR terms, however, having not publicly committed to the Bourn figure of 7,500 because the previous commitment of 6,500 was not yet reached, Pritchard said there was 'some discussion about the need for a settled future establishment, the lack of which is starting to affect plans for logistic support in the long term'.[183] The study contained detailed figures of the make-up of RUC officers along with future plans (see table 1).

If achieved, the study noted, it would give a ratio of police to population almost twice that of Merseyside, which itself held the highest ratio in Great Britain. The estimation did not take account of part-time reservists, civil-ianisation of administrative duties and overtime, so they concluded that 'current RUC estimates support the required strength of 7,500'. A greater degree of analysis was given to Catholic attitudes towards the police than during the Bourn investigation, partly because of the explicit recognition

Table 1 Future RUC requirements

	Present strength	Proposed future strength	Increase
Special Branch	256	413	157
CID	722	937	215
Operations – HQ	255	391	136
Traffic	231	721	490
SPG	313	632	319
Uniformed operational	3,069	4,216	1,147
Community relations	77	116	39
Administration, planning and training	295	392	97
Miscellaneous requirement	368	368	0
Total	**5,586**	**8,186**	**2,600**

Source: TNA, CJ4/1783, Security Forces' Capability: Royal Ulster Constabulary and Royal Ulster Constabulary Reserve, undated.

that improvement was needed for recruitment in the future. The idea of a virtuous circle of success and recruitment was reasserted, however, as was the significance of the attitude of Catholic leaders and the 'inhibiting factor' of PIRA activities. Some 9% of the police force was Catholic and there was clearly a long way to go before this mirrored the percentage of the general population. The study argued that the current approach of extending police activities, especially community relations work, was the key to increasing Catholic participation.[184]

Until the end of October 1977 Roy Mason had no involvement, though he knew that the review was taking place. Cubbon briefed him, recommending that future HR needs for the RUC be looked into, the expansion of the UDR's territorial responsibilities be carefully monitored and the MOD be asked to conduct a deeper study into the regiment's future shape and size.[185] Mason agreed to the recommendations, leaving Cubbon pleased with the exercise and proposing to repeat it the following year.[186] This fitted into a general pattern in the relationship between the permanent secretary and the Labour minister on security policy; with the exception of the 'intensification' initiative after the UUAC strike, all proposals for security reviews came from Cubbon and Mason simply approved their conclusions.

In November Mulley and Mason wrote to members of the ministerial committee on Northern Ireland arguing that the security situation had improved significantly since the spring, as had the public image of it. They proposed to reduce troop levels over the coming year. Towards the end of

1978 another resident battalion would arrive in Northern Ireland, matched by a reduction in a roulement unit of similar numbers. 100 Royal Military Policeman would be withdrawn to make room for the resident battalion and a further roulement unit would not be replaced when its tour ended in December 1978. This would result in a reduction in the force level from 14,200 to about 13,000.[187] Tellingly the ministerial committee discussed this only briefly, agreeing that further reductions should be considered if the security situation continued to improve in the New Year.[188] Debate on security within the committee was almost non-existent in 1977, with the exception of one meeting on the UUAC strike. The number of killings remained at a level much lower than the previous five years, the basic principles of police primacy and criminalisation held sway and neither Mason or Callaghan felt the need for discussion. Northern Ireland was a far less pressing problem for Labour ministers from 1977 onwards.

Conclusion

From 1976 there was a substantial shift in security policy which favoured the police over the army. While there had been attempts to move in this direction earlier, it was during this period that the long-term aspirations of Rees and senior civil servants in the NIO finally began to bear fruit. Following the Bourn proposals the RUC became increasingly professionalised. There were of course limitations; the outcome planned for required a great deal of time and resources to be achieved and violence remained high in 1976. This led senior army officers, such as David House, to call for further changes to the legal system to make convictions easier. More crudely, Airey Neave displayed the persistent temptation to reach for aggressive military solutions to the conflict. Both standpoints were resisted and in 1977 there was a significant improvement in the security situation which reinforced the principles of police primacy. The process was not one of Ulsterisation; the army remained prominent in republican areas and the UDR's role was far more limited than has been assumed.

Loyalist killings decreased dramatically during this period (from 120 deaths in 1976 to 26 in 1977 and 10 in 1978). The PIRA was also unable to maintain the level of violence that had pertained prior to the 1975 ceasefire. The number of deaths resulting from the conflict fell from 308 in 1976 to 116 in 1977 and 88 in 1978.[189] The reasons for this are many and difficult to rank in importance. It is questionable whether the high level of sectarian violence, prompted in part by the uncertainties surrounding the political future of Northern Ireland and the PIRA's ceasefire, was sustainable. It became increasingly apparent that direct rule would remain for the foreseeable future. The defeat of a second loyalist general strike was a particularly important moment for the Labour government and weakened the influence of Protestant paramilitaries. The new security strategy was thought to be a successful one, with much greater success in getting paramilitary volunteers through the court system and into the prisons. There are also likely to be numerous other aspects to the change which are currently (and will likely remain) incredibly difficult for the historian to reconstruct, particularly in the area of intelligence and covert activity.

Although it was an appealing explanation to some at the time, there is good reason to doubt the extent to which Roy Mason's appointment as Secretary of State for Northern Ireland was a factor. His reputation for conducting an aggressive campaign against the PIRA and facing down loyalist intransigence during the UUAC strike, a stance which Rees was deemed too weak-willed and indecisive to adopt, is not deserved. Security policies during Mason's tenure were almost entirely agreed before his appointment. Merlyn Rees, Frank Cooper and Brian Cubbon showed a commitment to the general principle of shifting away from military-minded security measures in order to remove some of the feelings of injustice that motivated militant republicans. Successive studies chaired by civil servants such as John Bourn and Anthony Pritchard produced proposals to achieve these objectives. Mason rarely took the initiative but, rather, sided with his officials against military advisors.

What Mason contributed was rhetoric. Rees's preference for secrecy was replaced with a bullish approach. Mason was preoccupied with the need to head off public criticism, whether by the press, Neave or from the unionist community. This played an important role in the failure of the UUAC strike, though the political context was more important. After the UUAC strike his 'intensification package' sought to head off criticism and gain the support of Ulster Unionists. The package in reality described decisions taken before his appointment with minor additions. Desiring public support, Mason made statements giving false hope for the eradication of terrorism. In the case of SAS activity, his statements were untruthful. The Pritchard review also marked the beginning of an acceptance within the NIO that police primacy and criminalisation could only have a limited effect on the PIRA's capacity to wage its campaign. There were still many limitations to the Labour government's strategy.

Notes

1 Hew Strachan, *The politics of the British army* (Oxford: Oxford University Press, 1997), p. 164.
2 James Callaghan, *Time and chance* (London: Politico's, 2006), pp. 387, 392–3.

3 Christopher Andrew, *The defence of the realm: the authorised history of MI5* (London: Allen Lane, 2009), p. 646.

4 The McGuinness quote was proudly included in the dustjacket of Mason's memoirs: *Daily Telegraph*, 18 April 2004; Roy Mason, *Paying the price* (London: Robert Hale, 1999).

5 Patterson, *Ireland since 1939*, p. 251; see also Edwards's similar description of 'a tough talking former miner who had no truck with terrorists': Aaron Edwards, '"A whipping boy if ever there was one"? The British army and the politics of civil–military relations in Northern Ireland 1969–79', *Contemporary British History*, 28:2 (2014), p. 177.

6 See also Peter Neumann, 'Winning the "war on terror"? Roy Mason's contribution to counter-terrorism in Northern Ireland', *Small Wars & Insurgencies*, 14:3 (2003), pp. 45–64.

7 TNA, CJ4/1197, MLO(76) meeting 1, 28 January 1976.

8 TNA, CJ4/1197, MLO(76) memo 3, undated.

9 TNA, CJ4/1197, Interim report of the official working party on law and order in Northern Ireland, undated.

10 TNA, CJ4/1197, MLO(76) meeting 2, 12 May 1976.

11 TNA, CJ4/1208, Webster to Barker, 25 March 1976.

12 TNA, CJ4/1779, GOC to CLF, 7 April 1976.

13 TNA, CJ4/1779, Newman to GOC, 16 April 1976.

14 Quoted in Andrew, *The defence of the realm*, p. 645.

15 TNA, CAB 134/4039, IN(76) memo 3, 20 May 1976.

16 TNA, CAB 134/4039, IN(76) memo 7, 24 May 1976.

17 TNA, CJ4/1198, Neave to Rees, 21 May 1976.

18 Hansard (Commons), 913, cols 37–41.

19 Hansard (Commons), 913, cols 46–55.

20 LSE, MERLYN-REES/1/10, Transcript of tapes, undated, p. 52.

21 LSE, MERLYN-REES/1/10, Transcript of tapes, undated, p. 7.

22 TNA, CJ4/1204, MLO memo 6, undated.

23 TNA, CJ4/1204, MLO memo 6, undated.

24 TNA, CJ4/1197, MLO meeting 3, 30 June 1976.

25 Hansard (Commons), 914, cols 880–4.

26 Hansard (Commons), 914, cols 906–913.

27 TNA, PREM 16/963, Thatcher to Callaghan, 6 July 1976.

28 TNA, PREM 16/963, Rees to Callaghan, 9 July 1976.

29 TNA, CJ4/1212, Bourn to Janes, 14 July 1976.

30 TNA, CJ4/1212, Bourn to Newman, 26 July 1976; TNA, CJ4/1212, Bourn to Janes, 12 July 1976.

31 TNA, CJ4/1201, Dromgoole to Bourn, 21 June 1976.

32 TNA, CJ4/1201, Bourn to Dromgoole, 23 June 1976.

33 TNA, CJ4/1806, Dromgoole to Hansford, 13 August 1976.

34 TNA, CJ4/1806, Hansford to Dromgoole, 25 August 1976.

35 TNA, CJ4/1806, Leech to Gatlish, 8 November 1976.

36 McKittrick *et al.*, *Lost lives*, p. 1553.

37 TNA, CJ4/1779, GOC to Cubbon, 22 June 1976.
38 TNA, CJ4/1779, Cubbon to Rees, 22 June 1976.
39 TNA, CJ4/1779, Rees to GOC, 23 August 1976.
40 TNA, CJ4/2521, GOC to Rees, 25 August 1976.
41 TNA, CJ4/1779, GOC to Rees, 1 September 1976.
42 TNA, CJ4/1779, GOC to Rees, 1 September 1976.
43 McKittrick *et al.*, *Lost lives*, pp. 669–70, 819.
44 *The Times*, 27 September 1976.
45 McKittrick *et al.*, *Lost lives*, pp. 663–5; TNA, PREM 16/1341, Hickman to Crosland, 25 July 1976.
46 Patterson, *Ireland's violent frontier*, pp. 100–3.
47 Patterson, *Ireland's violent frontier*, pp. 103–4.
48 *The Times*, 10 August 1976.
49 *The Times*, 19 August 1976.
50 TNA, CJ4/1779, Janes to England, 15 September 1976.
51 *The Times*, 28 September 1976.
52 TNA, CJ4/2521, Cubbon to Mason, 3 December 1976.
53 *The Times*, 10 August 1976; *The Times*, 6 October 1976; Hansard (Commons), 918, col. 687.
54 TNA, CJ4/2521, Cubbon to Mason, 3 December 1976.
55 TNA, CJ4/2521, Stewart to PS/PUS, 6 December 1976.
56 TNA, CJ4/1696, Cubbon to Stephens, 14 December 1976.
57 Hansard (Commons), 922, cols 1933–9.
58 Hansard (Commons), 922, cols 1947–9.
59 TNA, CJ4/1650, Buxton to Cubbon, 6 January 1977.
60 TNA, CJ4/1779, Cubbon to Mason, 14 January 1977.
61 TNA, CJ4/1651, Meeting between Mason, GOC and Chief Constable, 17 January 1977.
62 TNA, CJ4/1696, Stephens to Cubbon, 18 February 1977.
63 TNA, CJ4/1779, Meeting between the Permanent Under-Secretary of State (PUS), GOC and the Chief Constable, 28 February 1977.
64 TNA, CJ4/1779, Official security policy meeting, 16 March 1977.
65 TNA, CJ4/1779, Meeting between Mason, GOC and Chief Constable, 22 March 1977.
66 Graham Ellison and Jim Smyth, *The crowned harp: policing Northern Ireland* (London: Pluto, 2000), pp. 84, 104.
67 TNA, CJ4/1293, Directive for the General Officer Commanding Northern Ireland, 14 March 1973.
68 TNA, CJ4/1650, Joint Directive by General Officer Commanding Northern Ireland and Chief Constable Royal Ulster Constabulary, 12 January 1977
69 TNA, CJ4/1650, Cubbon to Mason, 21 December 1976.
70 TNA, CJ4/1651, Annex A of Stephens to PS/SSNI, 12 January 1977.
71 *Irish Times*, 13 May 1976; *The Times*, 7 Jun 1976.
72 Hansard (Commons), 926, cols 1491–1533.
73 TNA, CJ4/1653, Pritchard to PUS, 25 March 1977.

74 Robert White, *Ruairí Ó Brádaigh: the life and politics of an Irish revolutionary* (Bloomington: Indiana University Press, 2006), p. 255.
75 Patterson, *Ireland since 1939*, p. 250.
76 Tommy McKearney, *The Provisional IRA: from insurrection to parliament* (London: Pluto, 2011), pp. 139–40.
77 Neumann, *Britain's long war*, pp. 189–90.
78 Neumann, *Britain's long war*, p. 190; Peter Neumann, 'The myth of Ulsterisation in British security policy in Northern Ireland' in *Studies in Conflict & Terrorism*, 26 (2003).
79 TNA, CJ4/2294, Report of the working group to consider progress on security, undated; Neumann, *Britain's long war*, p. 190.
80 McKittrick *et al.*, *Lost lives*, p. 1552.
81 TNA, CJ4/1653, Pritchard to PUS, 25 March 1977.
82 TNA, CJ4/1653, Pritchard to PUS, 25 March 1977.
83 TNA, CJ4/1653, Cubbon to Pritchard, 4 April 1977.
84 Parliamentary Archives (PA), Airey Neave papers, AN/532, Statement by Airey Neave, 17 January 1977.
85 Hansard (Commons), 927, col. 1620.
86 PA, Neave, AN/531, Speech to Abingdon Conservatives, 12 March 1977.
87 PA, Neave, AN/531, Speech to Northern Area Young Conservatives, 2 April 1977.
88 TNA, CJ4/1653, Meeting between PUS, GOC and Chief Constable, 4 April 1977.
89 PA, Neave, AN/532, Speech to Abingdon Conservative Club, 23 April 1977.
90 TNA, PREM 16/1343, Molyneaux to Callaghan, 2 March 1977.
91 McKittrick *et al.*, *Lost lives*, pp. 702–9.
92 *News Letter*, 16 March 1977.
93 TNA, PREM 16/1343, Meeting between Callaghan and UUUC, 16 March 1977.
94 *Irish Times*, 25 April 1977; TNA, CJ4/1566, Elliott to Neilson, 25 April 1977.
95 TNA, CJ4/1566, Special security meeting, 25 April 1977.
96 TNA, CJ4/1566, Elliott to Neilson, 25 April 1977.
97 Kevin Hickson, *The IMF crisis of 1976 and British politics* (London: Tauris, 2005).
98 TNA, PREM 16/1344, Mason to Callaghan, 16 June 1977.
99 TNA, CJ4/777, Parkes to all permanent secretaries, 6 June 1974.
100 TNA, CJ4/777, ESC(74) meeting 1, 26 June 1974.
101 TNA, CAB 134/3779, IRN(74) memo 25, 21 November 1974.
102 TNA, CAB 134/3778, IRN(74) meeting 10, 4 December 1974.
103 TNA, CJ4/781, Meeting of the Emergency Steering Committee, 12 September 1975.
104 TNA, CJ4/781, England to PUS, 22 September 1975.
105 TNA, CJ4/781, Bourn to England, 13 October 1975.
106 CAB 134/3921, IRN memo 25, 7 November 1975.
107 TNA, CJ4/1566, Pritchard to Mason, 25 April 1977.

108 TNA, CJ4/1566, Special security meeting, 25 April 1977.

109 *The Times*, 26 April 1977.

110 TNA, CJ4/1566, Special security meeting, 26 April 1977.

111 TNA, CJ4/1566, Special security meeting, 26 April 1977.

112 TNA, CAB 134/4039, IN(77) meeting 2, 28 April 1977.

113 TNA, PREM 16/1344, Mason to Callaghan, 17 May 1977.

114 TNA, CJ4/1577, Meeting between Mason, Paisley and Baird, 2 May 1977.

115 TNA, CJ4/1567, Mason to Paisley, 3 May 1977.

116 TNA, CJ4/1567, Paisley to Mason, 3 May 1977.

117 TNA, CJ4/1572, Situation reports; TNA, CJ4/1573–4, NIOR log sheets.

118 TNA, CJ4/1567, PS/PUS to PS/SSNI, 4 May 1977.

119 TNA, CJ4/1573, NIOR log sheet, 2 May 1977.

120 TNA, CJ4/1572, Situation report at 1100 hours, 3 May 1977.

121 TNA, CJ4/1572, Situation report at 1600 hours, 3 May 1977.

122 TNA, CJ4/1567, Telephone conversation between Mason and Chief Constable, 3 May 1977.

123 TNA, CJ4/1572, Situation report at 1100 hours, 4 May 1977; TNA, CJ4/1572, Situation report at 1600 hours, 4 May 1977.

124 TNA, CJ4/1575, Special security meeting, 4 May 1977.

125 TNA, CJ4/1566, Special security meeting, 29 April 1977.

126 TNA, CJ4/1567, Telephone conversation with Lyons, 3 May 1977.

127 TNA, CJ4/1567, Telephone conversation with Lyons, 4 May 1977; TNA, CJ4/1567, Gilliland to Ford, 4 May 1977.

128 TNA, CJ4/1567, Meeting between Mason and Ballylumford workers, 5 May 1977.

129 TNA, CJ4/1653, Stephens to PS/PUS, 29 April 1977; TNA, CJ4/1653, Bourn to Stephens, 2 May 1977.

130 TNA, DEFE 13/1402, Dromgoole to Bourn, 3 May 1977.

131 TNA, CJ4/1567, Meeting between Mason and Ballylumford workers, 5 May 1977.

132 TNA, DEFE 13/1402, Dromgoole to APS/SSDEF, 6 May 1977; TNA, DEFE 13/1402, England to PS/SSDEF, 6 May 1977.

133 Mason, *Paying the price*, p. 187.

134 TNA, CJ4/1567, Ballylumford: 7/8 May, 8 May 1977.

135 TNA, CJ4/1567, Cubbon to Mason, 8 May 1977.

136 TNA, CJ4/1567, Meeting on political aspects of the security situation, 9 May 1977.

137 TNA, CJ4/1567, Buxton to Wicks, 10 May 1977.

138 McKittrick *et al.*, *Lost lives*, pp. 720–1.

139 TNA, CJ4/1567, Elliott to Ford, 11 May 1977.

140 TNA, CJ4/1572, Situation report at 1600 hours, 13 May 1977.

141 TNA, CJ4/1572, Note by Masefield, 4 May 1977; TNA, CJ4/1577, Note by Masefield, 5 May 1977.

142 TNA, CJ4/1577, Meeting between Concannon and Short Brothers and Harland & Wolff shop stewards, 4 May 1977.

143 TNA, CJ4/1577, Meeting between Concannon and Larne Harbour deputa-
     tion, 9 May 1977; TNA, CJ4/1577, Mason to Larne Harbour Deputation, 9
     May 1977; TNA, CJ4/1577, Note by Pritchard, 10 May 1977.
144 TNA, CJ4/1571, Meeting between officials and the Oil Industry Emergency
     Committee, 4 May 1977.
145 TNA, CJ4/1567, Permanent Secretaries meeting, 4 May 1977.
146 TNA, CJ4/1571, Meeting between officials and the Oil Industry Emergency
     Committee, 5 May 1977.
147 Mason, *Paying the price*, pp. 194–5.
148 TNA, CJ4/1567, Synopsis of meetings between Concannon and tanker driver
     representatives, 13 May 1977.
149 TNA, PREM 16/1344, Mason to Callaghan, 17 May 1977.
150 TNA, PREM 16/1344, Callaghan to Mason, 17 May 1977.
151 Mason, *Paying the price*, p. 197.
152 TNA, CJ4/1567, Waterfield to Janes, 11 May 1977.
153 TNA, PREM 16/1344, Mason to Callaghan, 17 May 1977.
154 *Irish Times*, 9 June 1977.
155 TNA, PREM 16/1343, Kenneally to Mulley, 6 May 1977.
156 TNA, CJ4/1654, Cubbon to Mason, 10 May 1977.
157 TNA, CJ4/1654, Meeting between Mason, the GOC and the Chief Constable,
     12 May 1977.
158 TNA, PREM 16/1344, Mason to Rees, 16 May 1977.
159 TNA, PREM 16/1344, Mason to Rees, 20 May 1977.
160 TNA, PREM 16/1344, Rees to Mason, 13 June 1977.
161 TNA, PREM 16/1344, Millan to Mason, 23 June 1977.
162 TNA, PREM 16/1344, Mason to Mulley, 18 May 1977.
163 TNA, CJ4/1654, Ford to Janes, 24 May 1977.
164 TNA, CJ4/1654, Meeting between Mason and Mulley, 24 May 1977; TNA,
     CAB 134/4039, Index, undated.
165 TNA, PREM 16/1344, Mason to Callaghan, 27 May 1977.
166 TNA, PREM 16/1344, Mason to Callaghan, 1 June 1977.
167 TNA, CJ4/1654, Newman to Pritchard, 21 May 1977; TNA, CJ4/1654,
     Meeting to discuss security policy, 27 May 1977.
168 TNA, PREM 16/1344, Mason to Callaghan, 1 June 1977.
169 *The Times*, 9 June 1977.
170 TNA, CJ4/1655, Neilson to Eliott, 20 June 1977.
171 *Irish Times*, 14 June 1977.
172 TNA, CJ4/1653, Meeting between PUS, GOC and Chief Constable, 4 April
     1977.
173 TNA, CJ4/1653, Cubbon to Pritchard, 4 April 1977.
174 TNA, CJ4/1781, Watkins to Pritchard and others, 19 May 1977.
175 TNA, CJ4/1781, WG(SF) meeting 1, 24 May 1977.
176 TNA, CJ4/1781, Ford to PUS, 9 June 1977.
177 TNA, CJ4/1781, Pritchard to PUS, 10 June 1977.
178 TNA, CJ4/1780, Meeting to discuss current security work, 17 June 1977.

179 TNA, CJ4/1783, Pritchard to Cubbon, 26 July 1977.

180 TNA, CJ4/1785, WG(SF) meeting 3, 19 July 1977.

181 TNA, CJ4/1783, Purkis to Pritchard, 8 August 1977.

182 TNA, CJ4/1783, Pritchard to Cubbon, 14 October 1977; TNA, CJ4/1783, Security forces' capability: Ulster Defence Regiment, undated.

183 TNA, CJ4/1783, Pritchard to Cubbon, 14 October 1977.

184 TNA, CJ4/1783, Security Forces' Capability: Royal Ulster Constabulary and Royal Ulster Constabulary Reserve, undated.

185 TNA, CJ4/1783, Cubbon to Mason, 28 October 1977.

186 TNA, CJ4/1783, Pritchard to Dromgoole, 2 November 1977; TNA, CJ4/1783, Cubbon to Newman, 4 November 1977.

187 TNA, CAB 134/4039, IN(77) memo 6, 11 November 1977.

188 TNA, CAB 134/4039, IN(77) meeting 3, 8 December 1977.

189 McKittrick *et al.*, *Lost lives*, pp. 1552–3.

8

'Positive direct rule': economic policy

In May 1976 Merlyn Rees argued that to remain acceptable 'direct rule needs to be seen to be "positive", emphasising 'good government' over 'constitutional aspirations and hobgoblins'.[1] The primary way in which this desire for 'positive direct rule' manifested itself was the attempt to strengthen Northern Ireland's weak economy. This came at a time when the United Kingdom's economy suffered acutely, enduring recession, a currency crisis, growing unemployment and high inflation. In 1976 the Chancellor, Denis Healey, was forced to negotiate his economic policies with the IMF in return for a loan.[2] A crucial issue to consider is the extent to which the Labour government shielded Northern Ireland from economic realities because of the conflict. There was substantial continuity with economic policy before the Labour government came to power but after March 1974 aspects of these policies were also informed by Labour's philosophy for governing Great Britain. Paul Bew *et al.* note that the high level of intervention by the British government and the expansion of the public sector in Northern Ireland has led some to speak of a 'workhouse economy', implying the creation of a dependency culture.[3] The origin of this perception lies during these crucial years. While 'workhouse economy' is too strong a term (and deliberately pejorative), Northern Ireland underwent an economic experience at odds with that of Great Britain that lasted beyond the life of the Labour government.

The economy and the conflict

The relative weakness of the Northern Ireland economy preceded the conflict; the region consistently suffered from the lowest average income and the highest percentage of unemployment in the UK.[4] Against this backdrop there was a record of government intervention.[5] In the mid-1960s these efforts evolved into a development programme which set a target of 30,000 new manufacturing jobs to be achieved by the end of the decade. The same figure was suggested, albeit more tentatively, for the service sector.[6] By mid-1969 the overall increase in employment was roughly 11,000, but as the working population rose so did unemployment, which was 0.3% higher than in mid-1964. A second report, the *Development programme 1970–75*, concluded that the growth planned for in the mid-1960s did not arrive for two reasons, both of which were also key to the economic struggles of the following decade; political unrest in Northern Ireland damaged prospects and the economy in Great Britain struggled, leading to a fall in consumer demand.[7]

Following the outbreak of violence in 1969 emergency measures were introduced, such as the raising of investment grants by 5% with Whitehall's assistance. Although the vast majority of firms were unaffected by the disturbances and good industrial relations were preserved, these facts naturally did not receive attention from the media, raising fears that investors would be discouraged. Initially, the promotion of 40,000 jobs by 1975 had been thought the 'minimum desirable' but the conflict made it 'an immensely formidable task'. Further courses of action were called for, namely an increase in public investment and assistance to private industry as well as 'an ambitious programme for expenditure on infrastructure'. Although the cost of creating jobs was high (£5,000 a year per job for public projects) and it was recognised that the British government would find it 'embarrassing and difficult…to make Northern Ireland a special case' (especially if this involved maintaining 'soup kitchens disguised as factories'), special measures were deemed necessary.[8]

In June 1971, with the PIRA's bombing campaign underway, another committee was appointed to consider economic and social development under the chair of Alec Cairncross, formerly a leading Treasury civil servant and economic advisor in the 1960s.[9] The Cairncross report concluded that economic indicators showed 'remarkably little sign of any serious effects on the economy'. Unemployment was high but industrial production stood higher than ever before and trade unions made 'an important contribution towards preserving industrial peace and maintaining the level of production'. There were, however, 'reasonable grounds' for believing the situation would deteriorate. The fact that production was at a high level showed that orders were carried out but there was an increasing hesitation to place orders in Northern Ireland because of the *perception* that industry was disrupted. Cairncross's report was doubtful that major improvements could be made: the immediate objective was 'to maintain as much as possible of the existing economic fabric of the Province, against the day when it will be possible to move forward again'. In 1971 the public–private sector balance was 'very much in line' with the UK as a whole, but Cairncross recommended enlarging public investment. As private and commercial investment was drying up this would lead to a significant shift in the balance between the public and private sectors, which Cairncross described as unsustainable; in the long run Northern Ireland would only improve its economic potential with private sector investment. To stem the tide he proposed the creation of the Northern Ireland Finance Corporation (NIFC) to offer financial assistance to businesses threatened with contraction or closure but which the NIFC judged to have 'reasonably good prospects' in the longer term.[10] The NIFC was introduced the following year alongside a number of other measures, including an acceleration of public works, special employment schemes, an expansion of industrial training, increases in industrial incentives, and measures to help the liquidity of retail and service businesses.[11]

In addition, the principle of parity in social services between Northern Ireland and Great Britain meant that an increasing subvention was made. A White Paper following the introduction of direct rule estimated that they totalled £133 million for the financial year 1972–73.[12] There was already a substantial degree of intervention in the Northern Ireland economy in the 1960s. While Labour was in opposition, and as the conflict gained momentum, this intervention increased and an important shift began to occur in the balance between public and private sectors.

Assisting industry

Between January and May 1974 economic affairs remained the prerogative of the Northern Ireland Executive. It was charged with the drafting of a five-year social and economic plan. When the executive collapsed the cost of their proposals stood at £425 million.[13] The question of whether this would have gone ahead had the executive survived is, of course, hypothetical but unofficial comments from the Treasury implied the figure was unrealistic.[14] After the executive collapsed the government sought to produce its own plan but preparations were disrupted by the worsening situation in Belfast's shipyards.

The UK shipbuilding industry was in decline generally but the conflict created an added dimension. Harland & Wolff suffered a steady decline from the Second World War and was heavily dependent on financial support from the government. Some £68 million of public money was spent keeping the 10,000 overwhelmingly Protestant employees in work between 1966 and 1974.[15] Nevertheless, the company continued to struggle and in May 1974 its chairman asked the Labour government to honour an undertaking by their Conservative predecessors to provide extra assistance, converting £10 million of debt into preference shares and providing an overdraft until the end of 1976.[16] On 4 June Harold Wilson publicly confirmed that support would be given but chastised 'the leading representatives of the employees' for denying 'hundreds of thousands of Ulster workers the right to work' during the UWC stoppage, adding that it was 'difficult to defend' the decision because of the employees' behaviour. Despite this, 'his constituents' and those of other MPs would 'pick up the bill' for such 'wantonly self-inflicted wounds'.[17] Wilson was contemptuous towards sections of the loyalist community who, he felt, demanded British money while showing contempt for the will of parliament. As on other occasions, his public statements offended the Protestant community and raised fears that his government would be less sympathetic to Northern Ireland's economic woes. Just as the number of troops deployed in the region was watched carefully by unionists for indications of withdrawal, so was the provision of economic support. Wilson's views did not, however, affect the government's treatment of Harland & Wolff.

In June 1974 Rees made a contradictory assertion to his ministerial colleagues that well captured the gap between the instincts of Labour ministers and actual government policy: 'Whether we shall wish to continue to provide support at anything like the present level will depend on whether there is movement towards political and social stability in Northern Ireland; yet withdrawal or marked reduction of our support would lead to economic collapse and social and political upheaval.'[18] It was felt that if Northern Ireland failed to measure up to British standards of political maturity then they should face the economic consequences, but such a punishment would have very dangerous consequences. Ultimately, decisions were based on the likely impact of government actions rather than an emotional distaste for the region's politics.

Rees proposed to continue support for Harland & Wolff despite its being certain that the company would operate at a loss. The government would accept liability for new debts over the following twelve months. Wilson asked whether 'these self inflicted wounds should be met by the people of Northern Ireland' but a discussion on imposing 'a special tax on one part of the United Kingdom' ended with the idea dismissed. Rees's proposals were approved with Wilson suggesting further consideration of 'certain wider aspects on the control of funding Northern Ireland'.[19] A memo prepared for the meeting showed that the subvention had increased to £310 million in 1973–74 and, with the addition of £66 million worth of loans, amounted to roughly 45% of Northern Ireland's public expenditure.[20]

A month later Rees's plan was rendered redundant by a new forecast of Harland & Wolff's financial position. In February 1974 the company had estimated it would lose £5.7 million but it now estimated the loss would be £32.8 million. Rees warned that it would be best to assume an even worse outcome. If they dealt with the problem on a purely commercial basis this would mean closing the yard but, he argued, to put 10,000 people out of work was 'socially unacceptable'. Rees claimed closure 'would very probably' lead to occupation by trade unions, possibly backed by loyalist paramilitaries, and they would need to deploy two extra battalions of troops in East Belfast. Rather than nationalisation in the strictest sense (which required legislation), Rees now recommended converting loans to the company into ordinary shares, giving them 90% equity which would be vested in Northern Ireland's Department of Commerce.[21] The ministerial committee approved the proposals with little debate, though Wilson once again remarked 'that the people of Northern Ireland could not continue to inflict damage on their economy and expect the United Kingdom taxpayers [*sic*] to meet an ever increasing bill'.[22]

Wilson's repeated complaints ignored the fact that Harland & Wolff's difficulties had little to do with the UWC strike. In addition to the generally bleak outlook for the shipbuilding industry in the UK, Rees highlighted the damaging effect of poor industrial relations due to incompetent management and resentment at the Heath government's compulsory incomes policy, which restricted wages.[23] The managing director was removed and a full examination of the company undertaken, with civil servants involved in fresh financial estimates. In March 1975 Rees noted that the estimate for prospective losses had increased again, this time to £60.5 million. Productivity was low and, most importantly, the yard was designed to build very large ships but the market for tankers had fallen dramatically. This time Rees proposed full nationalisation, compulsorily acquiring the remaining shares to the cost of £1 million and giving a grant of £41 million for future losses. A reconstructed board would then require his approval for new contracts, which would be rejected unless profitable, new plans for the yard would be developed and if these measures proved impracticable there would be a reduction of the workforce and a closure of facilities.[24] In August 1975 the Order nationalising the yard was passed in the Commons.[25]

In addition to the financial assistance given to the shipyard there was a distinctively left-wing aspect to Labour's approach, primarily due to the involvement of Stanley Orme. As a former union shop steward in the Amalgamated Engineering Union, Orme was particularly interested in introducing industrial democracy into the shipyards to improve relations between management and the workforce.[26] The concept, essentially amounting to worker participation in managerial decisions, received support from within the wider Labour party but was not implemented under the Labour government because business interests were opposed and trade unions divided on its merits.[27] On 22 July 1974 Orme told the Commons: 'we need to advance towards genuine worker participation in all the decision-making processes of the company'. He was convinced that participation in management would lay 'a solid foundation' for increased productivity.[28]

In March 1975 a discussion paper on industrial democracy for Harland & Wolff was published with a foreword from Orme. He remarked that they were 'entering upon an experiment'. A joint consultative council was already established but he advocated worker involvement in 'planning, production, marketing, employment and even redundancy'.[29] In April the Labour left newspaper *Tribune* asked 'will East Belfast's peaceful revolution take us all by storm?', adding that the conflict had 'thrown up something with deeper implications for the whole of Britain than anything to come out of Ulster over the last six years'.[30] In his own correspondence Orme remarked that the Harland & Wolff proposals 'cannot but have an effect upon British industry as a whole'.[31] While they did not have the ripple effect hoped for, Rees noted in mid-1976 that trade unions had agreed to full participation at all levels of the company, including the election of five worker directors to the board, which in his view put 'Harland and Wolff somewhere near the van in industrial relations in the United Kingdom'.[32]

Despite a new spirit of co-operation, problems remained. A broader interdepartmental study of the British shipbuilding industry for the ministerial committee on economic and industrial policy concluded that the outlook was 'bleak'. It decided that shipyards in Great Britain should also be nationalised, but Harland & Wolff would be excluded from the new British Shipbuilders Corporation. Rees cited the shipyard's 'tremendous importance' in Northern Ireland as 'a symbol of industry, employment and achievement'. This symbolism endowed the committee's decisions with a deeper significance: if Harland & Wolff was allowed to collapse this would be seen as 'clear proof of a planned British withdrawal'. This time Rees proposed a progressive rundown of the workforce to 40% of its existing size, making 5,500 workers redundant. Added to this was a particularly desperate recommendation that four bulk carriers be built without assurance that they would be sold. If a buyer could be found then £20.5 million would be needed on top of the previous £60 million but if the ships did not sell a total of £169 million was necessary. Rees admitted that it was unrealistic for the government to commit, but a decision on this extra idea was not necessary until mid-1977. He therefore asked that the committee agree on maintaining support and that they were in principle favourable to his longer-term plan.[33]

When the meeting on these proposals took place Rees again used the security situation to support his case, telling the ministerial committee that troops recently withdrawn from East Belfast might have to return if the yard were closed. Chancellor Denis Healey thought the commitment too large, remarking that he could not see 'how the government could justify giving to one firm in Northern Ireland shipbuilding aid on a scale which was comparable with that contemplated for the whole of Great Britain'. The firm had also failed to achieve productivity targets laid down in 1975 as a pre-condition for further government assistance and Healey warned that if speculative building were allowed then firms in Great Britain would want it too. James Callaghan approved Rees's plan minus the speculative shipbuilding.[34]

Many other, smaller companies sought financial help from the Northern Ireland Finance Corporation established under the Conservatives and, as with Harland & Wolff, the conflict influenced negotiations. A Treasury note described the NIFC arrangements as 'designedly more generous' than those for deprived parts of Great Britain. Assistance was limited to £6,000 to £7,000 per job and the amount of public money offered could 'not normally exceed 66.67% of the total injection of funds', requiring a significant private sector contribution. By July 1973, however, the Treasury recorded that Northern Ireland's Departments of Finance and Commerce had 'wrung from us' an agreement to go as far as 100% 'in exceptional cases'.[35]

In each exceptional case Northern Ireland departments emphasised political implications when dealing with the Treasury. In June 1974 the Treasury was asked to provide £250,000 of grants to Hughes Bakery. The company employed 400 men and 100 women in West Belfast and 80 men in Derry. The Department of Commerce concluded that the firm was not viable (a requirement for assistance). Two larger Protestant-owned firms had rationalised their production and were well placed to close the gap in West Belfast, but the Northern Ireland Permanent Secretary for Finance, David Holden, argued there was a political difficulty in the loss of a prominent Catholic-owned firm in West Belfast. As the NIO minister responsible for Commerce, Orme considered support 'absolutely essential' and Holden described him as 'deeply sensitive to the contrast which might be drawn between this case and that of the shipyard, should this help not be offered' (an allusion to how the zero-sum game of Northern Irish politics affected economic policy). Holden added that there was no commitment to keeping this assistance going for more than a year.[36] A week later Rees wrote to Joel Barnett, the Chief Secretary to the Treasury, mentioning the SDLP's concern for the company.[37] Pliatzky, the Treasury official concerned, advised Barnett that if he accepted the political case then the Treasury would not oppose the payment, even though the circumstances infringed normal rules, to which Barnett assented.[38]

Further businesses received exceptional assistance because of their geographical location or the religious composition of the workforce.

Electronics company Regna International was described as 'a Catholic firm' based on the western side of the river in Derry ('one of our most difficult areas…in both the political and the security sense') and was particularly significant in that it marked the first instance of 100% financing, beginning in 1973.[39] When the Treasury gave approval for further assistance in 1974 it was in spite of 'considerable reservations…because of doubts about the future viability of the company'.[40] These reservations were confirmed when receivers were called in to liquidate the company in March 1976, the level of assistance having reached £2.9 million.[41] For Diversified Industries, weavers of polypropylene, the issue was that it exceeded the limit per job by more than £2,000.[42] It received funding anyway because it was a new venture from an American company and the location was the unemployment black spot of Strabane.[43] Otis Engineering, which produced specialist equipment for oil and gas production, was a similar case for Derry.[44] The Treasury approved assistance for up to £9,000 per job on the condition that it was located in Derry rather than the more prosperous Bangor, which Otis also considered.[45] Lastly, Strathearn Audio was a company started by the NIFC in June 1973. The plan was to establish production at an industrial estate in Andersonstown (an almost exclusively Catholic area and one 'for which the 100% financing rules were designed'). It was hoped that the firm would initially employ 200 in 1975, rising to 1,200 by the end of the decade. Public expenditure was expected to reach £900,000 but the private sector contribution was 'slow to materialise' so the Department of Finance asked the Treasury to approve 100% ownership, which was given.[46]

The offer of grants and loans to maintain ailing businesses was not always an option. When Rolls-Royce decided to close its plant in Dundonald in November 1975, the government was unable to prevent this. The Dundonald case was particularly significant because the workforce of 800 was entirely Protestant and, the NIO believed, a 'good part…might be expected to be members of or give active support to the UDA'.[47] Despite the incentive of a possible security threat, there were 'very powerful economic reasons' for Rolls-Royce to withdraw from Northern Ireland so the government instead sought 'to look for alternative employment opportunities to match the skills of the workforce' while the operation was run down.[48] Orme hoped that Shorts and Harland, the aerospace company, would take up the factory and employ the same workforce.[49] Ultimately, this did not occur and despite writing to 1,400 firms in thirteen countries by July 1977 the search for a new tenant in the factory yielded no result.[50]

The Labour government's activity on the economic front was largely on an *ad hoc* basis. Rees 'agreed with and supported the broad strategy of the previous administration' (indeed, we have seen that many of the companies given public money either received or sought support before Labour returned to office). He warned, however, that 'in the light of current conditions and the atmosphere of disenchantment prevalent at Westminster in relation to Northern Ireland it was realistic not to expect to do overwell.' It was agreed that social and economic planning would continue but on the basis of public expenditure figures already established for 1974 with £150 million extra but minus assistance to the shipyards (rather less than the £425 million proposed by the power-sharing executive).[51]

In addition to the fiscal limitations on producing a social and economic plan, there were also political reasons for avoiding publishing detailed proposals. While constitutional agreement was unlikely to arise, the British government hoped that discussion on the economy in the Convention might lead to a greater appreciation of the similarities between the Northern Ireland parties. The discussion paper *Finance and the economy* was produced with the intention of informing these discussions. It described Northern Ireland's 'inter-dependence with Great Britain'. The unemployment situation was 'the worst of any United Kingdom region and among the worst of any region in the European Economic Community'. Production and manufacturing, which accounted for 63% of employment in 1950, had shrunk to 50% in 1973. Since the Second World War the three staples of the Northern Ireland economy (agriculture, textiles and shipbuilding) greatly declined. While this decline was experienced in Great Britain as well, the impact was worse in Northern Ireland because of the higher level of dependence on them. Great Britain accounted for 63% of sales by Northern Irish manufacturers. Of manufacturing firms employing 500 or more people in Northern Ireland, 45% were controlled from Great Britain, 20% by the United States, 20% by European Economic Community (EEC) members and just 22% from Northern Ireland. The paper further stressed the growing subvention to Northern Ireland. While the term 'inter-dependence' was used, the underlying purpose of the paper was to stress the weakness of Northern Ireland's economy and its dependence on Great Britain.[52] As Rees told his cabinet colleagues, 'Perhaps the single most important feature of the Northern Ireland economy is its dependence on the British economy.'[53] This was something that Rees particularly wanted to impress on those who thought independence would not mean the end of British financial support.[54]

The economic crisis in Britain

Northern Ireland's dependence on Great Britain further increased at a time when the UK as a whole was hit by economic crisis. As Artis *et al.* argue, economic growth was poor, 'inflation reached levels unparalleled in modern British history', staple industries declined severely and unemployment reached 'levels without precedent in postwar experience'.[55] On the right of the political spectrum the balance between public and private sectors was brought into question, with claims that government interference had damaged industrial competitiveness: '"Keynesianism" became a whipping-boy for all the perceived errors of economic policy'.[56] From the left, the Labour government was chastised for betraying socialism by first adopting a gradualist approach and then imposing tremendous spending cuts.[57]

While these views were (and continue to be) influential, Ian Tomlinson is right to highlight that the recession of the mid-1970s was 'largely a consequence of global forces'.[58] In March 1973 the Bretton Woods system of fixed currency exchange rates broke down after expansionary monetary policies by the United States to finance the Vietnam War and domestic social programmes led to inflation which the rest of the world (particularly Europe) was unwilling to import from the United States by keeping the value of the dollar fixed.[59] The outbreak of the Arab–Israeli War in October led the Organisation for Petroleum Exporting Countries to cut oil production and place an embargo on sales to the United States.[60] This in turn led to panic buying and the price of oil rocketed, increasing fourfold. Western economies were dependent on oil and so their real income, balance of payments and inflation rates worsened dramatically.[61]

During 1974 inflation increased from 13.5% in the first quarter to over 18% in the third.[62] An economic crisis combining recession with high inflation (a phenomenon termed 'stagflation') created new difficulties, as measures to alleviate unemployment would worsen inflation and vice versa.[63] As Dow notes, 'Neither the old Keynesian recipe nor any other had an answer to this; policy was about as much use as oars in a rowing boat on the Atlantic'.[64] Denis Healey prioritised curbing inflation. In January 1975 the government proposed to cut planned public spending by £1 billion (2%) for 1976/77 with a build-up to a reduction of £3.75 billion for 1978/79.[65] In April Healey produced a deflationary budget, raising income tax and Value Added Tax (VAT) while cutting public expenditure.[66] The following year three sets of cuts were proposed. The last of these, amounting to £3 billion, was required by the IMF in return for a loan.[67] The IMF were called in by Healey after a sharp decline in the value of sterling.[68] A shortfall in public spending of £1,600 million (as a result of inaccurate inflation forecasts being used as the basis for planning spending) meant that the actual spending cuts were larger than those negotiated with the IMF.[69] Less than half of the IMF loan was drawn as the economy improved significantly after this but the episode remained in the British national consciousness as a symbol of great economic decline.[70]

The public expenditure White Paper for 1975/76 noted that Northern Ireland had to 'bear its share of the reductions in the growth of public expenditure in line with the rest of the United Kingdom'. It recorded that 'inevitably a number of the improvements which were planned in various services will not now take place'. The NIO did, however, manage to increase expenditure on housing, job creation, and aspects of health and education that affected areas of special deprivation. Housing expenditure was projected to increase from £94.2 million to £110.8 million, Trade, industry and employment from £158.9 million to £165.4 million, health from £152 million to £160.8 million and education from £174.2 million to £191.9 million.[71] Indeed, overall the spending pattern remained favourable to Northern Ireland. In the first three years of the Labour administration real public expenditure for the region increased annually by 14.6%, 3.6% and 0.9%, whereas for the UK the figures were 8.5%, 1.2% and a decrease of 3.2%.[72] This exceptional treatment occurred because of the conflict and the need to ensure economic stability by maintaining the public sector regardless of the financial situation. Bew *et al.* rightly note: 'To have allowed an economic crisis to run alongside the political turmoil would have pushed the region into the abyss.'[73]

Developing a strategy

A more systematic economic plan for Northern Ireland was developed by the government from 1976 onwards, informed in part by Labour's policies for Great Britain. Secretary of State for Industry Tony Benn hoped to establish a National Enterprise Board (NEB) which would extend public ownership. Along with the left of the party, he proposed that the NEB should take equity in 25 of the top 100 private businesses in the UK, nationalising them and promoting investment and industrial democracy. Benn claimed that the mixed economy had failed and public ownership was the solution.[74] As Wickham-Jones argues, Harold Wilson 'carefully monitored' Benn's work and opposed his plans with support from the Treasury ministers Denis Healey and Joel Barnett.[75] Benn put forward a White Paper setting out his industrial strategy, but Wilson 'called Benn's draft "a sloppy and half-baked document, polemical, indeed menacing in tone"'. Healey attacked the plans, saying the NEB would not be profitable, that he opposed industrial democracy and the effect the proposals would have on the confidence of private industry would be hugely damaging. The cabinet sided against Benn. The government's White Paper, published in August 1974 and titled *The regeneration of British industry*, contained a far softer set of proposals. The NEB was a less aggressive entity requiring agreement for its acquisitions and with limitations placed on nationalisation. These proposals were further moderated when the Industry Bill was published in January 1975 and amended extensively before it received royal assent in November 1975 (after Benn had been moved to the Department of Energy). Ultimately, the NEB performed a similar role to that of the NIFC; '95% of its funds went on lame ducks'.[76]

The Industry Act established Welsh and Scottish Development Agencies to fulfil a similar set of functions as the NEB. Proposals were made to replace Northern Ireland's Finance Corporation with a Development Agency of its own. Emphasis was laid on industrial training and direct employment schemes for the preservation and reinforcement of the skill base. Rees said the NIFC 'had not fulfilled all the hopes that were placed in it' but he believed it had 'great potential' if 'properly staffed and with proper powers'.[77] In April 1976 Stanley Orme presented the Industries Development (Northern Ireland) Order to the Commons. He said the new Northern Ireland Development Agency (NIDA) would be 'a much more positive body' than the NIFC, operating as an 'agency for setting up State industries...especially in areas of high employment where private industry has so far failed to go' and taking steps 'to improve and strengthen existing Northern Ireland firms', such as finding 'new products and new processes suitable for introduction into Northern Ireland industry'. It would also give advice on 'management, finance and administration and, most important, marketing', which the Northern Ireland Economic Council (NIEC, a government-appointed advisory board including trade unionists, businessmen and other professionals) had highlighted as a key area where firms needed government assistance. As ever, it was promised that the NIDA would invest in projects 'only where it believes there is a reasonable prospect of viability', while not being 'over-cautious'.[78] The rebranding did not produce a tremendous change in character from the NIFC.

On 25 March 1976 Rees announced a review of economic and industrial strategy to the Commons, but warned that they did not 'expect to find any panacea'. As in the constitutional and security spheres he stressed there were 'no easy solutions'.[79] Rees remained downbeat in an assessment to cabinet colleagues in May: factors which had previously attracted outside investment 'had largely disappeared', labour was no longer significantly cheaper than in Great Britain, fuel costs were higher and transportation costs were increasing. Most bleak was the situation in the engineering industry. Standard Telephones and Cables was contracting with an estimated loss of 1,400 jobs in 1976, Rolls-Royce was set to close in early 1977 with the loss of 800 jobs and three defence establishments were being phased out with 2,000 jobs gone by April 1978. Some 5,000 redundancies were expected at Harland and Wolff over the next two to three years. All

of this, Rees warned, fed 'the politically dangerous belief that we are pursuing a policy of deliberate economic withdrawal.'[80]

In August 1976 Rees described the results of the review, chaired by the
Northern Ireland Department of Commerce's permanent secretary George
Quigley. The Quigley report depicted 'a serious and deteriorating unemployment situation', currently at 11.7% in Northern Ireland and 15.3%
outside Belfast. Rees warned that without action it would reach close to
20% overall and with the recent damage done to the engineering industry
any benefit from an upsurge in the UK economy was 'likely to be too little
and too late'. In 'very approximate terms', 40,000 jobs were needed to bring
unemployment down to 7% by 1980. While the objective 'must be...a
diversified industrial structure with a greater proportion of growth sectors',
the report said this was 'not realistic' in the medium term. It could only
be achieved in the future with 'supportive measures – with the State
playing a much greater role'. The Quigley team proposed an energy subsidy
to cut costs to businesses and encourage investment. They also suggested
measures to 'restore the effectiveness of Northern Ireland's incentives',
such as an increase in the maximum capital grant to 60%, a tax holiday on
export profits, tax exemption on profits obtained from within the UK and
a special scheme to encourage research and development. Treasury initiatives aimed at 'injecting the maximum amount of skill into the workforce
at all levels' should be continued with a further training centre set up in
Strabane, where male unemployment was 35%. The report concluded there
was 'no escape from the need for more resources'.[81]

The cost of these resources rather frightened the Treasury. Chief Secretary to the Treasury Joel Barnett aired concerns about the Quigley report's
public presentation. He stressed that, as the authors themselves emphasised, the report was 'no more than a useful "think-piece"', which did not
set out the financial implications of its content. He worried that it would
raise expectations 'which there is simply no possibility of meeting'. Barnett
suggested two options: either wait until after negotiations with the Treasury were complete and then publish ideas 'which are both feasible and
adequately costed' (with an explanation that these schemes 'could be introduced only where offsetting savings could be found') or circulate the document with certain contents removed. Barnett cited five proposals the
Treasury wanted omitted: subsidies towards energy costs, voluntary retirement for men at sixty-four (to free up jobs for the young), a tax holiday on
export profits, a tax exemption on profits earned in Northern Ireland but
reinvested there, and a request that the EEC adopt Northern Ireland as a
case for special treatment. Barnett argued the first four would provoke
similar demands from parts of Great Britain, while the fifth point 'would
be one for the government to consider as a UK initiative'.[82]

Rees understood Barnett's response, recording in his diaries that he 'saw it would shatter the Treasury; it was an Irish report, tax-free holidays, comparisons with the [Republic] and the whole thing was geared in the context as if it was not part of the UK'. His dismissive response to the work of NICS officials neglected the possibility that it could have been controlled more effectively with tighter terms of reference and Treasury involvement, which Rees could have ensured. Rees felt that they had to publish the report, so he proposed to 'put an introductory thing into it saying that this had a Green Paper tinge about it'.[83] Meanwhile, trade unions pulled out of the NIEC because they felt it was insufficiently independent from government and was not allowed to contribute enough to economic policy. Quigley cited the Secretary of State's role as chair and the use of civil servants to staff it as causing tension.[84] In his stock-taking minute to James Callaghan before moving to the Home Office Rees remarked that 'failure to deal with the unemployment situation could be the most important factor in destroying the improvements which we have achieved in the security and political situation'.[85]

Mason's big push

Mason's comments about the economy being Northern Ireland's biggest problem during his first press conference prompted *The Times* to write of a new initiative to make job creation a weapon against terrorism.[86] His public pronouncements on economic policy raised hopes, but privately he knew the extent of the difficulties the Labour government faced. Giving his first impressions to the prime minister, Mason reiterated that the economy 'is a very important, and perhaps at this moment even the most important issue in Northern Ireland'. He was about to discuss the Quigley report with trade unions and the Confederation of British Industry (CBI) but admitted: 'I fear... that I shall need more resources – and a greater measure of discretion in using them.'[87] Rees's caution and pessimism in public was replaced with a more forceful and assertive line from Mason but, as with security policy, such confidence was rarely expressed in private.

Officials lamented that options were limited in dealing with a regional economy: 'the classic remedy of devaluation was not available; the level of social security benefits blunted the incentive to mass emigration which might otherwise have restored the economic balance; and in general Northern Ireland could no longer offer cheap labour'. The two approaches identified by officials were to increase government aid to specific industrial projects ('but the difficulty was to find projects deserving support') and to adopt more attractive regional incentives.[88] Characteristically, Mason said relatively little in the ministerial committee on Northern Ireland, informing colleagues that he was 'devoting a great deal of time to consideration of these problems'.[89]

The Quigley report was published on 18 October 1976. Mason's preface described it as 'a valuable basis for discussion of the way forward'. All five of the proposals cited by Barnett were included. Quigley's team thought 'the most valuable contribution in terms of encouragement to existing industry' would be an across-the-board reduction in electricity costs to industrial and commercial users. The Department of Commerce advised that a reduction of 10% would cost £7 million a year. The voluntary retirement scheme suggested for those reaching sixty-four would provide a pension amounting to unemployment benefit plus half the difference between it and past earnings. They had not 'had the opportunity...to evaluate all the implications of the idea' or to estimate the cost, but felt it 'worthy of full exploration'. Both the tax ideas remained, as did the suggestion of EEC assistance. Contrary to the Treasury view, the report described the best 'short to medium term' prescription as 'a heavily subsidised Northern Ireland economy, with the state playing a much greater role, both direct and supportive'.[90] Ultimately, however, the Quigley recommendations were only implemented in part and, while the increase in both the role of the state and the subsidisation of Northern Ireland did take place, it did so by inches (ironically, the public sector reached its apogee in the mid-1980s under the Thatcher government).[91]

When Mason was asked for a statement on the Quigley report in the Commons on 28 October he said until discussions were completed he had nothing to add to his preface.[92] The NIEC was given the report but disbanded immediately afterwards and discussion was delayed while thought was given to its reconstitution. When unionist MP James Kilfedder accused Mason of stalling, Mason said he 'ought to put his tongue in his cheek and be grateful for the consideration and the priority that I have given from the outset' to the economy.[93] Such condescension ignored the difference between rhetoric and action. By March 1977 there was still no sign of change. Neave told the Commons that the Conservative party welcomed 'the government's special treatment of Northern Ireland' and congratulated Mason 'on having instilled a sense of urgency in dealing with these problems', but they still had 'no indication of the government's thinking on the Quigley report'. James Dunn, Parliamentary Under-Secretary at the NIO, simply argued that it needed 'to be looked at over a longer period and in greater detail than has so far been possible'. He said Mason was anxious that a new economic council be established to advise him on the report, adding that 'we must not jump too quickly'.[94]

On 28 March 1977 Douglas Janes told officials from other Whitehall departments that Quigley 'remained under examination', tellingly adding that 'a package of positive proposals was not easy to devise'. A week later Mason wrote to the ministerial committee that incentives for investment were less attractive than south of the border. The Republic of Ireland's tax holiday on export profits was the principal difference and the South had 'considerable success in attracting new projects' because of it. Mason also said Healey's employment measures had 'an essential role to play in keeping unemployment within bounds', a significant point because these were shortly due to end.[95] He 'sought no specific decisions at this stage', although NIO ministers were making frequent visits abroad 'to win investment from the United States and Europe'.[96] On 17 May Don Concannon announced that Denis Healey's employment subsidies would remain in place at a cost of £13 million.[97] Northern Ireland was able to keep these for longer than the rest of the UK.[98] Writing to Callaghan on 16 June, Mason said that the state of the Northern Ireland economy was still 'very grave'. In 1976, 31 manufacturing firms employing 2,600 closed and inward investment promoted only 431 jobs (compared with the Republic's 7,174).[99]

On 1 August, more than a year after the Quigley report was completed, Mason announced a five-year £950 million plan to stimulate Northern Ireland's economy. This included the write-off of £250 million of debt accumulated by the Northern Ireland Electricity Service and a grant of a further £100 million over five years to lower industrial tariffs. A further £600 million was earmarked to support industry.[100] The maximum industrial development grant was increased from 40 to 50%, interest relief from two to three years, the maximum period of rent-free occupation of government factories was increased from 3 to 5 years, and a new scheme was introduced which provided up to 50% grants towards research and development projects (up to £250,000). Some of these measures, such as interest relief and rent-free occupation, were available in parts of Great Britain such as Merseyside and the £600 million figure represented a set amount for a process that was usually *ad hoc* in nature but on the whole the package was more generous. Mason also announced the reconstitution of the NIEC. Absent from the changes were Quigley's EEC and tax suggestions.[101]

Arriving less than two months after Mason's 'intensification' initiative in the security field, the package provoked a similar response from the UUP; John Taylor described it as 'wonderful' and hoped that it would 'help all Ulstermen to emerge from seven dark years of division'. Far less enthusiastically, the SDLP's economic spokesman, Hugh Logue, said his party felt Mason was over-reliant on the stimulation of private industry (an unrealistic assessment in light of the wider economic context and the government's willingness to maintain public expenditure in Northern Ireland while cutting it in Great Britain).[102] Economists at Cambridge

University described the initiative as 'a bold one' but unlikely to bring enough investment into Northern Ireland to reduce unemployment. They pointed to the obvious attraction of the tax holiday in the Irish republic for investors and the slow rate of growth in Great Britain, which made an expansion of British manufacturing unlikely.[103]

Little debate took place in the Commons on the Quigley report and its outcome. In July 1978 Ian Paisley said all Northern Ireland MPs were 'dismayed that we have never had the opportunity of having a full-scale public debate on the report', to which Gerry Fitt added that 'it was no accident' that this happened.[104] Mason certainly showed reluctance to engage in direct debate with politicians, preferring to deal with the press instead. He did, however, inherit a flawed process. Barnett was right to suggest that the report be held back until they decided what would come of it. Despite the emphasis that it was merely a basis for discussion, the title *Economic and industrial strategy for Northern Ireland* implied greater substance. A more effective process would have been to include the Treasury from the start and produce a report that offered recommendations rather than suggestions for further investigation. No doubt this would have been difficult, but the production of a blueprint would have been far more useful both in terms of presentation and final outcome.

Meanwhile, there was a considerable drive to bring in new investment. In the first half of 1978 1,200 jobs were promoted, in contrast to a half-yearly average of 225 between 1972 and 1977. In July 1978 Don Concannon reported that General Motors would set up a £16 million seat-belt factory in Northern Ireland.[105] The operation of the new NIDA is illustrative of limitations to industrial policy, however. In December 1978 Raymond Carter, Parliamentary Under-Secretary at the NIO, remarked that during the first year of operation the NIDA was largely occupied 'with the problems of firms inherited from the former Northern Ireland Finance Corporation'.[106]

In March 1978 the government sought to transfer twenty firms, fourteen of which were in receivership, from the NIDA to the Department of Commerce. When Enoch Powell asked whether Commerce was the best home for them, Concannon said the department was 'the greatest keeper of albatrosses that Northern Ireland has had for a considerable time'.[107] The most prominent of these firms was Strathearn Audio. In October 1976 a management consultancy employed by the NIDA recommended a series of changes to the firm. Its audio equipment was reportedly of a high quality but the company was unable to produce it in sufficient volume.[108] The workforce was cut from 300 to 160, a far cry from the 1,200 originally intended.[109] An expenditure of nearly £11 million for a firm that provided only 160 long-term jobs was hardly a success.[110]

The most substantial, and notorious, case was DeLorean. As Graham Brownlow argues, the desperation for inward investment created opportunities for personal gain.[111] John DeLorean was a senior executive with General Motors before establishing the DeLorean Motor Company. In June 1978 he approached the Department of Commerce about establishing an assembly plant to produce his DMC12 sports car. From the start the process was rushed. He was already in negotiations with Puerto Rico and the Irish Republic, the latter having made him an offer due to expire in three days. On 19 June Quigley advised that 'if we are to get the project, we have only until sometime tomorrow to clinch the deal…there is no possibility of undertaking our usual detailed analysis'. DeLorean was assured that they would make 'a firm, definitive offer' before the Republic's deadline expired. Commerce and the NIDA hoped to make a combined commitment of over £40m on the basis that 'if the Republic, which has been attracting so many American projects, is prepared to regard this as worth securing, we (who are still fighting our way back in to the American market and have less choice) cannot logically take a more rigorous view'. It would also be 'an excellent project for West Belfast' and DeLorean 'may take a more relaxed view of such a location than some established companies would'.[112]

Mason told officials that they should not be influenced by the possible need to acquire extra public expenditure to finance the deal.[113] Quigley informed him that Commerce's Industrial Development Advisory Committee was unable to 'form a realistic view of the future viability of the project'. They considered it to be 'high risk but potentially rewarding', therefore requiring a decision 'on the basis of political judgement'.[114] On 21 June, the day of the Republic's deadline, Commerce and DeLorean signed heads of agreement. Commerce offered grants of £8.75 million for building expenditure and £24 million for machinery and equipment, in addition to loans of £14 million and the provision of both a site and factory in Twinbrook (a republican area of West Belfast). The NIDA offered to purchase £9.56 million of shares and give a loan of nearly £6.3 million.[115]

Difficulties remained, however, particularly as an offer to invest $18 million in the project by private business interests Oppenheimer was based on the assumption that the plant would be in Puerto Rico. When DeLorean switched to Northern Ireland, Oppenheimer withdrew this.[116] The NIDA made an offer to close the gap, taking $12 million as equity and giving the rest as a loan. Mason said he could only support the offer if it was 'a temporary safety-net' while DeLorean sought private investment elsewhere.[117] The Treasury said it would reserve judgement on the proposals until the whole financing package was clear, preferably with the Oppenheimer money made up by an American source.[118] On 13 July Under-Secretary J.H.

Parkes wrote that as the NIO were 'likely to receive an unhelpful reply' from the Treasury he had 'sought to postpone this' by waiting for further information before Mason discussed the project with Joel Barnett. After visiting the Twinbrook site DeLorean executives also said that more would be needed for it to meet their requirements, increasing the cost to Commerce by another £5 million.[119] The next day Mason's private secretary, Joseph Pilling, informed him that the Central Policy Review Staff in London 'have been asked to look at DeLorean and "their hair is standing on end".[120]

On 17 July Barnett told Mason that the Treasury could not support the project as a 100% investment of £50 million in a new company producing an untested car was extremely risky. Barnett said that Strathearn had set 'a very unpromising precedent for investing five times as much'. He insisted on private-sector participation, as 'a financial stake by the private sector is an indicator that a private commercial judgement regards the risk as worth investing its own money in'. Barnett promised they would reconsider if the $18 million could be replaced.[121] On 24 July James Callaghan proposed that the decision be made by the ministerial committee on economic and industrial policy.[122]

Two days later the committee supported the decision to invest in DeLorean, despite noting that 'the economics of the project were open to serious question'. The money was provided for essentially socio-political purposes.[123] Mason announced the deal to the press in August and said they hoped 'to move from cow pasture to production within 18 months'.[124] In October Oppenheimer reinvested in the project.[125] In March 1979 the deal was the focal point of a full-page week-long advertisement in the *Economist*, in which John DeLorean declared that 'Northern Ireland wrapped up our £65 million investment package in 45 days. 2 days later we were in the plant'.[126] When the first car came off the production line in January 1981 it cost $25,000 to buy, $11,000 more than planned. Sales were poor and a year later 1,100 redundancies were made, bringing the workforce down to 1,500.[127] The company collapsed in 1982.[128]

Conclusion

In February 1979 Roy Mason signed the foreword of *Economic and social progress in Northern Ireland: review and prospects*. The paper projected that employment in Northern Ireland in June 1981 would be 4,000 less than four years earlier. The combination of a UK-wide recession, the conflict and the inherent structural weaknesses of a regional economy reliant on manufacturing made the likelihood of attracting outside investors on anything like the scale of the Republic of Ireland remote.[129] During the lifespan of the Labour government public expenditure in the UK was cut dramatically before returning to a level in 1978–79 that was 0.74% higher than four years earlier. In Northern Ireland it was increased by 16%.[130] There was a limit to how much this expenditure could affect the situation and the desperation of both ministers and civil servants in trying to secure new jobs, as shown in the case of Strathearn and DeLorean, and the need to prop up failing concerns, as shown by Harland & Wolff, indicates how difficult the circumstances were. The significance of the conflict for economic policy is clearly shown by these enterprises; in all three cases they were aimed at communities identified with paramilitarism. The experience of the 1970s, and particularly under the Labour government, set the pattern for the following decades with a steadily increasing subvention from the rest of the United Kingdom and a growing dependence on the public sector, all at a time when the opposite trend took place in Great Britain. Positive direct rule in its economic manifestation was heavily focussed on preventing further violence. It did not lead to an improvement in the economy but had the aid not been provided a far worse scenario may well have occurred.

Notes

1 TNA, CAB 134/4039, IN(76) memo 5, 20 May 1976.
2 For an account of the IMF crisis see: Douglas Wass, *Decline to fall: the making of British macro-economic policy and the 1976 IMF crisis* (Oxford: Oxford University Press, 2008).
3 Paul Bew, Henry Patterson and Paul Teague, *Between war and peace: the political future of Northern Ireland* (London: Lawrence & Wishart, 1997), pp. 87–92.
4 *Northern Ireland development programme* (Belfast, 1970), pp. 3–5.
5 See Isles & Cuthbert, *An economic survey of Northern Ireland* (Belfast, 1957); *Report of the joint working party on the economy of Northern Ireland*, Cmd. 446 [NI], Belfast, 1962; *Belfast regional survey and plan*, Cmd. 451 [NI], Belfast, 1963.
6 *Economic development in Northern Ireland including the report of the economic consultant, Thomas Wilson*, Cmd. 479 [NI], Belfast, 1965.
7 *Northern Ireland development programme 1970–75* (Belfast, 1970).
8 *Northern Ireland development programme* (Belfast, 1970).
9 Alec Cairncross (www.oxforddnb.com, accessed 8 April 2016).
10 *Review of economic and social development in Northern Ireland: report of the joint review body*, Cmd. 564 [NI], Belfast, 1971.
11 Hansard (Commons), 846, cols 782–3.
12 *Northern Ireland: financial arrangements and legislation*, Cmnd. 4998, HC 1972–3.
13 PRONI, SOSEC/1/2, Social and economic planning, 21 June 1974.

14 Shaun McDaid, 'Northern Ireland: Sunningdale, power-sharing and British–Irish relations, 1972–75' (unpublished PhD thesis, Queen's University Belfast, 2010), p. 134.
15 TNA, CAB 134/3779, IRN(74), memo 20, 15 July 1974.
16 TNA, CAB 134/3778, IRN(74), memo 14, 7 June 1974.
17 Hansard (Commons), 874, cols 1046, 1054.
18 TNA, CAB 134/3778, IRN(74) memo 14, 7 June 1974.
19 TNA, CAB 134/3778, IRN(74) meeting 5, 12 June 1974.
20 TNA, CAB 134/3778, IRN(74) memo 15, 7 June 1974.
21 TNA, CAB 134/3779, IRN(74) memo 20, 15 June 1974.
22 TNA, CAB 134/3778, IRN(74) meeting 7, 17 July 1974.
23 TNA, CAB 134/3779, IRN(74) memo 20, 15 June 1974.
24 TNA, CAB 134/3921, IRN(75) memo 9, 12 March 1975.
25 TNA, CAB 134/3921, IRN(75) meeting 4, 19 March 1975; Hansard (Commons), 896, col. 2529.
26 Stanley Orme (www.oxforddnb.com, accessed 8 April 2016).
27 William Brown, 'Industrial relations' in Michael Artis and David Cobham (eds) *Labour's economic policies 1974–1979* (Manchester: Manchester University Press, 1991), p. 218; Mark Wickham-Jones, *Economic strategy and the Labour party: politics and policy-making 1970–83* (Basingstoke: Macmillan, 1996), p. 1.
28 Hansard (Commons), 877, col. 1062.
29 *Industrial democracy: a discussion paper on worker participation in Harland & Wolff* (Belfast: HMSO, 1975).
30 *Tribune*, 11 April 1975.
31 LSE, ORME/1/2, Orme to Graham, 23 April 1975.
32 TNA, CAB 134/4039, IN(76) memo 6, 21 May 1976.
33 TNA, CAB 134/4039, IN(76) memo 6, 21 May 1976.
34 TNA, CAB 134/4039, IN(76) meeting 1, 27 May 1976.
35 TNA, T341/737, Moore to Moody, 1 July 1974.
36 TNA, T341/737, Holden to Pliatzky, 19 June 1974.
37 TNA, T341/737, Rees to Barnett, 26 June 1974.
38 TNA, T341/737, Moody to PS/Chief Secretary, 2 July 1974; TNA, T341/737, Moody to Wilson, 12 June 1975.
39 TNA, T341/737, Note by Moody, 1 August 1974; TNA, T341/737, Rees to Barnett, 28 August 1974.
40 TNA, T341/737, Moody to Johnston, 31 July 1974.
41 *The Times*, 31 March 1976.
42 TNA, T341/737, Moody to Willott, 16 July 1974.
43 TNA, T341/737, Woods to Workman, 11 July 1974.
44 TNA, T341/737, Woods to Workman, 4 October 1974.
45 TNA, T341/737, Workman to Woods, 21 October 1974.
46 TNA, T341/737, Kidd to Workman, 23 October 1974; TNA, T341/737, Cousins to Kidd, 12 November 1974.
47 TNA, CJ4/1017, Bourn to Smith, 17 November 1975.

48   TNA, CJ4/1017, Press statement by Rees, 29 December 1975.

49   TNA, CJ4/1495, Meeting to discuss the Rolls-Royce Dundonald Plant, 23 January 1976.

50   Hansard (Commons), 925, col. 1632; Hansard (Commons), 935, col. 695w.

51   PRONI, SOSEC/1/2, SOSEC meeting, 19 July 1974.

52   *Northern Ireland: finance and the economy* (London: HMSO, 1974).

53   TNA, CAB 134/3921, IRN(75) memo 8, 18 February 1975.

54   LSE, MERLYN-REES/1/4, Transcript of tapes, undated, pp. 7, 34.

55   M. Artis, D. Cobham and M. Wickham-Jones, 'Social democracy in hard times: the economic record of the Labour government 1974–79', *Twentieth Century British History*, 3:1 (1992), pp. 32–3.

56   Jim Tomlinson, 'Tale of a death exaggerated: how Keynesian policies survived the 1970s' in *Contemporary British History*, 21:4 (2007), p. 442.

57   Artis *et al.*, 'Social democracy', p. 34.

58   Tomlinson, 'Tale of a death exaggerated', p. 441.

59   George Zis, 'The international status of sterling' in Michael Artis and David Cobham (eds) *Labour's economic policies 1974–79* (Manchester: Manchester University Press, 1991), p. 105; J.C.R. Dow, *Major recessions: Britain and the world 1920–1995* (Oxford: Oxford University Press, 1998), p. 295n.

60   Dow, *Major recessions*, p. 281.

61   Artis *et al.*, 'Social democracy', pp. 37–8.

62   Artis *et al.*, 'Social democracy', pp. 43–4.

63   Stagflation was originally coined by Iain Macleod in 1965: Hansard (Commons), 720, col. 1165.

64   Dow, *Major recessions*, p. 276.

65   Peter Jackson, 'Public expenditure' in Michael Artis and David Cobham (eds) *Labour's economic policies 1974–79* (Manchester: Manchester University Press, 1991), pp. 76–7.

66   Artis *et al.*, 'Social democracy', p. 44.

67   Jackson, 'Public expenditure', p. 78.

68   Artis *et al.*, 'Social democracy', p. 47.

69   Jackson, 'Public expenditure', pp. 84–5.

70   Artis *et al.*, 'Social democracy', p. 47.

71   *Public Expenditure to 1979–80*, Cmnd. 6393, HC 1975–76.

72   *The government's expenditure plans 1979–80 to 1982–83*, Cmnd. 7439, HC 1978–79.

73   Bew *et al.*, *Between war and peace*, p. 88.

74   Wickham-Jones, *Economic strategy*, pp. 63–4.

75   Wickham-Jones, *Economic strategy*, p. 143.

76   Wickham-Jones, *Economic strategy*, pp. 138–41.

77   TNA, CAB 134/3921, IRN(75) memo 8, 18 February 1975.

78   Hansard (Commons), 908, cols 1723–8.

79   Hansard (Commons), 908, cols 649–52.

80   TNA, CAB 134/4039, IN(76) memo 4, 20 May 1976.

81   TNA, CAB 134/4039, IN(76) memo 9, 2 August 1976.

82 TNA, PREM 16/1342, Barnett to Rees, 24 August 1976.

83 LSE, MERLYN-REES/1/12, Transcript of tapes, 8 September 1976, p. 1.

84 *Economic and social progress in Northern Ireland: review and prospects* (Belfast: HMSO, 1979).

85 Rees to Callaghan, 10 September 1976 (TNA, PREM 16/1342).

86 *The Times*, 30 September 1976.

87 TNA, PREM 16/1342, Mason to Callaghan, 1 October 1976.

88 TNA, CAB 134/4040, INO(76) meeting 2, 19 October 1976.

89 TNA, CAB 134/4039, IN(76) meeting 2, 28 October 1976.

90 *Economic and industrial strategy for Northern Ireland* (Belfast: HMSO, 1976).

91 Bew *et al.*, *Between war and peace*, p. 91.

92 Hansard (Commons), 918, col. 676.

93 Hansard (Commons), 918, cols 677–8.

94 Hansard (Commons), 927, cols 1719–20.

95 TNA, CAB 134/4039, IN(77) memo 3, 31 March 1977.

96 TNA, CAB 134/4039, IN(77) meeting 1, 5 April 1977.

97 Hansard (Commons), 934, col. 644; Hansard (Commons), 935, col. 1822.

98 *Economic and social progress in Northern Ireland: review and prospects* (Belfast: HMSO, 1979); Hansard (Commons), 947, col. 1649; Hansard (Commons), 934, col. 644; Hansard (Commons), 935, col. 1822.

99 TNA, PREM 16/1344, Mason to Callaghan, 16 June 1977.

100 *The Times*, 2 August 1977.

101 *Economic and social progress in Northern Ireland: review and prospects* (Belfast: HMSO, 1979).

102 *Irish Times*, 2 August 1977.

103 *The Times*, 10 August 1977.

104 Hansard (Commons), 953, cols 894–5.

105 Hansard (Commons), 953, col. 1707.

106 Hansard (Commons), 960, col. 181.

107 Hansard (Commons), 945, cols 1140–1.

108 *The Times*, 23 October 1976.

109 Hansard (Commons), 945, cols 1141.

110 Hansard (Commons), 965, col. 530w.

111 Graham Brownlow, 'Back to the failure: an analytic narrative of the De Lorean debacle', *Business History*, 57:1 (2015), p. 173.

112 TNA, CJ4/2016, Quigley to Minister, 19 June 1978.

113 TNA, CJ4/2016, Meeting about the DeLorean Motor Company, 20 June 1978.

114 TNA, CJ4/2016, Quigley to PS/SSNI, 21 June 1978.

115 TNA, CJ4/2016, Heads of agreement between the Northern Ireland Department of Commerce, the Northern Ireland Development Agency and the DeLorean Motor Company, 21 June 1978.

116 TNA, CJ4/2016, Bell to PS/SSNI, 30 June 1978.

117 TNA, CJ4/2016, Note for the record, 27 June 1978.

118 TNA, CJ4/2016, Jones to Bell, 4 July 1978.

119 TNA, CJ4/2016, Note for the record, 13 July 1978.

120 TNA, CJ4/2016, Quigley to Pilling, 14 July 1978.

121 TNA, CJ4/2016, Barnett to Mason, 17 July 1978.

122 TNA, CJ4/2016, Cartledge to Pilling, 24 July 1978.

123 TNA, CAB 134/4208, EI(78) meeting 20, 26 July 1978.

124 *The Times*, 4 August 1978.

125 TNA, CJ4/2016, Brown to Quigley, 9 October 1978.

126 *Economist*, 10–16 March 1979.

127 *The Times*, 20 February 1982.

128 Graham Brownlow, 'Back to the failure', p. 171.

129 *Economic and social progress in Northern Ireland: review and prospects* (Belfast: HMSO, 1979).

130 *The government's expenditure plans 1979–80 to 1982–83*, Cmnd. 7439, HC 1978–9.

9

Political inertia

While it was a logical conclusion that direct rule would have to continue indefinitely, the concept of 'positive direct rule' offered very little prospect of bringing about changes in the attitudes of nationalist and unionist political parties in Northern Ireland. Instead, the period that followed the end of the Convention was characterised by political inertia and when Mason replaced Rees it seemed to some that politics was pushed entirely to one side in favour of a focus on the economy and security. Scholars such as Patterson and Bew are right to identify Mason's basic enthusiasm for direct rule, embracing it as a desirable setup rather than merely the least bad option.[1] Although O'Leary claims that Mason 'pursued no significant power-sharing initiatives', there was some discussion of the concept of 'interim devolution'.[2] The hope of involving unionists and nationalists in administrative responsibilities as a stepping stone to a political settlement was never realised. Unionists continued to refuse to compromise. The Labour government was sharply criticised by the SDLP, which underwent a difficult period of fragmentation. Anger at the perceived lack of support from the Labour government and the belief that it had secretly struck a deal with unionists meant that relations with nationalists reached their lowest ebb under Mason.

After the Convention

Immediately after the Convention ended in March 1976 dialogue continued between the SDLP and unionists. Conversations between Gerry Fitt and Martin Smyth (Ulster Unionist and Grand Master of the Orange Order) led to secret talks between John Hume, Paddy Devlin, Austin Ardill and Smyth.[3] In the Commons Rees cautiously greeted talks between those 'who seek an equitable and durable agreement' and said he was 'ready to play a part at an appropriate time'.[4] Paddy Devlin told the NIO they had discussed 'only "simple issues"' and the real purpose was to undermine Ian Paisley's support.[5] In September the UUP publicly announced an end to the dialogue, saying there was no point continuing unless the SDLP gave ground. After receiving accounts from both sides, the NIO concluded that 'whatever their initial intentions, they had not got down to hard bargaining on the major issues.'[6]

Mason's arrival in September brought constitutional policy into question. Gerry Fitt was furious at the appointment. He bitterly told the BBC that the former Defence Secretary had proven 'completely partial to the British army in Northern Ireland.'[7] Relations between the two men proved especially fraught. Unionists, meanwhile, were hopeful that he would be more favourable than Rees. Harry West wrote an open letter to James Callaghan calling for the Convention proposals to be implemented but this was dismissed.[8] Giving his first impressions to Callaghan, Mason said there was 'no sign of a meaningful consensus'. He said they should not 'feel obliged to seek an early constitutional solution' but must remove any impression that they were 'deliberately putting constitutional proposals "on a long finger"'.[9] Brian Cubbon told other NIO officials that Mason 'did not appear to be changing Mr Rees's policies' but he was 'inclined to steer clear of political matters'.[10] His inclination and style were to have important consequences for relations with the Northern Ireland parties, much to the detriment of constitutional nationalism.

The SDLP endured very difficult circumstances in the context of unionist opposition to power-sharing and underwent a period of internal reflection that brought out divisions within the party.[11] Gerry Fitt told Mason in September that it was important he understand the difference between Belfast members such as himself and Paddy Devlin and those who came from Derry and rural border areas. The latter usually lived as the majority community and were accustomed to an existence that spanned both sides of the border but in Belfast 'Catholics were more conscious of the fact that they were a minority.'[12] The geographical distinction was not the only one; the name of the party indicated the inclusion of both social democrats and socialists and there were also those for whom nationalism remained the greatest part of their political identity. These three distinctions could map neatly onto each other (for instance, Fitt and Devlin as Belfast socialists in contrast to Hume the Derry social democrat) but were not always clear cut. Nevertheless, with no prospect of political power, the nationalistic side of the party became more prominent.

Sean Donlon, Secretary in the Irish Department of Foreign Affairs, warned that Seamus Mallon and others were pushing the SDLP towards a more radical constitutional position and if their faction 'got their way' then Fitt would leave the party and it would disintegrate.[13] This tension was clear to see at the 1976 annual conference in December. A motion in favour of British withdrawal was defeated, but by a relatively small margin of 153 to

111. Over half of the SDLP's Convention members favoured withdrawal, including Ivan Cooper, Paddy Devlin and Seamus Mallon. In contrast to Mallon's traditional nationalist position, Devlin and Cooper advocated independence, on which the party agreed to conduct a study. Gerry Fitt attacked both withdrawal and independence.[14] John Hume stuck to power-sharing and an all-Ireland dimension as the best option, with the *Irish Times* reporting his appropriate remark that 'We're all frustrated; but let not frustration be the basis for party policy.'[15] Technically SDLP policy remained the same but the party was hardly united.

These tensions were not helped by Roy Mason's adjustment to the vocabulary used in government statements on Northern Ireland. Brian Cubbon noted at an NIO seminar that central to Mason's thinking 'was surprise that the government and NI politicians had got "hooked" on power-sharing, as something to which the minority felt entitled.'[16] The term thus slipped out of usage in his statements, also to the annoyance of the Irish government. A parliamentary question was arranged in October 1976 for Mason to reaffirm constitutional policy. Airey Neave promised he would respond by reaffirming bipartisanship.[17] Douglas Janes, Deputy Secretary at NIO London, showed Irish ambassador Donal O'Sullivan the intended reply from Mason. Two days later the ambassador returned, saying that his government were 'seriously concerned' that the statement did not refer to power-sharing.[18] Janes told O'Sullivan that power-sharing 'had acquired very narrow connotations' and 'the form of words used was best designed to produce the desired result'. O'Sullivan asked that they insert 'partnership and participation' into the reply. Later that day he broke diplomatic protocol, telling William Whitelaw about this confidential exchange and the Irish government's unhappiness. Neave contacted the NIO, upset that the Irish government was allowed to interfere in preparing parliamentary answers.[19]

That evening O'Sullivan gave Downing Street a letter from the Taoiseach, Liam Cosgrave. It complained that the phrase 'widespread support throughout the community' was open to misinterpretation.[20] Janes advised that when replying they should tell O'Sullivan that his actions had been 'a serious breach' of confidence and 'made it quite impossible for them to agree to any changes.'[21] It was decided to insert 'participate' into the answer but to send Callaghan's reply to Cosgrave straight to Dublin, bypassing the ambassador.[22] When the question was finally asked on 28 October Mason said that any system must be one 'which will command widespread support throughout the community and in which both the majority and the minority will participate.'[23] Participation replaced power-sharing in the Labour government's vocabulary. For Mason, the distinction was one which indicated a less prescriptive attitude on the British side to a settlement which would still have to include nationalists as well as unionists. To nationalists it suggested Mason's lack of commitment to securing an acceptable settlement.

In November 1976 Brian Cubbon instigated discussion between officials on how the Northern Ireland parties might be brought together. The discussion brought out conflicting attitudes towards direct rule. Donald Middleton argued that it 'had the merit of impartiality'. He felt that involving the NICS in discussions with local politicians 'might be a better way of showing them their mutual interests than trying to drive them to agree on a devolved government through alienation and desperation'. The possibility of creating new local government institutions was raised, but officials agreed that this 'might run counter to our efforts to put pressure on NI politicians' to reach agreement and could also be construed as an integrationist approach.[24]

David Gilliland, head of information services in the NIO, prepared a paper on alternative policies which was rather more hostile to unionism and which feared that direct rule would drift into integration. Faced with the possibility of direct rule dragging on indefinitely, he felt there might 'be an argument for deciding that rather than having a sterile area in which nothing happens the wound should be allowed to go septic', leading in the long run 'to the amputation of a limb'. Unionists, he argued, claimed that only majority rule was democratic but refused to accept the will of 'the greater family of the United Kingdom'. Therefore, 'it should be made plain that certain consequences flow from such a refusal'. Gilliland believed that the present generation of politicians was 'finished'. He proposed that the government announce 'a progressive withdrawal of its interests'. They would then discuss with all representatives a future 'not within the United Kingdom, but within the context of the island of Ireland'.[25] Gilliland claimed that if the SDLP were to split and fuse with 'less extreme PIRA elements' the result might represent 'real Catholic feelings' and a similar development might happen on the Protestant side.[26]

Unsurprisingly, this was criticised; Gilliland had no solution for if the two communities failed to reach agreement and conflict continued.[27] Two civil servants from the Foreign and Commonwealth Office, John Hickman and G.W. Harding, were especially firm in opposing Gilliland's ideas.[28] Hickman stressed that the Irish government took it 'as axiomatic that the SDLP must be supported and kept in business...since they are the only moderate and constitutional voice of the Catholic minority'.[29] Harding pointed out that the British government had four strategic aims: 'to protect the health of Northern Ireland as part of the UK body politic', 'to minimize the threat to the citizens of the UK as a whole', 'to assist the people of Northern Ireland to find economic prosperity as well as political stability and peace', and 'to find a framework for harmonious symbiosis of Northern Ireland and the Republic and defuse the militant Republican tradition'. A more negative direct rule did not serve these objectives. Brian Cubbon concluded that even radical suggestions were 'premised on the belief that the people of Northern Ireland had ultimately to find a solution which worked and that we could only try to create favourable conditions in which they could do this'. He reaffirmed that any imposition by the British government would not work.[30] The discussion brought out the general powerlessness felt by those on the British side. Direct rule would have to continue for some time but it was incredibly difficult to see a way towards fostering a political settlement in the long term. There was no clear idea as to how more favourable conditions could be developed.

Administrative devolution

A new initiative followed in December 1976 but it began with the UUP rather than the Labour government. James Molyneaux called for an increase in Northern Ireland's representation in the Commons and the granting of administrative devolution. The call for greater representation was not new and was grounded in the region having proportionately fewer seats than Great Britain. Rees consistently opposed unionist pressure to change this, arguing that it should come only after 'the divide has been healed and the two groups are working for the good of Northern Ireland'.[31] More novel was Molyneaux's second proposal. He claimed that during fifty years of devolution Stormont was 'effectively bound by legislation passed in the United Kingdom'. Under direct rule it was 'the lack of control over the application and execution of the law which is intolerable'. As legislative devolution was not possible, he suggested that the British government should devolve administrative responsibilities instead.[32] Patrick Macrory, who headed a review of local bodies in 1970, wrote to *The Times* in January 1977 that 'the way back to peace, sanity and cooperation' might be found in the field of local government. His 1970 review concluded that a three-tier system of parliament, county councils and borough councils was an over-elaborate structure for a region with a smaller rates revenue than the city of Leeds. County councils were therefore abolished. Once Stormont was removed there was very little provision for democratic control of local services. Seven years later he proposed that county councils be re-established, to fill what had become known as the Macrory gap.[33]

On 18 January Bernard Donougue complained to Callaghan that Mason had not produced anything on paper about the political situation for Downing Street since October.[34] There was a steady decline in meetings of the Labour government's ministerial committee on Northern Ireland (11 in 1974, 9 in 1975, 5 in 1976, 3 in 1977, 3 in 1978 and 0 in 1979).[35] This occurred for multiple reasons. In a later interview with Peter Hennessy, Frank Cooper remarked that after a great deal of attention to Northern Ireland at cabinet level in the early years of the conflict 'it then got into the "too difficult" category'.[36] This appears to have been the case for Callaghan, who rarely intervened, and Mason was much less inclined towards debate than his predecessor. The context of the conflict was also a factor, in that meetings were far less obviously necessary than during 1974 and 1975 because of the differing problems faced by NIO ministers. Two days later Mason met Callaghan, telling him that he sought 'to prove that direct rule was purposeful'. Mason doubted that the SDLP would be willing to discuss Molyneaux's ideas. Callaghan said he was not pressing Mason to take any initiatives, but asked him to 'look ahead twelve or eighteen months'.[37]

A week later Douglas Janes wrote to Mason describing the Molyneaux proposals as 'an unclothed skeleton' which raised lots of difficult administrative questions, such as whether housing could be transferred back to an elected body after the previous record of unionist discrimination and whether the large sums of money involved in industry and commerce would be managed responsibly.[38] It also raised concerns in some sections of the UUP that Molyneaux was insufficiently committed to devolution. Harry West still held out for the Convention report, rejecting 'a purely administrative body masquerading as an Ulster government'. Molyneaux replied that he had been misunderstood and was not advocating a substitute for proper devolution but simply an upper tier of local government.[39] Afterwards Molyneaux told Mason's private secretary that he 'had not made a forceful intervention' when the Ulster Unionist Executive discussed his proposals because a direct confrontation with West might have split the party.[40] From March 1977 onwards NIO officials led by Janes began preparing a model for administrative devolution. They conceived of it primarily as an interim stage to devolution. An internal meeting chaired by Cubbon found that the main advantage of this was that major issues of contention 'could be put in cold storage, without seeming to be abandoned'. The consensus, however, was that 'the basic tactical position of the government should remain as it was'; there should be no initiatives and even if the parties agreed, the Labour government 'should have to react sceptically and cautiously'.[41]

Deals at Westminster

Around the same time, the Labour government's parliamentary majority was eroded after by-election defeats. The Conservatives tabled a motion of no confidence for 23 March 1977. Ultimately a pact was negotiated with the Liberals by Michael Foot but there was a less formalised change in the relationship between Labour and some Ulster Unionist MPs. Foot met Enoch Powell and James Molyneaux, who again asked for increased representation at Westminster and an upper tier of local government.[42] Foot was himself already sympathetic to representation. In September 1976, in light of a commitment to maintain the number of Scottish and Welsh constituencies in the event of devolution to the two countries, he suggested to Callaghan that they increase English and Northern Irish constituencies to bring about 'strict proportionality at Westminster'.[43] Powell and Molyneaux also met Callaghan. The prime minister said he was willing to consider an arrangement so he could carry out the government's economic policy. Molyneaux and Powell repeated their wishes. Callaghan's memoirs state that they did not promise a positive vote 'but if these issues were conceded there might be up to six abstentions'.[44]

During the debate on the motion of no confidence Callaghan announced that he was 'impressed' by Powell and Molyneaux's case on representation in the Commons. He proposed a Speaker's conference on the subject 'irrespective' of how Ulster Unionists voted that night. The sudden change after denying the unionist case for so long naturally led to accusations of bribery. Foot acknowledged in the Commons that security policy had been raised by Molyneaux but the government 'believed that it would be improper to make the question of security part of any such understanding'. Because of the Lib–Lab pact there was no need for the government to secure unionist votes and the motion was defeated by 322 votes to 298. Molyneaux voted against Labour but three Ulster Unionists abstained (Enoch Powell, John Carson and Harold McCusker).[45]

The following day Molyneaux wrote to Callaghan thanking him for the 'candour and the generosity of the passage about Northern Ireland' in his speech. Molyneaux thought it 'right that we should get down at once with Roy Mason to practical details' and said that Powell would be meeting Foot about this.[46] Mason wrote to Foot, remarking that a Speaker's conference and especially local government were 'fraught with dangers for me and indeed for [the government] generally'. On the concession of a Speaker's conference he said that they 'should hold the line there for the moment' and 'give no hostages to fortune about the precise details', while in the case of local government the unionists were 'trying to pick up what they did not pay for'. He cautioned: 'we must tread with extreme caution in this field'.[47] This point was reinforced on 29 March when Mason's private secretary warned Downing Street that his minister was anxious not to be 'rushed into hasty action'.[48] These exchanges are extremely important; despite Mason's reputation for overt sympathy towards unionists, he was clearly very conscious of the potential dangers involved in making concessions to the UUP. Callaghan wrote to Molyneaux that there were 'of course a lot of very complex problems involved.'[49]

At the end of May, following the collapse of the UUAC strike, Mason updated Callaghan. The SDLP, UUP and Alliance agreed to hold further talks with his officials but Mason said the DUP were 'as dogmatic and sectarian as ever and unwilling to contribute in any constructive sense.'[50] On 22 June he reported that the SDLP were 'highly suspicious of partial devolution', seeing a new tier of local government as a step towards integration and 'a device to secure the re-establishment of Protestant dominance'. Powell and Molyneaux, wrote Mason, were 'by no means at one with their colleagues across the water' either.[51] The Ulster Unionist Party continued to hanker after majority rule in spite of Westminster's repeated rejection of it.

The SDLP

Over the summer of 1977 the positions of both nationalist and unionist parties hardened. Added to the usual impact of the marching season, in August the Queen visited Northern Ireland to mark the silver jubilee. The nationalist community was affronted by what they saw as a triumphalist celebration by unionists. This prompted Callaghan to ask Mason to 'make some special effort with leaders of the Catholics'.[52] On 7 September Mason wrote that the UUP 'probably feel more confident and stronger than for some time'. They thought the Labour government were 'vulnerable to pressure' and felt 'less need to consider Catholic opinion'. In the SDLP there was 'a strong feeling that...they have little alternative but to fall back on a more nationalist stance'.[53] The tone of direct rule favoured unionists too much.

On 19 September the SDLP released a policy statement entitled *Facing Reality*. It attacked 'the shameful reality of a British Labour government entering into pacts and undertakings with unionists at Westminster'. The statement also proclaimed that attempts to solve the problem 'in a purely British context have failed and will continue to fail'. It demanded that the British pursue a policy to create 'an agreed Ireland; the essential unity of whose people would have evolved in agreement over the years; whose institutions of government would reflect both its unity and diversity'.[54] Peter McLoughlin aptly describes the change as the SDLP moving away from a belief 'in the feasibility of negotiating a local settlement for Northern Ireland' and towards promoting 'an inter-governmental' approach.[55]

Gerry Fitt told Callaghan that the past three months had been very bad for the Catholic population. Powell was 'making speeches to the effect that

the unionists were respected at last at Westminster', while 'Catholics had
no road to go down' without power-sharing. The Queen's visit 'placed him
in an impossible situation' and, Fitt said, the SDLP 'had gone green, on the
basis that if the unionists were going to go more Orange, there was only
one place for them to go'. There was little support for him within his party;
on its 17–man executive he claimed that 'two came from Belfast and the
rest from or near Crossmaglen' (an exaggeration but one which captures
the tendency within the party). Fitt feared that his party conference would
adopt a motion calling for British withdrawal, referring to the rest of the
SDLP leadership as 'green'.[56]

Paddy Devlin was expelled from the party during the summer. John
Hume told the Under-Secretary for information, D.R. Ford, that the main
reason for the rift had been Devlin's anger at not being selected as the
party's candidate for the European elections. Hume believed Devlin to be
'mentally unstable' and said on one occasion he 'attacked Austin Currie
with a chair'.[57] Devlin met Ford a few days prior to this conversation and
explained his plan to launch a cross-community workers' party and 'give
that ____ ____ John Hume a run for his money'. He launched into 'a long
and emotional tirade' against Hume, lambasting 'the way he manipulated
the SDLP towards his own ideas'.[58] In his memoirs Devlin later wrote that
the party was increasingly run on an autocratic basis by Hume and was
'stripped of its socialism and...taken over by unadulterated nationalists',
but admitted that he left in 'a most unworthy squabble in which I was not
the innocent party'.[59]

Seamus Mallon, meanwhile, told the NIO that the SDLP were in an
impossible position. They existed to persuade the Catholic minority that
there was an alternative to violence but having 'turned the cheek to loyalists time and again' the SDLP 'had no "honourable" alternative but to stand
square and call for British withdrawal'. When an NIO official remarked that
this would be the end of the party, Mallon agreed, but said it had already
been rendered ineffective and this way at least 'some honour could be
salvaged'. The officials were shocked, especially as he 'spoke calmly...without
animosity or rancour'.[60]

At the SDLP's annual conference in November Fitt was defiant. He
described Mason as a 'colonial administrator appropriately dressed in a
safari suit, walking through the streets of Belfast while the natives were
holed up in their sub-standard wigwams'. The party overwhelmingly
approved *Facing Reality*.[61] In September, Jack Lynch, who returned as
Taoiseach after Fianna Fáil won a majority in a July 1977 general election,
said that British policy 'seemed to be giving succour to the majority'. Callaghan promised they 'had not and would not ignore the SDLP' and there
'would not be a scintilla of a move...towards integration'. Lynch warned

that it would be dangerous if out of work politicians in the SDLP were compelled by 'enforced inactivity' to leave the political scene.[62]

Mason was keen to refute the claims of a pact between the Labour government and Ulster Unionists.[63] The NIO produced a list of key votes in the Commons, which the NIO believed 'fully substantiates the Secretary of State's belief that the [UUP] members…have given the government little support'. Molyneaux consistently opposed the Labour government but there were regular abstentions by Carson, McCusker and Powell. It was admitted that those 'who want to believe in a pact' would not be convinced. They could claim that the UUP did not have to actively support the government, and only when the party's votes 'make the difference between defeat and victory, will the pact come into play'.[64] Mason objected to Michael Foot that the belief in a pact was a major factor in the SDLP's shift towards a more nationalistic stance.[65] Foot replied that for his part he did 'not see how I could have been clearer or firmer in denying that a deal had been made' and said he had 'always been punctilious about keeping you informed of any action of mine'.[66] Mason privately warned Foot that some Ulster Unionists had 'a clear interest in hinting' that Northern Ireland policy was being influenced by them and the SDLP would 'be only too ready to believe it'.[67]

Interim devolution

On 4 November Cubbon provided Mason with a model for 'interim devolution'. He outlined a strategy for dealing with the parties: at first they should speak in general terms, reserving 'some of the tit-bits for both sides until we come to a crunch'. The advantage of having a model prepared was that they would already understand the implications of the negotiations as they unfolded. It outlined a system consisting of an elected assembly and committees for each government department. The chairships of the committees would be allocated according to the proportions of the assembly. The minority would be given the power 'to "pull the plug" on the whole system'.[68]

On 21 November Mason met the SDLP. He said it was in the government's interests to keep the party 'in a cohesive form' and insisted there had been no pact with the unionists. Mason said there was no chance of the Convention report being implemented and the pattern of votes by Ulster Unionists 'must surely make clear' that no pact existed. Mason gave a vague sketch of the model and said he was convinced that SDLP participation would not damage their long-term aspirations. Hume responded that they would not take part in talks unless there was a prospect of success and there had been no indication that the UUP was willing to make significant movement. Other members, such as Mallon, said they were disappointed that Mason allowed the unionists a veto on government policy and that the Irish dimension was being ignored.[69]

The following day Mason invited the DUP, SDLP, UUP and the Alliance party to talks with officials. It was fairly assumed that the DUP would reject any proposals and Alliance would automatically agree to them. Describing the proposed system as 'temporary in duration and only partial in the powers to be devolved', Mason informed colleagues on the ministerial committee on Northern Ireland that he was 'not optimistic about the chances of agreement on even this limited goal'.[70] Cabinet Secretary John Hunt advised Callaghan that Mason's approach was 'probably as good as any that can be devised'.[71] On 6 December Cubbon met the UUP. Harry West asked whether the ultimate aim was power-sharing. Cubbon replied that to talk about participation or partnership 'was to be bemused by labels' and the thing to do was examine what was on offer and if it 'was tolerable in itself'. The NIO was trying to cajole the parties into an interim settlement when the two sides had fundamentally opposing views of what it should be an interim to. West remained persistently unrealistic, asking whether it would 'not be better to avoid all this troublesome discussion and rely instead on the ballot box operating on a Westminster model'. Molyneaux was more willing to consider the scheme and asked detailed questions about how it would function.[72]

Austin Currie and Seamus Mallon met Cubbon for similarly unsuccessful discussions. Currie said they were 'interested only in a formula which contained the ingredients of a permanent settlement'. Again Cubbon talked of 'getting away from labels such as "partnership or participation"'. Mallon replied that the granting of a speaker's conference had led to a rethink in the SDLP and the British government should remember that power-sharing was not their fundamental objective; they wanted an administrative structure capable of evolving through peaceful means towards a united Ireland.[73] In the absence of success the SDLP resorted to traditional nationalist politics.

Meanwhile, a meeting was arranged between Callaghan and both Molyneaux and Powell. After finding this out Cubbon phoned the prime minister's office and asked that he meet Fitt as well.[74] A few days later the NIO suggested that Callaghan meet Hume as well because Fitt was not considered 'a reliable interlocutor'. Callaghan rejected this.[75] Seeing Fitt on 20 December, he opened by saying that he knew the SDLP had 'lingering fears' of a deal with the unionists but it was untrue. Fitt, departing from his public line, said he did not believe there had been a deal 'but some of his colleagues feared it'. Fitt acknowledged that neither side would get what they wanted but blamed the unionists for making no movement.[76]

When Callaghan met the UUP the next day, Molyneaux disingenuously said he was confused by the government's actions; they had seemed keen to fill the gap between local government and Westminster earlier in the year. Enoch Powell objected when Mason argued they should pursue a method 'acceptable to all parts of the community'. Both Ulster Unionists wanted local government 'in the proper sense of that term' but, Powell claimed, interim devolution 'would be of a different nature and would inevitably become an embryo government'. Powell remarked that unionists 'were not fool enough to accept a position where the majority and the minority were treated as being of equal weight'.[77] The talks led nowhere.

Jack Lynch

The chasm between the two parties widened further after a controversial RTÉ interview with Jack Lynch on 8 January 1978. Lynch described his hope that the talks between British officials and the parties in Northern Ireland would lead to devolution with power-sharing but he also said that the Irish government wanted Britain to acknowledge that it had little to offer Ireland as a whole and declare their interest in bringing the Irish people together. Asked whether he had put this to the government, Lynch affirmed that he had and said neither Heath, Wilson nor Callaghan was averse to unification. Lynch concluded by suggesting there was a possibility of amnesty for political prisoners if the conflict ceased.[78]

The following day Harry West publicly announced an end to talks with the Labour government, citing the Lynch statement as proving their real underhand intentions.[79] Mason responded swiftly that there would be no amnesty, adding that he was 'surprised and disappointed' by Lynch's 'unhelpful comments'.[80] John Hume thought Mason had overreacted, telling the NIO that his remarks were 'nothing less than disgraceful and represented an abandonment of the minority community'. He said 'there was no point in dealing with this government'. The party 'would wait until there was a majority government in Westminster'.[81] When the British ambassador met Sean Donlon to discuss Lynch's interview, the Irish official maintained that it contained nothing new or surprising and, as the ambassador complained, 'argued that we were being too theological (that, from an Irishman!)'.[82]

Mason was 'not very optimistic' but continued to believe that the interim framework offered 'the only possible way of showing a wish on our part for political progress'.[83] On 23 January Mason spoke with Fitt in the Commons lobby. Fitt said that 'against his inclinations and judgement, the

SDLP were rapidly becoming a deep shade of "green". Mason felt little sympathy, telling his private secretary that his inclination was 'to warn that Gerry's policy of "all take and no give" should be resisted'.[84] This was unfair; Fitt's party was being rendered redundant by unionist intransigence and the West Belfast MP suffered from being in many ways closer to the Labour government than his own political party.

On 3 February Mason suggested to Callaghan how to deal with the Irish government and its 'stepping up their traditional republican cries'. He said statements like Lynch's alienated unionists and encouraged 'the green element in SDLP', as well as the PIRA and their fundraisers in America. 'The distinction between the political aims of the Irish government, the SDLP and PIRA', he argued, 'is too subtle for the man in the street in Northern Ireland to appreciate or international interests to understand.' This 'lesson' could not be conveyed publicly as it would stir unionist fears, so he suggested that Callaghan make these points 'informally when opportunity offers'.[85]

Airey Neave, with rather less subtlety, accused the Irish government of nurturing 'the recovery of the terrorist element in Northern Ireland'. He claimed, with considerable inaccuracy, that 'thanks to the Irish government, a power-sharing administration in Northern Ireland is no longer practical politics'. In a marked change from previous bipartisan policy, Neave made an explicit bid for the UUP's support, promising an upper tier of local government to take away control from 'a socialist government…deeply offensive to a community which has no time at all for socialism'.[86] Molyneaux welcomed this as 'a more realistic attitude'.[87] Agreement was even less likely when the second party at Westminster actively sought to appeal to one community in Northern Ireland.

Relations between Mason and the SDLP were less antagonistic in private. When Fitt, Mallon and Currie met Mason in the Strangers' bar in Westminster a week later the conversation began with Currie ribbing the minister about a recent television profile, saying the diminutive Yorkshireman had 'come across as a "five foot four John Wayne"'. They nonetheless complained that the Labour government had 'done nothing for the party'. Mason objected that it was government policy to help them and 'challenged them to point to one issue on which [the government] had gone against the SDLP's interests'. They cited the granting of the speaker's conference. Mason argued that their 'basic problem was that they were continuing to sacrifice potential short term gains in the interests of long term aspirations, the reiteration of which simply served to alienate the unionists'.[88] Meanwhile, West continued what must have become a tedious exchange of correspondence for Mason. He continued to venerate the Westminster system, deploring the 'treasonable challenge' that the SDLP voiced in promising to resist it.[89] Distaste is a sentiment that the Northern Ireland Secretary would have been wise to indulge in only rarely but Mason had opportunities to do so more evenly and failed to take them.

Northern Ireland representation

February 1978 saw the publication of the speaker's conference report. It recommended an increase in Northern Ireland's Westminster seats from twelve to seventeen.[90] The SDLP was completely opposed. Mason said the issue of timing the legislation was 'very much a political decision'. His view was that they should 'move quickly', making it 'much easier to weather the inevitable protest from the SDLP'. Recognising that the UUP might have a part to play in sustaining a Labour government, he admitted there was also a political argument for delay: 'by keeping the six [UUP] MPs in a state of continuing suspense they will be the more reluctant to bring down the government until their eggs...are finally hatched'.[91]

Bernard Donoughue interjected that Mason had done little to consider how policy was perceived in Ireland and 'particularly among the Irish community which lives and votes in Britain'. The Speaker's conference report was 'seen by all Irish Catholics as a concession to the loyalists and a significant and a permanent move towards integration'. Donoughue said it was reasonable to argue that 'the proposals for greater representation are technically fair', 'the Irish Catholics always complain whatever we do' and, 'while we depend on the Ulster Unionists in parliament, we would be foolish to go out of our way to offend them on this', but there was a large number of Irish voters in Britain who could cost them an election. Donoughue admitted they could not reject the recommendations for extra seats, but the next parliamentary session was 'not so very far away'. If there was a full session they could legislate then, but if Callaghan called an autumn election they would not need unionist support any longer 'and may be relieved if we have not legislated and alienated the Irish vote in the meantime'.[92] In a further memo Donoughue referred to six marginal constituencies where the Irish population ranged from 5 to 12%.[93] This greatly overestimated the extent to which Irish voters in Great Britain voted as an ethnic bloc and on the basis of Northern Ireland policy.[94] The discomfort at rendering the SDLP so thoroughly estranged from the Labour government was, however, thoroughly merited.

On 8 March 1978 the ministerial committee on Northern Ireland discussed representation. Donoughue recorded in his private diaries that Mason referred to the Ulster Unionists by their first names but 'was offhand about the Catholics and scathing about the Republic'. When Mason put his case for immediate legislation Merlyn Rees, Denis Healey and Elwyn Jones all intervened to oppose him. According to Donoughue, Callaghan asked Mason to stay behind after the meeting and 'gave him firm instructions to lay off Lynch and improve his relations with the Catholics'.[95] A month later, Mason informed a full cabinet meeting that the ministerial committee had decided to accept the report and proposed an early announcement supporting the recommendations. Legislation would follow in the autumn.[96]

Mason told Gerry Fitt of the plan before it received approval in cabinet. Fitt said he had predicted this to his colleagues and 'the fact that he was going to be right would show them "that he sometimes knew what was going on at Westminster"'.[97] It was rather telling of the SDLP's changed stance when Hume told the NIO at the end of March that 'the policy of "fighting on new ground"...was going extremely well'. Rejecting a compromise with unionists, he argued that 'Only the British government had the power and the influence to bring them to heel and the only way forward was for the British government to declare its interest in the long term unity of Ireland'.[98] Hume had become happier with the comfortable ideological certainty of opposition politics, which the SDLP was set to endure regardless. In May Fitt complained to an NIO official 'that his party was now so green that it had stopped worrying about the reaction of unionists'. He was 'forever playing down unity and trying to bring the SDLP back to practical politics but he was very despondent about the way they were all going'.[99]

NIO officials in the London and Belfast branches disagreed over how to respond to the SDLP's new line. NIO London's N.R. Cowling produced a critique of the *Facing reality* document, describing it as 'unimpressive' and 'surprisingly slender and unpolished'.[100] D.R. Ford, who held regular meetings with local politicians as part of his role at NIO Belfast, replied that he was 'unhappy' with the tendency towards 'dismissive or perjorative [*sic*] epithets'. He said *Facing reality* should be treated as 'merely a strategic sketch' and argued that it 'will do us no good with Irish ministers if we are to assert that the SDLP are simply living in cloud cuckoo land and pretend that there is no basis for the feeling that the unionists have been and are intransigent'. Quite reasonably, he stressed the difficulties the party had experienced since the collapse of Sunningdale.[101]

Mason's view was closer to Cowling's, as shown by a note of his remarks on the SDLP document. The references to pacts at Westminster and Labour's abandonment of policies were accurately dismissed as 'simply not true', but Mason showed a lack of empathy in his analysis. In particular, his belief that the SDLP 'should not pass up short term gains' by objecting to the interim framework did not take into account the political conditions in which they had been operating over the past five years. Mason dismissed the idea of a cross-border institution because co-operation 'was already being done' and there was 'no need for elaborate institutions for their own sake'.[102] While there is some merit in questioning the practical value of such an institution (indeed Shaun McDaid has shown that during the formulation of proposals in 1973 civil servants from domestic departments in the Irish Republic did precisely this), Mason showed ignorance of its potential political value to nationalists willing to compromise in accepting an internal settlement.[103] The nature of the SDLP's more nationalistic stance made frustration understandable but the tone of dismissiveness was not similarly adopted for Harry West's repeated demands for a return to the old Stormont system.

La Mon and the Republic of Ireland

Relations with the Irish government further deteriorated with Mason becoming openly antagonistic towards the new Fianna Fáil administration. On 17 February 1978 the PIRA firebombed the restaurant of La Mon House, a hotel on the outskirts of East Belfast. Twelve Protestant civilians were burnt to death, many of them left unrecognisable.[104] Mason told the Commons that the men responsible for La Mon 'could easily have escaped across the border' and added that 'much of the home-made explosives' used by the PIRA and 'many of their weapons' came through the Republic.[105] The *Irish Times* responded that Mason was 'playing with Irish lives', while the *Irish Press* accused him of 'a Goebbels-like use...of the big lie'.[106] As Patterson notes, the British had previously been keen to restrict criticisms to private communication between the two governments and so 'public denunciation was a major shock'. The Republic's Department of Foreign Affairs continued to deny that a significant amount of PIRA violence had any connection to the border, despite individuals such as the Irish ambassador to London believing that British evidence to the contrary was largely correct.[107]

In this sense, Mason had a legitimate grievance but Bernard Donoughue fairly objected in his diaries that, since the La Mon atrocity, Mason had 'become spokesman of the Protestants' and blamed the Irish government for violence in Northern Ireland, prompting Callaghan to ask why he expected Jack Lynch to 'succeed in Dublin where you fail in Belfast'.[108] In April Mason sought to cancel a meeting with the Irish Minister for Foreign Affairs, Michael O'Kennedy, because there were 'real difficulties in my going to Dublin on the Irish terms'. Mason claimed that the Irish wanted the meeting 'as a demonstration for their own political interests' and that it would make the negotiating task harder in Northern Ireland by giving credence to the SDLP's use of the Irish government as a negotiating channel. Furthermore, he 'would be made to appear to be going cap in hand to Dublin' after a meeting a week earlier between Callaghan and Lynch at the European Council in Copenhagen.[109] At the meeting Lynch complained about Mason's public statements but was told that Callaghan had full confidence in him and would rather discuss Lynch's own interview which had prompted unionists to abandon talks. When Mason and O'Kennedy met in May the Irish objected to his suggestion that they were not fully supportive of border co-operation against the Provisionals. After Mason complained about Lynch's interview and other speeches on Irish unity for having driven unionists away from talks on interim devolution, the Fianna Fáil minister reacted with the traditional republican argument that long-term peace would only come through unification.[110] When Lynch and Callaghan spoke on the phone a few days later the Labour prime minister said the portrayal of their relationship in the press was 'silly' and Lynch replied that their personal relations were never in doubt. Callaghan assured him that there was no change in policy and promised there was no deal with the unionists.[111] The damage to Anglo-Irish relations was, however, very real.

'Neutrality'

Enoch Powell tried again to extract upper-tier local government from Labour in the build up to a vote on the government's finance bill. Michael Foot passed the proposals onto Mason but said 'he himself was well aware of the sensitivities'. Callaghan's 'immediate reaction' was that Powell's offer could not be accepted. They 'were now turning the screw' but the government 'had to think first and foremost of the impact on relationships in Northern Ireland'; 'there was a limit to the danegeld which the government could be expected to pay'. Callaghan said that 'if the government were defeated, they would have to take their own decisions on the implications'.[112] The government lost by 312 votes to 304 but was able to continue. Powell, Carson and McCusker all voted against the government.[113]

In June Molyneaux asked Mason and Foot if they might consider enhancing the powers of district councils. Mason 'made no commitment' but, oddly, said that if he could find scope in 'non-controversial areas' it might be worthwhile and 'could not be considered as integrationist or favouring the unionists because of the prominent position of the SDLP in some councils'.[114] This entirely ignored the SDLP's outlook, prompting Douglas Janes to warn that, while a few councils demonstrated partnership, 'the great majority still have all the worst features of dominant unionist rule'.[115]

Janes had been asked by Cubbon to chair a review of constitutional options open to a new Secretary of State after a general election.[116] The report, produced in July 1978, concluded that the government 'must preserve a posture of strict neutrality', reasserting the principle of self-determination within Northern Ireland and insisting that no settlement was possible without the support of both sides. It argued that 'the only solution likely to be acceptable is one that gives both sides something but not everything' and that this would likely mean some form of devolved government, either with executive participation from both sides or majority rule combined with an institutional link with the South.[117] Cubbon thought they would have to be extremely careful in dealing with this second option publicly. Most significantly, Cubbon suggested they 'should not fall into the trap of expecting as much from the unionists as from the SDLP, as though some even-handed arbitration has to be made'. He remarked that the unionists 'have more cards in their hands: time is on their side as direct rule drifts into something like integration, and they control the levers of economic power'.[118] Cubbon did not appreciate that the relative weakness of the SDLP meant that it needed more help rather than less.

The parliamentary situation was made more precarious when the Lib–Lab pact came to an end as the Commons broke for summer recess, with most anticipating an autumn general election.[119] Close advisors such as Bernard Donoughue were shocked on 7 September when Callaghan told the cabinet that he would wait until the following year.[120] After Callaghan's decision Mason wrote that he would continue pushing for the parties to engage in talks.[121] In the absence of an election they were also obliged to introduce the Bill to increase representation in the Commons.[122] Mason anticipated that Fitt, would 'probably put a lot of time and effort' into opposing it.[123]

When the ministerial committee met on 26 October the following remarks were made in discussion: 'It was questionable whether the Government could remain for much longer in its present negative position.' The government was being criticised for the lack of movement and while 'it was no doubt true that the majority of Catholics and Protestants...were content with direct rule', this might not always be the case. Alternatively, any hint of a major initiative 'would raise hopes which would almost certainly be dashed.' Callaghan concluded that until the parties showed signs they were ready to make progress 'in a way which would satisfy the criterion of political acceptability, there was little the government could do to relieve the political stalemate'.[124] In November Mason held talks with the parties but there was clearly no willingness to compromise. He told the

UUP that an upper tier of local government would 'put back the cause of a proper devolved government for years'. West again said his party could go no further than the Convention report and the SDLP could not be given a veto on constitutional developments.[125]

In November 1978 the Bill to increase Northern Ireland MPs at Westminster was debated. When Mason offered the case in favour, Gerry Fitt interjected that there were 'seven reasons present – sitting on the unionist bench'. He argued that unionists, having failed to obtain majority rule, were settling for the next best thing, an increase in seats that would in turn lead to further blackmailing of a government which would return power to Northern Ireland's local authorities, ensuring 'a return by the back door to unionist ascendancy'. Referring to UUP support for the UWC strike in May 1974, he described the legislation as 'the "Rehabilitation of Unionist MPs Bill"', because these were men who were involved in open conspiracy'. The nationalist community, he argued, saw 'my recompense for loyal support of the Labour Party, not only in the past four years, but since 1966, and they will ask what they have got out of politics'. Fitt then launched a personal attack on Michael Foot. He quoted Aneurin Bevan's vitriolic remarks about unionists voting against the creation of the NHS and asked if Bevan's biographer and close friend had thought 'Would Nye have tolerated such a descent into the gutter?' Fitt received support from a small number of Labour backbenchers but the Bill was easily passed.[126]

Conclusion

There was a tension within direct rule in that it was intended to remain only until agreement could be reached but gave little impetus to bring about the changes necessary for a restoration of devolution. Upon his arrival at the NIO, Mason did not abandon all hope of political progress, nor was he entirely pro-unionist. He was consistent on the need for SDLP participation in any settlement. Nearly all constitutional options had been exhausted by the time he came to office. The only one remaining was administrative devolution. Rather than integration, it was intended as a stepping stone to a political settlement involving both nationalists and unionists. Interim devolution was never likely to succeed as the parties were unwilling to side step its long-term implications.

Unprepared to compromise while violence continued, unionist politicians left the leaders of moderate nationalist opinion in the wilderness. The repeated rejection of power-sharing and all-Ireland institutions left the SDLP in a state of permanent opposition. In 1976 the party was disunited and its members turned to various radical suggestions. When it was able to articulate a clear policy from 1977 this was only because it resorted to a traditionalist nationalist position which matched the inflexibility of unionists. The situation at Westminster played a crucial role in justifying this. The granting of a speaker's conference on representation and the circumstances in which it came about naturally angered nationalists. Ulster Unionist MPs had no consequential impact on divisions in the Commons, but the overall trend of direct rule as administered by Mason seemed to be intrinsically favourable to them. His dismissive attitude to SDLP sensitivities gave the impression of an impatient, unsympathetic governor. These stylistic flaws were compounded by Brian Cubbon's acquiescence in the face of growing unionist confidence. The NIO could have done considerably more to push Mason towards a balanced approach.

Notes

1 Patterson, *Ireland since 1939*, p. 253; Bew, *Ireland*, p. 523.
2 O'Leary, 'The Labour government', p. 202.
3 TNA, CJ4/1440, Burns to Janes, 8 October 1976.
4 Hansard (Commons), 914, cols 627–8; Hansard (Commons), 916, col. 854.
5 TNA, CJ4/1433, Crooke to Counsellor, 12 July 1976.
6 TNA, CJ4/1440, Burns to Janes, 8 October 1976.
7 *The Times*, 11 September 1976.
8 TNA, PREM 16/1342, West to Callaghan, 15 September 1976; TNA, PREM 16/1342, Stewart to Meadway, 17 September 1976.
9 TNA, PREM 16/1342, Mason to Callaghan, 1 October 1976.
10 TNA, CJ4/2351, Unknown to PUS, 27 October 1976.
11 Murray, *John Hume and the SDLP*, p. 39; McLoughlin, *John Hume and the revision of Irish nationalism*, pp. 81–2; Campbell, *Gerry Fitt and the SDLP*, p. 213.
12 TNA, CJ4/2351, Meeting between Mason and Fitt, 29 September 1976.
13 TNA, CJ4/2351, Middleton to Leahy, 8 October 1976.
14 TNA, CJ4/2351, Elliott to Middleton, 8 December 1976.
15 *Irish Times*, 6 December 1976; McLoughlin, *John Hume and the revision of Irish nationalism*, p. 82.
16 TNA, CJ4/1385, Hillsborough seminar, 2 November 1976.
17 TNA, CAB 134/4039, IN(76) memo 10, 25 October 1976.
18 TNA, PREM 16/1342, Janes to Wright, 27 October 1976.
19 TNA, PREM 16/1342, Janes to Wright, 27 October 1976.
20 TNA, PREM 16/1342, Wright to Callaghan, 27 October 1976; TNA, PREM 16/1342, Cosgrave to Callaghan, 27 October 1976.
21 TNA, PREM 16/1342, Janes to Wright, 27 October 1976.
22 TNA, PREM 16/1342, Cubbon to Wright, 28 October 1976; TNA, PREM 16/1342, Callaghan to Cosgrave, 28 October 1976.
23 Hansard (Commons), 918, cols 689–90.

24 TNA, CJ4/1385, Hillsborough seminar, 2 November 1976.

25 TNA, CJ4/1385, 'A discussion paper', David Gilliland, undated.

26 TNA, CJ4/1385, Hillsborough seminar, 2 November 1976.

27 TNA, CJ4/1385, Hillsborough seminar, 2 November 1976.

28 Hansard (Commons), 905, cols 1653–7.

29 TNA, CJ4/2351, Hickman to Leahy, 4 November 1976.

30 TNA, CJ4/1385, Hillsborough seminar, 2 November 1976.

31 Hansard (Commons), 907, col. 1520.

32 Hansard (Commons), 922, cols 1042–5.

33 *The Times*, 21 January 1977.

34 TNA, PREM 16/1342, Donoughue to Callaghan, 18 January 1977.

35 See TNA, CAB 134/3778, CAB 134/3921, CAB 134/4039 and CAB 134/4237.

36 Peter Hennessy, *Cabinet* (Oxford: Basil Blackwell, 1986), p. 168.

37 TNA, PREM 16/1342, Wright to Stewart, 20 January 1977.

38 TNA, CJ4/1866, Janes to Mason, 27 January 1977.

39 *News Letter*, 25 January 1977; *Irish Times*, 25 January 1977; for tensions within the UUP see Patterson and Kaufmann, *Unionism and Orangeism*, pp. 186–94.

40 TNA, CJ4/1866, Ramsay to Mason, 3 February 1977.

41 TNA, CJ4/1866, Political meeting, 16 March 1977.

42 Kenneth Morgan, *Michael Foot: a life* (London: Harper Perennial, 2008), pp. 348–50; TNA, CJ4/2611, Meeting between Foot, Molyneaux and Powell, 3 March 1977.

43 TNA, CJ4/1852, Foot to Callaghan, 22 September 1976; for a detailed account of how Northern Ireland overlapped with constitutional proposals for Scotland and Wales see Walker and Mulvenna, 'Northern Ireland representation at Westminster', pp. 237–55.

44 Callaghan, *Time and chance*, pp. 453–4.

45 Hansard (Commons), 928, cols 1303–1428.

46 TNA, PREM 16/1343, Molyneaux to Callaghan, 24 March 1977.

47 TNA, PREM 16/1343, Mason to Foot, 25 March 1977.

48 TNA, PREM 16/1343, Ramsay to Wright, 29 March 1977.

49 TNA, PREM 16/1343, Callaghan to Molyneaux, 7 April 1977.

50 TNA, PREM 16/1344, Mason to Callaghan, 31 May 1977.

51 TNA, PREM 16/1344, Mason to Callaghan, 22 June 1977.

52 TNA, PREM 16/1344, Meadway to Ramsay, 15 August 1977.

53 TNA, PREM 16/1344, Mason to Callaghan, 7 September 1977.

54 The statement was formally adopted and published after the November SDLP conference: TNA, PREM 16/1344, Facing reality (SDLP), 19 September 1977; SDLP, *Facing reality* (Belfast, 1977).

55 McLoughlin, *John Hume and the revision of Irish nationalism*, p. 83.

56 TNA, PREM 16/1344, Meeting between Callaghan and Fitt, 20 September 1977.

57 TNA, CJ4/2352, Note for the record, 7 October 1977.

58 TNA, CJ4/2352, Note for the record, 4 October 1977.

59 Devlin, *Straight left*, pp. 278–84.

60 TNA, CJ/2352, Meeting with Seamus Mallon, 28 September 1977.

61 TNA, CJ/2352, Neilson to Ford, 7 November 1977.

62 TNA, PREM 16/1344, Extracts of a meeting between Callaghan and Lynch, 28 September 1977.

63 TNA, CJ4/2611, Brown to Wilson, 23 September 1977.

64 TNA, CJ4/2611, Wilson to PS/SSNI, 28 September 1977.

65 TNA, CJ4/2611, Mason to Foot, 30 September 1977.

66 TNA, CJ4/2611, Foot to Mason, 13 October 1977.

67 TNA, CJ4/2611, Mason to Foot, 11 November 1977.

68 TNA, CJ4/1863, Cubbon to Mason, 4 November 1977.

69 TNA, CJ4/1917, Meeting between Mason and the SDLP, 21 November 1977.

70 TNA, CAB 134/4039, IN(77) memo 7, 23 November 1977.

71 TNA, PREM 16/1721, Hunt to Callaghan, 7 December 1977.

72 TNA, CJ4/2362, Meeting between Cubbon and UUP, 6 December 1977.

73 TNA, CJ4/1917, Meeting between Cubbon and SDLP, 12 December 1977.

74 TNA, PREM 16/1721, Wood to Callaghan, 15 December 1977.

75 TNA, PREM 16/1721, Wood to Callaghan, 19 December 1977; TNA, PREM 16/1721, Meeting between Callaghan and Fitt, 20 December 1977.

76 TNA, PREM 16/1721, Meeting between Callaghan and Fitt, 20 December 1977.

77 TNA, PREM 16/1721, Meeting between Callaghan, Molyneaux and Powell, 21 December 1977.

78 TNA, PREM 16/1721, Haydon to FCO and NIO Belfast, 9 January 1978.

79 *The Times*, 9 January 1978.

80 *The Times*, 10 January 1978.

81 TNA, CJ4/2353, Telephone conversation between Ford and Hume, 10 January 1978.

82 TNA, PREM 16/1721, Haydon to FCO and NIO Belfast, 16 January 1978.

83 TNA, PREM 16/1721, Mason to Callaghan, 17 January 1978.

84 TNA, CJ4/2353, Ramsay to Cubbon, 24 January 1978.

85 TNA, PREM 16/1721, Mason to Callaghan, 3 February 1978.

86 PA, Neave, AN/532, Neave speech at Surbiton, 1 February 1978.

87 *Belfast Telegraph*, 1 February 1978.

88 TNA, CJ4/2353, Meeting between Mason and the SDLP, 9 February 1978.

89 TNA, CJ4/2363, West to Mason, 16 February 1978.

90 *Conference on electoral law*, Cmnd. 7110, H.C. 1977–8.

91 TNA, CAB 134/4237, IN(78) memo 1, 1 February 1978.

92 Churchill College archives, Cambridge, Bernard Donoughue papers, DNGH 1/1/24, Donoughue to Callaghan, 7 March 1978.

93 These were Luton, Glasgow Queen's Park, Hampstead, Acton, Coventry South West and Paddington: Bernard Donoughue papers, DNGH 1/1/24, Donoughue to Callaghan, 8 March 1978.

94 Indeed, this was not the case during the Irish War of Independence or afterwards: Mo Moulton, *Ireland and the Irish in interwar England* (Cambridge: Cambridge University Press, 2014), pp. 55–65, 260.

95 Bernard Donoughue, *Downing Street diary: with James Callaghan in no. 10*, volume 2 (London: Pimlico, 2008), pp. 298–9.

96 TNA, CAB 134/4237, IN(78) meeting 1, 8 March 1978; TNA, CAB 129/200, CP(78) memo 42, 10 April 1978; TNA, CAB 128/63, CP(78) meeting 14, 13 April 1978.

97 TNA, CJ4/2354, Meeting between Mason and Fitt, 15 March 1978.

98 TNA, CJ4/2354, Meeting between Ford and Hume, 30 March 1978.

99 TNA, CJ4/2354, Meeting between Ford and Fitt, 15 May 1978.

100 TNA, CJ4/2353, Wilson to Marshall, 23 February 1978.

101 TNA, CJ4/2354, Ford to Marshall, 28 February 1978.

102 TNA, CJ4/2353, Note for the record, 20 February 1978.

103 Shaun McDaid, 'The Irish government and the Sunningdale Council of Ireland: a vehicle for unity?', *Irish Historical Studies*, 36:150 (2012), pp. 283–303.

104 McKittrick *et al.*, *Lost lives*, pp. 745–6.

105 Hansard (Commons), 945, cols 997–1000.

106 TNA, PREM 16/1722, Haydon to FCO and NIO Belfast, 10 March 1978.

107 Patterson, *Ireland's violent frontier*, pp. 122–5.

108 Donoughue, *Downing Street diary*, volume 2, pp. 298–9.

109 TNA, PREM 16/1722, Mason to Callaghan, 14 April 1978.

110 Patterson, *Ireland's violent frontier*, pp. 127–8.

111 TNA, PREM 16/1722, Telephone conversation between Callaghan and Lynch, 8 May 1978.

112 TNA, PREM 16/1722, Meeting between Callaghan and Foot, 3 May 1978.

113 Hansard (Commons), 949, cols 918–20.

114 TNA, CJ4/2365, Note for the record, 9 June 1978.

115 TNA, CJ4/2365, Janes to Marshall, 13 June 1978.

116 TNA, CJ4/2139, Cubbon to Janes, 23 May 1978.

117 TNA, CJ4/2139, Options for Northern Ireland, undated.

118 TNA, CJ4/2139, Cubbon to Fergusson, 4 August 1978.

119 Donoughue, *Downing Street diary*, volume 2, p. 331.

120 Donoughue, *Downing Street diary*, volume 2, pp. 356–9.

121 TNA, PREM 16/1722, Mason to Callaghan, 13 September 1978.

122 TNA, CAB 134/4237, IN(78) memo 3, 24 October 1978.

123 TNA, PREM 16/1722, Mason to Callaghan, 13 September 1978.

124 TNA, CAB 134/4237, IN(78) meeting 3, 26 October 1978.

125 TNA, CJ4/2366, Meeting between Mason and UUP, 21 November 1978.

126 Hansard (Commons), 959, cols 236–362; Hansard (Commons), 960, cols 1879–1916.

10

The evolution of the long war

After the ceasefire the PIRA was in disarray and it struggled because of increased attrition by British security forces. In response, just as the Labour government adapted to the long haul ahead by formulating the policies of police primacy and criminalisation, republicans fashioned a 'long war' strategy which formed the basis of their armed struggle for the rest of the conflict. Sections of the Northern Ireland Office began to appreciate that the conflict would persist over a number of years because of the PIRA's ability to adapt to the new conditions. Pressure from the British army to revert to a more aggressive stance persisted and there was growing evidence that senior officers were only paying lip service to the Labour government's strategy. There were also a number of controversies over SAS operations, the growing protest in the prisons and interrogation techniques used by the RUC. Each of these illustrates the limitations on attempts to drive a wedge between the PIRA and the nationalist community. They also played a role in the timing of the Labour government's fall and the declaration of a general election in May 1979. The alienation of Gerry Fitt during Mason's tenure led him to passionately denounce Labour during the final no confidence debate at Westminster.

The Provisional IRA

The PIRA stutteringly moved towards a 'long war' strategy. Richard English briefly describes the final outcome: a Northern Command was established in November 1976 to oversee all operations and the traditional army structure was replaced with a cell system to increase security and specialisation.[1] This transition is depicted by the journalist Ed Moloney primarily as Gerry Adams's climbing of the greasy pole.[2] This is an oversimplification. Although Adams was heavily involved in some of the changes, the subsequent release of intelligence material makes it possible to reconstruct this process in greater detail and reveals a fluid situation in which a number of republicans contributed to the shift.

In March 1976 intelligence reports suggested there were 'still no signs from the Provisional leadership of any clear idea of long term objectives'.[3] There was dissent within the Belfast brigade, with only the Andersonstown battalion taking 'positive action'.[4] The following month the army believed there was 'sufficient intelligence' to indicate that the PIRA intended to escalate violence in the weeks leading up to Easter but did not do so because of dwindling local support, successes by the security forces (especially in Belfast where they had left the PIRA 'disorganised and demoralised'), and dissent both internally in Belfast and with Dublin.[5]

Despite the assassination of Ewart-Biggs in July 1976, August saw 'a remarkable falling off in Provisional morale' against the backdrop of increasingly successful security force operations, the failure of PIRA to escalate violence and the establishment of the Women's Peace Movement. Many reports indicated that the Provisionals, especially in Belfast, were 'in a state of some confusion and there is general dissension about what to do next'. Some in Belfast wanted to revert to attacks on the security forces and commercial targets but 3 PIRA (Ardoyne) and 4 PIRA (Markets) were reportedly 'pressing for an all-out attempt to create a state of civil war' while 'older Provisionals...want the campaign to be called off, claiming that the young thugs of today have lost sight of the republican ideals for which they claim to be fighting'.[6]

November saw the first indications of a shift in the PIRA structure. A 'reliable report' suggested Northern PIRA leaders had discussed a plan with the Provisional Army Council to form a Northern Command. Martin Meehan ('who is known to consider the present system to be too cumbersome') was reported to be the 'leading protagonist' in this initiative, though the Belfast brigade staff were divided in their support with some fearing it would create difficulties in obtaining arms and explosives from the South.[7] Reports of the growing dominance of 'hard-line military men' continued, as did indications that the Northern Command was being formed.[8] On 2 December the British army thought it 'still too early to assess the full implications of this decision, not least the acceptability to the present staffs of the Belfast and Londonderry Brigades of Martin McGuinness as overall commander'.[9] Early in 1977 a 'good report' suggested that the Northern Command would be imposed on the existing command organisation and would have specific responsibility for co-ordinating operations and resupply across Northern Ireland.[10] On 20 January Mason informed his cabinet colleagues of an intelligence assessment which predicted the new structure would lead to increased violence over the next few weeks. Mason proposed to continue with existing policy, emphasising that the key was good policing.[11]

The change did not herald a rise in violence, however. The loss of twenty-seven weapons prompted the West Belfast battalions to commit to 'tout-hunting' and there were 'sufficient reports' indicating that 'all is not well with the Belfast Brigade'. Some wanted Gerry Adams (released from prison on 14 February) to 'take over in Belfast again'.[12] James Glover, Brigadier-General Staff (Intelligence), concluded there had been a 'dearth of intelligence' that made it unable 'to make any substantive assessment' but argued that organisationally the PIRA was 'still in some disarray' and there were 'no signs that Martin McGuinness has yet been able to impose the authority of the new Northern Command'.[13]

In March Glover recorded that the majority of bombing attacks in Belfast were carried out by Martin Meehan's battalion in the Ardoyne, confirming earlier assessments that the other three battalions lacked qualified explosives officers. Despite the Provisional Army Council unanimously endorsing their strategy for 1977 the hierarchy had split. British intelligence suggested that Martin McGuinness (normally portrayed as one of the tougher leaders) and Billy McKee believed 'that military action will not achieve the political aim', whereas hardliners led by Seamus Twomey wanted to increase violence. Thus 'the Northern Command concept' was 'in disarray and clearly faltering'. Twomey was believed to be dominant and McGuinness, who took over as Brigade Commander in Derry, had been replaced as Director of Operations by Martin Doherty, 'who could well be a Twomey nominee carefully placed to stiffen up McGuinness'.[14] At the end of March 1977 three of the four PIRA battalions were operating in Belfast.[15] By May the fourth Belfast battalion returned to action, although the leadership was again in doubt as Ivor Bell was due for release. Bell, 'a dedicated terrorist' that had 'commanded the Belfast Brigade when it was at its peak' would possibly combine with Adams ('another hard man' that might 'be appointed "political advisor"').[16]

Over the summer of 1977 the main intelligence interest was in the Provisionals' plans for a royal visit in early August. In July Glover identified an increase in active service units (ASUs, smaller roving units) in rural areas and Derry, which might 'soon be reflected in Belfast'. Nonetheless, the capacity to mount 'a really damaging display of power' was 'open to doubt'.[17] A week before the visit Glover gave quite a detailed description of the Provisionals' plans. In Derry there would be only peaceful protests but in Belfast the plan was to bring the city to a standstill on the morning of the first day with a combination of hijackings, hoaxes and real bombs. He doubted, however, that they could implement them 'in the face of waning support, internal dissension, low morale and security forces [sic] attrition'.[18]

His assessment was proven correct. In September Glover wrote that the failure during the Queen's visit might prove 'in retrospect to have been another watershed in the campaign'; the Provisionals 'carried out a reappraisal of their tactics and a new leadership is emerging'. Glover could not 'yet assess the full implications of the leadership shake up in the North' but McGuinness appeared to be 'imposing a firmer control under the aegis of Northern Command (which we had thought was wasting out)'. In Belfast and Derry a cell-type system of ASUs containing more experienced volunteers was formed, with reports suggesting that these would be controlled by Northern Command and would delegate 'low level operations including hooligan activity' to the 'old brigade organisation' run on traditional military lines.[19]

Shortly after the visit Michael Smyth became Belfast Brigade commander, replacing Billy McKee who became chairman of the Army Council.[20] Smyth did not last long, however, as Gerry Adams's cousin, Kevin Hannaway, ousted him and 'began exerting a tighter grip'. Glover believed it would take time for the Provisionals to adapt to their reorganisation, though he expected an increase in attacks on the security forces.[21] Adams was the key figure involved in developing the cell-based ASUs, though there was a limit to his success, with Glover noting he was 'being thwarted in his attempts to set up a command structure which meets his needs'. In Belfast it appears the system made greater progress, though possibly because the company organisation had 'largely crumbled' already.[22] In October Adams was described as 'an influential member of the Provisional Army Council and the de facto leader of "Northern Command"'. Glover wrote that 'his intelligence, political awareness and ruthlessness make him arguably the most able leader the Republican movement has produced in this campaign'. The brutality of his cousin's activities, meanwhile, had 'aroused some local revulsion', but Glover thought he might 'achieve his aim of eradicating ill-discipline'.[23]

In December 1977 further details on the reorganisation emerged when Seamus Twomey was arrested in the Irish Republic while in possession of a PIRA document. Gerry Adams has been described as the author, though there is no clear proof of this.[24] The 'Staff Report' argued that police were 'breaking volunteers' and the PIRA were 'burdened with an inefficient structure of commands, brigades, battalions and companies'. Abandoning the structures of a traditional army, they should 'gear ourselves towards long term armed struggle based on putting unknown men and new recruits into a new structure'. Cells should consist of four people with no control over weapons and explosives and specialising in sniping, execution, bombing or robberies. In order to confuse British intelligence the cells

should 'operate as often as possible outside of their own areas'. The increased
importance of political activity by Sinn Féin was also described, stressing
that it should come under army organisation at all levels and be directed
to radicalise and agitate on social and economic issues to gain 'the respect
of the people'.[25] This document formed the basis for the PIRA's strategy,
representing the republican equivalent to Bourn's proposals for police
primacy.

At the start of 1978 Glover said the Provisionals had 'at last discarded
their traditional yet inefficient "army" organisation'. Northern Command
was 'exercising a control over PIRA activities which has been lacking for
some months', with the influence felt first in Belfast but having recently
'galvanised the Londonderry PIRA into action'. Glover concluded: 'The
improved professionalism of the PIRA, both in organisation and in method,
coupled with their improved security and revitalised motivation, persuades
us that they can sustain at least the existing level of violence almost indefinitely. They are not being contained'.[26] The consequences of the new system
varied geographically. Its greatest impact was in urban centres, as rural
units were already often small in size. The effect in the countryside was
rather different. Provisional IRA volunteer Tommy McKearney claims
Northern Command 'began regularly to visit country areas that had previously remained isolated from IRA officialdom'.[27] Such centralising tendencies created new opportunities for penetration by British intelligence in
the long term.

In November 1978 Glover produced a further paper, entitled 'Northern
Ireland future terrorist trends'. It acknowledged that the Provisional leadership was 'deeply committed to a long campaign of attrition…certainly for
the foreseeable future'. Glover concluded that, despite suffering from
'muddled political thinking', the PIRA possessed 'a strata of intelligent,
astute and experienced terrorists who provide the backbone of the organisation'. The rank and file were trained and used 'with some care', with the
ASUs mainly containing 'terrorists tempered by up to ten years of operational experience'. The PIRA could not attract 'the large numbers of active
terrorists they had in 1972/3. But they no longer need them.' The new cell
system meant that a small number of activists could 'maintain a disproportionate level of violence'. Glover foresaw a trend towards greater professionalism and selective targeting, concluding: 'The Provisionals' campaign
of violence is likely to continue while the British remain in Northern
Ireland'.[28]

Glover's report did, however, identify certain basic weaknesses, chiefly
the way in which arrests disrupted the organisation and attempts to reform
it. He noted the 'considerable turbulence among the leadership at the lower
levels'. This lack of continuity was endemic, as shown when 'following the

arrest of Adams, the prime architect of the new cellular system...there was a partial reversion towards the traditional brigade organisation' (membership charges against Adams were eventually dropped).[29] Nevertheless, Glover's report did not sit well with some other army officers, as he admitted to the journalist Peter Taylor: 'I always found it slightly ironic because I was accused of encouraging the enemy. I think it revealed for the first time the strength of the IRA's commitment to the "Long War".' According to Glover, the school of thought that military means alone were sufficient remained influential in the army.[30]

Pressures for change

Other members of this school included Airey Neave. In October 1977 he advocated the death penalty for 'terrorist killers'. Using rather puzzling logic, he argued that terrorism had changed the nature of the debate on capital punishment: 'The case for or against execution of terrorist killers as a deterrent has not the same importance...every time a terrorist killer is sentenced to imprisonment he or she becomes a symbol or a rallying point for a new campaign.'[31] That martyrs would be greater symbols than prisoners was an obvious counter-argument and such inflammatory policies were never adopted by the Labour government. Mason was nevertheless prone to responding to these demands by issuing bullish statements about the prospects of victory, telling the *Daily Express* in December 1977: 'We are squeezing the terrorists like rolling up a toothpaste tube.'[32]

Inevitably, such declarations earned Mason the reputation as a militarist. Curiously, in private he was not as optimistic. A month after his 'toothpaste' remarks he informed James Callaghan of the PIRA's restructuring, noting that the decline in violence over the summer of 1977 had been checked. In response to changing PIRA techniques, forces were deployed in districts where bombing was more likely, command and control of the security forces was improved and, as the developing threat was 'conspicuously an urban one', CID and Special Branch was reinforced in Belfast. Mason was 'anxious that the current misgivings in the Unionist ranks should not be permitted to develop into anything more dangerous'. He proposed to meet the Ulster Unionists and said he was 'willing' to see other leaders if they wanted him to, words which accurately reflected his imbalanced approach towards the Northern Ireland parties.[33]

In early March Callaghan, Mason and Mulley met Ulster Unionist MPs. Molyneaux claimed the RUC and the army did not have confidence in each others' intelligence gathering. Mason was naturally defensive and replied that the RUC and army had been 'working in close partnership', greater use was being made of the SAS and covert surveillance teams were now attached to each army unit; 'he was aware that there might be localised rivalries between the army and the RUC but this was to be expected during a period of transition'. Fred Mulley supported this, saying there was 'complete and unfettered exchange of intelligence' and though there might be local differences 'in general the collaboration was very close'.[34]

Afterwards James Callaghan requested an investigation into intelligence collaboration. Mason's private secretary reported that it was improvements in intelligence flow that had forced the Provisionals to adopt their new cell structure. The Director and Co-ordinator of Intelligence continued to work closely with RUC and army headquarters and, following the 1977 review of the machinery for co-ordinating intelligence, joint policy, assessment and review committees were established with joint intelligence groups 'at all levels down to RUC sub-division'. A Special Military Intelligence Unit was integrated with Special Branch at RUC headquarters and army personnel were posted to the RUC's Criminal Intelligence Units, which supported the regional crime squads. Co-operation and effectiveness varied geographically but the system 'although not faultless, has come a long way as part of the policy of putting the police in the lead'. It was claimed that there was not any mutual distrust of the reliability of shared intelligence, though the need to protect sources sometimes inhibited dissemination. Total sharing required full trust and confidence and the rotation of army personnel made this more difficult, though good relationships were 'quickly cemented and mutual confidence built up in most cases'. The differing nature of the army and the police caused difficulties but co-operation was 'generally effective'.[35] The nature of intelligence matters makes it is difficult to evaluate the assessment, but it certainly hinted at particular difficulties even while attempting to downplay them.

At a more strategic level, the tension between army headquarters and the NIO persisted despite reduced violence. In June 1978 Cubbon held a meeting to discuss the situation 'which might face a new Secretary of State after an October election'. It was recorded that they could not 'overlook the fact that terrorism was politically motivated and arguably incapable of elimination through ordinary criminal methods'. Nonetheless, as their primary aim was to isolate the paramilitaries from the bulk of the community, the strategy of working through the courts and giving the dominant role to the police was still seen as 'simply the best means of achieving this'. The point was raised that the minister sent to the NIO after a general election might find their assessment that violence 'would not disappear entirely over the next three to four years' displeasing. They might be asked to find means of eradicating it altogether. There was a consensus that draconian measures, although 'superficially attractive', would be counter-productive in the longer term and 'would retard the return to normality'.[36]

Looking ahead over the next two to three years they did not think that more than one or two army units could be removed, the RUC would 'probably make only a very gradual progress in gaining acceptability and in penetrating green areas' and the absence of special category status for paramilitary prisoners 'would continue to cause festering resentment among some 200–300 affected families'. The policy outlined by Bourn had been revealed as desirable but Cubbon said it 'had now reached a plateau'. He proposed a further stocktaking exercise along the same lines as Pritchard's review the previous year.[37]

In early July Cubbon made this proposal to Mason. In one of the first signs of friction to come he remarked that it 'would also have the advantage of flushing out any retrograde ideas which the army may be cooking up'.[38] Mason agreed and on 10 July Timothy Creasey, who replaced David House as GOC in November 1977, made the standard request that the group not be 'too narrow in their interpretation of the terms of reference'.[39] The task of chairing the review was given to James Hannigan, Pritchard's replacement as Deputy Secretary for NIO Belfast. When the working group met for the first time on 21 July, Anthony Stephens argued that the most significant changes in the security situation since the Bourn proposals had been a fall in the level of violence, an increase in the effectiveness of the security forces and an improvement in the morale of the population. Deputy Chief Constable Jack Hermon agreed, adding that sectarian murders had been reduced, PIRA activities were now limited because of lower support and police primacy was being achieved 'through a carefully planned and sensitive approach'. Brigadier Body said the army's view was more sombre; loyalist violence had been 'stamped out' but the PIRA's capability remained high. The situation in West Belfast, West Derry and South Armagh was 'particularly intractable' and progress had fallen short of that envisaged by Bourn.[40]

When in August the committee turned to future policy, the differing interpretation between the army, RUC and NIO became more apparent. Hermon argued that the five year timescale contemplated in the Bourn proposals was achievable, whereas Body responded that it would 'be at least 1985 rather than 1981 before the army would be able to revert to its peacetime garrison role'. Body's analysis was more realistic, but the list of proposals prepared by army officers was far less so.[41] Hannigan's brief judged the majority to be 'straightforwardly incompatible with the policy of progressive normalisation' or irrelevant to security policy. For instance, the first suggestion was the commitment of all civil government departments to the defeat of terrorism. The NIO believed that seeking to identify the civil administration with the security forces would undermine public confidence in its impartiality. Similarly, the suggestion of removing limitations on intelligence gathering, such as searching occupied houses and carrying out head checks, was contrary to 'the whole post-Bourn trend of normalisation'. Identification cards were dismissed 'because of the near certainty of mass boycott', various suggested modifications of the law had been rejected already, and proscribing Provisional Sinn Féin was deemed contrary to normalisation, ineffective and politically undesirable.[42] The Northern Ireland Office asked the Ministry of Defence for its view. One MOD representative on the committee was 'naturally somewhat guarded' but when the Assistant Secretary for security operations at NIO London, W.J.A. Innes, 'suggested lightly that the HQNI document had an air of 1972 rather than 1978...he rather wryly agreed with me'.[43] Later that month, a senior MOD official remarked that if the NIO produced a report which suggested the army should 'disentangle itself from a good deal' of the work in Northern Ireland, the MOD would acquiesce whatever HQNI's opinion.[44]

In October Hannigan's report was completed. It did not offer an 'immutable blue print for every detail of future strategy', recognising that this would be unrealistic in 'ever-changing circumstances'. A vast quantity of statistics was compiled, ranging from the number of deaths and punishment shootings to the number of discos held by the RUC's community relations branch. They showed a decline in the overall level of violence, a picture most clearly represented in figure 2.

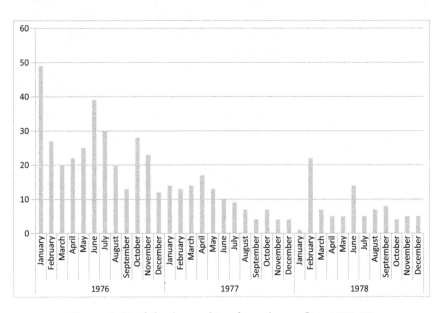

Figure 2 Total deaths resulting from the conflict, 1976–78

Shootings, bomb incidents and armed robberies were also shown to have declined. After the La Mon atrocity in February 1978 (which accounts for the spike in figure 2), the Provisionals shifted to attacks where the danger of civilian casualties was minimal. This general trend combined with a consistently high rate of attrition, especially in mid-1977 (see table 2). The conversion of charges to convictions was at a high rate: on average 75% were convicted as charged during this period and 13% were convicted of other offences, figures which did not vary substantially over time.[45]

Hannigan's analysis of the state of the PIRA was similar to Glover's. The Provisional Army Council contained 'a number of dedicated men, some of them highly capable', although they had shown themselves 'very reliant on the drive and organising ability of Gerry Adams'. His arrest had made it harder for his subordinates to make the same use of the co-ordinating functions of Northern Command. Meanwhile, loyalist terrorism was 'the extreme manifestation of unionism and depends upon community reaction and attitudes to an extent that is not the case with PIRA'. Progress in the security situation and the failure of the UUAC strike was thought particularly helpful in bring about its decline.[46]

The RUC's progress since the Bourn report was described glowingly. In each of the areas of expansion there was deemed to have been success, whether in terms of overall recruitment, specialist units such as CID, Special Branch and the SPG, or training and management. RUC regular strength went from 4902 on 1 January 1976 to 5,861 on 1 July 1978 and they expected to reach 6,500 by 1979. Similarly, RUC full-time reservists increased from 661 to 1,103, though this was offset by a similar reduction in part-time reservists. As for the army, they were deemed to be operating 'with increasing sensitivity and selectivity'. Covert capabilities were developed and, as planned by Mulley and Mason the previous year, the regular force level was reduced from 14,147 in January 1978 to 13,480 in July. The increase in the establishment figure for full-time members of the UDR had almost been met with an increase from 1,523 to 2,314 over two years. Contrary to the claims of Ulsterisation, the limitations on the UDR's role envisioned in the Pritchard review were supported with a further emphasis that the regiment should move towards only providing support on a contingency basis. Thus, it was recommended that the UDR not be expanded any further than the existing strength of 8,000 (despite the previous plan to reach 12,000).[47]

Although the overall analysis of progress was overwhelmingly positive, the review recognised a number of negative factors still in existence: there was 'no sign of PIRA giving up', disillusionment with the PIRA in many areas had not been converted into support for the security forces and

Table 2 Persons charged with terrorist offences, January 1976–June 1978

Offence	Jan.–March 1976	April–June 1976	July–Sept. 1976	Oct.–Dec. 1976	Jan.–March 1977	April–June 1977	July–Sept. 1977	Oct.–Dec. 1977	Jan.–March 1978	April–June 1978
Murder	40	10	22	48	17	40	52	22	14	29
Attempted murder	13	38	33	37	41	33	42	19	30	24
Firearms	70	111	91	81	71	98	70	62	67	44
Explosives	63	35	47	70	32	44	33	37	40	9
Armed robbery	45	32	50	61	42	51	58	52	45	40
Other	63	61	98	57	72	143	108	69	65	68
Total	**294**	**287**	**341**	**354**	**275**	**409**	**363**	**261**	**261**	**214**

Source: TNA, CJ4/2294, Report of the working group to consider progress on security, undated.

paramilitary organisations retained a hold over aspects of community life. The report endorsed the Bourn proposals as the 'right and practicable way forward' but for the next two years it did not foresee any withdrawal of the army from West Belfast or the west of Derry city. Similarly, the proximity of the border and the 'extent of PIRA's intimidatory hold over the local population' meant South Armagh was 'likely to remain chiefly a military problem.'[48] The army would remain the dominant force in key republican areas.

It was reasserted that the RUC 'should not take on, or be seen by the minority community to be acting in, a paramilitary role'. Despite this, they required the ability to act alone without army support and therefore would 'continue to need sub-machine guns, high velocity rifles and armoured landrovers'. The two positions were contradictory. The committee sought to circumvent this contradiction by arguing that such equipment should be used 'in a way sensitive to the community; thus except on rare occasions, it should not be used where the use of considerable fire power is an integral part of an offensive operation'. Instead, such operations should be conducted by the army. [49] In the Chief Constable's annual report for 1976 Ken Newman argued that the acquisition of M1 carbines should be seen as part of the police obligation to safeguard life and property, adding: 'A police force should not anyhow be characterised by the equipment necessary to enable it to discharge its duties but by its training, motivation and objectives. In these respects the RUC is enlightened and socially advanced.'[50] It was highly unlikely that the Catholic community would view the RUC as 'enlightened'. The recommendation that the RUC should avoid assuming a role contrary to their long-term development into a normal British police force was a difficult one to reconcile with the need to provide adequate protection to its officers.

Army Headquarters Northern Ireland disagreed on modifications to the law. It believed there were a number of changes which would make operations more effective. These included an increase in the responsibility of property owners giving them 'a positive duty to ensure that no part of one's property was being used for illegal purposes' and greater penalties for withholding information. The RUC, however, argued that the measures 'would be represented as a new and more repressive policy'. The review stated that 'any major increase in emergency powers would run counter to the main thrust of our present policy'.[51] The report also described a 'difference of philosophy and approach' on information policy which could not be resolved. The relevant under-secretary in the NIO, D.R. Ford, wrote that the aim of information policy was 'to project a realistic and balanced picture of the economic, social, security and political situations'. HQNI, on the other hand, wanted something more aggressive and claimed efforts had

been 'patchy over the last two years'. They complained that the Public Relations Co-ordinating Committee had only met twice in 1978, displaying a
'loss of momentum'.[52]

In response to a request from Cubbon, Anthony Stephens produced a
brief on the disagreements within the group.[53] It recorded that although
the report 'genuinely reflects the position reached in the group...some of
the agreement recorded (though by no means all of it) is precariously balanced upon a bare convergence of attitudes which remain quite capable of
diverging again'. He added:

> HQNI tend to think simply in terms of defeating PIRA – when that is done
> their task in Northern Ireland is over. The RUC have a longer-term view,
> seeing terrorism as a facet of crime which must be countered so far as is
> possible through the normal process of law and order and with due regard
> to community susceptibilities.

Army Headquarters Northern Ireland believed that the defeat of the
PIRA would not presently be achieved 'within a discernible time frame'.
They therefore proposed an intensification of activity, seeing the defeat of
terrorism as primarily a military problem 'to be achieved by military
means'. It was suggested HQNI were 'to some extent paying only lip service
to [police primacy] in that they see themselves in the front line in the hard
areas, de facto, if not de jure taking the lead'. As a result they were guilty
of 'simply ignoring community sensitivities', preferring to 'take a calculated
risk on the attitude of those who are uninvolved in terrorism but who will
nevertheless be affected by such activities'. The RUC and NIO, Stephens
wrote, believed there had been real progress and this should not be jeop-
ardised by 'an ill-considered intensification'. From the NIO members' perspective, however, the police seemed 'too euphoric about the speed of
progress and are over optimistic on the degree of movement there has been
in the attitudes of the minority community'. On occasion this optimism
pushed the army further into its entrenched position. The NIO also, on
occasion, 'had to put a brake on RUC tendencies towards developing markedly paramilitary capabilities'.[54]

Co-operation between the army and the RUC was reported as good at
headquarters and at the division/battalion level. The RUC still complained
about the army's turnover of personnel, claiming that its officers had 'difficulty in coming to grips with the subtleties of security policy'. While the
group endorsed the need for covert operations, 'the RUC and NIO were
throughout at pains to stress that such operations should not be conducted on the assumption that they should inevitably or even normally
lead to terrorists being killed'. The aim was to catch terrorists and killings
should occur 'only as an unavoidable use of force in accordance with the

law'. HQNI professed to accept this but Stephens noted that the point had to 'be continuously rammed home'.[55] This last issue was raised by Douglas Janes who complained that 'the army (and particularly the SAS) think of themselves "at war" and thus see the killing of the enemy as the first objective rather than capture'. Janes rightly pointed out that this could 'run counter to the objective of driving a wedge between terrorists and the community'. He complained that a sentence in the report which described terrorist deaths as 'a significant deterrent' was 'too much of a blessing'.[56]

With the report completed, the disagreements moved up the hierarchy. Both Brian Cubbon and Timothy Creasey strongly defended their respective positions when they met with Ken Newman to discuss the unresolved issues in the report. Creasey admitted that it was 'right that the army should be in support of the civil power' but 'the army did not see the defeat of PIRA as distinct from, or at odds with, the goal of bringing about a return to normality'. He argued that HQNI's proposals merely sought the maximum use of available resources. The Chief Constable sided with Cubbon, arguing that actions providing short-term advantage could be inconsistent with long-term objectives and 'part of our long-term aim was to eliminate terrorism in such a way that it did not return'.[57] When Cubbon prepared a draft submission to Mason and circulated it to Newman and Creasey, the latter complained that it 'attempted to paper over differences of which the Secretary of State should be aware'. Creasey also sought to use Mason's public statements against the NIO, referring to his public avowal that the government's aim was 'to defeat terrorism altogether'. He stressed that 'in SAS-type operations it was likely that arrest of terrorists would not always be possible', while expressing support for the rules on opening fire.[58]

On 17 October Cubbon emphasised the political context to Creasey in terms which, although resorting to crass national stereotyping, conveyed the basic political context which made defeating militant republicanism unachievable; 'for the foreseeable future we shall have the border, the long-standing republican tradition among the minority (backed by the South and considerable international opinion) and the Irish propensity for political emotionalism and violence'. Cubbon doubted 'that PIRA can be defeated by the effective harnessing of the total government effort on the security, political and socio-economic fronts'. He argued that 'powers in the political field are very limited and…we cannot see any steps that would defeat PIRA by totally removing their cause'. He rebutted Creasey's unrealistic suggestion that sanctions could be taken against the Irish Republic for failure to co-operate, saying that he was all for political pressure but this could go no further.[59]

The GOC had a formidable reputation, having served in Kenya, Aden and Oman. He told Cubbon that his political views had been 'formed as a result of the successes that the multi-national forces under my command achieved in the Dhofar war, where under similar circumstances to those here – or perhaps even more complex – we defeated a hydra headed communist attempt to conquer Oman'. The comparison was appended with pencilled exclamations of disbelief, though it is unclear whether these were Cubbon's – what *is* clear is that the Dhofar rebellion, far removed Western Europe, did not receive the same popular scrutiny.[60]

Cubbon's summary to Mason stated that he and the Chief Constable agreed 'that any general heightening of the profile or significant increase in the powers available to the security forces could alienate the more ambivalent sections of the community'. Adding Creasey as well, he said it was felt that there should be localised joint army–police studies conducted by the Divisional and Regional Action Committees to assess the capability of the RUC and community attitudes. The three agreed that army commanders should decide how a task given to them by the police was carried out but that the connection between the two forces should be such that the RUC could veto this upon hearing of the number of troops involved. The army should also have the right to decline an RUC request if deemed not to be a 'proper and suitable military task'. Cubbon reported that, while 'conscious of the substantial deterrent effect on PIRA' of the killing of terrorists during covert operations, they 'must recognise' that cases where someone other than a terrorist is killed 'threaten the public acceptance of…security policy'. HQNI's suggested law changes 'should not be taken further' and a more aggressive public relations campaign would raise the profile of the PIRA and the security situation. While the Public Relations Co-ordinating Committee had declined because the NIO and RUC thought frequent meetings unnecessary, they would henceforth be arranged on a monthly basis.[61]

When Mason replied on 23 November he was wholly supportive of his permanent secretary, remarking that 'purely security objectives should not be regarded as paramount'.[62] This was in stark contrast to his public declarations of confidence that the PIRA would be defeated. On 1 December Mason told James Callaghan of the conclusions of the review, describing them as an affirmation of existing policy.[63] The Cabinet Secretary John Hunt briefed the prime minister on the disagreements, omitted from Mason's letter: 'the real problem for Creasey has been the understandable dislike of a fighting general, who is regarded as one of the army's "stars", to accept the policy of police primacy and a low profile for the army'. This did not extend any further up the military hierarchy or pose problems at cabinet level. Mason talked privately to Mulley and Cubbon was in touch with the MOD permanent secretary Frank Cooper, who naturally understood the position having made the very same arguments when at the NIO. Hunt told the prime minister that the MOD did not 'want to appear hard on a good and respected commander' but there was general agreement that present policy should be maintained.[64] The long haul ahead was recognised and Mason again sided with his officials in rejecting a more aggressive security policy.

The SAS and 'shoot-to-kill'

Although senior army officers stated their support of the rules on opening fire during the Hannigan review, the NIO doubted their commitment to them. The actions of the SAS at times gave grounds for such concern. In its first year in Northern Ireland the regiment was considered a success, with the exception of an incursion into the Irish Republic. On the night of 5 May 1976 two armed SAS men dressed in civilian clothes were stopped at a vehicle check-point 300 yards into the Republic. Three hours later six SAS men went in search of the other two and reached the same check-point, also wearing civilian clothes and bearing arms. All eight were charged with possessing firearms without a certificate and with intent to endanger life.[65] Merlyn Rees told other Labour ministers that it was 'imperative to avoid an outcome of imprisonment'. He felt that Irish ministers 'realised the seriousness of the situation but could not lose face by appearing to yield to British pressure'. As Defence Secretary, Mason remarked that, if it appeared imprisonment was possible, the SAS men might not run the risk of standing trial. This of course would have great political implications and in the future British soldiers would not be granted bail by Irish courts.[66]

The court date was set for March 1977. Mason explained that the date had been announced publicly and, considering the PIRA's success in assassinating the British ambassador the previous summer, there was a real danger that the SAS men might be killed. It was unlikely that the men would be convicted of intent to endanger life but possession of firearms had a maximum penalty of five years. If the men were imprisoned, Mason remarked, 'parliamentary and public opinion would not understand how the government could allow men who were engaged in legitimate and dangerous operations...to be abandoned'. On the other hand, if they refused to attend the effect on British–Irish relations would be severe and it would be seen as 'clear confirmation of all the worst myths about the role of the SAS'. Mason proposed that the soldiers attend the hearing and plead guilty to possessing arms, which would likely result in a fine. This would be the best outcome provided they received assurances about security arrangements.[67] While there was a limit to what the Irish government could do because of the independence of the Director of Public Prosecutions, Labour ministers felt they had received sufficient assurances that security was being taken seriously and the men would not receive prison sentences.[68] When the case was concluded on 8 March the judge imposed a fine of £100 on each of the men.[69]

In 1976 the SAS killed one PIRA member, Peter Cleary, in controversial circumstances. Arrested at a house in South Armagh in April, the army claimed that Cleary fought with those guarding him and he was shot in the chest in self-defence. This was disputed by the republican's associates.[70] In November 1976 the Defence Secretary Fred Mulley claimed that the regiment had 'drastically curtailed' republican activities in County Armagh. Although Catholics were 'said to distrust the SAS' the minister believed this was 'largely confined to a minority' and he supported a request from the GOC to extend the regiment's activities to the rest of Northern Ireland.[71] John Hunt advised Callaghan that, the incursion across the border apart, SAS operations had 'not excited controversy'.[72] He supported the proposal and in early December it went ahead.[73]

A month later the SAS killed a second PIRA volunteer, again in disputed circumstances. On 16 January Seamus Harvey was shot dead in a gun-battle which republicans claimed the SAS started without warning. The army in turn claimed that as they moved to intercept Harvey, who was masked and wearing an ammunition belt, they were spotted by two other PIRA members and a gun-battle followed in which Harvey was killed.[74] On 21 June the SAS ambushed a PIRA unit planning to firebomb a post office depot in North Belfast. As the PIRA members stopped their car the SAS shot three dead plus a Protestant civilian walking nearby. None were armed though the army claimed the men were challenged at the depot and there was an exchange of fire.[75] The next month John Boyle, an innocent civilian, found an arms cache in a cemetery in County Antrim and told his father, who notified the police. Boyle was shot dead by two SAS soldiers when he returned to the graveyard. They were acquitted when the judge concluded that the men fired because they felt their lives were in danger, though he was critical of the military handling of the operation and deemed one of the soldiers untrustworthy.[76] Further deaths followed that year. In September a civil servant was killed by the SAS in Tyrone while on a duck-shooting expedition and in November a PIRA volunteer, Patrick Duffy, was killed in County Derry. Duffy was shot in the back in a house containing weapons. The house was staked out by the SAS and it later emerged that they had been present when the weapons were first placed there, raising questions as to why they had not attempted to apprehend those who brought them in.[77]

Such incidents led to claims that a 'shoot-to-kill' policy existed in Northern Ireland. What is clear is that the NIO's emphasis on the desirability of apprehending suspects did not mesh well with the nature of the SAS. As the journalist and former soldier Mark Urban has highlighted, 'Training emphasises the need to open fire, with the minimum of hesitation, if the target is recognised as hostile...SAS soldiers are scornful of civilians who believe that it is possible, western-style, to shoot out of a person's hand or to disable someone with shots to the legs.' Once an enemy is identified they are expected to put 'as many bullets into a person as is necessary to ensure that they will be unable to use their weapon.'[78] Although the term 'shoot-to-kill' in a literal sense misunderstands the nature of armed confrontations (if soldiers shoot they do so invariably with the intention of killing the target), and although the army were at pains to claim adherence to the rules on opening fire, there were instances where the SAS in particular were too quick to shoot. As the NIO rightly pointed out during the Hannigan review in 1978, such incidents undermined the government's strategy. The introduction of the SAS led to significant attrition against PIRA volunteers but was also followed by deaths which did political damage.

The prisons

Difficulties also arose from the ending of special category status, a crucial aspect of criminalisation which made confrontation in the prisons highly likely. Under special category status work was not obligatory, prisoners could wear their own clothing and they were entitled to receive one parcel, send one letter and have one visit of 30 minutes duration each week.[79] From 1 March 1976 persons convicted of offences committed after that date did not receive it, although those already possessing the status did not have it withdrawn and those found guilty of offences committed prior to March still received it. The phasing out of special category status was gradual in part because the government feared a violent reaction but also due to practical difficulties. Those under the new system were housed in cellular prisons rather than compounds. Merlyn Rees had initially hoped to provide one large prison at Maghaberry, making a clear break from the Maze because of its association with internment.[80] Maghaberry was not set to be completed until 1981, however. H-block prisons were built at the Maze, with two completed by December 1976 and a further six following by the end of the next year, providing a capacity for 800 prisoners.[81] This capacity was not enough to include special category prisoners and so they continued to be housed in compounds. In October 1977 Cubbon wrote that the special category population was expected to decline from 730 in 1978 to 230 in 1982. Any move against these prisoners in the short term would lead to violence but their 'ultimate objective' would be to move the prisoners to cellular accommodation once the numbers were low enough to make this possible.[82] This occurred in June 1988, when ninety prisoners were transferred.[83]

This in part explains why a prison protest took time to gather momentum. A month after the phasing out began the PIRA killed two prison officers but prisoners themselves did not respond until 14 September 1976, when PIRA volunteer Kieran Nugent refused to work or wear prison clothing.[84] Further republican prisoners joined him and by April 1977, wearing only blankets, the number had risen to ninety-seven.[85] That same month the protestors were separated from other prisoners, with the prison authorities claiming that conformists were being intimidated to join in. By July there were two occupants to a cell.[86] The protestors were punished with the withdrawal of radio access, free association with other prisoners and exercise. The prisoners also lost remission, delaying their release.[87] In the summer of 1977 officials were pleased to note that 'no public representatives are supporting the protestors, and there is hardly any outside activity seeking to draw attention.'[88]

In March 1978 the protestors, now numbering over 300, intensified their efforts by refusing to wash, use toilets, clean out their cells or empty their chamber pots. They smashed furniture and poured urine and excreta into the corridors, smearing the remnants on the walls.[89] The 'dirty protest' brought greater public attention. In May Amnesty International wrote to Mason. Amnesty said they were aware that the unpleasantness resulted from prisoners' refusal to accept discipline but there had been allegations which might constitute cruel, inhuman or degrading treatment. In two blocks it was alleged prisoners were confined to their cells for 24 hours a day with no exercise, that they were deprived of reading material and for three days had not been allowed 'to slop out and were given a restricted diet'.[90] Roy Mason replied with a strong defence of the prison system. He explained that exercise outdoors would be allowed if the protestor wore their prison clothes and the refusal to allow reading material was a consequence of their behaviour. Refusal to slop out and dietary restrictions had only been applied for 'more serious breaches of discipline'. Mason dismissed the conditions as the strikers' fault.[91]

Publicity increased in August when the Archbishop of Armagh, Tomás Ó Fiaich, argued 'one would hardly allow an animal to remain in such conditions, let alone a human being'. Ó Fiaich compared the H-blocks to the slums of Calcutta and said the refusal to wear uniform or do prison work should not entail the loss of such basic human needs as exercise and association. He placed responsibility with the government, claiming that the trials and the family backgrounds of the prisoners marked them out as 'in a different category from the ordinary.'[92] The NIO publicly responded by expressing surprise that Ó Fiaich made no reference 'to the essential fact that it is the prisoners themselves who have made conditions what they are.'[93]

James Hannigan wrote that international opinion was 'not greatly impressed by the dirty protest, with the exception of those people and bodies who are susceptible to PIRA propaganda'. Cellular confinement was ended and cells were cleaned on a regular cycle. Hannigan argued that the RUC, army, prison officers and 'the great bulk of people in Northern Ireland...would be very worried by' a significant change in regime. He nonetheless felt that humanitarian concern might make it vulnerable and suggested Mason consider whether it was worth making small changes on association or reading material.[94] Mason believed it was 'not the right time for humanitarian relaxations/concessions' and offering something 'to cleanse our conscience' might only find that 'the prisoners gobbled up the concessions and pressed on for more'.[95] The Conservatives, who were entirely supportive of the Labour government's response, inherited an escalating problem.[96] The number of prison officers killed rose dramatically from one in 1978 to nine in 1979 in a confrontation that prefaced the later hunger strikes.[97]

Police interrogation

The biggest controversy during the lifetime of the Labour government concerned RUC interrogations, with allegations surfacing that the police engaged in systematic brutality to obtain confessions. Allegations appeared in March 1977 during a BBC *Tonight* programme in which two men claimed to have been beaten by police interrogators.[98] In October the journalist Peter Taylor made a further documentary for Thames Television's *This Week*. The programme cited the importance of confessions in convicting for terrorist offences and was based on the complaints and medical reports of ten cases. One medical doctor who attended to people at Castlereagh interrogation centre said he believed the injuries he saw showed signs of ill-treatment. Taylor had difficulty persuading the Independent Broadcasting Authority to show the programme and it was only aired after his team agreed to allow the Chief Constable to give a prepared statement. Ken Newman remarked that while he could not rule out the possibility that police officers were sometimes tempted to 'overstep the mark', ill-treatment was not tolerated.[99]

The government's response to the documentary was hostile. Mason, speaking in the Commons, highlighted the 'specific safeguards' to prevent ill-treatment, such as the independent police complaints board. He claimed all complaints were thoroughly investigated and all allegations of criminal offence were referred to the Director of Public Prosecutions. He described the documentary itself as 'cheque-book television', 'riddled with unsubstantiated accusations' that placed every policeman's life 'at greater risk than before'.[100] Earlier that summer Newman wrote in his annual RUC report: 'terrorist organisations have adopted a deliberate policy of manufacturing allegations or contriving incidents, including self-inflicted injury'.[101]

The controversy prompted Amnesty International to launch an inquiry in November 1977. Its report, published in May 1978, dealt with seventy-eight people alleging maltreatment. Amnesty found 'a high degree of consistency among testimonials from numerous individuals' alleging mal-treatment. The doctors interviewed claimed the simulation of injury 'for the purpose of defaming the police was very rare'. Amnesty concluded that maltreatment of suspected terrorists had 'taken place with sufficient fre-quency to warrant the establishment of a public inquiry'.[102] On 8 June Mason described the basis for Amnesty's conclusions as 'incomplete evi-dence' and bemoaned that the anonymous basis on which the allegations were put forward made it impossible for a public inquiry to consider them. Amnesty was asked to give the names of the persons in confidence to the Director of Public Prosecutions (DPP) but they declined to do so. The government could not, therefore, carry out an inquiry into the allegations, but did agree to establish 'an independent and impartial investigation' on police practice and procedure, sitting in private.[103]

The following week Labour MP Phillip Whitehead asked if Mason agreed that 'we are unlikely to beat the terrorists unless we can do so without double standards and without dirty hands'. Mason replied 'I hope that my honourable friend does not accuse me of double standards'. Insist-ing that Amnesty International's investigation was predicated on a tiny sample of cases, he claimed he wanted 'to seek out the truth' but also 'discern the difference between truth and propaganda'.[104] Mason was bluntly dismissive of those who doubted the integrity of the security forces and refused to countenance the possibility that abuses might have taken place.

The Bennett report on police interrogation was completed in February 1979. It described a 'co-ordinated and extensive campaign to discredit the RUC' and said no other police force was called upon to deal with so much violent crime. It argued that reliance on admissions of guilt was also a common feature in England and Wales. Police officers were restrained from ill-treatment by law and by regulations and instructions. Similarly, medical examinations were offered to suspects upon arrival and before discharge, which could be conducted by the person's own general practitioner. The inquiry also found, however, that in early 1977 medical officers noted a large increase in injuries. The Association of Forensic Medical Officers made repeated representations to the Police Authority and senior police officers. The police denied ill-treatment and at one stage 'some of the medical officers who had examined prisoners...had reason to fear for their reputation'. Ultimately, a committee was established by Deputy Chief Constable Jack Hermon which offered the doctors' representatives direct access to the Chief Constable. Following this the medical officers 'were satisfied that the situation had improved'. In early 1978 concern arose again. After representations by the doctors to the Police Authority 'some changes were made in the personnel there, which brought about a situation satisfactory to the doctors'.[105]

After conducting their own inquiries, the Bennett committee found cases where prisoners 'clearly fabricated' ill-treatment or injuries were 'undoubtedly self-inflicted', but they also found instances where the injuries were 'inflicted by someone other than the prisoner himself...indicated beyond all doubt by the nature, severity, sites and numbers of separate injuries in one person'. The report nonetheless stressed that circumstances arose in which prisoners had to be physically restrained and so the committee were 'not to be taken as condemning these officers unheard'. They recommended a number of changes to the control of interrogation, such as installing CCTV cameras (which the Chief Constable's working party objected to because it would make the suspect more reluctant to speak) and allowing medical officers to see all suspects during each period of twenty-four hours in custody.[106]

In March an ITV documentary featured Dr Robert Irwin, secretary of the Northern Ireland Police Surgeons' Association. He claimed that at least 150 people had been beaten and tortured at Castlereagh.[107] Newman responded that Irwin himself had only examined 65 people who complained of ill-treatment and found only 10 cases of injuries consistent with the allegations.[108] Irwin replied that he had only referred 65 cases to the complaints body but had files on 150 because until April 1978 he and other doctors did not put notes on prisoners' files after a judge suggested he keep them privately for evidence.[109]

Just prior to Mason's statement on the Bennett report Gerry Fitt told the Commons of a *Daily Telegraph* article that morning containing accusations that Irwin was bitter towards the RUC because his wife had been raped. These accusations were reported as emanating from government officials in Whitehall. Fitt condemned this as a 'vicious smear, particularly if it emanated from the Northern Ireland Office'. Mason responded that he had made 'an urgent check' that morning and was certain the NIO had no involvement in the matter. He said the government accepted the 'broad conclusions' of the report and hoped to return in two to three months to describe the precise actions taken. Gerry Fitt, however, was extremely unhappy that the debate had been scheduled for a Friday, claiming that Mason had deliberately done so to ensure the chambers were practically empty and MPs had the report 'in our hands for only a few minutes'. He attacked the terms of reference, claiming they were designed to prevent it from speaking to people who had made allegations. Mason dismissed this saying there had been 'no cover-up' and Bennett had done a 'substantial, workmanlike job'.[110] Gerry Fitt's attempts to secure a full debate on the report were not successful and the episode played a decisive role in his decision to abstain on the motion of no confidence which brought the Labour government down.

The fall of the Labour government

The winter of 1978–79 did tremendous damage to the Labour government's position. Its policy of pay restraint collapsed with the Winter of Discontent. Beginning with the Ford motor company in September 1978, there were a series of strikes demanding pay increases as high as 30%.[111] In December the government won a vote of confidence by only ten votes.[112] Then, on 2 March 1979, referendums were held on Scottish and Welsh devolution. The Welsh voted overwhelmingly against while the Scottish result was 51.2% in favour, but on a turnout less than the 40% required. On 22 March Callaghan proposed party talks on devolution but the Scottish National Party (SNP) were not satisfied and produced a motion of censure against the government.[113] The Conservatives tabled a motion of no confidence for 28 March.

Labour needed votes from other parties to survive in power. The eleven SNP MPs were no longer supportive. The thirteen Liberals were also likely to oppose the government. Donoughue recorded that the three Plaid Cymru MPs 'implied that that they may vote for us'.[114] This left the twelve MPs for Northern Ireland, consisting of Gerry Fitt, the independent republican Frank Maguire and ten unionists. Callaghan was very reluctant to make any deals to ensure the survival of the government, much to the annoyance of Donoughue who approached him alongside fellow political advisor Tom McNally with a list of concessions that might win the vote.[115] In talks with Michael Foot, Enoch Powell asked for upper-tier local government as a condition for support but Callaghan vetoed Mason's request for permission to talk to him and West.[116]

The date 28 March saw frenetic activity in parliament. Roy Hattersley spent the entire day with UUP MPs John Carson and Harold McCusker.

They agreed to support the government in return for a Prices Commission inquiry in Northern Ireland (though, farcically, the agreement was retyped and signed again after the unionists objected to the green ink of Hattersley's pen). They also told Hattersley that other Ulster Unionists would consider abstaining in return for a gas pipeline running from Great Britain to Northern Ireland, Powell being particularly interested. Callaghan, however, again refused.[117]

Gerry Fitt had become completely alienated from the Labour government. Recent remarks by Mason on the nature of the SDLP added to his disaffection. In February Mason remarked on the radio about a poll showing increasing support for the Ulster Unionists: 'That reveals a picture that the moderate unionists and the Alliance party, bridging the sectarian gulf, are growing and those – the SDLP, who have in recent times turned a little more greener, wanting Irish unity above all, and the DUP, the extreme Protestants – they're losing ground.' Describing the Ulster Unionists as moderates led the SDLP to announce a boycott of Mason.[118] Fitt went to Downing Street a few days before the vote and Callaghan tried to gain his support but the SDLP MP said he could not offer it because of Mason's actions. Fitt later claimed that at this point Callaghan 'nodded at someone and they brought in a bottle of gin, a bottle of tonic, and sat it down on the table before me, and I didn't like that one little bit'. Hopes were therefore pinned on Frank Maguire, an independent republican MP for Fermanagh and South Tyrone who rarely attended the Commons. Jock Stallard, chosen as a Scottish Catholic, was assigned to Maguire and spent the entire day imploring him to save the government.[119]

When the debate began Callaghan attacked the opposition parties for co-operating against the government on issues about which they were fundamentally opposed.[120] The most dramatic speech of the debate was made by Gerry Fitt. He began: 'This will be the unhappiest speech I have ever made in this House.' He recounted how he had taken his place on the Labour benches as 'a committed socialist'. Over the following fourteen years he had 'never once voted in the Conservative lobby', but since the UWC strike the Labour government had 'not stood up to unionist and loyalist extremists as they should have done'. Mason was 'believed to be a unionist Secretary of State'. The granting of extra seats meant that the unionists would 'become the third major force in British politics', a decision which made all the less sense as having used the Labour government 'tonight they will try to bring about their downfall'. Fitt added: 'I want to see an election as soon as possible. I want to see the Labour Government win with such a majority that never again will they have to rely on the votes of the Unionists.' He said that his decision was made final when he received

the Bennett report on police interrogation in Northern Ireland and it was
not properly debated in the Commons. Fitt then made decisive remarks
about Maguire:

> There is a rumour circulating today, and if it is true it is despicable, that the
> hon. Member is somewhere within the building talking to someone from the
> Government Whips' office. He cannot talk to me in case I persuade him to
> do as I am doing tonight. I shall be watching very carefully, and if the hon.
> Member goes through the Government Lobby tonight it will be in opposition
> to everything that his constituents sent him here to do.[121]

The Labour government lost the vote by 311 to 310. The SNP and the
Liberals voted against the government, while the three Plaid Cymru MPs
gave their support. Of the ten unionists, eight voted against the government. Carson and McCusker voted with Labour but Powell joined the
Conservatives. Both Fitt and Maguire abstained, the latter after his wife
heard Fitt's speech from the gallery above the Commons and dragged him
away.[122] In May Labour lost the election and Margaret Thatcher became
prime minister.

Conclusion

It should be borne in mind that if the Labour government had survived
the no confidence debate it would likely have fallen a short time later.
Furthermore, if Mason had been able to adopt a policy that satisfied Fitt
and Maguire it is likely that Carson and McCusker would not have voted
with Labour. Mason later wrote that he found Fitt 'difficult' and that the
two 'never really got on'.[123] Fitt, however, was left in an isolated position
and received little sympathy from Mason. Mason at times showed dreadful
short-sightedness in viewing the SDLP as inflexible. He failed to appreciate
the nature of events prior to his appointment. Far more could have been
done to emphasise that the responsibility for the impasse lay primarily with
unionists. If increased representation had been refused, as under Rees, and
the Quigley and Bennett reports debated fully in the Commons, with a
greater admission of RUC misconduct in the case of the latter, Fitt might
have felt less rejected by a party to whom he was in many ways closer than
the one he led.

Despite security force attrition the PIRA gradually adopted a new strategy providing greater security and the means to wage a longer campaign.
The NIO was forced to repeatedly rebut arguments for a more aggressive
policy and the Hannigan review saw serious disagreements with army
officers. The NIO recognised that policies such as police primacy would
not end the conflict, but an aggressive response would only prolong it.

Criminalisation contributed significantly to attrition against the various paramilitary groups in a way less likely to provoke the Catholic community, forcing the PIRA to change its structural organisation in response. It did not, however, remove the political forces behind the conflict and, as Brian Cubbon rightly highlighted, the basic problem of the border could not be solved.

There were further flaws in the government's approach. A number of incidents involving the SAS led to accusations that a 'shoot-to-kill' policy existed. While this was not the case in the sense of a government-sanctioned strategy, unnecessary deaths occurred during SAS operations. Further difficulties arose from the government's strategy itself. The removal of special category status increased resistance in the prisons, which had enormous political effects in the following decade, and the manner in which CID detectives obtained confessions was brought into doubt by cases of physical abuse, undermining the moral credibility of the British government. Nevertheless, violence levels were much lower by 1979 and the core of security policy was in place for the remainder of the conflict.

Notes

1 English, *Armed struggle*, pp. 212–13.
2 Ed Moloney, *A secret history of the IRA* (London: Penguin, 2007), pp. 149–62.
3 TNA, DEFE 24/1226, PRE-NIOM meeting 9, 11 March 1976.
4 TNA, DEFE 24/1226, PRE-NIOM meeting 10, 18 March 1976.
5 TNA, DEFE 24/1226, PRE-NIOM meeting 14, 22 April 1976.
6 TNA, DEFE 24/1226, PRE-NIOM meeting 31, 25 August 1976.
7 TNA, DEFE 13/1401, PRE-NIOM meeting 41, 22 April 1976.
8 TNA, DEFE 24/1226, PRE-NIOM meeting 43, 18 November 1976; TNA, DEFE 24/1226, PRE-NIOM meeting 44, 25 November 1976.
9 TNA, DEFE 24/1226, PRE-NIOM meeting 45, 2 December 1976.
10 TNA, DEFE 24/1226, PRE-NIOM meeting 3, 20 January 1977.
11 TNA, CJ4/1651, Mason to Callaghan and annex, 20 January 1977.
12 TNA, DEFE 24/1226, PRE-NIOM meeting 7, 17 February 1977.
13 Freedom of Information request (FOI), Northern Ireland: weekly intelligence summary, 18 February 1977.
14 FOI, Northern Ireland: intelligence summary, 18 March 1977.
15 TNA, DEFE 24/1226, PRE-NIOM meeting 13, 31 March 1977.
16 FOI, Northern Ireland: fortnightly intelligence summary, 20 May 1977.
17 FOI, Northern Ireland: fortnightly intelligence summary, 20 July 1977.
18 FOI, Northern Ireland: interim intelligence summary, 4 August 1977.
19 TNA, DEFE 23/200, Northern Ireland: fortnightly intelligence summary: 9 September 1977.
20 FOI, Northern Ireland: interim intelligence summary, 26 August 1977.

21 TNA, DEFE 23/200, Northern Ireland: fortnightly intelligence summary: 9 September 1977.
22 FOI, Northern Ireland: intelligence summary, 7 October 1977.
23 FOI, Northern Ireland: intelligence summary, 28 October 1977.
24 Moloney asserts his authorship in factual terms while Smith states that the report was 'possibly written by Adams': Moloney, *A secret history*, p. 172; M.L.R. Smith, *Fighting for Ireland: the military strategy of the Irish Republican movement* (London: Routledge, 1995), p. 145.
25 Staff report, reprinted in Liam Clarke, *Broadening the battlefield: the H-blocks and the rise of Sinn Féin* (Dublin: Gill and Macmillan, 1987), pp. 251–3.
26 TNA, DEFE 23/200, Northern Ireland: Intelligence summary: 27 January 1978.
27 McKearney, *The Provisional IRA*, p. 142.
28 TNA, FCO 87/976, Northern Ireland Future Terrorist Trends, 2 November 1978.
29 TNA, FCO 87/976, Northern Ireland Future Terrorist Trends, 2 November 1978.
30 Taylor, *Provos*, pp. 215–17.
31 PA, AN/532, Speech at Wantage, Oxfordshire, 22 October 1977.
32 *Daily Express*, 5 December 1977.
33 TNA, PREM 16/1721, Mason to Callaghan, 26 January 1978.
34 TNA, PREM 16/1722, Meeting between PM and Official Unionist delegation, 3 March 1978.
35 TNA, PREM 16/1722, Ramsay to Cartledge, 22 March 1978.
36 TNA, CJ4/2290, Meeting to discuss the security/political outlook, 23 June 1978.
37 TNA, CJ4/2290, Meeting to discuss the security/political outlook, 23 June 1978.
38 TNA, CJ4/2290, Cubbon to Mason, 3 July 1978.
39 TNA, CJ4/2290, Pilling to Cubbon, 6 July 1978; TNA, CJ4/2290, Creasey to Cubbon, 10 July 1978.
40 TNA, CJ4/2290, WG(PS) 3, 21 July 1978.
41 TNA, CJ4/2290, WG(PS) 10, 3 August 1978.
42 TNA, CJ4/2291, Schulte to Hannigan, 16 August 1978.
43 TNA, CJ4/2290, Innes to Hannigan, 8 August 1978.
44 TNA, CJ4/2291, Buxton to Hannigan, 23 August 1978.
45 TNA, CJ4/2294, Report of the working group to consider progress on security, undated.
46 TNA, CJ4/2294, Report of the working group to consider progress on security, undated.
47 TNA, CJ4/2294, Report of the working group to consider progress on security, undated..
48 TNA, CJ4/2294, Report of the working group to consider progress on security, undated.

49 TNA, CJ4/2294, Report of the working group to consider progress on security, undated.
50 *Report of the Chief Constable of the Royal Ulster Constabulary for 1976* (Belfast, 1977), p. ix.
51 TNA, CJ4/2294, Report of the working group to consider progress on security, undated.
52 TNA, CJ4/2294, Report of the working group to consider progress on security, undated.
53 TNA, CJ4/2293, Cubbon to Hannigan, 2 October 1978.
54 TNA, CJ4/2293, Stephens to PS/PUS, 6 October 1978.
55 TNA, CJ4/2293, Stephens to PS/PUS, 6 October 1978.
56 TNA, CJ4/2293, Janes to PUS, 6 October 1978.
57 TNA, CJ4/2295, Meeting between PUS, GOC and the Chief Constable, 10 October 1978.
58 TNA, CJ4/2295, Meeting between PUS, GOC and the Chief Constable, 16 October 1978.
59 TNA, CJ4/2295, Cubbon to Creasey, 17 October 1978.
60 TNA, CJ4/2295, Creasey to Cubbon, 20 October 1978; Walter Ladwig, 'Supporting allies in counterinsurgency: Britain and the Dhofar rebellion' in *Small Wars & Insurgencies*, 19:1 (2008).
61 TNA, CJ4/2295, Cubbon to Mason, 14 November 1978.
62 TNA, CJ4/2295, Mason to Cubbon, 23 November 1978.
63 TNA, PREM 16/1722, Mason to Callaghan, 1 December 1978.
64 TNA, PREM 16/1722, Hunt to Cartledge, 13 December 1978.
65 TNA, CAB 130/864, GEN 17(76) memo 2, 21 May 1976; TNA, CAB 130/864, GEN 17(77) memo 1, 17 January 1977.
66 TNA, CAB 130/864, GEN 17(76) meeting 1, 24 May 1976.
67 TNA, CAB 130/864, GEN 17(77) memo 1, 17 January 1977.
68 TNA, CAB 130/864, GEN 17(77) meeting 2, 1 March 1977.
69 TNA, DEFE 11/917, Haydon to FCO, 8 March 1977.
70 McKittrick *et al.*, *Lost lives*, p. 640.
71 TNA, PREM 16/1342, Mulley to Callaghan, 26 November 1976.
72 TNA, PREM 16/1342, Hunt to Callaghan, 1 December 1976.
73 TNA, PREM 16/1342, Meadway to Facer, 6 December 1976.
74 McKittrick *et al.*, *Lost lives*, p. 699.
75 McKittrick *et al.*, *Lost lives*, p. 761.
76 McKittrick *et al.*, *Lost lives*, p. 763.
77 McKittrick *et al.*, *Lost lives*, p. 770.
78 Urban, *Big boys' rules*, p. 6.
79 TNA, CJ4/2213, Cubbon to Mason, 31 October 1977.
80 Hansard (Commons), 905, col. 1090.
81 Hansard (Commons), 922, col. 2043; TNA, CJ4/2213, Discussion of prison strategy, 10 October 1977.
82 TNA, CJ4/2213, Cubbon to Mason, 31 October 1977.
83 Hansard (Commons), sixth series, 134, col. 461W.

84 McKittrick *et al.*, *Lost lives*, pp. 639–41; TNA, CJ4/2216, Sanderson to Innes, 9 November 1978.

85 TNA, CJ4/2213, Prison protest report, 4 April 1977.

86 TNA, CJ4/2216, Sanderson to Innes, 9 November 1978.

87 TNA, CJ4/2213, Prison protest report, 4 April 1977.

88 TNA, CJ4/2213, Prison protest report, 9 August 1977.

89 TNA, CJ4/2216, Sanderson to Innes, 9 November 1978.

90 TNA, CJ4/2215, Oosting to Mason, 23 May 1978.

91 TNA, CJ4/2215, Mason to Oosting, 30 June 1978.

92 TNA, FCO 97/827, Haydon to FCO, 1 August 1978.

93 *Irish Times*, 2 August 1978.

94 TNA, CJ4/2215, Hannigan to PS/SSNI, 20 October 1978.

95 TNA, CJ4/2215, Pilling to PS/PUS, 23 October 1978.

96 Hansard (Commons), 963, col. 1468.

97 These figures were calculated using McKittrick *et al.*, *Lost lives*

98 PA, Neave, AN/531, Transcript of *Tonight* programme, 2 March 1977.

99 Peter Taylor, *Beating the terrorists? Interrogation at Omagh, Gough and Castlereagh* (London: Penguin, 1980), pp. 221–2.

100 Hansard (Commons), 939, cols 1734–6.

101 *Report of the Chief Constable of the Royal Ulster Constabulary for 1976* (Belfast, 1977), p. ix.

102 *Report of an Amnesty International mission to Northern Ireland* (London, 1978).

103 Hansard (Commons), 951, cols 229–234w.

104 Hansard (Commons), 951, cols 1165–8

105 *Report of the committee of inquiry into police interrogation procedures in Northern Ireland*, Cmnd. 7497, H.C. 1979.

106 *Report of the committee of inquiry into police interrogation procedures in Northern Ireland*, Cmnd. 7497, H.C. 1979.

107 *Irish Times*, 12 March 1979.

108 *Irish Times*, 14 March 1979.

109 *Irish Times*, 15 March 1979.

110 Hansard (Commons), 964, cols 965–9.

111 'Symposium: the winter of discontent' in *Contemporary Record*, 1:3 (1987), pp. 34–43; Colin Hay, 'Chronicles of a death foretold: the winter of discontent and construction of the crisis of British Keynesianism', *Parliamentary Affairs*, 63:3 (2010), pp. 446–70.

112 Of the ten unionist MPs only three voted (Paisley, Bradford and Kilfedder), all against the Labour government: Hansard (Commons), 960, cols 1044–51.

113 Donoughue, *Downing Street diary*, volume 2, p. 453; Callaghan, *Time and chance*, pp. 540–1; Hansard (Commons), 964, cols 1692–3.

114 Donoughue, *Downing Street diary*, volume 2, p. 466.

115 *A parliamentary coup*, BBC, 28 March 2009.

116 Donoughue, *Downing Street diary*, volume 2, p. 461.

117 *A parliamentary coup*, BBC, 28 March 2009.
118 *Irish Times*, 6 February 1979.
119 *A parliamentary coup*, BBC, 28 March 2009.
120 Hansard (Commons), 965, col. 471.
121 Hansard (Commons), 965, cols 515–22.
122 Hansard (Commons), 965, cols 584–7; *A parliamentary coup*, BBC, 28 March 2009.
123 Mason, *Paying the* price, pp. 165–6.

Conclusion

This book has attempted to critique a number of flawed perceptions of British policy during the Northern Ireland conflict. The Labour government's handling of the UWC strike was not as disastrous as has been portrayed. From an analysis of the context of the strike and the challenges it proffered it becomes clear that the government was limited in what it could achieve. The strike did not merely succeed because of indecisiveness or a lack of commitment to Sunningdale. This is reinforced by the experience of the UUAC strike three years later. The depiction of the two stoppages as symbolic of Rees and Mason's tenures as Secretary of State is inaccurate. In spite of a vastly different political context the UUAC strike was a close-run affair; after three years of planning difficulties remained.

It has also been shown that Labour did not seriously consider withdrawal from Northern Ireland, in spite of fears at the time. Wilson was preoccupied with the possibility of a complete breakdown and prepared plans to grant Dominion status, but the significance of these has been misunderstood. In the NIO and cabinet committees consideration was given to all possible options, including not just withdrawal but integration and many others. Rees viewed this process as serving to rule out everything except direct rule. While some Labour ministers favoured other options, the basic logic of his arguments and the political context meant that he won the argument. Rees was correct to conclude that no radical solution would work and to attempt to break the 'English' habit of trying to answer the 'Irish question.'

During the PIRA ceasefire the British government had a clearer strategy than was apparent to outside eyes. The belief was held that the longer the ceasefire lasted, the harder it would be for the PIRA to return to violence. This situation also assisted Rees's long-running ambition to end detention without trial and lower the profile of the army. The dialogue with the PIRA served these purposes but there was also an attempt to persuade the republican movement to engage with conventional politics. It was recognised, however, that there was only an outside chance of progress on this front. The ceasefire strategy seemed indeterminate and vacillating to critics for valid reasons. No government could have given sufficient assurance that they were not negotiating with militant republicans on larger political questions. Furthermore, violence did not cease and, because so much was invested in the ceasefire, statements by Rees attributing violent acts to 'loose cannons' naturally made him look weak.

After the ceasefire there was a fundamental shift in the balance of power between the security forces. The police assumed a greater role at the direction of Rees and following the formulation of proposals by a number of committees. While the RUC were enthusiastic, the army were resistant. They should not, however, be seen as uniformly opposed. The GOC, David House, was committed to the principles behind the approach but argued for aggressive security measures in the short term, not appreciating the contradiction. Following 1976 there was a substantial drop in the level of violence. This should not be attributed to a crackdown imposed by Mason, despite his subsequent reputation. There was certainly a greater degree of attrition by the security forces, in part because of the increasing ability to operate through the courts, but security policy continued to evolve within the parameters decided on during Rees's tenure. More significant was the changing dynamic of the conflict; the violence of the first half of the decade was unsustainable and it became increasingly apparent that there would be no final, successful push by republicans or an abandonment of the region by the British government. As anxiety decreased so did sectarian killings by loyalist paramilitaries.

This improvement, nevertheless, reached a plateau. The PIRA showed its ability to adapt to new conditions and benefited from the accumulation of expertise. Also crucial was the fact that the British government's strategy to separate the paramilitaries from the wider community was only partially achievable. Operations by the SAS led to unnecessary deaths and accusations of a 'shoot-to-kill' policy, while police interrogations were on occasion brutal, leading to great political damage. The growing protest in the prisons resulting from the ending of special category status (central to the policy of criminalisation) led to a political boost for Provisional Sinn Féin in the following decade when it culminated in the hunger strikes. Furthermore, the motivations and ideological commitment of the Provisionals allowed them to continue their campaign. Both the conflict and the historical dynamic in Northern Ireland meant a portion of the nationalist community remained sympathetic.

In the midst of this the Northern Irish economy suffered both as a result of a recession in Britain and because of the impact of the conflict. The Labour government continued to treat Northern Ireland favourably in order to prevent unemployment fuelling the conflict even more.

Meanwhile, the political situation turned stagnant. Mason failed to adopt a sufficiently neutral relationship with the parties in Northern Ireland. His attention turned primarily to the Ulster Unionists, not because of a pact at Westminster, but, rather, his personal perspective and the lack of an opportunity to break the constitutional deadlock. This alienated the SDLP. Attempts to bring the parties together continued but they remained irreconcilable. Interim devolution, the main initiative attempted since the Constitutional Convention, was not attractive because both the SDLP and the Ulster Unionists were, quite logically, preoccupied with what it might lead to. The SDLP underwent a process of change after suffering rejection by unionist politicians unwilling to compromise. Mason was too short-sighted, showing little sympathy and being too convinced of the merits of direct rule.

Throughout this book considerable thought has been given to the individuals involved in shaping government policy. As such it has served as a rebuttal for those who treat the views of the prime minister as synonymous with government policy. Harold Wilson's contributions were flawed but few and far between; beyond antagonising the Protestant population during the UWC strike and introducing the SAS into Northern Ireland he was largely irrelevant. James Callaghan, believing the possibility of progress to be slim, remained disinterested and preoccupied by other problems. Frank Cooper showed a commitment to the new approach to security policy that led him into confrontations with senior army officers and Brian Cubbon similarly did much to keep this process underway. Cubbon did not, however, advocate a sufficiently neutral approach to the political problem, which might have encouraged Mason to improve his relations with the SDLP. This would not have led to a political settlement including both nationalist and unionist politicians, but it could have at least minimised the disaffection of those who would ultimately have to compromise. Other civil servants, such as John Bourn, Anthony Pritchard, Anthony Stephens and James Hannigan, chaired important security reviews. They distilled the discussion of numerous other individuals but, especially in the case of Stephens and Hannigan, also had to resist arguments for a more aggressive, counter-productive, stance from the army. Accounts of government attempts to resolve or manage conflict should recognise the role of all such individuals and the parameters within which they operated. This last point is particularly important because of the prevalent tendency of many scholars of the conflict to evaluate ministers' quality by their media performance and to accept contemporary perceptions without investigating the government processes that occurred more privately.

The former Head of the Home Civil Service, Sir William Armstrong, made the following remark when asked about his thoughts during times of economic crisis: 'I have a very strong suspicion that governments are nothing like as important as they think they are, that the ordinary work of transport, manufacture, farming and mining is so much more important than what government does, that the government can make enormous mistakes and we can still survive.'[1] In Northern Ireland this condition was a tragic one. It has often been assumed that the British government, enjoying far more resources than other political actors in the region, had the capacity to impose a solution in Northern Ireland but lacked the insight to do so. A thorough and detailed historical analysis of the subject, however, reveals that all these resources could not overcome the political conditions in Northern Ireland during the years of the Labour government. For all the benefits of the Good Friday Agreement, the institutions, mechanisms and careful balancing contained within, it is in essence an agreement to disagree for the sake of peace. Those who believe it could have been achieved twenty years earlier while violence remained high utterly fail to understand the context of both the 1970s and the present. When Rees came to write an account of his time in Northern Ireland he wanted to call it 'No Solution' but the publisher did not find it appealing.[2] It was actually rather apposite.

Notes

1 Quoted in Peter Hennessy, *Whitehall*, p. 241.
2 *Independent*, 6 January 2006.

Bibliography

Government archives

The National Archives of the United Kingdom (TNA)

Cabinet Office	CAB
Foreign and Commonwealth Office	FCO
Ministry of Defence	DEFE
Northern Ireland Office	CJ
Prime Minister's Office	PREM
Treasury	T

Public Record Office Northern Ireland (PRONI)

Central Secretariat	CENT
Constitutional Convention	CONV
Office of the Executive	OE
Policy Co-ordinating Committee	PCC
Secretary of State's Executive Committee	SOSEC

Private papers

Papers of Bernard Donoughue, Churchill College, Cambridge
Papers of Brendan Duddy, NUI Galway
Papers of Airey Neave, Parliamentary Archives, Houses of Parliament
Papers of Ruairí Ó Brádaigh, NUI Galway
Papers of Stanley Orme, London School of Economics
Papers of Merlyn Rees, London School of Economics
Papers of Harold Wilson, Bodleian Library, Oxford
Papers of the Labour National Executive Committee, Labour History Archive and
   Study Centre, Manchester

Official publications

Hansard; House of Commons Official Report, Parliamentary Debates, 1974–
   1979.

Hansard; House of Lords Official Report, Parliamentary Debates, 1974–1979.

Isles & Cuthbert, *An economic survey of Northern Ireland* (Belfast, 1957).

Report of the joint working party on the economy of Northern Ireland, Cmd. 446 [NI], Belfast, 1962.

Economic development in Northern Ireland including the report of the economic consultant, Thomas Wilson, Cmd. 479 [NI], Belfast, 1965.

Text of a communiqué and declaration issued after a meeting held at 10 Downing Street on 19 August 1969 (London: HMSO, 1969).

Northern Ireland development programme 1970–75 (Belfast, 1970).

Review of economic and social development in Northern Ireland: report of the joint review body, Cmd. 564 [NI], Belfast, 1971.

Northern Ireland: financial arrangements and legislation, Cmnd. 4998, H.C. 1972–3.

Report of the Committee of Privy Counsellors appointed to consider authorised procedures for the interrogation of persons suspected of terrorism, Cmd. 4901, H.C. 1971–2.

Report of the commission to consider legal procedures to deal with terrorist activities in Northern Ireland, Cmnd. 5185, H.C. 1972–3.

Northern Ireland constitutional proposals, Cmnd. 5259, H.C. 1972–3.

Northern Ireland Constitution Act 1973 (London: HMSO, 1973.

The Sunningdale Agreement (London: HMSO, 1973).

The Northern Ireland Constitution, Cmnd. 5675, H.C. 1974–5.

Northern Ireland Act (London: HMSO, 1974).

Northern Ireland: finance and the economy, Discussion paper 1 (1974), London: HMSO.

Constitutional Convention: procedure, Discussion paper 2 (1974), London: HMSO.

Report of the Law Enforcement Commission to the Secretary of State for Northern Ireland and the Minister for Justice of Ireland, Cmnd. 5627, H.C. 1974–5.

Prevention of Terrorism (Temporary Provisions) Act 1974 (HMSO, London, 1974).

The Queen's regulations for the army, 1975 (London: HMSO, 1976).

The Government of Northern Ireland: a society divided, Discussion paper 3 (1975). London: HMSO.

Industrial democracy: a discussion paper on worker participation in Harland & Wolff (Belfast: HMSO, 1975).

Northern Ireland (Emergency Provisions) (Amendment) Bill (London: HMSO, 1975).

Report of debates: 8 May 1975 to November 1975: Northern Ireland Constitutional Convention (Belfast: HMSO, 1975).

Report of a committee to consider, in the context of civil liberties and human rights, measures to deal with terrorism in Northern Ireland, Cmnd. 5847, H.C. 1974–5.

The Northern Ireland Constitutional Convention, Cmnd. 6387, H.C. 1975–6.

Public expenditure to 1979–80, Cmnd. 6393, H.C. 1975–6.

Report, together with the proceedings of the Convention and other appendices: Northern Ireland Constitutional Convention, H.C. 1975–6.

Economic and industrial strategy for Northern Ireland (Belfast: HMSO, 1976).
Report of the Chief Constable of the Royal Ulster Constabulary for 1976 (Belfast, 1977).
SDLP, *Facing reality* (Belfast, 1977).
Conference on electoral law, Cmnd. 7110, H.C. 1977–8.
Report of an Amnesty International mission to Northern Ireland (London, 1978).
Report of the Committee of Inquiry into Police Interrogation Procedures in Northern Ireland, Cmnd. 7497, H.C. 1978–9.
Economic and social progress in Northern Ireland: review and prospects (Belfast: HMSO, 1979).
The government's expenditure plans 1979–80 to 1982–83, Cmnd. 7439, H.C. 1979–80.
Report of the Bloody Sunday Inquiry (London: HMSO, 2010).

Newspapers and periodicals

Belfast Telegraph
Daily Express
Daily Telegraph
Economist
Fortnight
Guardian
Independent
Irish News
Irish Times
New Statesman
News Letter
Observer
The Times
Tribune

Documentaries

'A modern rebellion', 14 May 1984 (Ulster Folk and Transport Museum, BBC NI Archive, #1663).
Wilson and Ulster, BBC Radio 4, 11 September 2008.
A parliamentary coup, BBC television, 28 March 2009.

Books, articles and theses

Alonso, Rogelio, *The IRA and armed struggle* (London: Routledge, 2003).
Anderson, Don, *Fourteen May days: the inside story of the loyalist strike of 1974* (Dublin: Gill and Macmillan, 1994).
Andrew, Christopher, *The defence of the realm: the authorized history of MI5* (London: Allen Lane, 2009).
Arthur, Paul, *Special relationships: Britain, Ireland and the Northern Ireland problem* (Belfast: Blackstaff, 2000).

Artis, M., Cobham, D. and Wickham-Jones, M., 'Social democracy in hard times': the economic record of the Labour government 1974–79', *Twentieth Century British History*, 3:1 (1992), pp. 32–58.

Aughey, Arthur, 'Conservative Party policy and Northern Ireland' in Brian Barton and Patrick J. Roche (eds), *The Northern Ireland question: perspectives and policies* (Aldershot: Avebury, 1994), pp. 121–50.

Aveyard, Stuart, 'The "English Disease" is to look for a "Solution of the Irish Problem"': British constitutional policy in Northern Ireland after Sunningdale 1974–76', *Contemporary British History*, 26:4 (2012), pp. 529–49.

Aveyard, Stuart, '"We couldn't do a Prague"': British government responses to loyalist strikes in Northern Ireland 1974–77', *Irish Historical Studies*, 39:153 (2014), pp. 91–111.

Aveyard, Stuart, 'Labour and police primacy in Northern Ireland' in Laurence Marley (ed.), *The British Labour Party and 20th Century Ireland: the cause of Ireland, the cause of Labour* (Manchester: Manchester University Press, 2015).

Bell, Geoffrey, *Troublesome business: the Labour Party and the Irish question* (London: Pluto, 1982).

Benn, Tony, *Against the tide: diaries, 1973–77* (London: Arrow, 1989).

Benn, Tony, *Conflicts of interest: diaries, 1977–80* (London: Arrow, 1991).

Bew, John, Frampton, Martyn and Gurruchaga, Iñigo, *Talking to terrorists: making peace in Northern Ireland and the Basque Country* (London: Hurst, 2009).

Bew, Paul, *Ireland: the politics of enmity, 1789–2006* (Oxford: Oxford University Press, 2007).

Bew, Paul and Dixon, Paul, 'Labour Party policy and Northern Ireland' in Brian Barton and Patrick J. Roche (eds), *The Northern Ireland question: perspectives and policies* (Aldershot: Avebury, 1994), pp. 151–65.

Bew, Paul and Gillespie, Gordon, *Northern Ireland: a chronology of the troubles, 1968–1999* (Lanham: Scarecrow Press, 1999).

Bew, Paul and Patterson, Henry, *The British state and the Ulster crisis: from Wilson to Thatcher* (London: Verso, 1985).

Bew, Paul, Gibbon, Peter and Patterson, Henry, *Northern Ireland 1921–2001: political forces and social classes* (London: Serif, 2001).

Bew, Paul, Hazelkorn, Ellen and Patterson, Henry, *The dynamics of Irish politics* (London: Lawrence & Wishart, 1989).

Bew, Paul, Patterson, Henry and Teague, Paul, *Between war and peace: the political future of Northern Ireland* (London: Lawrence & Wishart, 1997).

Bloomfield, Kenneth, *Stormont in crisis: a memoir* (Belfast: Blackstaff, 1994).

Bloomfield, Kenneth, *A tragedy of errors: the government and misgovernment of Northern Ireland* (Liverpool: Liverpool University Press, 2007).

Bogdanor, Vernon, *Devolution in the United Kingdom* (Oxford: Oxford University Press, 1999).

Boyce, D.G., *The Irish question and British politics, 1868–1996* (Basingstoke: Macmillan, 1996).

Brown, William, 'Industrial relations' in Michael Artis and David Cobham (eds), *Labour's economic policies 1974–1979* (Manchester: Manchester University Press, 1991), pp. 213–28.

Brownlow, Graham, 'Back to the failure: an analytic narrative of the De Lorean debacle', *Business History*, 57:1 (2015), pp. 156–81.

Bruce, Steve, *The red hand: Protestant paramilitaries in Northern Ireland* (Oxford: Oxford University Press, 1992).

Bruce, Steve, *Paisley: religion and politics in Northern Ireland* (Oxford: Oxford University Press, 2007).

Callaghan, James, *A house divided: the dilemma of Northern Ireland* (London: Collins, 1973).

Callaghan, James, *Time and chance* (London: Politico's, 2006).

Campbell, Sarah, *Gerry Fitt and the SDLP: 'in a minority of one'* (Manchester: Manchester University Press, 2015).

Catterall, Peter and McDougall, Sean, *The Northern Ireland question in British politics* (London: Macmillan, 1996).

Clarke, Liam, *Broadening the battlefield: the H-blocks and the rise of Sinn Féin* (Dublin: Gill and Macmillan, 1987).

Cochrane, Feargal, *Northern Ireland: the reluctant peace* (New Haven: Yale University Press, 2013).

Connor, Ken, *Ghost force: the secret history of the SAS* (London: Weidenfeld & Nicolson, 1998).

Cowper-Coles, Freddie, '"Anxious for peace": the Provisional IRA in dialogue with the British government 1972–75', *Irish Studies Review*, 20:3 (2012), pp. 223–42.

Cox, Michael, Guelke, Adrian and Stephen, Fiona, *A farewell to arms? Beyond the Good Friday Agreement* (Manchester: Manchester University Press, 2006).

Craig, Anthony, *Crisis of confidence: Anglo-Irish relations in the early Troubles* (Dublin: Irish Academic Press, 2010).

Craig, Tony, 'From backdoors and back lanes to backchannels: reappraising British talks with the Provisional IRA, 1970–1974', *Contemporary British History*, 26:1 (2012), pp. 97–117.

Craig, Tony, 'Laneside, then left a bit? Britain's secret political talks with loyalist paramilitaries in Northern Ireland, 1973–1976', *Irish Political Studies*, 29:2 (2014), pp. 298–317.

Craig, Tony, 'Monitoring the peace? Northern Ireland's 1975 ceasefire incident centres and the politicisation of Sinn Féin', *Terrorism & Political Violence*, 26:2 (2014), pp. 307–19.

Crossman, R.H.S. 'Introduction' in Walter Bagehot, *The English Constitution* (London: C.A. Watts, 1964).

Cunningham, Michael, 'Conservative dissidents and the Irish question: the pro-integrationist lobby 1973–94', *Irish Political Studies*, 10 (1995), pp. 26–42.

Cunningham, Michael, *British government policy in Northern Ireland, 1969–2000* (Manchester: Manchester University Press, 2001).

Currie, Austin, *All hell will break loose* (Dublin: O'Brien, 2004).

Cusack, Jim and McDonald, Henry, *UVF* (Dublin: Poolbeg, 2000).

Cusack, Jim and McDonald, Henry, *UDA: inside the heart of Loyalist terror* (Dublin: Penguin Ireland, 2004).

Dale, Iain (ed.), *Labour Party general election manifestos 1900–1997* (London: Routledge, 2000).

Devlin, Paddy, *The fall of the N.I. Executive* (Belfast: P. Devlin, 1975).

Devlin, Paddy, *Straight left: an autobiography* (Belfast: Blackstaff, 1993).

Dewar, Michael, *The British army in Northern Ireland* (London: Arms and Armour, 1985).

Dixon, Paul, 'The British Labour Party and Northern Ireland 1959–74' (unpublished PhD thesis, University of Bradford, 1993).

Dixon, Paul, '"The usual English double-talk": the British political parties and the Ulster Unionists 1974–94', *Irish Political Studies*, 9 (1994), pp. 25–40.

Dixon, Paul, '"A House divided cannot stand": Britain, bipartisanship and Northern Ireland', *Contemporary Record*, 9:1 (1995), pp. 147–87.

Dixon, Paul, *Northern Ireland: the politics of war and peace* (Basingstoke: Palgrave, 2001).

Donohue, Laura K., *Counter-terrorist law and emergency powers in the United Kingdom 1922–2000* (Dublin: Irish Academic Press, 2000).

Donoughue, Bernard, *Prime Minister: the conduct of policy under Harold Wilson and James Callaghan* (London: Jonathan Cape, 1987).

Donoughue, Bernard, *Downing Street diary: with Harold Wilson in no. 10* (London: Pimlico, 2005).

Donoughue, Bernard, *Downing Street diary: with James Callaghan in no. 10*, volume 2 (London: Pimlico, 2008).

Dow, J.C.R., *Major recessions: Britain and the world 1920–1995* (Oxford: Oxford University Press, 1998).

Edwards, Aaron, 'Social democracy and partition: the British Labour Party and Northern Ireland, 1951–64', *Journal of Contemporary History*, 42:4 (2007), pp. 595–612.

Edwards, Aaron, *A history of the Northern Ireland Labour Party: democratic socialism and sectarianism* (Manchester: Manchester University Press, 2009).

Edwards, Aaron, 'Misapplying lessons learned? Analysing the utility of British counterinsurgency strategy in Northern Ireland, 1971–76', *Small Wars & Insurgencies*, 21:2 (2010), pp. 303–30.

Edwards, Aaron, '"A whipping boy if ever there was one"? The British army and the politics of civil–military relations in Northern Ireland 1969–79', *Contemporary British History*, 28:2 (2014), pp. 166–89.

Ellison, Graham and Smyth, Jim, *The crowned harp: policing Northern Ireland* (London: Pluto, 2000).

English, Richard, *Armed struggle: the history of the IRA* (London: Pan, 2003).

English, Richard, 'Review: Shaun McDaid, *Template for peace*', *Irish Historical Studies*, 39:154 (2014), pp. 365–6.

Evelegh, Robin, *Peace keeping in a democratic society: the lessons of Northern Ireland* (London: C. Hurst, 1978).

Fallon, Ivan and Srodes, James, *Delorean: the rise and fall of a dream-maker* (London: Hamilton, 1983).

Faulkner, Brian, *Memoirs of a statesman* (London: Weidenfeld & Nicolson, 1978).

Fisk, Robert, *The point of no return: the strike which broke the British in Ulster* (London: André Deutsch, 1975).

FitzGerald, Garret, *All in a life: an autobiography* (Dublin: Gill and Macmillan, 1991).

FitzGerald, Garret, 'The 1974–5 threat of a British withdrawal from Northern Ireland', *Irish Studies in International Affairs*, 17 (2006), pp. 141–50.

Gildea, Robert, *France since 1945* (Oxford: Oxford University Press, 2002).

Gillespie, Gordon, 'Loyalist politics and the Ulster Workers' Council Strike of 1974' (unpublished PhD thesis, Queen's University Belfast, 1994).

Gillespie, Gordon, 'The Sunningdale Agreement: lost opportunity or an agreement too far?', *Irish Political Studies*, 13 (1998), pp. 100–14.

Guelke, Adrian, 'British policy and international dimensions of the Northern Ireland Conflict', *Regional Politics and Policy*, 1 (1991), pp. 140–60.

Haines, Joe, *The politics of power* (London: Jonathan Cape, 1977).

Haines, Joe, *Glimmers of twilight: murder, intrigue and passion at the court of Harold Wilson* (London: Politico's, 2003).

Hamill, Desmond, *Pig in the middle: the army in Northern Ireland 1969–1985* (London: Methuen, 1986).

Hanley, Brian and Millar, Scott, *The lost revolution: the story of the Official IRA and the Workers' Party* (Dublin: Penguin Ireland, 2009).

Hay, Colin. 'Chronicles of a death foretold: the winter of discontent and construction of the crisis of British Keynesianism', *Parliamentary Affairs*, 63:3 (2010), pp. 446–70.

Hayes, Bernadette C. and McAllister, Ian, 'British and Irish public opinion towards the Northern Ireland problem', *Irish Political Studies*, 11 (1996), pp. 61–82.

Hayes, Maurice, *Minority verdict: experiences of a Catholic public servant* (Belfast: Blackstaff, 1995).

Healey, Denis, *The time of my life* (London: M. Joseph, 1989).

Heath, Edward, *The course of my life: an autobiography* (London: Coronet, 1999).

Hennessy, Peter, *Cabinet* (Oxford: Basil Blackwell, 1986).

Hennessy, Peter, *Whitehall* (London: Secker & Warburg, 1989).

Hennessy, Peter, *Muddling through: power, politics and the quality of government in postwar Britain* (London: Weidenfeld & Nicolson, 1997).

Hennessey, Thomas, *The origins of the Troubles* (Dublin: Gill and Macmillan, 2005).

Hennessey, Thomas, *The evolution of the Troubles, 1970–72* (Dublin: Irish Academic Press, 2007).

Hickson, Kevin, *The IMF crisis of 1976 and British politics* (London: Tauris, 2005).

Hilton, Boyd, *A mad, bad and dangerous people? England 1783–1846* (Oxford: Oxford University Press, 2008)

Hume, John, *Personal views: politics, peace and reconciliation in Ireland* (Dublin: Townhouse, 1996).

Hume, John and Moss, Michael, *Shipbuilders to the world: 125 years of Harland and Wolff, Belfast, 1861–1986* (Belfast: Blackstaff, 1986).

Hyam, Ronald, *Britain's declining empire: the road to decolonisation* (Cambridge: Cambridge University Press, 2007).

Jackson, Alvin, *Home rule: an Irish history, 1800–2000* (London: Weidenfeld & Nicolson, 2003).

Jackson, Peter 'Public expenditure' in Michael Artis and David Cobham (eds), *Labour's economic policies 1974–1979* (Manchester: Manchester University Press, 1991), pp. 73–87.

Jeffery, Keith, 'Military aid to the civil power: an historical perspective' in Peter Rowe and Christopher Whelan (eds), *Military intervention in democratic societies* (Kent: Croom Helm, 1985), pp. 51–67.

Jeffery, Keith, 'Security policy in Northern Ireland: some reflections on the management of violent conflict', *Terrorism & Political Violence*, 2 (1990), pp. 21–34.

Jeffery, Keith and Hennessy, Peter, *States of emergency: British governments and strikebreaking since 1919* (London: Routledge & Kegan Paul, 1983).

Jenkins, Roy, *A life at the centre* (London: Macmillan, 1991).

Judt, Tony, *Postwar: a history of Europe since 1945* (London: Heinemann, 2005).

Kerr, Michael, *Imposing power-sharing: conflict and coexistence in Northern Ireland and Lebanon* (Dublin: Irish Academic Press, 2005).

Kerr, Michael, *The destructors: the story of Northern Ireland's lost peace process* (Dublin: Irish Academic Press, 2011).

Kitson, Frank, *Low intensity operations: subversion, insurgency, peace-keeping* (London: Faber and Faber, 1971).

Ladwig, Walter, 'Supporting allies in counterinsurgency: Britain and the Dhofar rebellion', *Small Wars & Insurgencies*, 19:1 (2008), pp. 62–88.

Lee, Joseph, *Ireland 1912–1985: politics and society* (Cambridge: Cambridge University Press, 1989).

Loughlin, James, *Ulster Unionism and British identity since 1885* (London: Pinter, 1995).

Lowe, Rodney, *The official history of the British civil service: reforming the civil service*, volume 1 (London: Routledge, 2011).

Lowry, Donal, 'Ulster resistance and loyalist rebellion in the British empire' in Keith Jeffery (ed.), *'An Irish empire'? Aspects of Ireland and the British empire* (Manchester: Manchester University Press, 1996), pp. 191–215.

McAllister, Ian, 'The legitimacy of opposition: the collapse of the 1974 Northern Ireland Executive', *Eire-Ireland*, 22 (1977), pp. 25–42.

McAllister, Ian, *The Northern Ireland Social Democratic and Labour Party: political opposition in a divided society* (London: Macmillan, 1977).

McDaid, Shaun, 'Northern Ireland: Sunningdale, power-sharing and British–Irish relations, 1972–75' (unpublished PhD thesis, Queen's University Belfast, 2010).

McDaid, Shaun, 'The Irish government and the Sunningdale Council of Ireland: a vehicle for unity?', *Irish Historical Studies*, 36:150 (2012), pp. 283–303.

McDaid, Shaun, *Template for peace: Northern Ireland 1972–75* (Manchester: Manchester University Press, 2013).

McGladdery, Gary, *The Provisional IRA in England: the bombing campaign* (Dublin: Irish Academic Press, 2006)

McGrattan, Cillian, 'Learning from the past or laundering history? Consociational narratives and state intervention in Northern Ireland', *British Politics*, 5 (2010), pp. 92–113.

McGrattan, Cillian, *Northern Ireland 1968–2008: the politics of entrenchment* (Basingstoke: Palgrave Macmillan, 2010).

McIntyre, Anthony, 'Modern Irish republicanism: the product of British state strategies', *Irish Political Studies*, 10 (1995), pp. 97–121.

McKearney, Tommy, *The Provisional IRA: from insurrection to parliament* (London: Pluto, 2011).

McKittrick, David, *Making sense of the troubles* (Belfast: Blackstaff, 2000).

McKittrick, David, Kelters, Seamus, Feeney, Brian, Thornton, Chris and McVea, David, *Lost lives: the stories of the men, women and children who died as a result of the Northern Ireland troubles* (Edinburgh: Mainstream Publishing, 2007).

McLoughlin, P.J., *John Hume and the revision of Irish nationalism* (Manchester: Manchester University Press, 2010).

Mansergh, Nicholas, 'Ireland and the British Commonwealth: the Dominion settlement' in Desmond Williams (ed.), *The Irish struggle 1916–1926* (London: Routledge & K. Paul, 1966), pp. 129–39.

Mansergh, Nicholas, *The unresolved question: the Anglo-Irish settlement and its undoing 1912–72* (London: Yale University Press, 1991).

Mason, Roy, *Paying the price* (London: Robert Hale, 1999).

Moloney, Ed, *A secret history of the IRA* (London: Penguin, 2007).

Morgan, Kenneth, *Callaghan: a life* (Oxford: Oxford University Press, 1997).

Morgan, Kenneth, *Michael Foot: a life* (London: Harper Perennial, 2008).

Morris, Gillian, *Strikes in essential services* (London: Mansell, 1986).

Moulton, Mo, *Ireland and the Irish in interwar England* (Cambridge: Cambridge University Press, 2014).

Mumford, Andrew, 'Covert peacemaking: clandestine negotiations and backchannels with the Provisional IRA during the early "Troubles", 1972–76', *Journal of Imperial and Commonwealth History*, 39:4 (2011), pp. 633–48.

Murray, Gerard, *John Hume and the SDLP: impact and survival in Northern Ireland* (Dublin: Irish Academic Press, 1998).

Neumann, Peter, 'British government strategy in Northern Ireland, 1969–98: an evolutionary analysis' (unpublished PhD thesis, King's College London, 2002).

Neumann, Peter, *Britain's long war: British strategy in the Northern Ireland conflict, 1969–98* (Basingstoke: Palgrave Macmillan, 2003).

Neumann, Peter, 'The myth of Ulsterization in British security policy in Northern Ireland', *Studies in Conflict & Terrorism*, 26 (2003), pp. 365–77.

Neumann, Peter, 'Winning the "war on terror"? Roy Mason's contribution to counter-terrorism in Northern Ireland', *Small Wars & Insurgencies*, 14:3 (2003), pp. 45–64.

Neumann, Peter and Smith, M.L.R., 'Motorman's long journey: changing the strategic setting in Northern Ireland', *Contemporary British History*, 19:4 (2005), pp. 413–35.

Newsinger, John, 'From counter-insurgency to internal security: Northern Ireland 1969–1992', *Small Wars & Insurgencies*, 6:1 (1995), pp. 88–111.

Ó Dochartaigh, Niall, *From civil rights to Armalites: Derry and the birth of the Irish troubles* (Cork: Cork University Press, 1997).

Ó Dochartaigh, Niall, '"Everyone trying", the IRA ceasefire, 1975: a missed opportunity for peace?' in *Field Day Review 7* (Dublin: Field Day, 2011), pp. 50–77.

O'Duffy, Brendan, *British–Irish relations and Northern Ireland: from violent politics to conflict regulation* (Dublin: Irish Academic Press, 2007).

O'Leary, Brendan, 'The Labour government and Northern Ireland, 1974–79' in Brendan O'Leary and John McGarry (eds), *The Northern Ireland conflict: consociational engagements* (Oxford: Oxford University Press, 2003), pp. 194–216.

O'Leary, Brendan and McGarry, John, *The politics of antagonism: understanding Northern Ireland* (London: Athlone Press, 1993).

Oppenheimer, A.R., *IRA: the bombs and the bullets, a history of deadly ingenuity* (Dublin: Irish Academic Press, 2010).

Patterson, Henry, *The politics of illusion: a political history of the IRA* (London: Serif, 1997).

Patterson, Henry, *Ireland since 1939: the persistence of conflict* (Dublin: Penguin Ireland, 2006).

Patterson, Henry, *Ireland's violent frontier: the border and Anglo-Irish relations during the Troubles* (London: Palgrave Macmillan, 2013).

Patterson, Henry and Kaufmann, Eric, *Unionism and Orangeism in Northern Ireland since 1945* (Manchester: Manchester University Press, 2007).

Pimlott, Ben, *Harold Wilson* (London: HarperCollins, 1992).

Prince, Simon, *Northern Ireland's '68: civil rights, global revolt and the origins of the Troubles* (Dublin: Irish Academic Press, 2007).

Purdie, Bob, *Politics in the streets: the origins of the civil rights movement in Northern Ireland* (Belfast: Blackstaff, 1990).

Ramsay, Robert, *Ringside seats: an insider's view of the crisis in Northern Ireland* (Dublin: Irish Academic Press, 2009).

Rees, Merlyn, 'The future of Northern Ireland', *Contemporary Review*, 223 (1973).

Rees, Merlyn, *Northern Ireland: a personal perspective* (London: Methuen, 1985).

Rose, Paul, *Backbencher's dilemma* (London: Muller, 1981).

Rose, Peter, *How the Troubles came to Northern Ireland* (Basingstoke: Palgrave, 2000).

Smith, M.L.R., *Fighting for Ireland? The military strategy of the Irish Republican movement* (London: Routledge, 1995).

Strachan, Hew, *The politics of the British army* (Oxford: Oxford University Press, 1997).

'Symposium: the winter of discontent', *Contemporary Record*, 1:3 (1987), pp. 34–43.

Taylor, Peter, *Beating the terrorists? Interrogation at Omagh, Gough and Castlereagh* (London: Penguin, 1980).

Taylor, Peter, *Provos: the IRA and Sinn Féin* (London: Bloomsbury, 1997).

Taylor, Peter, *Loyalists* (London: Bloomsbury, 1999).

Taylor, Peter, *Brits* (London: Bloomsbury, 2001).

Thorpe, Andrew, *A history of the British Labour Party* (London: Macmillan, 2015).

Todd, Jennifer, 'Two traditions in unionist political culture', *Irish Political Studies*, 2 (1987), pp. 1–26.

Tomlinson, Jim, 'Tale of a death exaggerated: how Keynesian policies survived the 1970s', *Contemporary British History*, 21:4 (2007), pp. 429–48.

Tomlinson, Mike, 'Walking backwards into the sunset: British policy and the insecurity of Northern Ireland' in David Miller (ed.), *Rethinking Northern Ireland: culture, ideology and colonialism* (London: Longman, 1998), pp. 94–122.

Tonge, Jon, 'From Sunningdale to the Good Friday Agreement: creating devolved government in Northern Ireland', *Contemporary British History*, 14:3 (2000), pp. 39–60.

Townshend, Charles *The British campaign in Ireland 1919–21: the development of political and military policies* (Oxford: Oxford University Press, 1975).

Townshend, Charles, *Britain's civil wars: counterinsurgency in the twentieth century* (London: Faber, 1986).

Urban, Mark, *Big boys' rules: the secret struggle against the IRA* (London: Faber and Faber, 1993).

Walker, Brian, *Parliamentary election results in Ireland: 1918–92* (Belfast: Institute of Irish Studies, 1992).

Walker, Graham, *A history of the Ulster Unionist Party: protest, pragmatism and pessimism* (Manchester: Manchester University Press, 2004).

Walker, Graham and Mulvenna, Gareth 'Northern Ireland representation at Westminster', *Parliamentary History*, 34:2 (2015), pp. 237–55.

Warner, Geoffrey, 'The Falls Road curfew revisited', *Irish Studies Review*, 14:3 (2006), pp. 325–42.

Wass, Douglas, *Decline to fall: the making of British macro-economic policy and the 1976 IMF crisis* (Oxford: Oxford University Press, 2008).

White, Robert, *Ruairí Ó Brádaigh: the life and politics of an Irish revolutionary* (Bloomington: Indiana University Press, 2006).

Whitelaw, William, *The Whitelaw memoirs* (London: Aurum, 1989).

Whyte, John, 'How much discrimination was there under the Unionist regime, 1921–68?' in T. Gallagher and J. O'Connell (eds), *Contemporary Irish studies* (Manchester: Manchester University Press, 1983), pp. 1–35.

Whyte, John, *Interpreting Northern Ireland* (Oxford: Oxford University Press, 1990).

Wickham-Jones, Mark, *Economic strategy and the Labour Party: politics and policy-making 1970–83* (Basingstoke: Macmillan, 1996).

Wilson, Harold, *Final term: the Labour government, 1974–6* (London: Weidenfeld & Nicolson, 1976).

Wood, Ian S., *Crimes of loyalty: a history of the UDA* (Edinburgh: Edinburgh University Press, 2006).

Wright, Frank, *Northern Ireland: a comparative analysis* (Dublin: Gill and Macmillan, 1987).

Zis, George, 'The international status of sterling' in Michael Artis and David Cobham (eds), *Labour's economic policies 1974–1979* (Manchester: Manchester University Press, 1991), pp. 104–20.

Index

CPSIA information can be obtained
at www.ICGtesting.com
Printed in the USA
JSHW021339270120
3827JS00003B/43